DISEASE SHRINKS ONE'S WORLD AND LESSENS RESPONSIBILITIES. HEALTH FREES THE ORGANISM TO REALIZE ITS CAPACITIES. ANXIETY IS THE BRIDGE BETWEEN THE TWO!

Rollo May provides new concepts and sound insights into the theorizing and **The Meaning of Anxiety.**

"Competition for success is the greatest source of anxiety in our culture," says Rollo May. "Success being the dominant cultural value, it is also the dominant criterion for self-valuation. Whatever threatens this goal is, therefore, a cause of profound anxiety.

"Every person experiences continual shocks and threats to his existence; indeed, self-realization occurs only at the price of moving ahead despite such shocks. Anxiety, from the positive point of view, is an indication of new possibility for the development of the self."

Alcoholism, compulsive sexual activity and compulsive work are among neurotic ways of dealing with anxiety, Rollo May points out. Compulsive work is perhaps the most common way of allaying anxiety and can be called in this country a "normal neurosis."

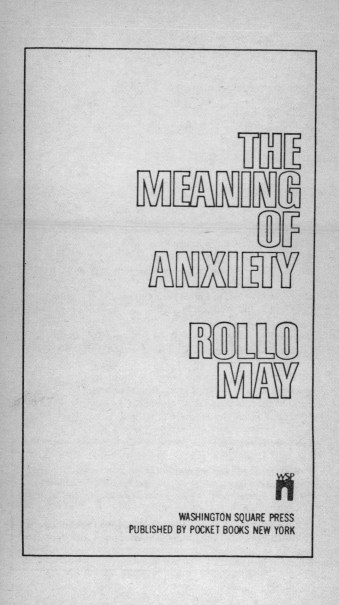

THE MEANING OF ANXIETY

ROLLO MAY

WSP

WASHINGTON SQUARE PRESS
PUBLISHED BY POCKET BOOKS NEW YORK

A Washington Square Press Publication of
POCKET BOOKS, a division of Simon & Schuster, Inc.
1230 Avenue of the Americas, New York, N.Y. 10020

Published by arrangement with W. W. Norton & Co., Inc.
Library of Congress Catalog Card Number: 77-1359

ISBN: 0-671-60385-X

First Pocket Books printing May, 1979

10 9 8 7 6 5

WASHINGTON SQUARE PRESS, WSP and colophon are
registered trademarks of Simon & Schuster, Inc.

Printed in the U.S.A.

Acknowledgments

I wish to acknowledge the courtesy of the following authors and publishers in permitting quotations from their publications.

Academic Press, for excerpts from Charles Spielberger, editor, *Anxiety and Behavior,* copyright 1966; from Eugene Levitt, "A Brief Commentary on the Psychiatry Breakthrough," in Charles Spielberger, editor, *Anxiety: Current Trends in Theory and Research,* copyright 1972 by Academic Press; from Richard Lazarus and James Averill, "Emotion and Cognition: With Special Reference to Anxiety," also in Charles Spielberger, cited above.

American Book Company, for excerpts from Kurt Goldstein, *The Organism: A Holistic Approach to Biology,* copyright 1939 by American Book Company.

Mr. W. H. Auden, for excerpts from *The Age of Anxiety: A Baroque Eclogue,* copyright 1947 by W. H. Auden, and published by Random House.

Ballantine Books, for excerpts from Gregory Bateson, *Steps to an Ecology of Mind,* copyright 1972 by Chandler Publishing Co.

The Blakiston Company, for an excerpt from R. R. Grinker and S. P. Spiegel, *Men under Stress,* copyright 1945 by The Blakiston Company.

Clark University Press, for an excerpt from R. R. Willoughby, "Magic and Cognate Phenomena: An Hypothesis," in Carl Murchison, editor, *A Handbook of Social Psychology,* copyright 1935 by Clark University.

Columbia University Press, for excerpts from Helen

Flanders Dunbar, *Emotions and Bodily Changes,* revised edition, copyright 1935, 1938 by Columbia University Press; and from Abram Kardiner, *The Psychological Frontiers of Society,* copyright 1945 by Columbia University Press.

Erich Fromm, for excerpts from *Escape from Freedom,* copyright 1941 by Erich Fromm, and published by Rinehart & Co., Inc.; also for excerpts from *Man for Himself,* copyright 1947 by Erich Fromm, and published by Rinehart & Co., Inc.

Grune and Stratton, for excerpts from Lauretta Bender, "Anxiety in Disturbed Children"; also for excerpts from Paul Tillich, "Anxiety-Reducing Agencies in Our Culture," (both) in Paul Hoch and Joseph Zubin, editors, *Anxiety,* copyright 1950 by Grune and Stratton.

Harcourt, Brace and Company, Inc., for excerpts from Karl Mannheim, *Man and Society in an Age of Reconstruction,* copyright 1941 by Harcourt, Brace and Company, Inc.; and from R. H. Tawney, *The Acquisition Society,* copyright 1920 by Harcourt, Brace and Company, Inc.

Harvard University Press, for excerpts from Kurt Goldstein, *Human Nature in the Light of Psychopathology,* copyright 1940 by Harvard University Press.

Henry Holt & Company, Inc., for excerpts from Herman Hesse, *Steppenwolf,* translated by Basil Creighton, copyright 1947 by Henry Holt & Company, Inc.

Journal of the History of Ideas and Paul Tillich for an excerpt from "Existential Philosophy," *Journal of the History of Ideas,* copyright 1944 by Journal of the History of Ideas.

Alfred A. Knopf, Inc., for excerpts from Otto Rank, *Will Therapy,* copyright 1936 by Alfred A. Knopf, Inc.

Mr. Howard S. Liddell, for excerpts from a paper read before the American Psychopathological Association at its meeting of June 4, 1949.

Liveright Publishing Corporation and Sigmund Freud Copyrights, Ltd., for excerpts from Sigmund Freud, *Introductory Lectures on Psychoanalysis,* published by Liveright, New York; copyright renewed 1948; 1920, 1935 by Edward L. Bernays; copyright © 1965, 1964, 1963 by James Strachey.

McClelland and Stewart, Ltd., for excerpts from Hans Selye, *Stress without Distress,* copyright 1974 by Hans Selye.

McGraw-Hill Co., for excerpts from Hans Selye, *The Stress of Life*, copyright 1956 by Hans Selye.

Mr. O. H. Mowrer, for excerpts from various articles and addresses, published and unpublished.

W. W. Norton & Company, Inc., for excerpts from Walter B. Cannon, *The Wisdom of the Body*, revised and enlarged edition, copyright 1939 by Walter B. Cannon; from Karen Horney, *New Ways in Psychoanalysis*, copyright 1939 by W. W. Norton & Company, Inc.; also *The Neurotic Personality of Our Time*, copyright 1937 by W. W. Norton & Company, Inc.; and *Our Inner Conflicts*, copyright 1945 by W. W. Norton & Company, Inc.; from Sigmund Freud, *New Introductory Lectures in Psychoanalysis*, copyright 1933, by Sigmund Freud; and *The Problem of Anxiety*, copyright 1936 by The Psychoanalytic Quarterly Press.

The Peter Pauper Press, for excerpts from *Pascal's Pensées*, edited and translated by G. B. Rawlings.

Princeton University Press, for eleven illustrative extracts from Søren Kierkegaard, *The Concept of Dread*, translated by Walter Lowrie, copyright 1944 by Princeton University Press, and one excerpt from *Sickness unto Death* by the same author and translator, copyright 1941 by Princeton University Press.

Random House for excerpts from Robert Jay Lifton, *History and Human Survival*, copyright 1961, 1962, 1965, 1968, 1969, 1970 by Robert Jay Lifton.

Rinehart & Company, Inc., for excerpts from C. Landis and W. A. Hunt, *The Startle Pattern*, copyright 1939 by Carney Landis and William A. Hunt.

The Ronald Press Company, for excerpts from Leon J. Saul, "Physiological Effects of Emotional Tension," in J. McV. Hunt, editor, *Personality and the Behavior Disorders*, copyright 1944 by The Ronald Press Company.

W. B. Saunders Co., for excerpts from George Engel, *Psychological Development in Health and Disease*, copyright 1962 by W. B. Saunders Co.

Simon and Schuster for excerpts from Robert Jay Lifton, *The Life of the Self*, copyright 1976 by Robert Jay Lifton.

University of Chicago Press, for excerpts from Paul Tillich, *The Protestant Era*, copyright 1947 by University of Chicago Press.

The Viking Press, Inc., for an excerpt from Norman

Cousins, *Modern Man Is Obsolete,* copyright 1945 by Norman Cousins.

John Wiley and Sons, for excerpts from D. B. Coates, S. Moyer, L. Kendall, and M. G. Howat, "Life-Event Changes and Mental Health," from J. J. Groen and J. Bastiaans, "Psychological Stress, Interhuman Communication and Psychosomatic Disease," from Richard Lynn, "National Difference in Anxiety," and from Yona Teichman, "The Stress of Coping with the Unknown Regarding a Significant Family Member," all in Irwin Sarason and Charles Spielberger, editors, *Stress and Anxiety,* Vol. IV, copyright 1977 by Hemisphere Publishing Corp., Vol. III, copyright 1976 by Hemisphere Publishing Corp., Vol. II, copyright 1975 by Hemisphere Publishing Corp., Vol. I, copyright 1975 by Hemisphere Publishing Corp.

Yale University Press, for excerpts from Ernst Cassirer, *An Essay on Man,* copyright 1944 by Yale University Press, and Carl Jung, *Psychology and Religion,* copyright 1938 by Yale University Press.

Contents

ix

PART II

CLINICAL ANALYSIS OF ANXIETY

PART III

THE MANAGEMENT OF ANXIETY

ſ

Foreword to the First Edition

This book is the result of several years of exploration, research, and thought on one of the most urgent problems of our day. Clinical experience has proved to psychologists and psychiatrists alike that the central problem in psychotherapy is the nature of anxiety. To the extent that we have been able to solve that problem, we have made a beginning in understanding the causes of integration and disintegration of personality.

But if anxiety were merely a phenomenon of maladjustment, it might well be consigned to the consulting room and the clinic and this book to the professional library. The evidence is overwhelming, however, that we live today in an "age of anxiety." If one penetrates below the surface of political, economic, business, professional, or domestic crises to discover their psychological causes, or if one seeks to understand modern art or poetry or philosophy or religion, one runs athwart the problem of anxiety at almost every turn. The ordinary stresses and strains of life in the changing world of today are such that few if any escape the need to confront anxiety and to deal with it in some manner.

For the past hundred years, for reasons which will appear in the following chapters, psychologists, philosophers, social historians, and other students of humanity have been increasingly preoccupied with this nameless and formless uneasiness that has dogged the footsteps of modern man. Yet in all that time, to my knowledge, only two attempts have been made in book form—one essay by Kierkegaard and one by Freud—to present an objective picture of anxiety and to indicate constructive methods of dealing with it.

This study seeks to bring together in one volume the theories of anxiety offered by modern explorers in different areas of our culture, to discover the common elements in these theories, and to formulate these concepts so that we shall have some common ground for further inquiry. If the synthesis of anxiety theory presented here serves the purpose of producing some coherence and order in this field, a good part of my goal will have been achieved.

It is of course clear that anxiety is not merely an abstract theoretical concept, any more than swimming is to a person whose boat has capsized a mile from shore. A discussion of anxiety that was not geared to immediate human problems would not be worth either writing or reading. Hence the theoretical synthesis has been tested by investigation of actual anxiety situations and selected case studies to discover what concrete evidence there may be to support my conclusions as to what anxiety means and what purpose it serves in human experience.

In order to keep this study within manageable limits, I have restricted its scope to the observations of persons who are our contemporaries in all important respects, and even within these limits only the most significant figures. These are persons who represent Western civilization as we experience it, whether they are philosophers like Kierkegaard, psychotherapists like Freud, novelists, poets, economists, social historians, or others with keen insight into human problems. These restrictions in time and space serve to bring the problem of anxiety into sharp focus, but they should not be taken to imply that anxiety is exclusively a modern problem or solely a Western one. I hope that this book will stimulate similar surveys in other parts of the field.

Because of the vital general interest in the subject of anxiety, I have stated my findings so that they will be clear not only to professional readers but also to students, to social scientists, and to readers who seek a psychological understanding of modern problems. This book is in fact pertinent to the concerns of intelligent citizens who feel on their own pulse the tensions and anxiety-creating conflicts of our day and who have asked themselves what the meaning and causes of this anxiety may be and how the anxiety can be dealt with.

For those interested in a comparative survey of modern schools of psychotherapy, this volume should serve as a convenient textbook, presenting as it does the views of a dozen leaders in this field. There is no better way to understand these various schools than to compare their theories of anxiety.

During the years I was working on this book, my ideas on anxiety were sharpened and broadened by discussions with many professional colleagues and friends, too numerous to be mentioned here. But I wish to express appreciation to Dr. O. H. Mowrer, Dr. Kurt Goldstein, Dr. Paul Tillich, and Dr. Esther Lloyd-Jones, who read the manuscript at its various stages and who discussed with me through many stimulating hours the problem of anxiety in the fields they represent. I am also indebted for direct and indirect help in this study to Dr. Erich Fromm and other colleagues in the William Alanson White Institute of Psychiatry, Psychoanalysis and Psychology. A final word of appreciation is directed to the psychiatrist and the social workers at the institution in which the case studies of unmarried mothers were made. These colleagues gave expert help in the understanding of the cases, though for obvious reasons they must remain anonymous.

ROLLO MAY

New York, New York
February, 1950

Foreword to the Revised Edition

Since the first edition of this book appeared in 1950, there has been an enormous amount of research and interest in anxiety. In contrast to the fact that only two books were written on anxiety before 1950, a score of volumes were published in the last quarter century. And in contrast to the half-dozen papers exploring the subject before 1950, it has been estimated that at least 6,000 studies and dissertations on anxiety and tangential subjects have appeared since 1950. Anxiety has certainly come out of the dimness of the professional office into the bright light of the market place. I am gratified that the original *Meaning of Anxiety* spurred some of this surge of interest.

But with all the devoted efforts on the part of gifted persons, I know of no one who would claim that the riddle of anxiety has been solved. Our knowledge has increased but we have not learned how to deal with anxiety. Though the concept of normal anxiety, as advanced in the first edition of this book, has been generally accepted in theory, the implications of it have not been faced. We still cling to the illogical belief that "mental health is living without anxiety." We seem unaware that the delusion of living without anxiety reveals a radical misperception of reality— a point made inescapably clear in our day of atomic radiation and the hydrogen bomb.

Anxiety has a meaning. Though part of this meaning can be destructive, another part also can be constructive. Our very survival is the result of steps taken long ago to confront anxiety. Originally, primitive man, as both Freud and Adler have said, experienced anxiety as a warning of the threat to his life from the teeth and claws of wild animals. Anxiety played a prominent part in our forefather's development of his capacity to think and his ability to use symbols and tools to extend his protective reach.

But in our day we still see our major threats as coming from the tooth and claw of physical enemies when they are actually largely psychological and in the broadest sense spiritual—that is they deal with meaninglessness. We are no longer prey to tigers and mastodons but to damage to our self-esteem, ostracism by our group, or the threat of losing out in the competitive struggle. The form of anxiety has changed, but the experience remains relatively the same.

Anxiety is essential to the human condition. For a personal example, I experience anxiety before every lecture even though I have given hundreds of them. One day, tired of enduring this tension, which seemed so unnecessary, and with the help of a strong resolve, I proceeded to condition myself out of the anxiety. That evening I was perfectly relaxed and free from tension when I mounted the platform. But I made a poor speech. Missing were the tension, the sense of challenge, the zest of the race horse at the starting gate—those states of mind and body in which normal anxiety expresses itself.

The confrontation with anxiety can (note the word *can* and not *will*) relieve us from boredom, sharpen our sensitivity, and assure the presence of the tension that is necessary to preserve human existence. The presence of anxiety indicates vitality. Like fever, it testifies that a struggle is going on within the personality. So long as this struggle continues, a constructive solution is possible. When there is no longer any anxiety, the struggle is over and depression may ensue. This is why Kierkegaard held that anxiety is our "best teacher." He pointed out that whenever a new possibility emerged, anxiety would be there as well. These considerations point to a topic that has barely been touched in contemporary research—namely, the relation between anxiety on the one hand and creativity, originality, and intelligence on the other. Part III of this book, dealing albeit briefly with these topics, has been entirely rewritten for the present volume.

I believe a bold theory is necessary that will comprehend not only our normal and neurotic anxiety but anxiety in literature, art, and philosophy as well. This theory must be formulated at our highest level of abstraction. I propose that this theory be founded on the definition that anxiety is the *experience of Being affirming itself against Nonbeing.* The latter is that which would reduce or destroy Being, such as aggression, fatigue, boredom, and ultimately death. I have rewritten this book in the hope that its publication will aid in the forming of this theory of anxiety.

It is a pleasure to express my gratitude to the graduate students and colleagues who have urged me on in the revision of this book, a task that turned out to be considerably more rewarding than I had expected. I am especially grateful to my research associate Dr. Joanne Cooper, who has given me indispensable aid in the library explorations of this subject, and also in her penetrating suggestions.

ROLLO MAY

Tiburon, California
June, 1977

I saw that all the things I feared and which feared me had nothing good or bad in them save in so far as the mind was affected by them.

—Spinoza, *Treatise on the Correction of the Understanding*

I would say that learning to know anxiety is an adventure which every man has to affront if he would not go to perdition either by not having known anxiety or by sinking under it. He therefore who has learned rightly to be anxious has learned the most important thing.

—Kierkegaard, *The Concept of Dread*

There is no question that the problem of anxiety is a nodal point at which the most various and important questions converge, a riddle whose solution would be bound to throw a flood of light on our whole mental existence.

—Freud, *Introductory Lectures on Psychoanalysis*

PART

I

MODERN
INTERPRETATIONS
OF ANXIETY

CHAPTER
1

Anxiety in
Mid-Twentieth Century

Now there are times when a whole generation is caught
. . . between two ages, two modes of life, with the consequence that it loses all power to understand itself and
has no standards, no security, no simple acquiescence.

—Herman Hesse, *Steppenwolf*

Every alert citizen of our society realizes, on the basis of
his own experience as well as his observation of his fellow-men, that anxiety is a pervasive and profound phenomenon in the twentieth century. From 1945 and the birth
of the atom bomb, anxiety shifted from a covert to an
overt problem. The alert citizens were then aware not
only of the more obvious anxiety-creating situations such
as uncontrolled atomic warfare, radical political and economic upheaval, but also the less obvious, deeper, and
more personal sources of anxiety in themselves and their
fellow-men. This latter includes the inner confusion, alienation, psychological disorientation, and uncertainty with
respect to values and acceptable standards of conduct.
Hence to endeavor to "prove" the pervasiveness of anxiety
in our day is as unnecessary as the proverbial carrying
coals to Newcastle.

Since the implicit sources of anxiety in our society are
generally recognized, our task in this introductory chapter
is to point out how anxiety has emerged, and has to some
extent been defined, as an *explicit* problem in many different areas in our culture. One had the impression that

3

in the middle decade of this century the explorations and investigations in such diverse fields as science and poetry, religion and politics were converging on this central problem of anxiety. Whereas the period of two or three decades before might have been termed the "age of covert anxiety" —as I hope to demonstrate later in this chapter—the middle of our century may be called, as Auden and Camus called it, the "age of overt anxiety." This emergence of anxiety from an implicit to an explicit problem, this change from anxiety as a matter of "mood" to a recognition that it is an urgent issue which we must at all costs try to define and clarify—these are the significant phenomena.

Not only in the understanding and treatment of emotional disturbances and behavioral disorders had anxiety become recognized as the "nodal problem," in Freud's words, but it was then seen likewise to be nodal in such different areas as literature, sociology, political and economic thought, education, religion, and philosophy. I shall cite examples of testimony from these fields, beginning with the more general and proceeding to the more specific concern with anxiety as a scientific problem.

IN LITERATURE

If we were to inquire into anxiety as exhibited in the American literature, say, of 1920 or 1930, we would be forced to occupy ourselves with symptoms of anxiety rather than with overt anxiety itself. But though signs of open, manifest anxiety were not plentiful in that period, certainly the student could find plenty of symptomatic indications of underlying anxiety. Recall, for example, the pronounced sense of loneliness, the quality of persistent searching—frantically and compulsively pursued, but always frustrated—in the writings of a novelist like Thomas Wolfe. In the cases demonstrating anxiety in this book, it will be observed that anxiety frequently—and, in many cases, basically—hinged on the issue symbolically expressed in Wolfe's title, *You can't go home again*. We shall observe that neurotic anxiety occurred because these characters were unable to accept the psychological meaning of not going home again—namely, psychological autonomy. One could wonder (realizing that literary artists symbolically express, often with remarkable fidelity, the unconscious assumptions and conflicts of their culture) whether these symbols in Wolfe's writing could be taken to mean that many people in the late 1920's and early 1930's were beginning to realize not only that one cannot go home again, but that it was impossible to depend for security on past economic, social, and ethical criteria. The upshot of this realization was the increasing emergence of overt anxiety as a conscious problem, along with a feeling of "homelessness." If we take this as speculation about the central symbols of the home and the mother, it may usefully raise a problem that we shall be confronting, in more specific form, time and again in this study of anxiety.

In 1950, anxiety emerged into overt statement in contemporaneous literature. W. H. Auden entitled his poem with the phrase which he believed most accurately characterized that period, *The Age of Anxiety*.[1] Though Auden's interpretation of the inner experience of the four persons in this poem is set in the time of war—when "necessity is associated with horror and freedom with boredom"[2]—he makes it clear that the underlying causes of the anxiety of his characters, as well as of others of that age, must be sought on deeper levels than merely the occasion of war. The four characters in the poem, though different in temperament and in background, have in common certain characteristics of our times: loneliness, the feeling of not being of value as persons, and the experience of not being able to love and be loved despite the common need, the common effort, and the common but temporary respite provided by alcohol. The sources of the anxiety were to be found in certain basic trends in our culture, one of which, for Auden, was the pressure toward conformity which occurs in a world where commercial and mechanical values are apotheosized:

> We move on
> As the wheel wills; one revolution
> Registers all things, the rise and fall
> In pay and prices. . . .[3]

> . . . this stupid world where
> Gadgets are gods and we go on talking,
> Many about much, but remain alone,
> Alive but alone, belonging—where?—
> Unattached as tumbleweed.[4]

And the possibility facing these four characters is that they too will be drawn into the mechanical routine of meaninglessness:

> . . . The fears we know
> Are of not knowing. Will nightfall bring us
> Some awful order—Keep a hardware store
> In a small town. . . . Teach science for life to
> Progressive girls—? It is getting late.
> Shall we ever be asked for? Are we simply
> Not wanted at all?[5]

What has been lost is the capacity to experience and have faith in one's self as a worthy and unique being. At the same time, these characters, symbolizing all of us, have lost the capacity for faith in, and meaningful communication with, other selves, their fellow human beings.[6]

In a phrase parallel to Auden's, Albert Camus designated this age as "the century of fear," in comparison with the seventeenth century as the age of mathematics, the eighteenth as the age of the physical sciences, and the nineteenth as that of biology. Camus realized that these characterizations were not logically parallel, that fear is not a science, but that "science must be somewhat involved, since its latest theoretical advances have brought it to the point of negating itself while its perfected technology threatens the globe itself with destruction. Moreover, although fear itself cannot be considered a science, it is certainly a technique."[7] Our period is also often called the "century of psychology." Whether there is some necessary connection between fear and psychology, and whether fear is what requires people to examine their psyches, are questions to be kept in mind throughout this book.

Another writer who poignantly expressed the anxiety and anxiety-like states of people in this period was Franz Kafka. The remarkable surge of interest in the 1940's and '50's in the writings of Kafka is important for our purposes here because of what it shows in the changing temper of the time. The fact that increasing numbers of people discovered that Kafka speaks significantly to them must indicate that he was expressing some profound aspects of the prevailing experience of many members of the society. In Kafka's novel *The Castle*, the chief character devotes his life to a frantic and desperate endeavor to communicate with the authorities in the castle who control all aspects of the life of the village, and who have the power to tell him his vocation and give some meaning to his life. Kafka's non-hero is driven "by a need for the most primitive requisites of life, the need to be rooted in a home and a calling, and to become a member of a community."[8] But the authorities in the castle remain inscrutable and inaccessible, and Kafka's character is left without direction or integration in his own life and remains isolated from his fellows. What the castle specifically symbolizes could be debated at length, but it is clear that the authorities in the castle represent the epitome of bureaucratic efficiency which exercises such power that it quenches both individual autonomy and meaningful interpersonal relations. We may confidently assume that Kafka is writing of those aspects of his bourgeois culture of the late nineteenth and early twentieth centuries which so elevated technical efficiency that personal values were largely destroyed.

Herman Hesse, writing less in literary symbols than Kafka, was more explicit about the sources of modern man's anxiety. The awareness of traumatic social change in the twentieth century occurred in Europe before it did in America; thus what Hesse wrote was more relevant to conscious problems in this country in the 1940's, than in 1927, the date of *Steppenwolf*. He presents the story of Haller, his chief character in this novel, as a parable of our age.[9] Hesse holds that Haller's—and his contemporaries'—isolation and anxiety arose from the fact that the bourgeois culture in the late nineteenth and early twentieth centuries emphasized mechanical, rationalistic "balance" at the price of the suppression of the dynamic, irrational elements in experience. Haller tries to overcome his isolation and loneliness by giving free rein to his previously suppressed sensuous and irrational urges (the "wolf" in the title). But this reactive method yields only a temporary relief. Indeed, Hesse presents no thoroughgoing solution to the problem of the anxiety of contemporaneous Western man, for he believes the present period to be one of those "times when a whole generation is caught . . . between two ages." That is to say, bourgeois standards and controls had broken down, but there are as yet no social standards to take their place. Hesse sees Haller's record

as a document of the times, for Haller's sickness of
the soul, as I now know, is not the eccentricity of a
single individual, but the sickness of the times themselves, the neurosis of that generation to which Haller
belongs . . . *a sickness which attacks . . . precisely
those who are strongest in spirit and richest in gifts.*[10]

IN SOCIAL STUDIES

Here, too, anxiety came to the fore. The awareness of
anxiety as an overt sociological problem in an American
community during the third and fourth decades of our
century was shown in the comparison of the Lynds' two
studies of Middletown.[11] In the first study, made in the
1920's, anxiety is not an overt problem to the people of
Middletown, and the topic does not even appear in the
index of the Lynds' volume. But anyone reading this study
from a psychological viewpoint would suspect that much
of the behavior of the citizens of Middletown was symptomatic of *covert anxiety*—for example, the compulsive work
("businessmen and workingmen seem to be running for
dear life" in the endeavor to make money[12]), the pervasive struggle to conform, the compulsive gregariousness
(the great emphasis on "joining" clubs), and the frantic endeavors of the people in the community to keep their
leisure time crammed with activity (such as "motoring"),
however purposeless this activity might be in itself. On a
Sunday afternoon the regular practice of many people was
to get in their cars, drive fifty miles, and then drive back
again. One is reminded of Pascal's description of some
symptoms of covert anxiety: the constant endeavor of
people to divert themselves, to escape ennui, to avoid
being alone, until "agitation" becomes an end in itself.
Only one citizen in this first volume—whom the Lynds
describe as a "perspicacious" observer—looked below
these symptoms and sensed the presence of covert apprehension. Of his fellow townsmen he observed, "These
people are all afraid of something; what is it?"[13]

But the later study of the same community made in the
1930's presented a very different picture. *Conscious anxiety
is now present.* "One thing everybody in Middletown has
in common," the Lynds observed, "is insecurity in the face
of a complicated world."[14] To be sure, the immediate, out-

—

ward occasion of anxiety was the economic depression. But it would be an error to conclude that the inclusive *cause* of the emerging anxiety was economic insecurity. The Lynds accurately related this insecurity in Middletown to the *confusion of role* which the individual was then experiencing. The citizen of Middletown, they write, "is caught in a chaos of conflicting patterns, none of them wholly condemned, but no one of them clearly approved and free from confusion; or, where the group sanctions are clear in demanding a certain role of a man or woman, the individual encounters cultural requirements with no immediate means of meeting them."[15]

This "chaos of conflicting patterns" in Middletown was one expression of the pervasive social changes occurring in our culture, which, I will submit in a later chapter, were intimately connected with the widespread anxiety of our times.[16] The Lynds observed that, since "most people are incapable of tolerating change and uncertainty in all sectors of life at once,"[17] the tendency in Middletown was toward a *retrenchment into more rigid and conservative economic and social ideologies*. This ominous development as a symptom of, and defense against, anxiety points toward the discussion of the relation between anxiety and political totalitarianism in the following section.

Robert Lifton, who may be considered a social psychiatrist, has given us many insights into the process of brainwashing,[18] which has become a prominent form of social turmoil throughout the world in the decades since 1950. Without going into Lifton's seminal research in many relevant areas, I wish only to quote one reference bearing on our topic of anxiety:

> John S. Dunne, the distinguished Catholic theologian, posits as the new religion of our time "a phenomenon we might call 'passing over.'" Dunne describes this process as "a going over to the standpoint of another culture, another way of life, another religion, . . . followed by an equal and opposite process we might call 'coming back,' coming back with new insight to one's own culture, one's own way of life, one's own religion."[19]

There is a darker side, however, to that same process. Considerable anxiety can be generated by the very multiplicity of possibilities in "passing over" and in the Protean style in general. That anxiety around diffuseness can in turn contribute to the kind of quest for certainty we now see so widely expressed in fundamentalist religious sects and various totalistic spiritual movements.[20]

The "Protean Man" refers to Lifton's analysis of the contemporary personality as continually changing its identity. Proteus, in the Greek myth, was able to change his shape —"from wild boar to lion to dragon to fire to flood. . . . But what he could not do, unless seized and chained, was to *commit himself to a single form.*" This drive to don a number of masks, to be in incessant change, to reflect continuously the environment, with no idea of "where I belonged and no idea of myself,"[21] as one young modern protean put it, bespeaks a dizzily changing cultural situation. Whether one looks upon this with approbation or despair, it is undeniable that this condition also expresses the radical upheaval in our society.

Lifton himself speaks of the modern anxiety, as shown in fear of atomic warfare, for example, as a process of *numbing.* This defense is an emotional withdrawal in which people who can do nothing else dull their sensitivities, cut off their awareness of threat. The shrinking of consciousness seems to work temporarily in the warding off of anxiety. Whether one must pay later is an open question; with the survivors of the *Pueblo* incident, this was true. One who studied them writes, "It is possible that adjustment on a short-term basis was due to marked repression and denial and that the price must be paid later,"[22] i.e., in such things as suicide or psychotic depression.

IN THE POLITICAL SCENE

The ideal relation between politics and anxiety is expressed in Spinoza's insight into the political aspect of "freedom from fear." He held that the purpose of the state is "so to free each man from fear that he may live and act with full security and without injury to himself or his neighbor." But when we turn to the actual political arena, we find pronounced anxiety in both symptomatic and overt forms. Without going into the complex determinants of fascism, we need only note that it is born and gains its power in periods of widespread anxiety. Paul Tillich, who experienced in his own life in Germany the rise of Hitler, described the situation in Europe in the 1930's out of which German fascism developed:

> First of all a feeling of *fear* or, more exactly, of indefinite anxiety was prevailing. Not only the economic and political, but also the cultural and religious, security seemed to be lost. There was nothing on which one could build; everything was without foundation. A catastrophic breakdown was expected every moment. Consequently, a longing for security was growing in everybody. A freedom that leads to fear and anxiety has lost its value; better authority with security than freedom with fear![23]

In such periods, people grasp at political authoritarianism in their desperate need for relief from anxiety. Totalitarianism in this sense may be viewed as serving a purpose on a cultural scale parallel to that in which a neurotic symptom protects an individual from a situation of unbearable anxiety. An observer of Italian and Spanish fascism, Herbert L. Matthews, wrote: "Fascism was like a jail where the individual had a certain amount of security, shelter, and daily food."[24] With some very significant differences, communistic totalitarianism fulfills a similar function. Arthur M. Schlesinger, Jr., told us: "[Communism] has filled the 'vacuum of faith' caused by the waning of established religion; it provides a sense of purpose which heals internal agonies of anxiety and doubt."[25] As I shall indicate later in this study, such forms of totalitarianism are not only economic phenomena, but are also the product of the spiritual, ethical, and psychological vacuum which characterized the breakdown of the bourgeois tradition in Western Europe. As Martin Ebon phrased it, communism is a product of "the desperate wish to find a purpose in what seems confusion and emptiness."[26] In this confusion and emptiness one thing did exist, namely anxiety. Totalitarianism gains its foothold to a considerable extent because, like a symptom, it "binds" and provides some relief from this anxiety.[27]

In addition to anxiety in the above symptomatic forms,

unsystematized anxiety had been increasingly evident in the sociopolitical scene in that decade. The frequent references to Franklin D. Roosevelt's sentence in his first inaugural, "The only thing we have to fear is fear itself," testify to the fact that large numbers of people have become increasingly aware of "fear of fear"—or, more accurately, anxiety—in the face of the radical sociopolitical changes in our century.[28]

The emergence of the Atomic Age brought the previously inchoate and "free-floating" anxiety of many people into sharp focus. The stark possibilities of modern man's situation were stated in an impassioned expression of anxiety by Norman Cousins just after the first atomic bombs were dropped:

> The beginning of the Atomic Age has brought less hope than fear. It is a primitive fear, the fear of the unknown, the fear of forces man can neither channel nor comprehend. This fear is not new; in its classical form it is the fear of irrational death. But overnight it has become intensified, magnified. It has burst out of the subconscious into the conscious, filling the mind with primordial apprehension. . . . Where man can find no answer, he will find fear.[29]

Even if we are to escape being confronted with actual death in a shooting and atom-bomb war, the anxiety inhering in our portentous world situation would still be with us. The historian Arnold Toynbee stated his belief that overt warfare on a world scale was not probable in our lifetime, but that we would remain in a "cold" war for a generation. This means a perpetual condition of tension and worry. To live in a state of anxiety for a generation (or more, as it turned out) was, indeed, a horrendous prospect!

But the picture is not inevitably black. Toynbee held that the tension in the persistent cold war can be used constructively as our motivation for bettering our own socioeconomic standards in the West. I agree with Toynbee that our political and social survival depends both on our capacity for tolerating the anxiety inherent in the threatening world situation and on our capacity for turning this anxiety to constructive uses.

Toynbee gave an analogy which is such a vivid parable

of the constructive uses of anxiety that I summarize it here. Fishermen bringing in their herring from the North Sea were faced with the problem of the fish becoming sluggish in their tanks and thus losing some of their market value for freshness. Then one fisherman conceived the idea of placing a couple of catfish in the herring tanks. Because of the threat of death in the presence of these catfish, the herring not only did not grow sluggish but became even more active and flourishing.[30] Of course, whether the reaction of the West to the catfish (China or Russia) would be constructive or not is another question; in other words, whether we would use the anxiety in our world situation predominantly for constructive purposes remains largely to be seen.

Anxiety in the situation is increased by the fact that there is no clear-cut villain, no "devil" on which to project our fears. Anxiety is further increased by our being ourselves involved, subjectively and objectively, in the problem. As Peanuts says, "We have met the enemy and he is us."

IN PHILOSOPHY AND THEOLOGY

Anxiety had also emerged as a central problem in contemporaneous philosophy and religion not only as a general, but also a specific, indication of the prevalence of anxiety in the culture. Anxiety had become most prominent in the thought of those theologians, like Reinhold Niebuhr, who were most intimately concerned with the economic and political issues of the day, and in those philosophers, like Paul Tillich and Martin Heidegger, who had experienced in their own lives the cultural crises and upheavals of Western society in the past three decades.

In the light of Nietzsche's idea that the philosopher is a "physician of culture," the thinking of these philosophers and theologians is to be regarded not as the product of ivory-tower speculation, but as a diagnosis of the condition of our culture

Tillich described anxiety as man's reaction to the threat of *nonbeing*. Man is the creature who is self-consciously aware of his being, but he is also aware that at any moment he might cease to be. This concept of Tillich's was, of course, formulated before the emergence of the atomic age, but that is undoubtedly a vivid symbol by which many more people are able to comprehend the immediate threat of nonbeing. In philosophical terms, anxiety arises as the individual is aware of being as over against the ever-present possibility of non-existence. This, we will see, is parallel to Kierkegaard's description of anxiety as the "fear of nothingness." "Nonbeing" does not mean simply the threat of physical death—though probably death is the most common form and symbol of this anxiety. The threat of nonbeing lies in the psychological and spiritual realms as well—namely, in the threat of *meaninglessness* in one's existence. Generally the threat of meaninglessness is experienced negatively as a threat to the existence of the self (the experience of the "dissolution of the self" in Goldstein's term). But when this form of anxiety is confronted affirmatively—when the individual both realizes the *threat* of meaninglessness and takes *a stand against the threat*—the result is a strengthening of the individual's experience of selfhood. This is also a strengthening of his perception of himself as a being who is distinct from the world of nonbeing or objects.

Niebuhr made anxiety central in his theological doctrine of man. To Niebuhr every act of man, creative or destructive, involves some element of anxiety. Anxiety has its source in the fact that man is, on one hand, finite, involved like the animals in the contingencies and necessities of nature. But, on the other hand, man has freedom. Unlike "the animals he sees this situation [of contingency] and anticipates its perils," and to this extent man transcends his finiteness. "In short, man, being both bound and free, both limited and limitless, is anxious. Anxiety is the inevitable concomitant of the paradox of freedom and finiteness in which man is involved."[31] Much will be said later in the present study about anxiety as the precondition of neurosis; but here it is significant that Niebuhr, in parallel theological terms, makes anxiety "the internal precondition of sin. . . . Anxiety is the internal description of the state of temptation."[32]

IN PSYCHOLOGY

"Anxiety is the most prominent mental characteristic of Occidental civilization," the social psychologist R. R. Willoughby asserted. He then presented statistical evidence for this assertion in the form of the rising incidences in three fields of social pathology which he believes may reasonably be understood as reactions to anxiety, namely *suicide,* the *functional forms of mental disorder,* and *divorce.*[33] Suicide rates for the last 75 to 100 years showed a steady increase in the majority of the countries of continental Europe. With regard to the functional forms of mental illness, Willoughby held, "it seems probable . . . that there is a real rise in incidence of mental disease even when the greatest reasonable allowance is made for increasing facilities for hospitalization and insight in diagnosis."[34] The divorce rates for every country except Japan have shown a steady upward trend in the twentieth century. Willoughby believes that the incidence of divorce is a measure of the inability of the members of the culture to tolerate the additional stress of the critical marital adjustment, and the higher incidence must presuppose a considerable load of anxiety in the culture. An important fact in America is that divorces for "cruelty" were "solely responsible for the increase, all other causes steadily declining." Willoughby interpreted "cruelty" as a matter of increase of anxiety—"if the conduct of the spouse is such as to exacerbate anxiety, it is 'cruel.' "

Willoughby's purpose in introducing these statistics to substantiate the "commonsense proposition that there is in our civilization a large and increasing incidence of anxiety," cannot be questioned. But there might rightly be considerable question as to whether the relation between these statistical evidences and anxiety is as direct as he holds. The rising incidence of divorce would seem to be due to changing social attitudes toward divorce as well as to the prevalence of anxiety. It seems more logical to *regard rising divorce, suicide, and mental disease rates as symptoms and products of the traumatic transition of our culture, and to regard anxiety also as a symptom and product of that transitional state.*

To trace one of these, divorce, down to the present day, we note that "three or four times as large a proportion of first marriages are ending in divorce among Americans now in their late twenties as among those of similar age 45 years ago," according to statistics published in 1976.[35] The divorce rate has more than doubled in the last twelve years. However we look upon these statistics, they are surely indicative of a culture in radical upheaval, and hence a culture open to widespread anxiety.

Since in subsequent chapters we shall be concerned in detail with the study of anxiety in the various fields of psychology, we shall here only cite, in line with our introductory purpose, that anxiety has gradually come to be seen as a central problem in learning theory, in dynamic psychology, and specifically in psychoanalysis and other forms of psychotherapy. While it long has been recognized that apprehensions and fears, particularly those related to approval or punishment from parents and teachers, exerted much power over the child in school, not until recently have there been scientific recognitions of the innumerable subtle expressions and influences of anxiety permeating the child's educational and classroom experience. For this appreciation of anxiety as a focal problem in learning theory, and the scientific formulation thereof, we are early on indebted to such learning psychologists as Mowrer, Miller, Dollard, and a host of others following them.[36]

More than three decades ago, Freud singled out anxiety as the crucial problem of emotional and behavioral disorders. Further development of psychoanalysis has only substantiated his proposition, until it is now recognized on all sides that anxiety is the *"fundamental phenomenon of neurosis,"* or, in Horney's term, the *"dynamic center of neuroses."* But not only in psychopathology is this true. In the actions of "normal" people as well as the "abnormal" it is now recognized that anxiety is much more prevalent than was suspected several decades ago. Whether we are concerned with "normal" or pathological behavior, Freud was correct in saying that the solution to the "riddle" of anxiety must cast "a flood of light upon our whole mental existence."[37]

PURPOSE OF THIS BOOK

Despite the fact that anxiety has become a central problem in so many diverse areas in our culture, the attack on the problem has been handicapped by the fact that the various theories and studies of anxiety have, to date, been uncoordinated. In spite of the industrious work by skilled psychologists, this is as true in 1977 as it was in 1950. As is evident to anyone reading the papers from various symposia on anxiety, we do not even use the same language. Freud's description of the state of the problem in the opening paragraph of his chapter on anxiety published in 1933 is still largely accurate: "You will not be surprised to hear that I have a great deal of new information to give you about our hypotheses on the subject of anxiety . . . and also that none of this information claims to provide a final solution of these doubtful problems." What is necessary at the present stage of the understanding of anxiety is "the introduction of the right abstract ideas, and of their application to the raw material of observation so as to bring order and lucidity into it."[38]

The purpose of the present study is to bring, so far as we are able, some "order and lucidity" into the presently uncoordinated field of anxiety theory. I propose to bring together the various theories of anxiety and to view them in their cultural and historical as well as their biological and psychological aspects. I shall then seek the basic common denominators in these theories, assess the points of disagreement, and, so far as possible, synthesize the various viewpoints into a *comprehensive theory of anxiety.* The case studies in this book are presented for the purpose of observing anxiety theory clinically—that is, for illustrating and demonstrating, or questioning, various aspects of a comprehensive, contemporary theory of anxiety.

CHAPTER
2

Philosophical Interpreters
of Anxiety

> I have no desire to speak in strong terms about this age
> as a whole, but he who has observed the contemporary
> generation will surely not deny that the incongruity in it
> and the reason for its anxiety and restlessness is this, that
> in one direction truth increases in extent, in mass, partly
> also in abstract clarity, whereas certitude steadily decreases.
>
> —Søren Kierkegaard, *The Concept of Dread*

Until the coming of Freud and the other depth psychologists, the problem of anxiety lay in the provinces of philosophy, especially in its branch of ethics, and in religion. The philosophers who dealt most explicitly with anxiety and fear were those whose primary concern was not with the formation of an abstract intellectual system, but rather with the existential conflicts and crises of living human beings. They could not escape confronting anxiety, as the living human being cannot. It is thus no historical accident that the most penetrating insights into anxiety and its related problems should have come from those thinkers whose interests were both religious and philosophical, such as Spinoza, Pascal, and Kierkegaard.

An inquiry into the philosophical backgrounds of the problem of anxiety is of help in understanding contemporaneous anxiety in two respects. The first and most obvious help is in the actual insights into the meaning of anxiety to be found in the writings of these philosophers —insights which, as seen in Kierkegaard, not only often antedate Freud's theories but in some respects predict developments after Freud. Second, such an inquiry illuminates one phase of the historical background of the problem of anxiety in our society. Since an individual's anxiety is conditioned by the fact that he stands at a particular point in the historical development of his culture, it is indispensable to have some understanding of the individual's culture, including the dominant ideas which formed the atmosphere in which he grew up, if we are to understand his anxiety.[1] Thus, our investigation in this chapter should cast light on the genesis of certain cultural issues and attitudes which are crucial for much contemporaneous anxiety.

One such issue, for example, is the dichotomy between mind and body, which was enunciated in its dominant modern form by Descartes and other thinkers of the seventeenth century. This not only produced psychological disunity and anxiety for large numbers of people in the late nineteenth and twentieth centuries, but in some respects specifically set the problem of anxiety for Freud.[2]

Another such issue has been the tendency in our culture to be preoccupied with "rational," mechanical phenomena and to suppress so-called "irrational" experience. Since anxiety is always partially irrational, there has been a tendency in our culture to repress the experience. We may approach this issue by means of two questions: Why did anxiety not emerge as a specific problem until the middle of the nineteenth century? And why was anxiety not dealt with as a problem in the various schools of psychology (excepting psychoanalysis) until the latter 1930's, despite the fact that during the previous half-century the study of fears had been prominent in psychology? Among the varied legitimate answers to these questions, an important one is our widespread tendency since the Renaissance to look askance at "irrational" phenomena. We tend to admit in our own experience as well as to accept as a legitimate area for investigation only those aspects of experience which can be made to appear "rational"—that is, aspects of experience for which intellectual "reasons" can be presented. This tendency, for example, appeared in several of the cases in the study of anxiety in unmarried mothers presented in this book. See especially that of Helen, who had strong anxiety arising from her extramarital pregnancy but who sought to repress this anxiety beneath a continual concern for the quasi-scientific "facts" of pregnancy. Helen's need to exclude from conscious awareness all ideas and feelings which were not intellectually "acceptable" and explicable is typical of many persons in our society.

Since fears are experienced as specific and definite, we can present "logical" reasons for them, and we can study them by mathematical means; but anxiety is generally experienced by an individual as a profoundly irrational phenomenon. The tendency to suppress anxiety because it seems irrational or to rationalize it in terms of "fears," is by no means limited to sophisticated intellectuals in our culture. It continually crops up in clinical or psychoanalytic work as a major hurdle in therapy with anxiety problems. The case of Helen in this book (Chapter 9) is a good example. For an understanding of the genesis of such tendencies, we must inquire into the background of the accepted attitudes and normative ideas of our society.

In the discussion which follows, I do not treat philosophical formulations as either cause or effect, but rather as one expression of the total cultural development of the period. The particular philosophers whose formulations have become important for their own and subsequent centuries (such as those we shall refer to in this chapter) are those who were successful in penetrating and expressing the dominant meaning and direction of development of their culture. It is in this sense that the formulations made by the intellectual leaders of one century become the common currency, in the form of unconscious assumptions, of large numbers of people in succeeding centuries.[3]

We begin with the seventeenth century because in that century the systems of thought which have been dominant for the major part of the modern period were formulated. Many of the formative principles which guided the scientists and philosophers of that century had emerged in the Renaissance, but it was in the seventeenth century—that remarkable classical period of Descartes, Spinoza, Pascal, Leibnitz, Locke, Hobbes, Galileo, Newton—that they received their systematic formulation.

The philosophies of the seventeenth century had one theme in common with respect to the understanding of human nature: they presented the "rationalistic solution to the problem of man."[4] The common denominator was the confidence that each man was a rational individual who could arrive at autonomy in his intellectual, social, religious, and emotional life. Mathematics was conceived as the chief tool of reason. This belief in "autonomous reason," as Tillich calls it, or "mathematical reason," in Cassirer's phrase, was the guiding intellectual principle of the cultural revolution which, beginning in the Renaissance, resulted in the overthrow of feudalism and absolutism and ultimately led to the supremacy of the bourgeoisie. It was believed in that age that autonomous reason would make possible the control of the individual's emotions (e.g., Spinoza). Autonomous reason would also make possible the mastery of physical nature—a confidence which was later to be thoroughly substantiated by far-reaching progress in the physical sciences. Descartes gave impetus to this development by his sharp distinction between mind and the processes of thought (intension) on one hand and physical nature (extension) on the other.

The crucial point was in a corollary to Descartes' dichotomy—namely, that *physical nature, including the body, could be understood and controlled by means of mechanical, mathematical laws*. The way was thus paved for the preoccupation in modern times with phenomena susceptible to mechanical and mathematical treatment. This preoccupation was to be accompanied both by an endeavor to extend the application of the methods of mechanics and mathematics to as many areas of experience as possible, and by a tendency to omit from consideration those aspects of experience which were not susceptible to such methods of treatment. The suppression of the nonmechanical and "irrational" aspects of experience went hand in hand, both as cause and effect, with the needs of the new industrialism following the Renaissance. What could be calculated and measured had practical utility in the industrial, workaday world, and what was "irrational" did not.

The confidence that physical nature and the human body were mathematically and mechanically controllable had vast anxiety-dispelling effects. This was true not only in meeting man's material needs and overcoming the actual threats of physical nature but also in freeing the human being from "irrational" fears and anxiety. A way was opened for dissolving the multitude of fears of devils, sorcerers, and forms of magic which had been the foci of pervasive anxiety in the last two centuries of the Middle Ages as well as in the Renaissance itself. Tillich points out that the Cartesians, by means of their assumption that the soul could not influence the body, were able to "disenchant the world." The persecution of witches, for example, which had occurred throughout the Renaissance up to the early eighteenth century, was overcome through such Cartesian formulations.

The confidence in the power of the autonomous, rational individual, which had emerged at the Renaissance and was more explicitly formulated in the seventeenth century, thus had on one side its anxiety-dispelling effects. But on the other side, since the confidence in reason was inseparably connected with the individualism of the Renaissance, it brought in its train new sources of anxiety in feelings of psychological isolation on the part of the individual.[5] In some ways, in fact, the doctrine of autonomous reason was in itself an intellectual expression in the seventeenth century of Renaissance individualism. Descartes' classical phrase, "I think; therefore, I exist," shows the emphasis on rational processes as a criterion of existence, but it also implies that one arrives at belief in one's own existence *in vacuo* as far as the community is concerned. Compare the present psychological concept that the experience of identity of the self occurs when the child becomes aware of other people as distinct from himself. W. H. Auden phrases this social origin of the self in succinct poetic terms:

> . . . for the ego is a dream
> Till a neighbor's need by
>   name create it.[6]

If this "neighbor's need" is not taken into consideration, the way is opened for new anxiety.

This problem of isolation of the individual was also confronted in the thought of the seventeenth century, and the solution presented had far-reaching effects in allaying anxiety. The solution consisted of the belief that the liberation of reason in every person would lead to a realization of a universal humanity and to a system of harmony between individuals and society. That is to say, the individual need not feel isolated, for if he courageously pursued his own reason, his conclusions and his interests would ultimately be in accord with those of his fellow-men and a harmonious community would be achieved. Moreover, even a metaphysical basis for overcoming isolation was presented—namely, that the pursuit of universal reason would lead the individual into accord with "universal reality." As Cassirer put it, *"mathematical reason was the bond between man and the universe."*[7]

Both the individualistic character of the thought of this period and the factors compensating for it can be seen in Leibnitz. His basic doctrine of the "monads" is individualistic in the sense that the monads are unitary, separated; but the compensating element is given in his doctrine of "pre-established harmony." Tillich expressed this graphically:

> In the system of harmony the metaphysical solitude of every individual is strongly emphasized by the doctrine that there are "no doors and windows" from one "monad" to the other one. Every single unit is lonely in itself, without any direct communication. The horror of this idea was overcome by the harmonistic presupposition that in every monad the whole world is potentially present and that the development of each individual is in a natural harmony with the development of all the others. This is the most profound metaphysical symbol for the situation in the early periods of bourgeois civilization. It fitted this situation because there was still a common world, in spite of the increasing social atomization.[8]

These anxiety-dispelling ways of thought are essential to understanding why the specific problem of anxiety is so rarely confronted by the thinkers of the seventeenth century. I shall demonstrate in the writings of Spinoza that the confidence that fear could be overcome by reason did serve to a considerable extent to obviate the problem of anxiety. We shall also discuss Pascal, a representative of the period who could not accept the prevalent confidence in the power of autonomous reason and for whom anxiety was therefore a central problem.

SPINOZA: REASON OVERCOMING FEAR

An eminent example of the method of dealing with fear in terms of mathematical reason is found in the writings of Baruch Spinoza (1632–1677). Spinoza "ventures to make the last and decisive step in this mathematical theory of the world and the human mind," remarks Cassirer; "Spinoza constructs a new ethics . . . a mathematical theory of the moral world."[9] It is well known that Spinoza's writings are replete with acute psychological insights which are remarkably close to contemporary scientific psychological theories, such as his statement that mental and physical phenomena are two aspects of the same process.[10] We can be sure that if Spinoza does not concern himself with anxiety, it is not because of lack of psychological discernment. At many points he anticipates later psychoanalytic concepts, as, for example, when he states that a passion (he uses "passion" to mean an emotional complex, not as Kierkegaard uses it to mean commitment) "ceases to be a passion when one has formed a clear and distinct idea of it."[11] This is a curious prediction of a later psychoanalytic technique, i.e., clarifying an emotion.

Spinoza believed that fear is essentially a subjective problem—that is, a matter of one's state of mind, or attitudes. He defines fear in juxtaposition to hope: they are both characteristic of the person in doubt. Fear is an "uncertain pain" arising from the idea that something we hate may befall us, and hope is an "uncertain pleasure" arising from the idea that a good we wish may come to pass. "It follows from these definitions," he adds, "that fear cannot be without hope, nor hope without fear."[12] Fear *"arises from a weakness of mind and therefore does not appertain to the use of reason."*[13] Hope also is a weakness of mind. "Therefore the more we endeavor to live under the guidance of reason, the less we endeavor to depend on hope, and the more to deliver ourselves and make ourselves free from fear and overcome fortune as much as possible, and finally to direct our actions by the certain advice of reason."[14] Spinoza's guidance on how to overcome fear is consistent with the general rational emphasis of the time, in which emotion is not repressed but rather made amenable to reason. It is true, he holds, that an emotion can be overcome only by a contrary, stronger one. But this can be done by paying attention to the "ordering of our thoughts and images." "We must think of courage in the same manner in order to lay aside fear, that is, we must enumerate and imagine the common perils of life and in what manner they may best be avoided and overcome by courage."[15]

At several points in his analysis Spinoza stands on the threshold of the problem of anxiety, as, for example, when he defines fear in juxtaposition to hope. The simultaneous presence of fear and hope within a given individual, perpetuated over a period of time, is one aspect of the psychic conflict that is seen by later writers, including myself, as anxiety.[16] But Spinoza does not cross the threshold into the problem of anxiety itself. In marked contrast to Kierkegaard in the nineteenth century, he does not see conflict between hope and fear as persistent or necessary; fears can be overcome by courageous dedication to reason, and hence the problem of anxiety does not confront him.

A similar difference between Spinoza and philosophers of the nineteenth century is evidenced in the treatment of confidence and despair. In Spinoza's terms we are confident when the cause of doubt has been removed from our hope—i.e., we are certain the good event will occur. And we are in despair when the element of doubt is removed from our fear—i.e., when we are certain that the evil event will occur or has occurred. For Kierkegaard, in contrast, confidence is not the removal of doubt (and anxiety) but rather the attitude that we can move ahead *despite* doubt and anxiety.

In Spinoza it is that word *certain* which strikes us so boldly. If one believed, as apparently Spinoza in his century could believe, that such intellectual and emotional certainty could be achieved, enviable psychological security would result. This belief, of course, underlay Spinoza's constructing a *mathematics* of ethics; one should be as certain about an ethical problem as one is about a proposition in geometry. The essential point is that for Spinoza the removal of doubt and the attainment of certainty is possible if we direct ourselves by the "certain advice of reason."

The central problem of anxiety does not intrude itself into Spinoza's thought. One cannot escape the conclusion that, given the cultural situation in which he lived, his confidence in reason served him satisfactorily.[17]

PASCAL: THE INADEQUACY OF REASON

Though representative of the eminent intellectuals of the seventeenth century in his mathematical and scientific genius, Blaise Pascal (1623–1662) was the exception in that he did not believe human nature, with all its variety, richness, and contradiction, could be comprehended by mathematical rationalism. He believed that rational certitude about man was not in any sense identical to rational certitude in geometry and physics. Thus he sounds to us like a contemporary, while Spinoza sounds like a man from a different age. The laws that operate in human life are, to Pascal, laws of chance and "probabilities." Hence he was impressed by the contingency of human existence.

> When I consider the brief span of my life, swallowed up in the eternity before and behind it, the small space that I fill, or even see, engulfed in the infinite immensity of spaces which I know not, and which know not me, I am afraid, and wonder to see myself here rather than there; for there is no reason why I should be here rather than there, now rather than then.

> On beholding the blindness and misery of man, on seeing all the universe dumb, and man without light, left to himself, as it were, astray in this corner of the universe, knowing not who has set him here, what he is here for, or what will become of him when he dies, incapable of all knowledge, I begin to be afraid, as a man who has been carried while asleep to a fearful desert island, and who will wake not knowing where he is and without any means of quitting the island. And thus I marvel that people are not seized with despair at such a miserable condition."[18]

Pascal was thus directly concerned with not only anxiety which he himself experienced but which he believed he observed underneath the surface of the lives of his contemporaries, evidenced by the "perpetual restlessness in which men pass their lives."[19] He noted the unceasing endeavors of people to divert themselves, to escape ennui, to avoid being alone, until "agitation" becomes an end in itself. The great bulk of diversions, he felt, were actually endeavors of people to avoid "thoughts of themselves," for if they should pause for self-contemplation, they would be miserable and anxious.

In his preoccupation with the contingent and uncertain

aspects of human experience, Pascal took cognizance of the fact that reason was offered by his contemporaries as a guide to certainty; but he believed that reason is undependable as a practical guide. It is not that he devaluated reason as such. On the contrary, he believed it to be the distinctive quality of man, the source of man's dignity in the midst of unthinking nature, and the source of morality ("to think well . . . is the principle of morality"[20]). But in practical life reason is undependable because it is "pliable to every sense," and sense reports are notoriously deceptive. Moreover the usual confidence in reason is faulty, he held, because it fails to take into account the power of the emotions.[21] Pascal conceived of the emotions in both a positive and a negative sense. He saw values in the emotions that were not comprehended in rationalism, expressed in this beautiful and justly quoted sentence: "The heart has reasons which the reason knows not of." On the other hand, the emotions often distort and override reason, and reason becomes mere rationalization. Overconfidence in reason often facilitates the abuse of reason to support mere custom, or the power of kings, or to rationalize injustice. In practice, reason is often a matter of "Truth on this side of the Pyrenees, error on that."[22] He was impressed with the frequency with which self-interest and vanity are the actual motivations of men, and are then justified by "reason." Greater trust could be placed in reason, he remarks epigrammatically, if "reason were only reasonable." In all these qualifications of the prevalent confidence in reason, it is clear that Pascal valued very highly what he termed a "genuine love of and respect for wisdom," but he felt that love of and respect for wisdom are rare phenomena in human life. Hence he saw the human situation much less optimistically than his contemporaries. "We are placed in a vast medium," he observed, "ever floating uncertainly between ignorance and knowledge."[23]

We have suggested that the confidence in reason, as interpreted by the intellectual leaders of the seventeenth century, served to dispel anxiety. It is some support for this hypothesis that Pascal, the one who could not accept the rationalistic solution to human problems, was at the same time the one who could not avoid anxiety.

Pascal stands as an exception, however, to the prevalent formulations of his day, and to the central stream of the philosophical developments in the modern period.[24] On the whole, the belief that through reason Nature could be mastered and man's emotions ordered served the intellectual leaders of that day relatively satisfactorily, so that the problem of anxiety rarely is confronted in their thought. I suggest that the cultural position in which Spinoza and the other thinkers of this classical phase of the modern period found themselves *did not result in the inner trauma which was to occur to comparable intellectual leaders in the nineteenth century and to vast numbers of people in the twentieth century.* The central belief in the power of autonomous reason gave a psychological unity to the culture which was not to be threatened with serious disintegration until the nineteenth century.

KIERKEGAARD: ANXIETY IN THE NINETEENTH CENTURY

In the nineteenth century we can observe on a broad scale the occurrence of fissures in the unity of modern culture which underlie much of our contemporary anxiety. The revolutionary belief in autonomous reason which had been central in the inception and structuralization of modern culture was now supplanted by "technical reason."[25] The rapidly increasing mastery over physical nature was accompanied by widespread and profound changes in the structure of human society. The economic and sociological aspects of these changes concern us in a later section, but here it is important to note the changes at that time in people's views of themselves.

This was the era of "autonomous sciences." Each science developed in its own direction: but a unifying principle, as Cassirer phrases it, was lacking. It was against the consequences of "science as a factory" that Nietszche warned; he saw technical reason progressing rapidly on one hand and the disintegration of human ideals and values on the other, and he feared the nihilism which would result. The views of man presented in the nineteenth century are not divorced, in most cases, from the empirical data produced by the advancing sciences; but since science itself was without a unifying principle, there was great variance in the interpretations of man. "Each individual thinker," Cassirer remarks, "gives us his own picture of human nature"; and whereas each picture is based upon empirical evidence, each "theory becomes a Procrustean bed on which the empirical facts are stretched to fit a preconceived pattern."[26] Cassirer continues:

> Owing to this development our modern theory of man lost its intellectual center. We acquired instead a complete anarchy of thought. . . . Theologians, scientists, politicians, sociologists, biologists, psychologists, ethnologists, economists all approached the problem from their own viewpoints. To combine or unify all these particular aspects and perspectives was impossible . . . every author seems in the last count to be led by his own conception and evaluation of human life.

Cassirer feels that this antagonism of ideas constituted not only "a grave theoretical problem but an imminent threat to the whole extent of our ethical and cultural life."[27]

The nineteenth century was marked by a cultural *compartmentalization*, not only in theories and in the sciences but in other phases of culture as well. In aesthetics, there was the "art for art's sake movement" and an increasing separation of art from the realities of nature—a development attacked toward the end of the century by Cézanne and Van Gogh. In religion there was a separation of theoretical beliefs and Sunday practices from the affairs of weekday life. The compartmentalization in family life is vividly portrayed and attacked by Ibsen in *A Doll's House*. With respect to the psychological life of the individual, the nineteenth century is broadly characterized by a separation of "reason" and "emotions," with voluntaristic effort (will) enthroned as the method of casting the decision between the two—which resulted generally in a denial of the emotions.

The seventeenth-century *belief in the rational control* of the emotions had now become the *habit of repressing* the emotions. In this light it is easy to understand why the less acceptable emotional impulses, such as sex and hostility, should have undergone particularly widespread repudiation. It is this psychological disunity which set the problem for the work of Sigmund Freud. His discoveries relating to unconscious forces and his techniques designed to assist the individual to find a new basis for psychological unity can be adequately understood only when seen against the background of compartmentalization of personality in the nineteenth century.[28]

In view of this psychological disunity, it is not surprising that anxiety should have emerged as an unavoidable problem in the nineteenth century. It is not surprising also that in the middle of that century we should find Kierkegaard producing the most direct, and in some ways the most profound, study of anxiety to appear up to that point in history. The disunity itself was, of course, anxiety-creating. The search for a new basis for unity of personality, as pursued by Kierkegaard and later by Freud, necessitated first of all confronting, and so far as possible solving, the problem of anxiety.

This breakdown in the unity of thought and culture was keenly felt by a number of sensitive and prophetic thinkers of the nineteenth century, many of whom can be grouped under the term Existentialists. The existentialist movement dates from the German philosopher F. W. J. Schelling's Berlin lectures in 1841, delivered before a distinguished audience including Kierkegaard, Engels and Burckhardt.[29] In addition to Schelling and Kierkegaard, existential thinking is represented on one wing by the "philosophers of life"—Nietzsche, Schopenhauer, and later Bergson—and on its sociological wing by Feuerbach and Marx.[30] "What all philosophers of Existence oppose is the 'rational' system of thought and life developed by Western industrial society and its philosophical representatives."[31] Tillich characterized the endeavors of these existential thinkers as "the desperate struggle to find a new meaning of life in a reality from which men have been estranged, in a cultural situation in which two great traditions, the Christian and the humanistic, have lost their comprehensive character and their convincing power." Tillich continues:

During the last hundred years the implications of this system have become increasingly clear: a logical or naturalistic mechanism which seemed to destroy individual freedom, personal decision and organic community; and analytic rationalism which saps vital forces of life and transforms everything, including man himself, into an object of calculation and control. . . .[32]

In their rejection of traditional rationalism, the existential thinkers insisted that reality can be approached and experienced only by *the whole individual, as a feeling and acting as well as a thinking organism.* Kierkegaard felt that Hegel's system, which confuses abstract thought with reality, was nothing short of trickery. Kierkegaard and others in this line believed that passion (using this word as meaning full commitment) cannot be divorced from thinking. Feuerbach wrote, "Only that which is the object of passion really is."[33] Said Nietzsche, "We think with our bodies."

Thus, these thinkers sought to overcome the traditional dichotomy between mind and body and the tendency to suppress the "irrational" aspects of experience. Pure objectivity is an illusion, Kierkegaard held; and even if it weren't, it would be undesirable. He emphasizes "the word 'interest' *(inter-est),* which expresses the fact that we are so intimately involved in the objective world that we cannot be content to regard truth objectively, i.e., disinterestedly."[34] Kierkegaard reacted strongly against rigid definitions of such terms as "self" and "truth"; he felt they could be defined only dynamically, i.e., dialectically, as continuously developing among living people. "Away from speculation," he cried, "away from 'the System' and back to reality."[35] He insisted that "truth exists for the particular individual only as he himself produces it in action."[36] This sounds like a radical subjectivity, which on the surface it is; but it must be remembered that Kierkegaard and the others in this movement believed that this was the way to a genuine objectivity as opposed to the *artificial* objectivity of the "rationalistic" systems. As Tillich expressed it, these thinkers "turned toward man's immediate experience, toward 'subjectivity,' not as something opposed to 'objectivity,' but as that living experience in which both objectivity and subjectivity are rooted."[37] Also, "They tried to discover the creative realm of being which is prior to and beyond the distinction between objectivity and subjectivity."

It was the aim of these thinkers to overcome the compartmentalization of their culture by a *new emphasis on the individual as a living, experiencing unity*—i.e., the individual as an organism which thinks, feels, and wills at the same time. The existentialists are important in this study, not only because the dichotomy between psychology and philosophy is broken down in their thought, but also because now for the first time in the modern period *anxiety comes directly into the foreground as a specific problem.*

We turn now directly to Søren Kierkegaard (1813–1855). He is regarded on the Continent, according to Brock, as "one of the most remarkable psychologists of all time, in depth, if not in breadth, superior to Nietzsche, and in penetration comparable only to Dostoievski."[38]

The keystone idea in Kierkegaard's little book on anxiety,[39] published in 1844, is the relation between anxiety and freedom. Kierkegaard held that "anxiety is always to be understood as oriented toward freedom."[40] Freedom is the goal of personality development; psychologically speaking, "the good is freedom."[41] Kierkegaard defines freedom as *possibility.* This he views as the spiritual aspect of man; indeed, it is not inaccurate to read "possibility" whenever Kierkegaard writes "spirit." The distinctive characteristic of the human being, in contrast to the merely vegetative or the merely animal, lies in the range of human possibility and in our capacity for self-awareness of possibility. Kierkegaard sees man as the creature who is continually beckoned by possibility, who conceives of possibility, visualizes it, and by creative activity carries it into actuality. What the specific content of this possibility is, in psychological terms, I shall discuss below in dealing with Kierkegaard's ideas of expansiveness and communicativeness. It suffices here to emphasize that this possibility is human freedom.

Now this capacity for freedom brings with it anxiety. Anxiety is the state of the human being, says Kierkegaard, when he confronts his freedom. Indeed, he describes anxiety as "the possibility of freedom." Whenever possibility is visualized by an individual, anxiety is potentially present in the same experience. In everyday experiential terms, this may be illustrated by our recalling that every person has the opportunity and need to move ahead in his development—the child learns to walk, and moves on into school, and the adult moves into marriage and/or new jobs. Such possibilities, like roads ahead which cannot be known since you have not yet traversed and experienced them, involve anxiety. (This is "normal anxiety," and is not to be confused with "neurotic anxiety," which will be considered below. Kierkegaard makes it clear that neurotic anxiety is a more constrictive and uncreative form of anxiety which results from the individual's *failure* to move ahead in situations of normal anxiety.) [42] There is anxiety in any actualizing of possibility. To Kierkegaard, the more possibility (creativity) an individual has, the more potential anxiety he has at the same time. Possibility ("I can") passes over into actuality, but the intermediate determinant is anxiety. "Possibility means *I can*. In a logical system it is convenient enough to say that possibility passes over into actuality. In reality it is not so easy, and an intermediate determinant is necessary. This intermediate determinant is anxiety . . ."[43]

Viewing anxiety developmentally, Kierkegaard begins with the original state of the infant. This he terms the state of innocence, in which the infant is in immediate unity with its natural condition, its environment. The infant has possibility. This entails anxiety, but it is anxiety without specific content. In this original state anxiety is a "seeking after adventure, a thirst for the prodigious, the mysterious."[44] The child moves ahead, actualizing his possibilities. But in the state of innocence he is not self-consciously aware that the possibility of growth, for example, also involves crises, clashes with, and defiance of his parents. In the state of innocence, individuation is a potentiality which has not yet become self-conscious. The anxiety connected with it is "sheer possibility," i.e., without specific content.

Then in human development comes self-awareness. Kierkegaard cites the story of Adam as a presentation in myth form of this phenomenon. Disposing immediately of the deteriorated view of this myth as a historical event, he insists that "the myth represents as outward that which occurred inwardly."[45] In this sense the myth of Adam is re-enacted by every human being somewhere between the ages of one and three. Kierkegaard interprets it as a portrayal of the individual's inner awakening into self-consciousness. At some point in development there occurs the "knowledge of good and evil," as the myth puts it. Then *conscious choice* enters the picture of possibility. There occurs a heightened sense both of the portentous nature of possibility and of the responsibility that goes with it. For now the possibility of conflict and crises confronts the individual; possibility is negative as well as positive. Developmentally, the child now moves toward individuation. And the road over which he moves is not one of immediate harmony with environment or specifically with parents, but a road which continually skirts the edges of defiance of this environment; and indeed in many cases the road must move *directly through* actual experiences of conflict with parents. The threat of isolation and powerlessness and the consequent anxiety arise at this point in the child's development (discussed on pages 55–56 ff. below). Individuation (becoming a self) is gained at the price of confronting the anxiety inherent in taking a stand *against* as well as *with* one's environment. Describing the moment of this heightened awareness of the possibility of freedom, Kierkegaard speaks of "the *alarming* possibility of being able."[46]

It may be helpful to point out here that Kierkegaard's central problem when he writes psychologically is how a person can will to be himself. *To will to be himself is man's true vocation.* Kierkegaard holds *that we cannot specifically define this self* one is to be, *for the self is freedom.* But at considerable length he points out how people try to avoid willing to be themselves: by avoiding consciousness of the self, by willing to be some one else or simply a conventional self, or by willing to be oneself defiantly, which is a form of tragic, stoic despair and, therefore, doomed to fall short of full selfhood. His word "will" is not to be confused with nineteenth-century voluntarism, which consisted chiefly of repression of unacceptable elements within the self. Rather, this *willing is a creative decisiveness, based centrally on expanding self-awareness.* "Generally speaking, consciousness, i.e. consciousness of self, is the decisive criterion of the self," he writes. "The more consciousness, the more self. . . ."[47]

This is not a foreign language to anyone conversant with modern psychotherapy. One basic aim of therapy is to enlarge self-awareness by means of clarifying inner self-defeating conflicts which have existed because the individual has been forced to block self-awareness at earlier times.[48] It is clear in therapy that these blockages in self-awareness have occurred because the person has been unable to move through accumulations of anxiety at various points in his growth. Kierkegaard makes it clear that selfhood depends upon the individual's capacity to *confront anxiety and move ahead despite it.* Freedom, to Kierkegaard, is not a simple accretion, nor does it occur as spontaneously as the plant grows toward the sun when the rocks that block it are removed (as the problem of freedom is sometimes oversimplified in deteriorated forms of psychotherapy). *Freedom, rather, depends on how one relates oneself to oneself at every moment in existence.* This means, in present-day terms, that freedom depends on how responsibly and autonomously one relates to oneself.

When Kierkegaard speaks of the awakening of self-awareness following the state of innocence of the child, one is tempted to compare this with the data of contemporary psychology. The difficulty in such a comparison is that the equivalence is never entirely complete. For example, Kierkegaard's idea of the *self* is only partially contained in the psychological term *ego,* which is its nearest equivalent. But we can say that the awakening of self-awareness is roughly parallel to what is now meant in some psychological quarters by the "emergence of the ego." This occurs generally somewhere between the ages of one and three; we can observe in babies that this self-awareness does not exist, whereas it is discernible in the child of four or five. So far as Kierkegaard's own view goes, he believed this change is a "qualitative leap," and cannot, therefore, be adequately described by scientific methods. Kierkegaard's aim is to describe phenomenologically the human situation—of an adult, for example—which he finds as a state of conflict (self-awareness) set against a backdrop of innocence.[49]

As a consequence of this "leap" into self-awareness, anxiety becomes reflective—that is, it now has more content. Anxiety "in the later individual is more reflective as a consequence of the participation of the individual in the history of the race."[50] Self-awareness makes possible not only self-directed individual development, but also self-conscious historical development. Just as the individual now sees himself as not merely at the mercy of his environment and his natural condition, but as possessing the capacities of choice and independence, so he sees himself likewise as something more than an automaton, swallowed up in a meaningless historical development. Through self-awareness man can mold and to an extent transform his present historical development. This does not annul the determining influences of one's historical environment. "Every individual begins in a historical nexus," Kierkegaard writes, "and the consequences of natural law are still as valid as ever."[51] But what is of crucial significance is how a person relates himself to his historical nexus.

Kierkegaard's argument up to this point may be summarized as follows: In the state of innocence there is no separation of the individual from his environment, and anxiety is ambiguous. In the state of self-awareness, however, there occurs the possibility of separation as an individual. Anxiety is now reflective; and the individual can through self-awareness partially direct his own development as well as participate in the history of the race.

We now come to a crucial point. Anxiety involves inner conflict; this is another and important consequence of self-awareness. Anxiety "is afraid," says Kierkegaard, "yet it maintains a sly intercourse with its object, cannot look away from it, indeed will not. . . ."[52] (Our author adds, for reasons the reader can well understand, "If to one or another this may appear a difficult saying, I can do nothing about it.") And again, anxiety

is a desire for what one dreads, a sympathetic antipathy. Anxiety is an alien power which lays hold of an individual, and yet one cannot tear oneself away, nor has a will to do so; for one fears, but what one fears one desires. Anxiety then makes the individual impotent.[53]

This inner conflict which characterizes anxiety is familiar in modern clinical psychology; it has been described specifically by Freud, Stekel, Horney, and others. Ample illustrations of it can be cited from clinical data, especially in its exaggerated form in neurosis: a patient has sexual or aggressive desires, yet he fears these very desires (including the consequences of them), and a persistent inner conflict is engendered. Every person who has been seriously ill physically knows that he has severe anxiety lest he not get well, yet he flirts with the prospect of remaining sick; *he is sympathetic,* in Kierkegaard's words, *to the prospect he hates and fears most.* This is a phenomenon more profound than the mere desire for the "secondary gain" of illness, be it emotional or physical. Possibly Freud was struggling with this phenomenon when he postulated the much questioned formulation of the "death instinct" as in conflict with the "life instinct." It would seem that Otto Rank comes closer to Kierkegaard (and at the same time avoids the less acceptable elements in Freud's postulation) in his concept of the conflict between the "life will" and the "death will."[54] The conflict occurs not only *in* anxiety, but is itself the product of anxiety—i.e., one has such conflict to the extent that one already has anxiety in the situation.

In any case, Kierkegaard makes it clear that he would not limit this inner conflict to neurotic phenomena. He believes that in every possibility, in every experience of anxiety beyond infancy, the conflict is present. In every experience the individual wishes to move ahead, actualizing his possibilities; but at the same time he plays with the prospect of not doing so—i.e., there is in him a wish *not* to actualize his possibilities. Kierkegaard would describe the difference between the "neurotic" and "healthy" state by saying that the healthy individual moves ahead despite the conflict, actualizing his freedom, whereas the unhealthy person retrenches to a "shut-in" condition, sacrificing his freedom. The radical distinction between fear and anxiety appears at this point: in fear one moves in one direction, *away* from the feared object, whereas in anxiety a persistent inner conflict is in operation and one has an ambivalent relation to the object. Kierkegaard always insists that although anxiety in the reflective stage has more content, it can never be assigned a wholly specific content, for it describes an inner state, a state of conflict.

Another consequence of self-awareness is that responsibility and guilt feeling enter the picture.[55] Guilt feeling is a difficult and perplexing problem, to Kierkegaard as well as in contemporary psychology, and to my mind it is often evaded by oversimplification. We can understand Kierkegaard's ideas on the relation between guilt and anxiety only by emphasizing that he is always speaking of anxiety in its relation to creativity. One has anxiety because it is possible to create—creating one's self, willing to be one's self, as well as creating in all the innumerable daily activities (and these are two phases of the same process). One would have no anxiety if there were no possibility whatever. It is valuable to let patients in therapy know this—to point out that the presence of anxiety means a conflict is going on, and so long as this is true, a constructive solution is possible.

Now creating, actualizing one's possibilities, always involves destructive as well as constructive aspects. It always involves destroying the status quo, destroying old patterns within oneself, progressively destroying what one has clung to from childhood on, and creating new and original forms and ways of living. If you do not do this, you are refusing to grow, refusing to avail yourself of possibilities; you are shirking your responsibility to yourself. Hence refusal to actualize one's possibilities brings guilt toward one's self. But creating also means destroying the status quo of one's environment, breaking the old forms; it means producing something new and original in human relations as well as in cultural forms (e.g., the creativity of the artist).[56] Every experience of creativity has its potentiality of aggression or denial toward other persons in one's environment or toward established patterns within one's self. To put the matter figuratively, in every experience of creativity something in the past is killed so that something new in the present may be born. Hence, for Kierkegaard, guilt feeling is always a concomitant of anxiety: both are aspects of experiencing and actualizing possibility. The more creative the person, he held, the more anxiety and guilt are potentially present. "The greater the genius," writes Kierkegaard, "the more profoundly he discovers guilt."[57]

Although sex and sensuality are often made the content for this guilt, Kierkegaard did not believe that sex and sensuality are in themselves sources of either anxiety or guilt. Sex is significant, rather, because it stands for the problem of *individuation and community*. In Kierkegaard's culture as well as in ours, sex is often the clearest fulcrum of the problem of being a self—e.g., having individual desires, urges, yet being in expanding relationships with others. The complete fulfillment of these desires involves other persons. Sex may thus express this individuality-in-community constructively (sex as a form of interpersonal relatedness), or it may be distorted into egocentricity (pseudo-individuality) or into mere symbiotic dependence (pseudo-community). In what we may take as an analogy, Kierkegaard speaks of anxiety culminating in the woman at the birth of a child, because "at this instant the new individual comes into the world." *Anxiety and guilt are potentially present at every instant that individuality is born into community.* And this is not only in the figurative sense of the birth of a child, but in the birth of new phases of one's own individuality. According to Kierkegaard, one is, or ought to be, continually creating his own selfhood every instant of his life.[58]

The belief in fate, says Kierkegaard, is often used as a method of avoiding the anxiety and guilt feeling in creativity. Since "fate is a relation of spirit (possibility) to something external," such as misfortune, necessity, or chance, the full meaning of anxiety and guilt are not felt. But Kierkegaard holds that this taking of refuge in a doctrine of fate sets limits to creativity. Thus he believed that Judaism, in which the problem of guilt was frankly faced, represents a higher level than Hellenism, which rested with a belief in fate. The creative genius in the highest sense does not seek to avoid anxiety and guilt through recourse to belief in fate; he creates by moving *through* anxiety and guilt.

One form of the loss of freedom is the state of "shut-upness." "Shut-upness" is a graphic term for the processes of blocked awareness, inhibition, and other common neurotic reactions to anxiety.[59] This is the state, points out Kierkegaard, that has been characterized historically as the "demoniacal," and since he cites some biblical cases of hysteria and muteness, we know that he is referring to various clinical forms of neurosis and psychosis. The trouble in such cases he felt to be an "unfree relation to the good." Anxiety takes the form of "dread of the good"; the individual endeavors to shut out freedom and constrict his development. Indeed, "freedom is precisely the expansive," Kierkegaard holds; "freedom is constantly communicating," he adds, foreshadowing the concepts of Harry Stack Sullivan.[60] In the demoniacal state, "unfreedom becomes more and more shut-up and wants no communication."[61] Kierkegaard makes it clear that he is not referring, in the phrase "shut-upness," to the reserve of the creative person, but to shut-upness as withdrawal and as a form of continual negation. "The demoniacal does not shut itself up *with* something, but shuts *itself* up."[62] Hence he also holds that the shut-up is the tedious (the impression of being extinct) and the vacuous. The shut-up person has anxiety when confronted with freedom or the "good" (these two terms are used as synonyms at this point). The "good" in Kierkegaard's sense signifies to the shut-up person a challenge to reintegrate himself on the basis of freedom. The "good" furthermore, he describes as expansiveness, ever increasing communicativeness.

Kierkegaard believed that it is a false compassion to view the shut-up personality as a victim of fate, for this implies that nothing can be done about it. A real compassion involves facing the problem with guilt (i.e., responsibility). This is responsibility on the part of all of us, whether shut-up or not. The courageous man prefers, when ill, to have it said, "this is not fate, this is guilt," for then his possibility of doing something about his condition is not removed from him. For "the ethical individual," Kierkegaard continues, "fears nothing so much as fate and aesthetic folderol which under the cloak of compassion would trick him out of his treasure, *viz.*, freedom" (*ibid.*, p. 108 n.). I can illustrate this experientially from a realm which is supposed in our culture to be even more closely referable to fate than psychological disturbances—i.e., infectious illnesses. When I was ill with tuberculosis (before the days of drugs to cure the disease), I noticed, in observing myself and many other patients, that we were often reassured by well-meaning friends and medical personnel that the disease was due to an accident of infection by the tubercle bacillus. This explanation on the basis of fate was thought to be a relief to the patient. But actually it threw many of the more psychologically sensitive patients into greater despair. If the disease were an accident, how could we be certain it would not occur again and again? If, on the other hand, the patient feels that his own pattern of life was at fault and that this was one of the causes of his succumbing to the disease, he feels more guilt, to be sure, but at the same time he sees more hopefully what conditions need to be corrected in order to overcome the disease. From this point of view, guilt feeling is not only the more accurate attitude, but it is also the one yielding the more genuine hope. (Needless to say, Kierkegaard and I are referring to *rational*, not *irrational* guilt. The latter has unconscious dynamics, is unconstructive, and needs to be weeded out.)

Shut-up states, in the last analysis, are based upon illusions: "it is easy to see that shut-upness *eo ipso* signifies a lie, or, if you prefer, untruth. But untruth is precisely unfreedom. . . ."[63] He suggests that those who work with shut-up personalities should realize the value of silence, and should always keep their "categories very clear." He believed that the shut-up state can be cured by inward revelation, or "transparency," and his references to this on the psychological level are not unlike contemporary ideas of catharsis and clarification.

Freedom may also be lost psychosomatically. To Kierkegaard "the somatic, the psychic, the pneumatic" (possibility) are so interrelated that "a disorganization in one shows itself in the others."[64] He adds a third determinant to the customary psyche and soma, namely the self. It is this "intermediate determinant" which involves possibility and freedom. He did not believe that personality is a mere synthesis of psyche and soma. If it is to be developed to its larger capacities, personality depends upon *how the self relates itself to both psyche and soma.* This is another indication that Kierkegaard's concept of the self is not to be identified with merely a portion of the psyche such as the ego. The self is in operation when an individual is able to view both psyche and soma with freedom and to act on this freedom.

Other examples of the loss of freedom as a result of anxiety are seen in the rigid personalities. These are the personalities, writes Kierkegaard, who lack inward certitude.

A partisan of the most rigid orthodoxy may be demoniacal. He knows it all, he bows before the holy, truth is for him an ensemble of ceremonies, he talks about presenting himself before the throne of God, of how many times one must bow, he knows everything the same way as does the pupil who is able to demonstrate a mathematical proposition with the letters *ABC*, but not when they are changed to *DEF*. He is therefore in anxiety whenever he hears something not arranged in the same order. And yet how closely he resembles a modern speculative philosopher who found a new proof for the immortality of the soul, then came into mortal danger and could not produce his proof because he had not his notebooks with him.[65]

The kind of anxiety which is related to lack of inward certitude may show itself on one hand by wilfulness and unbelief—the negating attitude; and on the other hand by superstition. "Superstition and unbelief are both forms of unfreedom."[66] The bigot and the unbeliever are in the same category with respect to the form of anxiety underlying their frame of mind. Both lack expansiveness; "both lack inwardness and dare not come to themselves."[67]

It is not surprising to Kierkegaard that people should do everything possible to avoid anxiety. He speaks of his "cowardly age" in which "one does everything possible by way of diversions and the Janizary music of loud-voiced enterprises to keep lonely thoughts away, just as in the forests of America they keep away wild beasts by torches, by yells, by the sound of cymbals."[68] For anxiety is an exceedingly painful experience. And again we quote, because of its vividness and aptness, his description of this painfulness:

> And no Grand Inquisitor has in readiness such terrible tortures as has anxiety, and no spy knows how to attack more artfully the man he suspects, choosing the instant when he is weakest, nor knows how to lay traps where he will be caught and ensnared, as anxiety knows how, and no sharpwitted judge knows how to interrogate, to examine the accused, as anxiety does, which never lets him escape, neither by diversion nor by noise, neither at work nor at play, neither by day nor by night.[69]

But attempts to evade anxiety are not only doomed to failure. In running from anxiety you lose your most precious opportunities for the emergence of yourself, and for your education as a human being. "If a man were a beast or an angel, he would not be able to be in anxiety. Since he is a synthesis he can be in anxiety, and the greater the anxiety the greater the man. This, however, is not affirmed in the sense in which men commonly understand anxiety, as related to something outside a man, but in the sense that man himself produces anxiety."[70]

Kierkegaard writes in his most engaging vein about anxiety as a "school." Anxiety is an even better teacher than reality, for one can temporarily evade reality by avoiding the distasteful situation; but anxiety is a source of education always present because one carries it within. "Even in relation to the most trifling matters, so soon as the individuality would make an artful turn which is only artful, would steal away from something, and there is every probability that it will succeed, for reality is not so sharp an examiner as anxiety—then anxiety is at hand."[71] Accepting anxiety as a teacher may seem a foolish counsel, he admits, especially to those who boast of never having been in anxiety. "To this I would reply that doubtless one should not be in dread of men, or of finite things, but *only that man who has gone through the anxiety of possibility is educated to have no anxiety.*"[72]

On one side—which we may term the negative side—this education involves facing and accepting the human situation frankly. It means facing the fact of death and other aspects of the contingency of existence, and from this *Angst der Kreatur* one learns how to interpret the reality of one's human situation. "When such a person, therefore, goes out from the school of possibility, and knows more thoroughly than a child knows the alphabet that he can demand of life absolutely nothing, and that terror, perdition, annihilation, dwell next door to every man, and has learned the profitable lesson that every anxiety which alarms [*Aengste*] may the next instant become a fact, he will interpret reality differently, he will extol reality. . . ."[73]

On the positive side, going to school to anxiety enables one to move through the finite and petty constrictions and to be freed to actualize the infinite possibilities in personality. The finite to Kierkegaard is that which "shuts up" freedom; the infinite refers in contrast to "opening up" doors to freedom. The infinite, therefore, is part of his concept of possibility. Finiteness can be defined as one experiences it in the innumerable constrictions and artificial limitations that we observe in the clinic as well as in our own lives. The infinite cannot be so defined, because it represents freedom. In facing anxiety, Kierkegaard extols the attitude of Socrates who

> solemnly flourished the poisoned goblet . . . as a patient says to the surgeon when a painful operation is about to begin, "Now I am ready." Then anxiety enters into his soul and searches it thoroughly, constraining out of him all the finite and the petty, and leading him hence whither he would go.[74]

In such confronting of anxiety the individual is educated to faith, or inward certitude. Then one has the "courage to renounce anxiety without any anxiety, which only faith is capable of—not that it annihilates anxiety, but remaining ever young, it is continually developing itself out of the death throe of anxiety."

To the scientifically minded reader, it may seem that Kierkegaard in the above quotations is speaking in poetic and paradoxical figures of speech. This is, of course, true; but his meaning may be summarized in clear, experiential terms. On one hand he is anticipating the contention of Horney and others that anxiety indicates the presence of a problem which needs to be solved; and in Kierkegaard's mind, anxiety will dog the steps of the individual (if he does not engage in complete neurotic repression) until it is resolved. But on the other hand, Kierkegaard is proclaiming that "self-strength" develops out of the individual's successful confronting of anxiety-creating experiences. This is the way one becomes educated to maturity as a self.

What is so amazing in Kierkegaard is that despite his writing 130 years ago, and despite his lack of the tools for interpreting unconscious material—which tools have been available in their most complete form only since Freud—he so keenly and profoundly anticipated modern psychoanalytic insight into anxiety. At the same time he placed these insights in the broad context of a poetic and philosophical understanding of human experience. In Kierkegaard one finds a promise of the dawning of that day for which the French physiologist Claude Bernard yearned, the day when "the physiologist, the philosopher and the poet will talk the same language and understand each other."

CHAPTER
3

Anxiety Interpreted Biologically

The planning function of the nervous system, in the course of evolution, has culminated in the appearance of ideas, values, and pleasures—the unique manifestations of man's social living. Man, alone, can plan for the distant future and can experience the retrospective pleasures of achievement. Man, alone, can be happy. But man, alone, can be worried and anxious. Sherrington once said that posture accompanies movement as a shadow. I have come to believe that anxiety accompanies intellectual activity as *its* shadow and that the more we know of the nature of anxiety the more we will know of intellect.

—Howard Liddell, *The Role of Vigilance in the Development of Animal Neurosis*

In this chapter we inquire: What happens to an organism when it is confronted with a danger situation? We will make our inquiry from the biological viewpoint, biology as including not only the reflexive responses to danger but also the broader sense of the organism as a biological whole responding to a threat.

I am aware that, in the study of anxiety, there have occurred during the last two decades a great number of researches into relatively isolated phases of neurology and physiology. Indeed, the progress in the development of more sophisticated instruments, for example, to study endocrinology, has been great indeed. Each of these researches is like an individual brick to be used in the building of a house. But where is the design for the house? *Where, in other words, is the synthesis, the integration, the pattern into which all these discrete bricks are to be placed?*[1]

Our great need, as the authors of the many papers in symposia on anxiety seem universally to agree, is for an integrating design which will bring, as Freud said half a century ago, some "order and lucidity" into the field. Our heterogeneous, isolated, segmented knowledge has vastly increased; our understanding of anxiety as a whole has scarcely increased at all. The pattern which would include all these different phases seems still to elude us.

Eugene E. Levitt, for example, describes an article in the *Scientific Monthly* in 1969, in which the author, Ferris Pitts, claimed to have found the chemical source of anxiety, consisting of high concentrations of lactate in the blood. This was announced as a "breakthrough," similar to the announcement every four or five years of a "breakthrough" in the cause of schizophrenia. These breakthroughs then are forgotten, to be mentioned only in obituaries. Levitt summarizes it with these words, "Breakthrough research is low caliber work masquerading as top drawer work."[2]

The reason these "discoveries" so often turn out to be disappointing is that the "cause" of a condition of life like anxiety can never be found in an isolated neurological or physiological reaction. What is necessary is a new pattern which will include all the different approaches. The neurological and physiological aspects of anxiety cannot be understood by themselves, but they must be seen in reference to the question, *What needs is the organism trying to fulfill in its struggle with its world?* By world I mean not only physical environment but more than that: the psychological and attitudinal environment as well.

This means that the neurophysiological processes need to be seen as one phase of the *hierarchy of organization* of the organism. It means what Adolph Meyer called "a subordination of physiology to the integrating functions and particularly by means of the use of symbols."[3]

There are many empirical supports for this summary statement of Adolph Meyer. Aaron Beck states that the "stressful life situations, per se, are less important in the production of anxiety and physical disorders than the way in which these situations are *perceived* by the individual."[4]

In their studies of anxiety in soldiers in the Vietnam War, three authors, Bourne, Rose, and Mason, summarize that what causes the variation in anxiety is not the physiology per se, but the "characteristic life style" of the particular soldier. In other words, the manner in which the individual perceives the threat is more important than the threat itself. In the life style of the person the *integrative* dynamism is of great importance. Mason points out that many illnesses may be *disorders of this integrative mechanism*. It is this integrative mechanism by which the person symbolically interprets the situations as threatening or nonthreatening.

Contrasting the "elementalistic" approach in biology, John Mason states, "The premise underlying the 'integrative' or 'synthetic' approach . . . is that ultimate understanding of the living organism lies not only in knowing its ultimate component parts, but that a unique and fundamental task in biology is to determine how the many separate bodily parts or processes are integrated with the organism as a whole."[5]

The aim of an integrating pattern must be kept in mind in this chapter. We must ask how each research fits into the whole, if we are to avoid the quicksand lying in wait for all researches in physiology and neurology.

THE STARTLE PATTERN

We begin by noting a protective response which, although not fear or anxiety, is a precursor of these emotions—the startle pattern. The study of the startle pattern by Landis and Hunt is of particular interest, since it casts light on the order of emergence in an organism of protective response, anxiety, and fear.[6]

If one shoots off a gun behind a person, or in other ways gives a loud, sudden stimulus, the person will bend quickly, jerk his head forward, blink his eyes, and in other ways exhibit the "startle response." This response is a primary, innate, involuntary reaction which precedes the emotions of fear and anxiety. Landis and Hunt performed varied experiments to elicit the startle pattern, using mainly a pistol shot for the stimulus and cinemaphotography to record the instantaneous reactions. The startle pattern has as its most prominent feature a general flexion of the body, "which resembles a protective contraction or 'shrinking' of the individual."[7] The startle pattern always is marked by a blinking of the eyes, and in the normal picture it includes "head movement forward, a characteristic facial expression, raising and drawing forward of the shoulders, abduction of the upper arms, bending of the elbows, pronation of the lower arms, flexion of the fingers, forward movement of the trunk, contraction of the abdomen, and bending of the knees . . . It is a basic reaction, not amenable to voluntary control, is universal, and is found in Negroes as well as whites, infants as well as adults, in the primates and in certain of the lower animal forms."[8] Neurologically, the startle pattern involves an inhibition of the higher nervous centers, since the latter are unable to integrate a stimulus of such suddenness. That is to say, we startle before we know what threatens us.

The startle response is not fear or anxiety as such. "It seems best to define startle as pre-emotional," Landis and Hunt rightly remark.[9] "It is an immediate response to sudden, intense stimulation which demands some out-of-the-ordinary treatment by the organism. As such it partakes of the nature of an emergency reaction, but it is a rapid, transitory response much more simple in its organization and expression than the so-called 'emotions.' "[10] Emotion proper may *follow* the startle reflex. The adult subjects in the Landis and Hunt experiments showed such secondary behavior (emotion) as curiosity, annoyance, and fear after the startle. The authors suggest that this secondary behavior is a "bridge from the innate and unlearned response over to the learned, socially conditioned, and often purely voluntary type of response."[11]

Significantly, *the younger the infant in these experiments, the less secondary behavior accompanied the startle*. During the first month of life the infant showed very little reaction except startle, "while our work shows," continue Landis and Hunt, "that as the infant develops, more and more secondary behavior appears. . . . Crying and escape behavior—either a turning of the head away from the sound source or actual turning of the body and creeping away—became increasingly frequent with age."[12]

A great deal can be deduced from the startle pattern as a pre-emotional response of anxiety and fear. For example, Lawrence Kubie finds in this pattern the "ontogeny of anxiety." He holds that the startle pattern is the first indication that *a gap exists between the individual and his world. The fetus, Kubie holds, cannot experience startle; in the fetus there is no interval between stimulus and response. But the infant and the startle pattern are born at the same moment. Thereafter there exists a "distance" between the individual and his environment. The infant experiences waiting, postponement, frustration. Anxiety and the thought processes both arise out of this situation of "gap" between the individual and the world, Kubie holds, with anxiety preceding the development of thought. "Anxiety in the life of the individual stands as a bridge between the startle pattern and the dawn of all processes of thought."*[13]

This startle pattern, according to Landis and Hunt, belongs to the general type of response which Goldstein calls the "catastrophic reaction." We view the startle pattern as a primal, unlearned protective response, the precursor to the emotional reactions of the organism which are later to become anxiety and fear.

ANXIETY AND THE CATASTROPHIC REACTION

The contribution of Kurt Goldstein is important for our present purposes because it yields a broad biological base for the understanding of anxiety.[14] Goldstein's concepts arise out of his work as a neurobiologist with diverse mental patients, but especially with patients with brain injuries. As director of a large mental hospital in Germany during World War I, Goldstein had the opportunity to observe and study many soldiers who had had part of their brains shot away. These patients, whose capacities for adequate adjustment to the demands of their environment were limited by their brain lesions, responded to a wide variety of stimuli with shock, anxiety, and defense reactions. By observing them, as by observing normal individuals in crisis situations, we can gain insights into the biological aspects of the dynamics of anxiety in all organisms.[15]

Goldstein's central thesis is that *anxiety is the subjective experience of the organism in a catastrophic condition.* An organism is thrown into a catastrophic condition when it cannot cope with the demands of its environment and, therefore, feels a threat to its existence or to values it holds essential for its existence. The "catastrophic condition" must not be seen as always referring to high emotional intensity. It may come with just a thought running through one's mind of a threat to his existence. The degree of intensity is not the issue; it is a *qualitative* experience.

The brain-injured patients Goldstein studied devised innumerable ways of avoiding catastrophic situations. Some, for example, developed compulsive patterns of orderliness: they kept their closets in perfect order. If placed in surroundings in which the objects were in disarray—i.e., if someone changed the arrangement of their shoes, clothes, etc.—they were at a loss to react adequately and exhibited profound anxiety. Others, when asked to write their names on a paper, would write in the extreme corner of the paper; any open space (any "emptiness") represented a situation with which they could not cope. Any changes in environment were avoided by these patients, for they were unable to evaluate new stimuli adequately. In all these situations we see the patient unable to cope with the demands of his world and unable to actualize his essential capacities. The normal adult, of course, is able to cope with a much wider range of stimuli, but the problem of *organism-in-catastrophic-condition* remains essentially the same. The objective aspect of being in such a condition is disordered behavior. *The subjective aspect is anxiety.*

Goldstein denies that an organism is to be understood as a composite of various "drives," the blocking or disturbing of which results in anxiety.[16] Rather, there is only one trend in an organism—namely, *to actualize its own nature.* (We note the similarities between this view and Kierkegaard's concept of self-realization.) Each organism's primal need and tendency are to make its environment adequate to itself and itself adequate to its environment. Of course, the nature of organisms, animal or human, varies widely. Each has its own essential capacities, which determine both what it has to actualize and how it will endeavor to do so. A wild animal may actualize its own nature successfully in its jungle habitat, but placed in captivity in a cage it is often unable to react adequately and exhibits frantic behavior. Sometimes an organism overcomes the hiatus between its own nature and the environment by sacrificing some elements in its nature—presumably the wild animal above learns to avoid the catastrophic condition in the cage by sacrificing its need to roam freely. An inadequate organism may seek to shrink its world to that in which its essential capacities are adequate, thus avoiding the catastrophic situation. As an example, Goldstein mentions that Cannon's sympathetomized cats stayed near a radiator because their capacity to react adequately to cold (and thus preserve their existence) had been curtailed by the cutting of the sympathetic nervous chain.

It is not merely or even centrally the threat of pain, according to Goldstein, that causes the catastrophic condition and consequent anxiety. Pain can often be born without anxiety or fear. Likewise anxiety is not cued off by *any* danger. It is that particular danger which threatens the existence of the organism—"existence" here meaning not merely physical life but psychological life as well. The threat may be to *values the organism identifies with its existence.* We may note, apart from Goldstein's analysis, that in our culture the so-called "drives"—be they psychophysical like sex or psychocultural like "success"—are often identified in various ways with the psychological existence of the individual. Hence one person may be thrown into anxiety by the frustration of certain sexual desires and another may feel himself to be in a catastrophic situation when his success in terms of money (and prestige) falls below a certain level.

To one student a particular examination may be breezed through without anxiety, whereas to another student, whose life career depends on passing the examination, the situation may be traumatic and catastrophic, and reacted to with disordered behavior and anxiety. There are thus two sides to the basic concept of organism-in-catastrophic-situation: one is the objective situation itself, and the other is the nature of the organism involved. In even the normal anxiety of everyday life, in the "black threat that grips us in the pit of the stomach," each of us can recognize the threat of the catastrophic situation.

Human beings vary enormously with respect to their capacity for meeting crisis situations. Why some individuals are so ill-prepared for crises because of conflicts within themselves is more strictly the psychological problem and is discussed in the next chapter. Let it suffice here to point out that every human being has his "threshold" beyond which additional stress makes the situation catastrophic. Grinker and Spiegel have illustrated this threshold in their studies of soldiers who have broken down in battle.[17] Also Bourne, Rose and Mason, studying combat soldiers in the Vietnam War, illustrate a similar situation. The function of the various defenses of the soldiers—self-reliance to the extent of believing themselves invincible, compulsive activities, faith in the strength of the leader—all can be seen as protections of the individual from the catastrophic condition.[18]

Anxiety and the Loss of the World

We now turn to Goldstein's interesting discussion of *why anxiety is an emotion without a specific object.* He agrees with Kierkegaard, Freud, and others that anxiety is to be distinguished from fear in that fear has a specific object, whereas anxiety is a vague and unspecific apprehension. The puzzling problem in contemporary psychology is not this definition but the rationale for it. So far as the phenomenon goes, it is readily observable that a person in severe anxiety is unable to say, or to know, what "object" he is afraid of.[19] This "objectlessness" is clear in patients at the onset of psychoses, says Goldstein, but the same phenomenon can be seen in less extreme cases. When clients are in anxiety states in psychoanalysis (like Harold Brown, to be described below), they will report that their inability to know what they are afraid of is precisely what makes the anxiety so painful and disconcerting.

Goldstein suggests that "it seems as if, in proportion to the increase of anxiety, objects and contents disappear more and more." And he asks, *"Does not anxiety consist intrinsically of that inability to know from whence the danger threatens?"*[20] In fear we are aware of ourselves as well as of the object, and we can orient ourselves spatially with reference to the thing feared. But anxiety "attacks us from the rear," to use Goldstein's phrase, or, I would say, from all sides at once. In fear, your attention is narrowed to the object, tension is mobilized for flight; you can flee from the object because it occupies a particular point spatially. In anxiety, on the other hand, your efforts to flee generally amount to frantic behavior because you do not experience the threat as coming from a particular place, and hence you do not know where to flee. As Goldstein phrases it:

> In fear, there is an appropriate defense reaction, a bodily expression of tension and of extreme attention

to a certain part of the environment. In anxiety, on the other hand, we find meaningless frenzy, with rigid or distorted expression, accompanied by withdrawal from the world, a shut-off affectivity, in the light of which the world appears irrelevant, and any reference to the world, any useful perception and action is suspended.

Fear sharpens the senses. Whereas anxiety paralyzes the senses and renders them unusable, fear drives them to action.[21]

Goldstein observed that when the brain-injured patients were in anxiety, they were unable to evaluate external stimuli adequately, and hence they were neither able to give an accurate account of their objective environments nor were they able to see realistically their own positions in relation to these environments. "The fact that the catastrophic condition involves the impossibility of ordered reactions," he remarks, "precludes a subject 'having' an object in the outer world."[22] Everyone has noticed in his own experience how anxiety tends to confuse not only his awareness of himself but at the same time to confuse his perception of the objective situation. It is understandable that these two phenomena should go together, for, in Goldstein's words, "to be conscious of one's self is only a correlate of being conscious of objects."[23] *The awareness of the relationship between the self and the world is precisely what breaks down in anxiety.*[24] Hence it is not at all illogical that anxiety should appear as an objectless phenomenon.[25]

In the light of the above discussion, Goldstein holds that severe anxiety is experienced by a person as a disintegration of the self, a "dissolution of the existence of his personality."[26] Thus it is not strictly accurate to speak of "having" anxiety; rather one "is" anxiety, or "personifies" anxiety.

Origins of Anxiety and Fear as Seen by Goldstein

What is the relation, speaking developmentally, between anxiety and fears? In Goldstein's view, anxiety is the primal and original reaction and fear a later development. The first reactions of infants to threats are diffuse and undifferentiated—i.e., anxiety reactions. Fears are a later differentiation as the individual learns to objectivate and to deal specifically with those elements in his environment which might throw him into the catastrophic condition. In an infant, even an infant in the first ten days of life, one can observe obvious anxiety—diffuse, undifferentiated reactions to threats to its security. Only later, as the growing infant becomes neurologically and psychologically mature enough to objectivate—i.e., to distinguish those items in its environment which might give rise to the catastrophic condition—do specific fears appear.

Proceeding into his more specific formulation of the relation between fear and anxiety, Goldstein makes a statement which may seem confusing to many readers. *"What is it then that leads to fear?"* he asks, and then asserts, *"Nothing but the experience of the possibility of the onset of anxiety."*[27] Thus fear, he holds, is actually an apprehension that one might be thrown into the catastrophic condition. This may be illustrated by the case study to which we have already referred—that of Harold Brown (Chapter 8 of this book). At different times this young man needed to pass certain examinations if he was to be permitted to proceed in his academic life. On one occasion he felt at the moment of writing the examination that he could not succeed and was seized with panic that he might be dropped from the university and would then again be a "failure." The very pronounced tension and conflict, with all his old symptoms of profound anxiety, were the subjective reactions to his experience of being in a "catastrophic condition."

At another time, however, approaching a similar situation of examinations, he felt apprehension but moved ahead, steadily doing his work, and ultimately succeeded in writing the tests without being thrown into panic. The apprehension on this latter occasion we may define as fear. Now what was he afraid of? Namely, that he would again be thrown into the catastrophic condition described in the first instance. Thus, Goldstein holds, fear represents a warning that if the dangerous experience is not coped with adequately, one might be thrown into a situation of danger to the whole organism. Fear boils down to apprehension of specific experiences which might produce the more devastating condition, namely anxiety. Fear, in Goldstein's formulation, is fear of the onset of anxiety.

Part of the reason Goldstein's formulations at this point

may seem confusing is that the tendency in much of our past psychological thinking is to regard fear as the generic term and anxiety as a derivative from fear.[28] Goldstein's viewpoint is the opposite: fear is a differentiation from anxiety and a later development in the maturation of the organism. He asserts that the customary procedure of understanding anxiety as a form of fear, or the "highest form of fear," is incorrect. "Thus it becomes clear that anxiety cannot be made intelligible from the phenomenon of fear, but that only the opposite procedure is logical."[29] To be sure, fear may pass into anxiety (when the individual finds he cannot cope with the situation) or anxiety may pass into fear (as the individual begins to feel he can cope adequately). But when increasing fear turns eventually into a state of anxiety, for example, Goldstein contends that a qualitative change is occurring—that is, *a change from the perception of the threat as coming from a specific object to an apprehension which engulfs the whole personality so that the person feels his very existence is endangered.*

We need to remark that since anxiety is the much more discomforting state, there is always a tendency to "rationalize" anxiety in terms of fears. This is done unrealistically and unconstructively in the phenomena of phobias and superstitions. But it can be done constructively, as is shown in therapeutic sessions in which the individual learns to view his dangers realistically and at the same time develops confidence that he can meet them adequately.

With regard to the origin of fears and anxiety, Goldstein obviously disagrees with the various theories of hereditary anxiety and inherited fears of certain objects. Stanley Hall went back so far as to assume that children's fears were inherited from the animal ancestors of man. Stern refuted this, but he held, with Groos, that the child has an instinctive fear of the "uncanny." Goldstein feels that this cannot be true, since the child learns by moving ahead into unfamiliar situations. Stern held that certain peculiarities of objects lead to the child's fears of them: sudden appearance, rapid approach, intensity of the stimulus, and so forth. All these have one factor in common, says Goldstein: they make an adequate stimulus evaluation difficult, if not impossible.[30] "For an explanation of anxiety in childhood," Goldstein sums up the question, "it suffices to assume that the organism reacts to inadequate situations with anxiety, and did so in the days of his ancestors, as well as today."[31] This explanation, we might add, saves us from becoming lost in that labyrinth of futility, the "heredity vs. learning" debates, which have heretofore bedeviled much of the discussion of fears and anxiety. Goldstein's view is clarifying in that it becomes no longer necessary to view the individual as a carrier of certain fears, but rather as an organism needing to make itself adequate to its environment and its environment adequate to itself. When this cannot be done, as stated above, anxiety results; and fears, rather than being hereditary, are objectivated forms of this capacity for anxiety. It is the biological *capacity to have apprehension* which is inherited, not the specific fears.

The Capacity to Bear Anxiety

Goldstein points toward the constructive use of anxiety when he states, *The capacity to bear anxiety is important for the individual's self-realization and for his conquest of his environment.* Every person experiences continual shocks and threats to his existence; indeed, *self-actualization occurs only at the price of moving ahead despite such shocks. This indicates the constructive use of anxiety.* Goldstein's view is here similar to that of Kierkegaard, who, as indicated in the previous chapter, emphasized that anxiety, from the positive point of view, is an indication of new possibility for development of the self. Goldstein holds that the freedom of the healthy individual inheres in the fact that he can choose between various alternatives, can avail himself of new possibilities in the overcoming of difficulties in his environment. In moving *through* rather than *away from* anxiety the individual not only achieves self-development but also enlarges the scope of his world.

Not to be afraid of dangers which could lead to anxiety—this represents in itself a successful way of coping with anxiety. . . .[32]

Courage, in its final analysis, is nothing but an affirmative answer to the shocks of existence, which must be borne for the actualization of one's own nature.[33]

The normal child has less power to cope with his world than the adult, but the child also has a strong tendency toward action—this inheres in the child's nature, says Goldstein. Hence he moves ahead, growing and learning despite shocks and dangers. This is the essential difference between a normal child and a brain-injured patient, though they both represent limited powers of coping with anxiety-creating situations. The capacity to bear anxiety is found least of all in the brain-injured patient, more in the child, and most of all in the creative adult. *The creative person, who ventures into many situations which expose him to shock, is more often threatened by anxiety but, assuming the creativity is genuine, he is more able to overcome these threats constructively.* Goldstein quotes with approval Kierkegaard's statement, "The more original a human being is, the deeper is his anxiety."[34]

Culture is the product of man's conquest of anxiety in that culture represents man's progressive making of his environment adequate to himself, and himself adequate to his environment. Goldstein disagrees with Freud's negative view of culture—*viz.*, that culture is a result of the sublimation of repressed drives, a result of the desire to avoid anxiety. Creativity and culture, from the positive viewpoint, Goldstein holds, *are associated with the joy of overcoming tasks and shocks.* When creative activities are a direct product of the individual's anxiety, or the substitute phenomena into which the individual is forced by his anxiety, there is evident a stress on partial aspects of action, compulsiveness, and lack of freedom. Hence ". . . as long as these activities are not spontaneous, are not outlets of the free personality, but are merely the sequelae of anxiety, they have only a pseudo-value for the personality." He continues:

> This can be illustrated by the difference between the sincere faith of the really religious man, which is based upon willing devotion to the infinite, and superstitious beliefs. Or by the difference between the open-minded scholar who bases his beliefs upon facts and is always ready to change his conceptions when faced with new facts, and the dogmatic scientist. . . .[35]

Goldstein adds a comment on the age-old pattern by which people, in ancient as well as modern countries under totalitarianism, are enslaved:

Shaken on the one hand by uneasiness about the present situation and by anxiety for their existence, deceived on the other by the mockery of a brilliant future as the political demagogue depicts it, a people may give up freedom and accept virtual slavery. And it may do this in the hope of getting rid of anxiety.[36]

NEUROLOGICAL AND PHYSIOLOGICAL ASPECTS OF ANXIETY

As I mentioned earlier, in most discussions of the neurophysiological aspects of anxiety, the procedure is to describe the functioning of the autonomic nervous system, and the bodily changes for which this division is the medium, and then to assume implicitly or explicitly that this adequately takes care of the problem. While I agree that an understanding of the function of the automatic system is one very important step in the inquiry into the neurophysiology of anxiety. I indicated why such a procedure is not in itself adequate. Anxiety is a reaction in the organism so pervasive and fundamental that it cannot be relegated to a *specific* neurophysiological base. As we shall see in the subsequent discussion of psychosomatics, anxiety almost always involves a complex constellation of neurophysiological interrelationships and "balances." In the present section, therefore, we shall proceed from the simpler levels of the question—e.g., the functioning of the automatic system when the organism is subjected to threat—to the more complex levels as the organism is seen as a reacting totality in its environment.[37]

When an organism is subjected to threat, bodily changes occur which prepare the organism for fighting or fleeing from the danger. These changes are effected by way of the *autonomic* nervous system. Called "autonomic" because it was believed not to be subject to direct conscious control,[38] this system is the medium by which emotional changes occur in the body. It has been called "the bridge between psyche and soma." As will be discussed more fully below, the autonomic system consists of two divisions which work in opposition to or balance with each other. The *parasympathetic* division stimulates digestive, vegetative, and other "upbuilding" functions of the organism. The affects connected with these activities are of the comfortable, pleasurable, relaxing sort. The other division, the *sympathetic,* is the medium for accelerating heartbeat, raising blood pressure, releasing adrenaline into the blood, and the other phases of mobilizing the energies of the organism for fighting or fleeing from danger. The affects connected with the "general excitement" of sympathetic stimulation are typically some form of anger, anxiety, or fear.

The bodily changes induced through activity of the autonomic nervous system are known to everyone in his own experiences of anxiety or fear. The pedestrian feels his heart pounding heavily when he has stepped on the curb after having been narrowly missed by a speeding taxi. The student feels an urgency to urinate before a crucial examination. Or a speaker finds his appetite strangely absent at the dinner after which he must make an important and crucial address.

Originally in the time of primitive man, these responses had a clear purpose in protecting the person from wild animals and other concrete perils. In modern society man has few direct threats; the anxiety mainly concerns such psychological states as social adequacy, alienation, competitive success, and so on. But the mechanisms for coping with threats remain the same.

These and many other physical expressions of anxiety-fear can be conveniently linked in the framework of Cannon's "flight-fight" mechanism.[39] The heartbeat is accelerated in order to pump more blood to the muscles which will be needed in the impending struggle. The peripheral blood vessels, near the surface of the body, are contracted and the blood pressure thereby raised to maintain arterial pressure for the emergency needs. This peripheral contraction is the physiological aspect of the popular expression "blanching with fear." The "cold sweat" occurs preparatory to the warm sweat of actual muscular activity. The body may shiver and the hairs of the body stand on end to conserve heat and protect the organism from the increased threat of cold caused by the contraction of peripheral blood vessels. Breathing is deeper or more rapid in order to insure a plentiful supply of oxygen; this is the "pant" of strong excitement. The pupils of the eyes dilate, permitting a better view of threatening dangers; hence the expression "eyes wide with fear." The liver releases sugar to provide energy for the struggle. A substance is released into the blood to effect its more rapid clotting, thus protecting the organism from the loss of blood through wounds.

As a part of placing the organism on this emergency footing, digestive activity is suspended, since all available blood is needed for the skeletal muscles. The mouth feels dry, because of a decreasing of the flow of saliva corresponding to the suspending of the flow of gastric juices in the stomach. The smooth muscles of internal genital organs are contracted. There is a tendency toward voiding of bladder and bowels—again recognized in vernacular expressions—which has the obvious utilitarian function of freeing the organism for strenuous activity.

Perception of Danger

The impulses moving to the autonomic nervous system go through the lower and middle brain centers—i.e., the thalamus and diencephalon—the last-named being the "coordinating apparatus" for the sympathetic stimuli involved in anxiety and fear. These lower and middle brain centers are, in turn, interrelated with the cerebral cortex —i.e., the higher brain centers which involve the function of "awareness" and "conscious interpretation" of situations.

When we are afraid, for example, crude sensory stimuli cause an automatic reaction relayed through the hypothalamus to the reticular activating system of the brain. This regulates our alertness and permits us to fight or flee. The thalamus also sends impulses to the cortex for interpretation.

This function of the cerebral cortex, or psychologically speaking, conscious awareness, is of great importance in clinical dealing with anxiety, since the apprehension depends centrally on how the individual *interprets* potential dangers. The central difference, neurologically speaking, between animals and human beings is that in the latter the cerebral cortex is vastly larger. This is the neurological correlate of the fact that the problems of anxiety in the human organism involve intricate and complex interpretations which the person makes of his danger situation.[40] For example, Harold Brown experienced profound anxiety whenever he engaged in a minor argument or a bridge game, because any suggestion of competition set off associations connected with his early competition with his sisters which had been a great threat to his close dependency on his mother. (Of course, we do not mean that an individual like Brown is consciously aware of all the determinants which go into his interpretations; the influence of unconscious factors is more strictly the psychological problem and falls in the next chapter.) Thus a relatively harmless situation, objectively speaking, may become the occasion for great anxiety because of the complex ways, involving past experiences, in which the individual interprets his situation.

The stimuli which the person interprets as dangerous may be *intrapsychic* as well as external. Certain inner promptings of a hostile or sexual nature, for example, may be associated with past experiences in which the carrying out of these promptings produced guilt feelings and fear of punishment or actual punishment. Hence whenever the promptings occur intrapsychically again, guilt feelings and consequent expectation of punishment may arise and the individual may experience intense and undifferentiated anxiety.

Normally, the cortex exercises an inhibitory control over the lower centers by which the organism tones down and controls the intensity of the anxiety, fear, or rage responses. This control is proportionate to the maturity of cortical development. Infants, for example, respond to a variety of stimuli with an intensity of undifferentiated rage or anxiety. The closer to the infant state an organism is, the more its reactions take the reflexive or undifferentiated form. "Maturing" in this sense means developing increasing cortical differentiation and control. When the cortex is surgically removed from animals, we observe the automatic and excessive "sham rage" reaction (Cannon). Intense fatigue or illness may also weaken the control of the cortex. Hence we find tired or sick persons responding to threats with a greater degree of undifferentiated anxiety. In psychoanalytic terms, we would speak of this as regression.

The matter of cortical direction and control has important bearings on learning theory and maturation which can only be mentioned here. We have noted that on the infant level (and in animals with their cortexes surgically removed) the stimuli of threat are responded to in an undifferentiated or reflexive way. "As the cortex becomes

better developed with the process of growth and maturing," Grinker and Spiegel hold,

> it establishes increasing inhibition over these indis-
> criminate responses. At first only secondarily aware of
> the reflex response to stimuli, it attempts on succeed-
> ing repetitions of such stimuli to modify the response,
> segregating those stimuli which are truly dangerous
> from those which can be dealt with, and learning by
> trial and error how to deal with the former.

When the individual is confronted with a situation beyond
his degree of control (e.g., because of the suddenness of
the stimuli or their traumatic nature), he may be thrown
back into the state of less differentiated response. Grinker
and Spiegel hold that this is equivalent to a "regression"
to the infant stage when, neurologically speaking, there
was no cortical control over the emotional response.[41]

Balance in the Autonomic System

It is necessary, now, to expand a point mentioned earlier
—namely that the sympathetic and parasympathetic divisions work in opposition to each other. These two branches
of the autonomic system are "balanced," as Cannon suggests, somewhat like extensor and flexor muscles. The
sympathetic is stronger in the sense that it is capable of
overruling the parasympathetic. In other words, a moderate
amount of fear or anger will inhibit digestion, whereas it
requires a considerable degree of parasympathetic stimulation (e.g., eating) to overcome a moderate amount of
anger or fear.

A slight degree of stimulation of the opposing nervous
division, however, may simply serve to "tone up" the activity the organism is engaged in. For example, a low
degree of anxiety or fear, amounting to what we may call
the feeling of "adventure," may serve to heighten the
pleasure in eating or sexual relations. Folklore tells us that
"stolen fruit tastes sweeter," and it is the common experience of many persons that the element of adventure
adds zest to sexual activities. This, of course, may very
easily take a neurotic form if carried to any extreme, but
it has its normal phase as well. An analogy is seen in the
fact that the arm performs better in its extensor move-

ments if there is a slight flexor tension at the same time. This discussion points to our later discussion of the constructive uses of moderate amounts of anxiety and fear.

The fact that these two nervous divisions are set in balance against each other is of crucial importance in the understanding of anxiety in psychosomatic phenomena. With some persons, for example, anxiety seems to be a cue to begin eating. Clinical literature yields frequent cases of overeating, and consequent obesity, as a result of anxiety states. This may have much to do, of course, with eating as an expression of the need for infantile dependency cued off by anxiety, but it also has its clear neurological corollary in the fact that a considerable amount of parasympathetic stimulation may quiet sympathetic activity.

A parallel phenomenon can be seen in the area of sex. The early stages of sexual arousal involves the sacral, or parasympathetic, division; the nervi erigentes, which stimulate erection, are part of this division. This is the neurological correlate of the feelings of tenderness and comfort experienced in the earlier stages of sexual activity. It is common knowledge that some persons masturbate as well as engage in other sexual activity in order to quiet anxiety. Interestingly enough, it is said that masturbation was prevalent among the Romans while the enemy barbarians were encamped about the city. Socrates remarks in the last pages of the *Phaedo*, on the day he was to drink the hemlock, that it was a customary practice of the condemned to spend their last day in eating and sexual relations. This was, no doubt, not only for the purpose of getting their last taste of human pleasures, but also for the anxiety-quieting effect such activities afforded.

As regards sexual activity as a form of allaying anxiety, it is significant that the sexual ejaculation and orgasm are mediated by the opposite or sympathetic division; this division innervates the seminal vesicles. This is the neurological aspect of the experience of aggression or rage often felt at the height of sexual activity; Havelock Ellis spoke of the "love-bite." From a sheer neurological viewpoint, sexual experience serves to allay anxiety only up to the point of orgasm. Though the orgasm does release tension, and in normal situations does not produce anxiety, it may leave the individual who engages in masturbation or other sexual activity for anxiety-allaying purposes more anxious than he or she was to begin with. I do not wish to advance any of these psychoneurological correlations as hard and fast. The neurological functioning is so generally influenced, and so often contravened, by complex psychological factors in the picture that it is necessary to emphasize continually that behavior in a given case can be understood only by viewing that particular organism in the total situation to which it is reacting.

Sympathetic stimulation results in a *general* state of excitement of the whole organism. This is effected neurologically by the condition that the sympathetic division has a large number of connecting and bridging fibers, resulting in a "diffuse, widespread discharge of nerve impulses through sympathetic channels, as contrasted with the limited, sharply directed discharge to specific organs in the functioning of the cranial and sacral divisions."[42] The sympatin and adrenin (for which the trade name is Adrenalin) poured into the blood stream also have this generalized effect on the organism. Cannon speaks of adrenin working in "partnership" with direct sympathetic stimulation. "Since secreted adrenin has a general distribution in the blood stream, the sympathetic division, even if it did not have diffuse effects because of the way its fibers are arranged, could have such effects by the action of adrenin."[43] These facts are the neurological and physiological correlates of the experience everyone has observed in himself—that anger, fear, and anxiety are felt as generalized, "over-all" emotions.

Since sympathetic stimulation leads simply to a general state of excitement in the organism, it is impossible to predict on the basis of neurophysiological data alone whether the emotion will take the form of fear, anxiety, anger, or hostility, or something else like challenge or sense of adventure. Except in the reflexive reactions, like the startle pattern, the form of the emotion will be determined by the interpretation the organism makes of the threatening situation. Speaking in general terms, if the danger is interpreted to be one which can be mastered by attack, the emotion will be anger. Then the activities of the organism become "fight" rather than "flight," and certain physical changes follow from that interpretation. In anger, for example, the lids of the eyes are often narrowed to restrict the vision to that part of the environment the organism seeks to attack. If the situation is seen as one which cannot be overcome by assault but can be avoided by flight, the emotion will be fear. Or, if the danger is interpreted as putting the organism in a dilemma of helplessness, the emotion will be anxiety.

Certain physical changes likewise occur as a result of these interpretations. In fear and anxiety the eyelids, for example, are generally opened very wide to give the organism opportunity to see every possible route of escape. Thus the psychological factor in how the organism relates itself to the threat is essential in the defining of an emotion as such.

Since an emotion consists of a certain relation between the organism and its environment, and since the sympathetic neurophysiological processes are general rather than specific, it is misleading and erroneous to reason either *from* a so-called specific neurophysiological process *to* a specific psychological experience like fear or anxiety or vice versa. The intricately balanced neurophysiological apparatus is capable of being employed in an infinite variety of combinations, depending on the needs and patterns of the organism at the time. Likewise, it is erroneous to *identify* a neurophysiological process with an emotion. An illustration of this latter error is seen when one psychologist writes as follows: "the initiation of antagonism between strong excitatory and strong inhibitory nervous excitation throws the organism into a condition of generalized activity, as if a general nervous irradiation or overflow were in process. . . ." The "generalization of excitation," he suggests, "should be equated with anxiety."[44] No, I do not believe that anxiety can be equated with any generalization of neurophysiological excitation. Anxiety is not a biochemical entity like steam. It is, rather, *a term for a certain relation (e.g., one of helplessness, conflict, etc.) existing between the person and the threatening environment, and the neurophysiological processes follow from this relationship.* The error arises from the fallacy which confounds the physiological mechanism through which psyche operates with the fundamental etiology.

This idea is based upon Freud's first theory—i.e., that anxiety is the converted form of repressed libido. Now it must be agreed that this theory lends itself to thinking of anxiety as a physiochemical entity. Freud's works, however, reveal an ambivalence with respect to the identification of physiological processes with emotion. On the one hand, Freud minces no words in insisting that a description of neurophysiological processes was not to be confused with the psychological understanding of the phenomena. In his chapter on anxiety in the *General introduction to psychoanalysis* he writes:

> Interest there [in academic medicine] centers upon anatomical processes by which the anxiety condition comes about. We learn that the medulla oblongata is stimulated, and the patient is told that he is suffering from a neurosis of the vagal nerve. The medulla oblongata is a wondrous and beauteous object. I well remember how much time and labor I devoted to the study of it years ago. But today I must say I know of nothing less important for the psychological comprehension of anxiety than a knowledge of the nerve-paths by which the excitations travel. (pp. 341–42)

He cautions the psychoanalyst to "resist the temptation to play with endocrinology and the autonomic nervous system, when the important thing is to grasp psychological facts psychologically." But on the other hand, his libido theory, a physiochemical concept whether one accepts it as referring to actual chemical processes or as an analogy, opens the way for such fallacies as equating anxiety with a neurophysiological process. I would simply underline Freud's own statement that *the important thing is to grasp psychological facts psychologically.*

VOODOO DEATH

The condition of traumatic fear and anxiety may be so crucial and devastating for the organism that actual death results. The phrase "scared to death" is not an exaggerated description of what happens in some cases. Some years ago, Cannon discussed the phenomenon of "voodoo" death in this light.[45] He cites several competently observed cases of death occurring to natives who were the victims of some powerful symbolic act held by the tribe to be lethal, such as the magic "bone-pointing" of the witch doctor, or the eating of tabooed food which the community believed would result in death. Observing the Maoris of New Zealand, Tregear, an anthropologist, notes: "I have seen a strong young man die the same day he was tapued [tabooed]; the victims die under it as though their strength ran out like water."[46] The native believed, as his community believed, that the taboo carried the power to cause his death. It may well be true, says Cannon, that an "ominous and persistent state of fear can end the life of a man."[47]

There is like testimony from Africa. Leonard (1906) has written an account of the Lower Niger and its tribes in which he declares:

> I have seen more than one hardened old Haussa soldier dying steadily and by inches because he believed himself to be bewitched; no nourishment or medicines that were given to him had the slightest effect either to check the mischief or to improve his condition in any way, and nothing was able to divert him from a fate which he considered inevitable. In the same way, and under very similar conditions, I have seen Krumen and others die in spite of every effort that was made to save them, simply because they had made up their minds, not (as we thought at the time) to die, but that being in the clutch of malignant demons they were bound to die.[48]

The physiological aspects of "voodoo" death are not difficult to understand. The reported symptoms of natives dying from voodoo bone-pointing or from having eaten tabooed food are in accord with those of an organism experiencing profound and persistent sympathetic-adrenal stimulation. If this stimulation continues without corresponding outlet in action—and the voodoo victim, paralyzed by anxiety since he himself believes he will die, lacks any effective outlet for action—death may result. Cannon found in his experiments with decorticate cats, which lacked the usual moderating effects of the cortex on emotional excitement, that after several hours of "sham rage" the cat expired. "In sham rage, as in wound shock, death can be explained as due to a failure of essential organs to receive a sufficient supply of blood or, specifically, a sufficient supply of oxygen, to maintain their services."[49]

There is also evidence of similar occurrences in our own day. Engel tells of "young, healthy soldiers in combat who die without injury and persons trapped in disasters who succumb when they give up hope. . . . In folklore and fact, a person may be said to 'die of grief.' "[50] And, we could add, from "voodoo" beliefs and many things other than physical causes.

But the psychological questions in "voodoo" death—such as what interpretation the native makes of his environment that leads him to experience such severe threat—are not so easy to answer, chiefly because we lack data on the subjective experiences of the particular natives involved. Cannon suggests one psychological explanation from William James's idea of being "cut dead" when the others in one's group ignore one. The primitive victim of taboo is certainly "cut dead," and he must experience powerful psychological suggestion from the fact that his entire community not only believes he will die but, in fact, behaves toward him as though he were already dead. Dying as the consequence of overwhelming anxiety has likewise been observed in other situations, such as death from shock in war when "neither physical trauma nor any of the known accentuating factors of shock could account for the disastrous condition."[51]

Cannon refers to the work of Mira, a psychiatrist in the Spanish War of 1936–1939, who has reported fatal results in patients afflicted with "malignant anxiety." Mira observed in these patients signs of anguish and perplexity, accompanied by a permanently rapid pulse, rapid respiration, and other symptoms of excessive sympathetic-adrenal stimulation. Mira mentions as predisposing conditions "a previous liability of the sympathetic system" and "a severe mental shock in conditions of physical exhaustion due to lack of food, fatigue, sleeplessness, etc."[52] Whatever the psychological determinants of such experiences may be, it is clear *that a threat to an individual's existence can be so powerful that the individual possesses no way of coping with the threat short of giving up his existence—namely, dying.*

PSYCHOSOMATIC ASPECTS OF ANXIETY

Of more practical interest is the great variety of psychosomatic disorders in which the organism suffering anxiety maintains its struggle for existence but does so by means of a somatic alteration of function.[53] All through history it has been recognized in folklore and by observers of human nature that emotions like anxiety and fear have a profound and pervasive interrelationship with the sickness and health of the organism. In recent years the studies in psychosomatic relations have begun the scientific exploration of this area and have yielded new illumination on the dynamics and meaning of fear and anxiety. Psychosomatic symptoms may be viewed as "one of the modes of expression of the emotional life, especially of the unconscious emotional life—one of its languages, like dreams, slips of the tongue, and neurotic behavior."[54]

Psychosomatic ailments have also been described as arising from inhibited communication, since "input into the organism must be followed by an adequate output. When verbal or motor components of emotional states are partly or completely inhibited the organism tends to *substitute* other forms of behavior along other output channels."[55]

There are frequent instances of the overproduction of sugar in the body and ensuing diabetes mellitus in states of anxiety and fear.[56] It is not surprising that many heart conditions are found accompanying anxiety, since the heart in everyone is directly sensitive to emotional stress. Oswald Bumke holds that most of the "so-called 'cardiac neuroses' are nothing but a somatic manifestation of anxiety."[57]

Many cases of excessive appetite (bulimia) and consequent obesity accompanying chronic anxiety have been cited. Saul describes one in which the desires to eat "were displacements to food of intense frustrated desires for love. . . ." A number of such patients were found to have been children of overprotective mothers—a childhood situation which often predisposes the child to anxiety. The opposite condition, pathological lack of appetite (anorexia nervosa), has been found in persons in whom there were intense frustrated wishes for love and attention from the mother which led to hostility toward the mother and consequent guilt because of the hostile feelings.[58] The frequent association of diarrhea with anxiety is well known. Saul cites a case from his own analytic practice of a young physician who had been overprotected by his parents as a child. When he graduated from medical school and began to assume his own professional responsibilities, he reacted with anxiety and diarrhea. The diarrhea, remarks Saul, was an expression of his hostility that he should be forced to be independent and responsible. Thus the hostility was a reaction to his anxiety.[59]

Though essential hypertension (elevated blood pressure without evidence of other disease) is generally associated in psychosomatic literature with suppressed rage and hostility, a pattern of anxiety is often found underlying the aggressive affects. Saul cites cases of hypertension to illustrate that the rage and hostility are reactions to situations of conflict on the part of persons who were predisposed to anxiety by excessive dependence on a parent and who were, at the same time, submissive to this parent.[60] As regards asthma, Saul remarks on the basis of a number of studies, "It appears that the outstanding personality traits of asthmatics are over-anxiety, lack of self-confidence, and a deep-seated clinging dependence upon the parents which is often a reaction to parental oversolicitude." Asthma attacks "bear a relationship to anxiety and to crying (weeping changing to wheezing)."

Frequency of urination has been found accompanying anxiety connected with competitive ambition.[61] Though epilepsy, to the extent that it can be viewed psychosomatically, is generally conceded to represent a mass discharge of repressed hostility, there is evidence in some cases of epilepsy that anxiety attacks and anxiety-provoking feelings (sometimes specifically related to the mother) underlie the hostility.[62]

An Example: Gastric Functions

That stomach functions and other gastrointestinal activities are closely related to emotional states has been known throughout history. Folk language is rich in expressions like "not being able to stomach" something or being "fed up" with a situation. The neurophysiological aspects of this interrelationship have been pointed out by Pavlov, Cannon, Engel, and others. Psychosomatically, the basic consideration is the close association of gastrointestinal functions with desires for care, support, and a dependent form of love—all of which are related genetically to being fed by one's mother. Conflict situations, such as in anxiety, hostility, and resentment, accentuate these receptive needs. But these needs are bound to be frustrated, partly because of their excessive character and partly because in our culture they have to be repressed under the façade of the "he-man" who is characterized by ambition and conscientious striving. In the ulcer patients and in Tom, these receptive needs took the somatic expression, as we shall see, of increased gastric activity, and hence gastric ulcers.

A psychoanalyst, a psychiatrist, and a physician—Mittelmann, Wolff, and Scharf—carried on interviews with thirteen ulcer subjects, during which physiological changes in the patient were recorded. By inducing the person to discuss topics such as marriage or vocation which were known from the case history to be anxiety-creating, the experimenters were able to correlate the accompanying changes in gastroduodenal function. It was discovered that when conflicts involving anxiety and related emotions were touched upon, the patients regularly exhibited accelerated gastric activity. Increased stomach acidity, increased peristaltic motility, and hyperaemia (increased blood supply) were evidenced. These conditions are known to be ulcer-producing. But in interviews in which the doctors reassured the person and allayed his anxiety, gastric activity was restored toward normal and the symptoms were eliminated. It was clearly demonstrated that the gastric activities which cause or exacerbate the ulcer-formation were *increased by anxiety and were decreased as security supplanted anxiety in the patient's affective condition.*[63]

Whether this kind of reaction to anxiety occurs only with persons of a particular psychophysical type, whether it is a general occurrence in our culture or a general human reaction, are still open questions. The thirteen control cases investigated in this study—persons who were healthy and without special anxiety—exhibited in general similar gastric responses to emotional stress but of lesser magnitude and duration than those of the ulcer patients. At any time of basic change in their life pattern—such as divorce, being assigned to a totally new location in one's employment—people will experience more or less anxiety and stress. Those who have characteristics described above often have stomach symptoms, whereas other types react with a different "language" of symptoms.

The Case of Tom

Equally significant for our present inquiry is Tom, whose gastric activities during periods of emotional stress could be observed through a fistula in his stomach. Tom was studied intensively by S. G. Wolf and H. G. Wolff over a period of seven months.[64] Now a fifty-seven-year-old man of Irish stock, Tom had drunk some boiling hot chowder as a boy of nine which caused his esophagus to close. Following this accident, an enterprising physician had made an aperture surgically through his abdomen and into his stomach. For almost fifty years he had fed himself successfully by means of a funnel through this fistula. Since Tom was an emotionally labile individual who ran through the gamut of fear, anxiety, sadness, anger, and resentment, Wolf and Wolff had abundant opportunity to observe through the aperture the interrelation of these emotions with Tom's gastric functions.

In periods of fear, Tom's gastric activity was sharply *decreased:*

> Sudden fright occurred one morning during a control period of accelerated gastric function, when an irate doctor, a member of the staff, suddenly entered the room, began hastily opening drawers, looking on shelves, and swearing to himself. He was looking for protocols to which he attached great importance. Our subject, who tidies up the laboratory, had mislaid them the previous afternoon, and he was fearful of detection and of losing his precious job. He remained silent and motionless and his face became pallid. The mucous membrane of his stomach also blanched from a leve' of 90 to 20 and remained so for five minutes until the doctor had located the objects of his search and left the room. Then gastric mucosa gradually resumed its former color.[65]

Other affects associated with such hypofunctioning of the stomach were sadness, discouragement, and self-reproach. Tom and his wife had made tentative arrangements to move into a new apartment, a change they very much desired. But mainly because of their own negligence, the landlord leased the desired apartment to someone else. The morning after this discovery, Tom was downcast, uncommunicative, and sad. He felt defeated and had no desire to fight back; his dominant mood was self-reproach. That morning his gastric activity was markedly decreased.

But in periods of anxiety, Tom, like the ulcer patients, showed *accelerated gastric activity:*

The most marked alterations in gastric functions which were encountered were associated with anxiety provoked by our failure to inform the subject how long he might expect an income from the laboratory. He had been receiving government aid prior to his employment with us, and the rise in his family's standard of living since his new job meant a great deal to him. The subject of how long his job would last had come up in a discussion between his wife and himself the previous evening. He decided to inquire about it the next morning. Both he and his wife were so anxious about the answer, however, that neither of them slept at all. The next morning the values for vascularity and acidity were the highest encountered in any of the studies. . . .[66]

This illustrates a pattern which was regularly found with Tom. "Anxiety and the complex conflicting feelings found associated with it were regularly accompanied by hyperaemia, hypersecretion, and hypermotility of the stomach."[67]

In experiences of hostility and resentment Tom likewise exhibited increased stomach activity. Two different instances are cited when he felt aspersions had been cast upon his ability and conscientiousness by members of the hospital staff. In these situations, his gastric secretions were greatly increased. During one of these periods when Tom was diverted from his hostile feelings by conversation, the overactivity subsided, but it rose afterward when he again lapsed into brooding over his wounds.

Though Tom did not have peptic ulcers, the pattern of his personality was in many ways similar to that of the patients in the prior study. As a child he had been very dependent on his mother, though apparently he did not experience much emotional warmth in his relation with her. "He had a fear and a love for his mother," write Wolf and Wolff, "such as he had for the Lord."[68] He was seized with panic when she died, after which he became dependent on his sister. A like ambivalence was shown in his relation to the doctors: he exhibited considerable dependence, and he frequently reacted with hostility toward them when this dependence was frustrated. He placed great emphasis on being the "strong man," the successful provider for his family. "If I couldn't support my family," he remarked, "I'd as soon jump off the end of the dock." This sentence is a vivid revelation of how profound a psychological value was at stake in Tom's façade of the strong, responsible man. He could not release his emotions in crying, since there was the need to keep a firm appearance of strength. This personality pattern, characterized by affective dependence covered over by the need to appear strong, presumably bears a decisive relationship to the fact that Tom reacted to anxiety and hostility with acceleration of his gastric functions.

This accelerated gastric activity as a response to conflict situations may be viewed in two ways. First, it may be a somatic expression of the psychologically repressed needs of the organism to be cared for. The person endeavors to resolve anxiety and hostility and gain security through eating.[69] Second, it may represent a form of aggression and hostility toward those who deny the comfort and solace desired. Eating as a form of aggression is common in animal life—e.g., "eating up" the prey.[70]

These studies demonstrate that it is an oversimplification, and an inaccuracy, to relegate anxiety solely to automatic nervous activity. The neurological functions in anxiety cannot be understood except as we see them in the light of the needs and purposes of the organism confronting its threat. "It is not possible with the evidence at hand," remark Wolf and Wolff, "to attribute the pattern of bodily changes observed solely to vagus or sympathetic activity. It seems more profitable to consider gastric changes which accompany emotional disturbances as part of a general bodily reaction pattern."[71] Mittelmann, Wolff, and Scharf state the same thing in a different way: "The question as to which parts of the nervous system will dominate under stress is of secondary importance; of primary importance is *the interplay or combination which will best serve the needs of the animal in meeting a given life situation.*"[72]

CULTURE AND THE MEANING OF DISEASE

Having a disease is one way of resolving a conflict situation. Disease is a method of shrinking one's world so that, with lessened responsibilities and concerns, the person has a better chance of coping successfully. Health, on the contrary, is a freeing of the organism to realize its capacities.

George Engel puts this pithily when he writes that "health and disease may be seen as phases of life."[73] He adds, "thinking of disease as an entity separate from oneself has a great appeal to the human mind." In other words, I believe that people utilize disease in the same way older generations used the devil—as an object on which to project their hated experiences in order to avoid having to take responsibility for them. But beyond giving a temporary sense of freedom from guilt feeling, these delusions do not help. Health and disease are part and parcel of our continuous process throughout life of making ourselves adequate to our world and our world adequate to ourselves.

When a person experiences a conflict situation which continues and which cannot be resolved on the level of conscious awareness, somatic symptoms of various types typically appear. These are a kind of "body language." One type is the *hysterical conversion* symptom, such as hysterical blindness in situations of terror (the person can't bear to *see* it), or the hysterical paralysis of certain muscles. Having a fairly direct psychological etiology, hysterical symptoms may involve any part of the neuromuscular apparatus. In contrast, the *psychosomatic* type of symptom, in its limited sense, is a dysfunction mediated by the autonomic nervous system. But from a broader perspective anxiety may be involved in any illness whether or not it takes specifically hysterical or psychosomatic forms. An example of this third type is the infectious diseases. The susceptibility of the organism to such diseases is influenced by anxiety as well as other affects. It is possible that deterioration diseases like tuberculosis may be associated with repressed discouragement following chronic conflict situations which have not been soluble by the person on the level of direct awareness or on the specifically psychosomatic level.[74]

What determines whether a person will be able to resolve his conflict in conscious awareness or will have to manifest psychosomatic or hysterical symptoms or a different form of disease? This complicated question can be answered only by a thorough study of the person concerned. Certainly the answers would involve constitutional factors, the person's experiences in infancy as well as other past experiences, the nature and intensity of the immediate threat, and the cultural situation. In every case, however, the organism is to be viewed as endeavoring *to resolve a conflict situation, a conflict characterized in its subjective aspect by anxiety and in its objective aspect by illness*. The symptom—when it is present—is one expression of the organism's endeavor at resolution of the conflict.

Cultural factors are intimately related to the anxiety underlying psychosomatic disorders. Demonstrations of this could be cited from almost any of the psychosomatic illnesses. I take again the case of peptic ulcer. The high incidence of ulcer has often been related to the excessively competitive life in modern Western culture. It is particularly a "disease of the striving and ambitious of Western civilization." The most likely explanation is that men in the forties were expected to repress their dependent needs under a façade of independence and strength, whereas women were permitted to give vent to their feelings of helplessness, as in weeping. In some circles expression of dependence on the part of women was even considered a virtue. In the early nineteenth century there was a high incidence of ulcer—so far as statistics can be relied upon —in women in their twenties. Mittelmann and Wolff suggested that this is related to the fact that in that culture women experienced considerable need to compete in getting a husband; the prospect of remaining unmarried, dependent on relatives, created marked anxiety. In that period men, on the contrary, occupied the "strong" position vocationally and were able at the same time to express their need for dependence within the family circle. The fact that in the forties ulcers were found more than ten times as frequently in men as in women but that women now are almost equal to men presents interesting cultural questions. Now, as women play more assertive roles in our society, female incidence of ulcers has increased.

It will be recalled that the control cases (patients without ulcers) studied by Mittelmann, Wolff, and Scharf exhibited the same hyperfunction of gastric activities in periods of emotional conflict, though in lesser degree than the ulcer patients. Tom, also not an ulcer patient, exhibited the same reactions. These data would point to a hypothesis that this psychosomatic reaction pattern is not only a matter of individual type but occurs with some frequency in Western culture. Whether there is a specifically American cultural factor present is also an interesting question. In discussing the relation between the repressed needs for dependency and gastrointestinal symptoms frequently found in their work with soldiers in conflict situations, Grinker and Spiegel remark on the accentuated desire to drink milk on the part of these soldiers. The "particular food so intensely desired is that associated with the earliest signs of maternal affection and care," and they add that "drinking milk is a cultural trait of most Americans."[75] There is presumptive evidence for the hypothesis that the emphasis upon individual competition in Western culture took root with special influence in the American branch of that culture.

Since the individual lives and moves and has his being in a given culture, with his own reaction patterns having been formed in terms of that culture and with the conflict situation confronting him likewise given in terms of that culture, it is readily understandable that cultural factors should be interrelated with psychosomatic as well as other behavior disorders. It would seem that the affects, biological needs, and forms of behavior *most repressed in a given culture are the ones most likely to give rise to symptoms.* In the Victorian period Freud found the repression of sex central in symptom-formation. In American culture in the forties, as Horney held, the repression of hostility was more common than the repression of sex and thus could have been expected to be frequently related to psychosomatic symptoms. It would certainly not be gainsaid that our competitive culture generates considerable hostility.

As shifts in cultural emphasis occur, corresponding shifts in the incidence of various diseases likewise occur. Examples are the rise in incidence of cardiovascular disturbances and the decline of hysterical cases in World War II from World War I. Another significant point is that in our culture it is considered much more acceptable to have an organic illness than an emotional or mental disorder; this would influence the fact that anxiety and other emotional stresses in our culture so often take a somatic form. In short, the culture conditions the way a person tries to resolve his anxiety, and specifically what symptoms he may employ.

It is very rare that we get hysterical persons these days in psychotherapeutic practice, except in out-patient clinics located in frontier situations where people are isolated from the self-consciousness of our time. Most of our patients are compulsive-obsessional and/or depressed. This is related to the hyper-self-consciousness in our day. Almost everyone in the educated populations of the cities (from which our private patients come) knows enough about psychotherapy so that there are no more surprises as there were in Freud's day. Also, to point out another influence of culture on disease, it was found in World War I that officers, who by and large were able to communicate about themselves and their experiences, had less hysterical breakdowns than the less educated and less verbally adept enlisted men. This accords with the emphasis of Groen and Bastiaans that psychosomatic disorders are directly related to blocked communication.

The psychosomatic studies throw light upon the *distinction between, and the relative importance of, the various emotions*. First, take the distinction between *anxiety* and *fear*. In some treatments of anxiety and fear there has been a reluctance to make a distinction between these two affects, since it was assumed that they had the same neurophysiological base.[76] But when the person is viewed as a functioning unit in a life situation, very important distinctions between anxiety and fear surely appear. In the instance of Tom, we recall that his neuropsychological behavior was radically different in fear from what it was in anxiety. His affects which came with a withdrawal without inclination to struggle—such as fear, sadness, self-reproach—were accompanied by a suspension of gastric activity. But in situations in which Tom was engaged in conflict and struggle—when the affect was anxiety, hostility, or resentment—the gastric functions were employed overtime. This is the *opposite* to what would be expected on the basis of the conventional analysis of neurophysiological processes (i.e., anxiety identified with sympathetic activity). I therefore submit that the distinction between fear and anxiety must be made if we are to understand the organism as a behaving unit endeavoring to adjust to a given life situation. How this distinction may be made I propose to summarize in Chapter 7 below. One added observation, however, may be offered at this point: *Fear ordinarily does not lead to illness if the organism can flee successfully.* If the individual cannot flee, but is forced to remain in a conflict situation which cannot be resolved, fear may turn into anxiety and psychosomatic changes may then accompany the anxiety.

A distinction is to be drawn between anxiety and the aggressive affects, such as anger and hostility. Though repressed rage and hostility are specific etiological factors in certain psychosomatic disorders, it is significant that rage and hostility can frequently be discovered on more thorough analysis of the patient to be reactions to an underlying anxiety. (Cf. the above discussion of hypertension and epilepsy.) The rationale of this situation can be suggested as follows. Anger does not lead to illness unless it cannot be expressed in fighting or some other direct form. When it must be repressed—because of the dangers to the organism if the aggression were carried out in action—psychosomatic symptoms like hypertension may appear. *But if underlying anxiety were not present, the hostility would not have to be repressed in the first place.* This accords with our emphasis that the basic picture is that of the organism in a conflict situation, the conflict being represented on the psychic side by anxiety. There is ground, then, for Felix Deutsch's statement that "every disease is an anxiety disease," if we mean by this that anxiety is the psychic component of every disease.

The most intricate problem in the relation of anxiety to somatic changes is *the meaning of the organ symptom.* Somatic symptoms may be approached through two questions, both of which are necessary for an understanding of why the anxiety takes a somatic form. First, how does the organ symptom function in the organism's struggle to cope with the threatening situation, or, to put it somewhat figuratively, what is the organism trying to do via the symptom? Second, what are the intrapsychic mechanisms by which this interrelationship of anxiety and symptom takes place?

Several pertinent clinical observations throw light upon these questions. *There tends to be an inverse relation between the individual's capacity to tolerate conscious anxiety and the appearance of psychosomatic symptoms.* Whereas conscious anxiety and fears are aggravating factors, there is evidence that the anxiety and fears and conflicts which have been excluded from consciousness are of the greatest significance—that is, those most likely to be etiological in illness. The more overt the anxiety and the greater its manifestation in neurotic behavior, the less severe the organic disease. While the person is endeavoring to master the conflict consciously he may be experiencing considerable conscious anxiety, but he is still confronting the threat through direct awareness. "In general it may be stated that the existence of anxiety implies lack of serious disintegration. . . . It may be compared with the prognostic significance of fever."[77] But when the conscious struggle can no longer be tolerated, either because of its increasing severity or because of its lack of success, symptomatic changes in the organism take place. These relieve the strain of the conflict and make a quasi- or pseudo-adjustment possible when the conflict cannot actually be solved. Thus it may be said that *the symptoms are often ways of containing the anxiety; they are the anxiety in structuralized form.* Freud rightly remarks about psychological symptoms: "The symptom is bound anxiety," or, in other words, anxiety which has been crystallized into an ulcer or heart palpitations or some other symptom.

In the case of Brown (page 228), we observe that the progression taken by anxiety states was roughly as follows: First he reported an organ symptom, such as momentary spells of dizziness, about which he had no conscious anxiety except the discomfort of the symptom itself. Several days subsequently anxiety dreams began to appear. Later came conscious anxiety, with considerable dependence and many demands upon the therapist. As the anxiety came more into consciousness, he was more severely discomforted *but the organ symptom disappeared.*

Now it is significant that the patients with ulcer symptoms discussed above were not aware of conscious anxiety. The symptom is in this sense a protection against the anxiety-creating situation. This is why, practically speaking, it is often dangerous to remove the symptoms of anxiety patients until the anxiety itself can be clarified. The existence of the symptom indicates roughly that the subject has not been able to handle his anxiety, and it may be a protection against a worse state of deterioration.

It is extremely interesting that *when people become ill in organic ways, anxiety tends to disappear.* When, in the midst of this study, I became ill with tuberculosis at a time when drugs were not available for its treatment, I observed a curious phenomenon in patients around me with the same disease. When a patient became aware that he was seriously ill, a considerable amount of anxiety associated with his behavior patterns before the illness seemed *to disappear.* Conscious anxiety often reappeared as the patient neared the state of physical health when he could return to work and responsibilities. One could remark superficially that the disease served to relieve him from responsibilities, afforded him protection, etc. But the phenomenon seems to be more profound. Assuming that succumbing to the disease in the first place was partly the result of chronic unsolved conflicts, *the disease itself may represent one way of shrinking the scope of the conflicts to an area in which they might be solved.* This may throw light on the clinically observed phenomenon that when the disease appears, there is a lessened awareness of anxiety, and when the disease is overcome, anxiety may reappear.[78]

The problem of the interchange of symptoms and anxiety is explained by writers using Freud's first anxiety hypothesis in terms of the libido theory. F. Deutsch, for example, holds that the organ symptom results from dammed-up libido. If libido cannot be discharged normally, it takes the form of anxiety, and this anxiety may discharge itself in the form of a somatic symptom. *Hence, "psychologically speaking, to remain or to become organically healthy the individual must either invest his libido or get rid of his anxiety."*[79] The viewpoint I take here is that anxiety occurs not because the individual is a "carrier of libido" but because he is confronted with a threatening situation with which he cannot deal and which therefore throws him into a state of helplessness and inner conflict. It may well be that the presence of the libido—e.g., sexual drives—pushes the person into the conflict; but it is important to remember that the problem is *the conflict and not the sex. Thus our conclusion is that the purpose of the symptom is not to protect the organism from dammed-up libido, but rather from the anxiety-creating situation.*

I suggest the following rough schema as a framework which brings together the points of this chapter. First, the organism interprets the reality situation which it confronts in terms of *symbols and meanings.* Second, these produce attitudes toward the reality situation. And third, the attitudes, in turn, involve the various emotions (and the neurophysiological and hormonal components thereof) as *preparations for activity* in meeting the reality situation. I have already emphasized the importance of symbols and meanings by which the human being interprets situations as anxiety-creating. We noted at the outset of this chapter Adolph Meyer's emphasis on "the integrating functions" and "the use of symbols as tools." It is these to which neurology and physiology are subordinated.

We have also noted that these interpretations occur chiefly in the cortex, that part of the human being's neurological apparatus which grossly distinguishes him from animals. Cannon's work on sympathetic activity, which is the basis for most discussions in which the neurophysiological aspects of anxiety are identified with sympathetic activity, was done chiefly with animals. Thus one cannot reason from these studies to human behavior without making clear the qualification that the animal reactions represent a parallel to human reactions only when certain aspects of the human being are isolated out of this total context.[80]

It is possible, then, to avoid three common errors in psychology. The first is the error, on one side, of identifying an emotion with a neurophysiological process. The second is the error in the middle of "neurologizing tautology" (e.g., merely describing sympathetic activity as the neurophysiological aspect of anxiety). And the third is the error on the other side of assuming a simple dichotomy between neurophysiological and psychological processes.

The reader may recognize that these three errors are parallel to three viewpoints which recur in historical philosophy and science as endeavors to solve the mind-body problem: (1) physiological mechanism (making psychological phenomena merely the epiphenomena of physiological processes); (2) psychophysical parallelism; and (3) dualism.

Both in psychology and philosophy we need to move toward an integrated theory of mind-body, which will presumably be found by going back to the dimension out of which both mind and body arise. The way we seek to do this in this book is through the hierarchy of symbols, attitudes and neurology and physiology. Meyer's organismic approach is, to my mind, one approach that seeks to do this.

CHAPTER
4

Anxiety Interpreted
Psychologically

Anxiety is the fundamental phenomenon and the central problem of neurosis.

—Sigmund Freud, *The Problem of Anxiety*

DO ANIMALS HAVE ANXIETY?

The investigations of anxiety-like reactions in animals have shed important illumination on the problem of anxiety in human beings. We use the term "anxiety-like reactions" because there is considerable difference of opinion as to whether animals experience anxiety or not. Goldstein believed animals do have anxiety, but he was using the term to refer to undifferentiated fright reactions, parallel to the "normal" anxiety which may be seen in the two-week-old human infant. Harry Stack Sullivan held animals do not have anxiety. O. Hobart Mowrer, in his early studies of the "anxiety" of rats (which will be reviewed later in this chapter), used the terms "fear" and "anxiety" interchangeably. But later on, he concluded that the apprehension his animals were experiencing was fear, and that animals did not have anxiety except as they were placed in a special psychological relationship with human beings, such as the experimenters. In contrast to Goldstein, however, Mowrer was using the term "anxiety" to refer to *neurotic* anxiety, which by definition presupposes the capacities for self-consciousness, repression, and so forth which are uniquely the possessions of the human mammal.

84

It is Howard Liddell, in my judgment, who cuts the Gordian knot of this controversy. In a paper which is remarkably pertinent to our study of anxiety, based on his extensive work in experimental neurosis with sheep and goats, Liddell held that animals do not have anxiety in the meaning of that term as applied to human beings, but they do have a primitive, simple counterpart—namely *vigilance*.[1] When an animal is in a situation that involves a possible threat—such as the sheep in the laboratory expecting an electric shock, or the seal sleeping in its natural habitat having to awake every ten seconds to survey the landscape lest Eskimo hunters sneak up on it—the animal exhibits an alertness and a general expectancy of danger. It is as though the animal were asking, "What is it?" This vigilance is characterized by generalized suspiciousness (indicating that the animal does not know whence the danger may arise), with tendencies to act but without any clear-cut direction for acting. Such behavior, as will readily be seen, is the parallel on the animal level to the vague and generalized apprehensive behavior of the human being in anxiety.

Liddell holds that Goldstein was describing this vigilance in his concept of the "catastrophic reaction," but he adds that the fact that Goldstein pegged the reactions at a high level of intensity has kept other investigators from identifying the catastrophic reaction. This seems very true. In conditioning experiments, vigilance may be shown not only at a high intensity—as in experimental neurosis, when the animal gives a very clear picture of Goldstein's catastrophic condition. But it is also shown through all gradations down to such a low intensity as a "small movement of the eyes or a slight acceleration of the heart."

It is this vigilance, states Liddell, *which supplies the power for the conditioned reflex.* While Pavlov was astonishingly accurate in his description of the neurophysiological *mechanics* of conditioning, Liddell believes he was inaccurate when he contended that the motive power for the conditioning came from instinctual sources—e.g., the dog's instinctual desire to get food or to avoid pain and discomfort. Liddell writes that "the conditioning machinery is not powered, as Pavlov believed, by a leakage of energy along a newly formed pathway or channel from a highly energized unconditioned reflex center to a sensory center feebly energized by sensory impulses set up by the condi-

tioned stimulus." Rather, *it is powered by the animal's
capacity for vigilance* or, in other words, by the animal's
capacity as a behaving organism to be alert to, and sus-
picious of, its environment. Liddell's distinction here,
which places the problem on a psychobiological rather
than a neurophysiological level, is the point we have emphasized in the previous chapter—namely that the neurophysiological *media* by which behavior occurs must not be
confused with the *causes* of the behavior. If the animal
is to be conditioned—i.e., if it is to learn to behave in an
orderly fashion—it must be able to get some reliable answer to its question, "What is it?" Thus in conditioning
experiments consistency is all-important.

Within its limitations (e.g., the sheep can keep track of
time, can "plan for the future," only up to about ten minutes, and the dog up to about half an hour), the animal
must also be able to get some answer to a second question,
"What happens next?" When, as in the laboratory experiments designed to produce the experimental neurosis,
the animal cannot get these answers, but continues in tension as though asking, "What is it? What is it? What is
it?"; when, in other words, the animal is kept in a constant, unrelieved state of vigilance, its behavior soon becomes frantic, disordered, and "neurotic." This, on the
animal level, is parallel to what happens when human
beings break down under the burden of severe and constant anxiety. Though Liddell cautions that we cannot
identify the disturbed behavior of animals with human
anxiety, it is possible to state that *conditioned reflex behavior in animals bears the same relation to experimental
neurosis as intelligent action in human beings bears to
anxiety.*

The reader will be aware that we here step, with Liddell, from the realm of physiology—i.e., instincts—to the
organismic realm. It is so easy to think and talk in terms
of "energy" released by the instincts as though we were
dealing with a species of electricity, and it were some
specific power we could measure and hopefully harness.
Liddell makes it very clear that the reality is quite different: we are concerned with a defensive reaction of the
total organism as seen in Liddell's dogs and sheep, including their senses of sight, hearing, smelling, touching, etc.,
as well as the neurological and physiological media for
transmitting the signals. These capacities add up to vig-

ilance on the part of the animals, the precursor of human anxiety.

This brings Liddell to some exceedingly stimulating and suggestive thoughts about the relation between intelligence and anxiety in human beings. Pavlov had believed that the "What is it?" response was the rudimentary form of human inquisitiveness, which in its flowering became man's capacity for scientific investigation and realistic exploration of his world. Liddell is able to carry this line of thought further, and also to make it more precise, by his distinction between the *sentinel* function of the neurological system—i.e., "What is it?"—and the *planner* function—i.e., "What happens next?" The latter function plays a much greater role in human behavior than in animal. Man is the mammal who can foresee, can plan for the future, can retrospectively enjoy past achievements. By these means, human beings construct culture. This capacity to plan for the future has culminated in the human being's unique capacity for living by means of ideas and values.

The capacity to experience anxiety, Liddell states, *and the capacity to plan are two sides of the same coin.* He holds that "anxiety accompanies intellectual activity as its shadow, and that the more we know of the nature of anxiety, the more we will know of intellect." Thus Liddell states one aspect of the problem, which was attacked by Kierkegaard and Goldstein, and with which we shall wrestle again and again in this book, of the relation between creative potentialities and the potentiality for experiencing anxiety. The human being's capacity for imaginative reality-testing, for dealing with symbols and meanings, and for changing behavior on the basis of these processes —all are processes which are intertwined with our capacity to experience anxiety.[2]

It remains only to note that Liddell, like myself and so many other investigators cited in the present study, see the social nature of the human being as the source of our uniquely creative intellectual capacities as well as our capacity for anxiety. ("Social" is defined here as interpersonal and *intra*personal.) Liddell asserts "that both intellect and its shadow, anxiety, are products of man's social intercourse."[3] This social intercourse would not be possible, I must also emphasize, without the inner potentialities which we associate with individuality.

fear of Falling

THE STUDY OF CHILDREN'S FEARS

If we think of children's fears as responses to specific threats, on the apparently sound assumption that the child will fear things that have actually been of danger to him or her in their past experience, we are in for some surprises. Fear of apes, polar bears, tigers—animals the child will never have encountered except in rare visits to the zoo—will appear most in the reports of children's fears. Dangers from mysterious agents like ghosts, witches, and the occult, which again the child has never encountered, also bulk large in the reports of fears. Why should the things feared be so largely imaginary? These and similar questions which bear on the relation of fears to anxiety encourage us to probe more deeply into the origin of childhood fears and anxiety.

Several decades ago the chief problem of the psychology of fear was to discover the original, unlearned stimuli which give rise to fears, and to account for these fears by instinctive processes. The child was supposed to have instinctive fears of darkness, animals, large bodies of water, slimy things, and so forth—many of these assumed by Stanley Hall to have been inherited from the animal ancestors of man. Then it became the task of many psychologists to disprove these "inherited fears" one after another, until in John B. Watson's behaviorism the field was reduced to two. Says Watson of the infant, "there are just two things which will call out a fear response, namely, a loud sound, and loss of support."[4] All subsequent fears, this hypothesis contended, are "built in"—i.e., established by conditioning.

But later students of children's fears have pointed out that Watson's view was a gross oversimplification. Various investigators have been unable to find these two "original fears" with any consistency in infants. As Jersild writes, "the fear stimulus cannot be described as consisting of an isolated stimulus. . . . The circumstances that may give rise to so-called 'unlearned' fears in the infant include not simply noises and loss of support, but any intense, sudden, unexpected, or novel stimulus for which the organism appears to be unprepared."[5] That is to say, situations to which the organism cannot react adequately constitute a threat and are reacted to with anxiety or fear.

I submit that the debate on "original fears," represented by the instinctivists on one hand and the behaviorists on the other, was a tilting at windmills. The endeavor to determine what specific fears the infant is born with causes us to become lost in a labyrinth of misleading questions. The fruitful question, rather, is: What capacities (neurological and psychological) does the organism possess for meeting threatening situations? With respect to inheritance, we need only assume that the organism reacts to situations for which its capacities are inadequate with anxiety or fear, and did so in the days of our ancestors as well as today. The problem of the acquisition of anxiety and fears after birth boils down to the two questions of *maturation* and *learning*. I also question whether these reactions of the infants described by Watson ought accurately to be called "fears" at all. Are they not, rather, *undifferentiated defensive reactions properly to be termed anxiety?* Such a hypothesis would account for the unspecific character of the reactions—i.e., that the "fear" is not found consistently even in the same child in response to a specific stimulus.

Maturation in Anxiety and Fears

Another defect in the Watsonian approach to children's fears was its neglect of the factor of maturation. As Jersild observed in this connection, "If a child at a certain stage of development exhibits behavior that was not shown at an earlier time, it does not follow that the change in behavior is due primarily to learning."[6]

It will be recalled from the discussion of the startle pattern above that in the early weeks of life the infant exhibited the startle response and little or nothing which could be called the emotion of fear. But as the infant developed, more and more secondary behavior (anxiety and fear) appeared. Jersild found in his studies that at about five or six months the child showed occasional signs of fear at the approach of a stranger, while before that level of development the child showed no such reaction.

Gesell's account of the reaction of the infant at different ages to confinement in a small pen is illuminating. At ten weeks the child was complaisant; at twenty weeks he showed mild apprehension, one sign of which was persistent head-turning. (To me, this "persistent head-turning" is a significant picture of vigilance and mild anxiety; the infant is disquieted, but it cannot spatially locate the object of its apprehension.) At thirty weeks his response to the same situation "may be so vigorously expressed by crying that we describe his reaction as fear or fright."[7] As Jersild expresses it, "the tendency to respond to an event as actually or potentially dangerous is relative to the child's level of development."[8]

It seems clear that the level of maturation is one determinant in the infant's or child's response to danger situations. The data suggest that the earliest reactions are of the reflexive variety (i.e., startle) and of diffuse, undifferentiated apprehension (anxiety). Though this diffuse apprehension may be elicited in the early weeks of the infant's life in response to certain stimuli (e.g., falling), it is more frequent as the infant develops greater capacity to perceive danger situations. As regards specific fears, are not these the latest to appear in the scale of maturation of the infant? As Goldstein has indicated, responding with a specific fear presupposes the capacity to objectivate— i.e., to discriminate between specific objects in the environment; and this capacity requires greater neurological and psychological maturation than to respond in a diffuse, undifferentiated way.

René Spitz has coined the phrase "eighth-month anxiety" for the apprehension shown by a baby between eight and twelve months when it is confronted by a stranger. The baby may respond with a look of bewilderment, may cry, or may turn and try to crawl to its mother. Spitz explains that this is due to the fact that the child, through his gradual maturation, has learned to put together his observations so that he recognizes mother and familiar objects. But this perception is not yet solidified and is easily upset by the appearance of another person in the field where mother ought to be. Hence the anxiety aroused when his perceptions are disturbed by a stranger.[9]

As the child develops after the infant period, Jersild points out, new and significant changes occur in the kinds of stimuli which give rise to fears. "With the development of the child's imaginative abilities, his fears become increasingly concerned with imaginary dangers; with the development of understanding of the meaning of competition and of awareness of one's own status as compared with others, there frequently come fears of loss of prestige, ridicule, and failure."[10]

It seems clear that in the latter of these apprehensions—those related to competition—the child is engaging in a more or less complex interpretation of environmental situations. Such interpretive processes presuppose a certain amount of maturation, but they also patently involve the experience and conditioning which occur as the culture makes impact upon the child. Not only has it been found that fears related to competitive status increase as the child matures, but also, interestingly enough, that adults reporting on their remembered childhood fears gave a much higher percentage of apprehensions related to competitive status than any of the groups of children studied. This is rightly explained as due to the tendency of the adults to "read back" into their childhood the fulcra of fear and anxiety which had become increasingly important to them in adulthood.

It is unnecessary to review in detail the results of Jersild's comprehensive studies of children's fears. But two problems arise as one contemplates these results. We cite these problems because of the illumination they shed upon the relation of fears to underlying anxiety.

First, Jersild's results show the *"irrational" qualities* of children's fears. There was a sharp discrepancy between the fears the children reported and what they described, later in the interview, as the "worst happenings" in their lives.[11] The worst happenings were cited as illnesses, bodily injuries, misfortunes, and other experiences that had actually befallen the children. Their fears, on the other hand, were "predominantly described in terms of somewhat vague calamities that might occur." Actual terrifying experiences with animals constituted less than 2 per cent of the "worst happenings," whereas fears of animals accounted for 14 per cent. The animals feared were chiefly remote creatures like lions, gorillas, and wolves. Being left alone in the dark and being lost were given as 2 per cent of the actual experiences, while fears of such situations amounted to about 15 per cent. Fears of mysterious agents like ghosts, witches, and the occult accounted for over 19 per cent (the largest group) of the total fears expressed. As Jersild sums it up, a *"large proportion of fears that were described have little or no direct relation to misfortunes that actually have befallen the children."*[12]

The above data are puzzling. One would expect the child to fear what actually had given him trouble. Noting that the "imaginary fears" of the child increase with age, Jersild suggests as one explanation the fact that "imaginative capacities" of the child are developing. Such maturing capacities may explain why the child deals in imaginary material. But in my judgment this does not adequately account for the fact that these imaginary things should, in such large measure, be *feared*.

A second problem raised by Jersild's data is the *unpredictability of fears*. Jersild notes that his data emphasize how difficult it is to predict when a child will be afraid:

> the same child may face a given situation at a certain time without showing fear but at a later time, with no grossly apparent intervening causal factors, the same situation gives rise to fear. . . . A certain noise causes fear and another does not; a child is taken to one strange place and exhibits no fear, while in another strange situation he does show fear.[13]

It is significant that "fear of strange persons" is most often mentioned as a fear that appears in certain situations and not in other similar situations. Since a child's fears shift unpredictably, some process is occurring that is vastly more complicated than the usual concept of conditioning. But the question of what this process is remains unanswered.

Fears Masking Anxiety

I submit that these two problems—the irrational and unpredictable qualities of children's fears—become intelligible if many of these so-called "fears" are regarded not as specific fright reactions (that is, fears as such) but rather as *appearances in objectivated form of underlying anxiety*. Fear is regularly defined as a specific reaction, and it is apparent that something is occurring in these "fears" which cannot be explained as a specific response inseparably and intrinsically related to a specific stimulus. If the hypothesis is made that these fears are rather expressions of anxiety, the high percentage of "imaginary" fears becomes understandable. It is well known that the anxiety of children (as well as of adults) is often displaced upon ghosts, witches, and other objects which do not have a specific relation to the child's objective world but do fulfill significant functions for his subjective needs, specifically in relation to his parents. In other words, *fears may mask anxiety.*

In some cases, for example, the process is to be understood as follows: the child feels anxiety about his relation to his parents. He cannot face this directly, in such terms, for example, as "I am afraid my mother does not love me," for such a realization would markedly increase his anxiety. Or he is aided in covering up the direct form of the anxiety by reassurances from the parents, which often have little to do with the real fulcrum of anxiety. The anxiety is then displaced upon "imaginary" objects. I have placed the term "imaginary" in quotation marks frequently in this immediate discussion because it would no doubt be found on more profound analysis of the mysterious fears, that the imagined object stands for something all too real in the child's experience. Adults, of course, likewise engage in a similar pattern of displacement of anxieties, but adults are much more skilled in rationalizing the anxieties so that the objects become more apparently "logical" or "reasonable."

Our hypothesis, that these fears are the expression of underlying anxiety, would also make clear why the fears of animals were not of animals actually encountered by the child but remote ones like gorillas and lions. Fears of animals are often projections of anxieties the child feels in relations with objects or persons (such as parents) who are by no means remote. Freud's case of Little Hans is a classic example.[14] I here suggest that fears of animals may also be projections of the child's own hostile feelings toward members of his family, feelings which entail anxiety because of the probability of punishment or disapproval if these hostile tendencies were carried into action.

Our hypothesis likewise throws light upon the unpredictability and shifting quality of children's fears. If these fears are appearances in objectivated form of underlying anxiety, the anxiety could focus now on this object and now on that. What appears as inconsistency on superficial analysis would then be quite consistent when viewed on a deeper level. Jersild himself notes this shifting character of fears when the fears are an expression of underlying anxiety:

As long as there are underlying difficulties that press upon the child from many sides, the elimination of one particular expression of fear may shortly be followed by other fears of a slightly different cast.[15]

Several years after the first edition of this book was published, Jersild remarked to me in personal conversation that he agreed with my conclusion that these fears really expressed anxiety. He was surprised that he had never seen this earlier. I think his not seeing it shows how hard it is to get out of our traditional ways of thinking.

Another indication that anxiety rather than fear is occurring in many children is in the observation that studies indicate the frequent *ineffectiveness of verbal reassurance* in overcoming ("in contrast to covering up") children's fears. As Goldstein held, if the emotion is a specific fear, it can normally be allayed by verbal reassurance. If the child who has a fear that the house is on fire receives adequate demonstration that such is not the case, the fear vanishes. But if this apprehension is actually an objectivated form of anxiety, either the terror will not be allayed, or it will shift to a new object.

There is indirect presumptive support for the hypothesis that anxiety often underlies children's fears in the close relationship between children's "fears" and those of their parents. Hagman's study yields a correlation of .667 between the gross number of children's fears and the gross number of mothers' fears.[16] Jersild found "a good deal of correspondence between the frequency of fears of children of the same family; the correlations ranged from .65 to .74"[17] It would seem that something more is occurring than the parents' fears having an "influence," as Jersild puts it, upon the fears of the children—i.e., that the child learns to fear certain things because the parents do. It has been so frequently pointed out as to become a platitude that the development of anxiety in children arises centrally out of their relations with their parents.[18]

I suggest that the close relationship between children's fears and those of their parents, and between fears of children of the same family, can be understood more clearly as a carry-over on the anxiety level. In other words, in families in which the parents have a good deal of anxiety, the interpersonal relations with children will be disrupted by this anxiety, and there will be greater anxiety (i.e., increased tendency to have "fears") on the part of the children.

The purpose of this discussion of children's fears, in addition to throwing light upon the specific problem of fear as such, has been to demonstrate that *the study of fears leads inexorably to the study of anxiety. The particular hypothesis suggested here is that many children's fears are objectivated forms of underlying anxiety.*[19]

A NOTE ON STRESS AND ANXIETY

Hans Selye's first book, *Stress,* was published, interestingly enough, the same year as the first edition of my *Meaning of Anxiety,* 1950, the exact middle of the century. This marked the beginning of the extensive concern with stress in psychological and medical thinking. In a book six years later, Selye defined biological stress as an "adjustment through the development of an antagonism between an aggressor and the resistance offered to it by the body." Stress is the response to "the rate of wear and tear in the body."[20]

He proposed a General Adaptation Syndrome (called G.A.S.). The G.A.S., through our various internal organs (endocrine glands and nervous system), helps to adjust us to the constant changes which occur in and around us. "The secret of health and happiness lies in successful adjustment to the ever-changing conditions on this globe; the penalties for failure in this great process of adaptation are disease and unhappiness."[21] Each person, he believes, is born with a certain amount of adaptation energy.[22]

This may well be true physiologically, but I question it psychologically. Is not energy partially a product of the zest and commitment of the person for the task at hand? Do we not now find, in our studies of gerontology, that persons grow senile not wholly as a function of age but also because psychologically they have nothing to interest them? And that the brain depends considerably on commitment to tasks which call forth zest, if it is to retain its energy?

A statement needs to be made about the tendency among psychologists to use the word "stress" as a synonym for anxiety. Books purportedly on anxiety use the word "stress" instead; conferences seemingly on anxiety now are entitled interchangeably with the term "stress." I will here argue against the identification of stress and anxiety, and will hold that stress is not an adequate substitute for describing the apprehension we ordinarily refer to as anxiety. This is not an argument against the classical work of Selye, whose field and insightful work is in experimental medicine and surgery. In his field the term surely fits; in psychology I do not believe "stress" encompasses the rich meaning of anxiety.

The word stress is borrowed from engineering and physics. It seems to have become popular in psychology because it can be defined readily, handled easily, and generally measured satisfactorily, all of which are difficult with the term "anxiety." It would seem relatively easy to define the point at which a person will break under stress. Our culture is obviously one which subjects its citizens to great and increasing stress, arising from the radical changes in technology, loss of values, and so on. These are obviously related to the prevalence of stress disorders like cardiac problems, arteriosclerosis, ad infinitum. No cocktail party occurs these days without people talking about stress and the ill effects it causes. "Mental stress" has become an acceptable term even though it appears only eighth on the list of meanings of "stress" in my dictionary.

But the problem with the term "stress" as a synonym for anxiety is that it puts the emphasis on what happens *to* the person. It has an objective but not a genuinely subjective reference. I am aware that many users of the word "stress" uphold its use for inner experience as well. George Engel holds stress can come from inner problems and mentions grief as one example. But normal grief arises, let us say, from the death of someone we love, obviously outside us. Stress still emphasizes chiefly what happens *to* and *on* the person. Grief at the fact that I will die someday in the future is anxiety, not stress. A neurotic form of anxiety would be the state of the person who has so much grief about a past accident his child suffered that he never lets the child go out of the house to play.

Even though its users state that they mean to include psychology in their definition, the term "stress" is still weighted heavily on what happens *to* and *on* the person. This makes sense in its original use in the areas from which it is borrowed—in engineering the concern is how much stress a heavy car makes *on* the bridge, or whether a building can withstand the stress *on* it from an earth-quake. In the area of engineering, consciousness is irrel-evant. Anxiety, on the other hand, is uniquely bound up with consciousness and subjectivity. Even Freud defines anxiety as having to do with one's inner feelings, in con-trast to fear which has to do with objective things.

Psychologically speaking, how the person *interprets* the threat is crucial. Aaron Beck has pointed out that stressful life situations per se are less important in the production of anxiety than the way in which these situations are per-ceived by the individual.[23] As Bourne, Rose, and Mason also say in their article on anxiety in combat soldiers in Vietnam (in this case, operators of helicopters), flying, or even death, cannot be interpreted as stress without con-sideration of the manner in which each individual per-ceives the threat.[24] "Perceive" and "interpret" are subjec-tive processes, rightly included in anxiety but not in stress.

If, furthermore, we use stress as a synonym for anxiety, we cannot *distinguish between the different emotions.* Protracted anger or protracted guilt-feeling causes stress as much as protracted fear; we blur this distinction if we use stress as the catch-all term. We also cannot distinguish between fear and anxiety. In the case of Tom, as we saw above (p. 71), when Tom was responding with fear (i.e., after he had misplaced some valuable papers in the doc-tor's laboratory), his gastric readings were very low. The stomach, so to say, shut off. Whereas when he responded with anxiety, as when he lay awake all night worrying about how long his job would continue, his gastric read-ings were the highest of any time in the study. Opposite to how it functioned in fear, the stomach now worked overtime. If we lump both of these together under "stress," we will have lost a crucial distinction for our understand-ing.

No matter how strongly Selye argues against it in his recent book, his earlier statement, "any stress produces damage" is taken, it seems in America, as meaning that all stress should be avoided. Or at least as often as pos-sible. Selye saw this problem when he dedicated one of his books to those "who are not afraid to enjoy the stress of a full life, nor too naïve to think that they can do so without intellectual effort."[25] But let us remind our-selves of the remark attributed to Hudson Hoagland, "Getting up in the morning is a great cause of stress." Yet we don't stay in bed.

Furthermore, let us recall that additional stress may also bring a great relief from anxiety. In wartime Great Britain, amid the bombing, painful austerity, and other great stress, there was a clear diminution of neurosis.[26] This situation has been demonstrated in many countries. The neurotic problems are allayed in times of stress because the persons have something definite on which to pin their inner turmoil, and they can thus focus on concrete pressures. Indeed, in such cases stress and anxiety work directly opposite to each other. *When there is great stress there may be freedom from anxiety.*

Finally, we can see the inadequacy of the term "stress" used as a synonym for anxiety in Liddell's statement that "anxiety accompanies intellect as its shadow, and the more we know of the nature of anxiety, the more we will know of intellect." If we say "stress accompanies intellect as its shadow," we do not make sense. The same is true when we consider the basic statement made by Kubie: "Anxiety precedes the development of thought." To say "Stress precedes the development of thought" does not at all do justice to Kubie's meaning, i.e., that the gap between stimulus and response, self and object makes thought necessary. "Stress" is, as Selye used it, chiefly a physiological term.

Anxiety is how the individual relates to stress, accepts it, interprets it. Stress is a halfway station on the way to anxiety. Anxiety is how we handle stress.

Gregory Bateson has bemoaned the fact that psychologists so often confuse a part with the whole; "God help the psychologist if he thinks the part is real!" I propose that stress is a *part* of the threat situation and that the term "anxiety" is essential when we wish to refer to the whole.

The substitution of other words for anxiety is not a very rewarding process. There is richness to the word "anxiety" which, even though it presents problems for psychologists, is central in literature, art, and philosophy in its form and experience of "dread." When Kierkegaard says, "Anxiety is the dizziness of freedom," he is saying something that every artist and every man of letters knows, even though the terms are difficult for psychology.

RECENT RESEARCH ON ANXIETY[27]

During the last two decades, thousands of articles, plus a deluge of dissertations, have appeared in the literature on anxiety and stress. Charles Spielberger's indefatigable efforts to bring together major contributors to the field in several symposia led to the publication of no less than seven volumes of research.[28] Although these studies have contributed to our understanding of aspects of anxiety, they create an even greater need for an integrated theory of the meaning of anxiety. I cannot hope to do justice to all of these studies. Instead, I trust the reader will permit me to mention a few of the inquiries that seem most significant to me. I do this, with appropriate anxiety, as an exercise in moving ahead *in spite of* the fact that one cannot cover everything.

Four areas of current research stand out as leading to new understanding of what contributes to anxiety in human beings. First, cognitive theorists, such as Richard Lazarus and James Averill[29] and Seymour Epstein,[30] concerned about the person's perception of reality, believe that an individual's appraisal of the threat serves as a key to understanding anxiety. The significance of these studies is that cognitive theorists place man-as-perceiver at the center of anxiety theory. Although Lazarus and Averill describe anxiety as an emotion based on cognitive mediators between the situation and the personal response, they emphasize that anxiety does not arise from pathology, but humanity. Much of their work, however, seems to be on the effects of psychological stress rather than anxiety.[31] Epstein describes expectancy as the basic parameter in determining the level of arousal, defining anxiety as "acutely unpleasant diffuse arousal following the perception of threat." Anxiety is seen as unresolved fear, resulting in diffusion of the threat. Epstein and Fenz[32] studied sport parachutists, finding that experienced parachutists had high focused arousal, which served to expand their awareness prior to the jump. Novices, on the other hand, had a defensiveness against stimulation which was experienced as aversive, causing them to be overwhelmed by jumping. Epstein's most interesting finding seems to us to be the linkage of anxiety to low self-esteem.[33] Similar to Goldstein's view of the "catastrophic situation," Epstein states that "people have an integrated self theory subject to collapse."[34] Acute psychotic reactions can facilitate the development of an individual's new, more effective self theory. Epstein continues: "acute anxiety is produced by threats to the integrative capacity of the self system." A person with low self-esteem collapses more easily than a person of high self-esteem. Epstein elaborates: "Increases in self esteem produce increases in feelings of happiness, integration, energy, availability, freedom and expansiveness. Decreases in self esteem produce increases in feelings of unhappiness, disorganization, anxiety and constriction."[35]

A second area of significant current research is Spielberger's differentiation between "state" and "trait" anxiety. This has inspired literally hundreds of studies. He sees state anxiety as a transitory emotional condition associated with autonomic-nervous-system activity. Trait anxiety is anxiety proneness, or frequency of the manifestation of anxiety over a long period of time.[36] This model has been used by many researchers to differentiate between arousal and underlying anxiety. Those experiences which have most influence on raising the level of trait anxiety probably date back to childhood, Spielberger believes, and involve parent-child relations in which the child is punished. This points in the direction of the thesis of my own research in Chapter 9, that anxiety proneness has its roots in maternal rejection. Norman Endler believes that both trait and state anxiety are multidimensional, posing a Person-Situation-Interaction model for anxiety. He sees anxiety an an interaction between interpersonal or ego threat (situational factor) and level of interpersonal A-Trait (personality factor).[37]

A third area of current research, that on the relationship between anxiety and fear, is one which has led to many debates among theorists. Conditioning theorists, equating anxiety with fear, have developed various systems of behavior therapy based upon learning theory. It should be noted that their greatest success is with phobics. But a phobia is, by definition, a crystallization of anxiety around some external event, and is by common consent, a neurotic fear covering up anxiety. (See case of Hans in Chapter 5.) It is not difficult to change the focus of fear. But to deal with the underlying anxiety seems to be avoided in the strict behaviorist technique. My point of view is close to that of H. D. Kimmel who criticizes the behaviorists who equate anxiety with fear. Kimmel believes that Pavlov's "experimental neurosis" should have been termed anxiety.[38] He maintains that conditioned fear cannot serve as a model for the acquisition of anxiety because it is built upon the principle of certainty, whereas anxiety has as its core uncertainty and lack of controllability.

Another of the great contributions that researchers have made to our understanding of anxiety has come from studies of individuals in actual life situations. Yona Teichman, studying the responses of family members of soldiers missing in action in the 1973 Middle East War, demonstrated that parents, wives and children have different styles of coping with personal loss. Parents typically maintained a highly personal experience of grief, at first refusing to share it with others. Most responses centered around their need for personal courage and their feelings of bitterness. Despite extreme withdrawal for a week or so, no perpetuation into pathological, long-lasting withdrawal was reported. Wives, though similar to the parents in desiring to be strong, maintained a milder form of bitterness. Typically they were preoccupied with practical problems and dependent on supporting figures. Children, on the other hand, reacted to the general stress of the home rather than the specific loss. Since children did not express their grief continuously, they received parental hostility because of their "unfeeling" attitude.[39] These role comparisons are interesting to view in the light of Lifton's *Protean Man*.[40] Charles Ford's descriptions of the anxieties of those involved in the Korean *Pueblo* incident have demonstrated that men who maintained a faith in their commanding officer, religion, or country coped much more successfully with the anxieties of their incarceration. More than half the men reported significant anxiety from the unpredictability of their treatment. Ford concluded that massive repression was evoked as an acute defense mechanism. More significantly, however, was the finding that the long-range psychological response to severe anxiety may be much greater than the acute response.[41] Richard Lynn's cross-cultural studies of national differences in anxiety, used increased alcohol consumption, rising suicide rates, and the frequency of accidents as some indicators of anxiety.[42]

Observations of life event changes and anxiety in mental

health demonstrate that any change in one's familiar life pattern, for better or worse, calls for adaptation, often mobilizing anxiety.[43]

I hope that these inquiries into the cognitive and multi-dimensional studies of living people in crisis may help us appreciate how protean are the aspects of anxiety.

ANXIETY AND LEARNING THEORY

O. Hobart Mowrer's work is taken for our chief emphasis here because he spans, in his own metamorphosis, the gamut of schools of psychology. Beginning as a staunch behaviorist, Mowrer contributed some of the best formulations of his time of anxiety in stimulus-response psychology. (He is still quoted by Eysenck, who is apparently unaware of Mowrer's later changes.) This led Mowrer to learning theory, the area in which many psychologists find his most significant contribution. Learning theory was a bridge for him to clinical psychology via the problem of how and why rats learn delinquent behavior. This, in turn, led him to a concern with the problems of time, symbols and ethics. The last underlie his preoccupation, in the latter part of his writings, with guilt and responsibility and their implications for therapy. Such a radical metamorphosis must indeed have been difficult to assimilate. This is one reason Mowrer's work is especially revealing.

If we express this in another way, Mowrer's first stage is behaviorism, the second is anxiety and learning theory, and the third is his concern with guilt feeling and its implications for psychology. The changes in his concerns reflect several significant levels in the broadening approach to anxiety in this country. The material reviewed here is mainly in his *second* period.

Mowrer's analyses of anxiety, which interest us here, are based centrally upon his researches in learning theory. In view of the frequently proposed assumption that the ultimate bridge between psychoanalysis on one hand and experimental and academic psychology on the other will probably be learning theory, it is presumable that the learning theory base of Mowrer's work gives his conceptualizations of anxiety greater cogency.

In his early stimulus-response formulations, written when he was still a behaviorist, Mowrer explicitly characterized anxiety as a "psychological problem to which the habits known as 'symptoms' provide solutions."[44] Anxiety was defined in his first paper as "the conditioned form of the pain reaction."[45] That is to say, the organism perceives the danger signal (the stimulus), and the conditioned response which then follows in anticipation of the danger—a response characterized by tension, organic discomfort, and pain—is anxiety. Any behavior which reduces this anxiety is rewarding, and hence, by the law of effect, such behavior becomes "stamped in," i.e., learned. This analysis has two important implications. First, anxiety is seen as one of the central motivations of human behavior. And, second, as a corollary, the process by which neurotic symptoms are acquired is placed squarely on a basis of learning theory—symptoms are learned because they are anxiety-reducing.

Mowrer's next researches in anxiety were experiments with rats and guinea pigs, verifying the above hypothesis that reduction in anxiety serves as a reward and is positively correlated with learning.[46] This hypothesis is now widely accepted in the psychology of learning.[47] It has the practical merit not only of emphasizing how important and pervasive anxiety is as a motivation in education, but it also sheds light on healthy and constructive methods of management of that anxiety in the classroom.[48]

These early approaches of Mowrer to the problem of anxiety have two elements of definition in common. First, no specific distinction is made between fear and anxiety. In the first paper the terms are used synonymously, and in the second the factor of anxiety is defined as the animals' expectation of the electric shock—a state that could be termed fear as accurately as, if not more accurately than, anxiety.[49] Second, the threat which cues off anxiety is defined as the threat of organic pain and discomfort. Obviously, during the period when these papers were written, Mowrer was endeavoring to define anxiety in physiological terms.[50]

But radical changes occurred in Mowrer's conception of anxiety following his further researches in learning theory. The changes came particularly after his inquiry into the question: Why do people learn nonintegrative ("neurotic," consistently punishing) behavior? Experimenting with animals, he demonstrated that rats exhibited "neurotic" and "criminal" behavior because they were incapable of anticipating future, long-time rewards and punishments and balancing them against the immediate consequences of their behavior.[51]

In his stimulating discussion of the findings of his many studies, Mowrer concludes that the essence of integrative behavior is *the capacity to bring the future into the psychological present*. Human beings have this capacity for integrative learning in a form vastly different from animals because they are able to bring the "time determinant" into learning, to weigh future against immediate consequences. This gives human behavior flexibility and freedom and, by inference, responsibility. Mowrer refers to Goldstein's observations that the most characteristic loss of patients with cortical injuries was the capacity to "transcend concrete (immediate) experience," to abstract, to deal with the "possible." Hence these patients were limited to rigid, inflexible behavior. Since the cortex represents the distinctive neurological difference between man and animals, this capacity which the cortically impaired patients lost may be assumed to be the distinctively human capacity.

Our human capacity for transcending the present in the light of future consequences depends upon several distinctive qualities which set us "well apart" from animals, in Mowrer's phrase. One is the capacity to *reason,* to use *symbols.* We communicate by means of symbols, and we think by means of setting up "emotionally charged" symbols in our minds and reacting to them. Another quality is our distinctive *social, historical* development. Weighing the long-time consequences of one's behavior is a social act in that it involves the question of values for the community as well as for one's self (if, indeed, these two can be separated).

Mowrer's findings imply a new emphasis on the *historical* nature of man, on the human being as the "time-binding" being.[52] As he phrases it,

the capacity, then, to bring the past into the present as a part of the total causal nexus in which living organisms behave (act and react) is the essence of "mind" and "personality" alike.[53]

To be sure, the importance of the individual's own genetic past—the fact that he carries into the present the experiences from his childhood, for example—has long been generally accepted in clinical psychology. But there is another implication of this emphasis on man as the "time-binding" being which is relatively new in clinical work: namely, since the human being weighs his behavior in terms of symbols which have been developing through many centuries in the history of his culture, he can be understood only in the context of that history. These findings meant for Mowrer a new interest in history in general, and in particular a new interest in ethics and religion, which are the history of the human endeavor to transcend immediate consequences in terms of long-time universal values.

Through his discussion of integrative learning, Mowrer makes an exceedingly useful distinction between the terms *integrative* and *adjustive*. All learned behavior is in some sense adjustive: neuroses are adjustive; defense mechanisms are ways of adjusting to difficult situations. Mowrer's "neurotic" rats gave up taking food, and his "criminal" rats took it despite the future punishment, each group "adjusting" to a difficult situation. But neuroses and defenses, like the behavior of these rats, are not *integrative* in the sense of preparing the person for future learning. Neuroses and defenses do not permit the further constructive development of the individual.[54]

The implications of the above considerations for anxiety theory are profound. *The problem of neurotic anxiety is placed squarely in its cultural and historical nexus, and is related specifically to man's distinctive problems of social responsibility and ethics. This is in radical contrast to Mowrer's previous definition of anxiety as response to the threat of organic pain or discomfort.* For Mowrer now the "social dilemma [as illustrated in the child's ambivalent relation to his parents] is a precondition for anxiety."[55] If animals have neurotic anxiety at all, Mowrer holds, it is only in artificial environments (e.g., the "experimental neurosis") in which they have become to some extent domesticated, "socialized." That is, by virtue of their relationship with the experimenters, the animals have become something more than "just" animals. This does not imply, in Mowrer's writings or in my own attitude, any depreciation of the value of animal experiments or laboratory studies of human beings, but it does place such methods of study in perspective. In the study of neurotic anxiety, we find the essence of our problem in precisely those characteristics which distinguish human beings from animals. If we limit ourselves to the areas in human behavior which are identical with the infrahuman or to those elements which can be isolated in the laboratory, or, indeed, if we center our study around the strictly biological and organic impulses and needs of man, the essential significance of anxiety for human beings will elude us.

We shall now turn to Mowrer's later presentation of his concept of anxiety. He notes that the beginning of the "social dilemma" is in the child's early relations with his parents. The child cannot avoid anxiety cued off in the family situation by simple flight (like the animal in nature), for the anxious child is dependent upon his parents at the same time that he fears them. Mowrer agrees with the Freudian theory that repression occurs in the child because of real fears—generally the fear of punishment or deprivation (withdrawal of love). Indeed, Mowrer wholly accepts Freud's description of the *mechanism* by which anxiety occurs: a real fear→repression of this fear→neurotic anxiety→symptom formation as a solution to the anxiety. But *mechanism* is a different thing from *meaning.* Mowrer contends that Freud "never succeeded in fully comprehending the essential nature of anxiety itself"[56] because of his endeavor to explain anxiety in terms of instincts and his failure to understand the social context of personality. In the maturing of the human individual, social responsibility normally becomes (or *should* become) a positive, constructive goal. By and large, Mowrer holds, the conflicts which are most likely to cause anxiety are of an ethical nature—a point seen by Kierkegaard but not by Freud. The "ethical accomplishment of untold past generations," writes Mowrer, "as imbedded in the conscience of modern men and women, is not a stupid, malevolent, archaic incubus, but a challenge and a guide for the individual in his quest for self-fulfillment and harmonious integration."[57] The sources of the conflicts are social fear and guilt. What the individual fears is social punishment and withdrawal of love and approval on the part of the significant other persons in his constellation of relationships. It is these fears and the guilt associated with them which become repressed. In their repressed state they become neurotic anxiety.

Anxiety is a product, states Mowrer, "not of too little self-indulgence and satisfaction . . . but of irresponsibility

acceptance

guilt, immaturity." It arises from "repudiated moral urgings,"[58] or, in Freudian terminology, anxiety is caused by "repression of the superego," not, as Freud would have it, the reverse. This viewpoint, of course, has radical implications for dealing with anxiety in therapy. Mowrer points out that the endeavor of many psychoanalysts to dilute and "analyze away" the superego (and concomitantly the individual's sense of responsibility and guilt) only too often results in a " 'deep narcissistic degression' rather than in the growth in personal maturity, social adequacy, and happiness which one has a right to expect from a really competent therapy."[59]

One of the significant implications of Mowrer's viewpoint is that anxiety is seen as playing a constructive, positive role in human development. He writes:

> There is a common tendency in our day, both on the part of professional psychologists and laymen, to look upon anxiety as a negative, destructive, "abnormal" experience, one which must be fought and if possible annihilated. . . . Anxiety, as conceived in these pages, is not the cause of personal disorganization; rather is it the outcome or expression of such a state. The element of disorganization enters with the act of dissociation or repression, and anxiety represents not only an attempted return of the repressed but also a striving on the part of the total personality toward a re-establishment of unity, harmony, oneness, "health."[60]

And, again,

> Nothing could be truer in the light of my own clinical, as well as personal, experience than the proposition that psychotherapy must involve acceptance of the essential friendliness and helpfulness of anxiety, which, under such treatment, will eventually again become ordinary guilt and moral fear, to which realistic re-adjustments and new learning can occur.[61]

guilt + moral fear

PERSONAL COMMENTS

As I have been working on this chapter, some ideas have been running through my mind that I thought would be valuable to share. The first has to do with the problem of experimentally induced anxiety.

In a paper in 1950 Mowrer remarked, "There is at present no experimental psychology of anxiety and one may even doubt whether there ever will be."[62] Not only was it true that the problem of human anxiety had been absent from the strictly experimental specialties of psychology, but until the 1950s it had largely been omitted from the other branches of academic and theoretical psychology as well. In searching psychological books written earlier than 1950 (except those concerned with psychoanalysis), it is almost impossible to find the topic of anxiety even listed in the indexes. What Kierkegaard wrote over a hundred years ago remained true in the first half of the twentieth century: "One almost never sees the concept of anxiety dealt with in psychology."[63] True, there had been a plenitude of studies of *fears* in the experimental and academic psychology of this century, for fears can be made specific and can be counted. But on the threshold where the problem of fears moves into the problem of anxiety, the psychological inquiries had halted.

The practical reasons for this, Mowrer believed, were that the effects of inducing anxiety experimentally in the laboratory would be too damaging. But Mowrer either underestimated the ingenuity of psychologists (and their personal defense mechanisms) or overestimated the human sensitivity of some of them. In any case, of the thousands of researches on anxiety which have sprung up since 1950, many utilize some form of experimentally induced anxiety, generally with students as the subjects.

When my colleague and I went through many of these, we found that some psychologists induce anxiety by setting up an experiment where the student is threatened by shock and others capitalize on the threat of failure. It turned out that threat of failure was definitely more potent in getting the desired reaction from students, so that the majority of later studies induced anxiety by threatening failure. The typical set-up would be roughly as follows: the student comes in with an attitude of respect and trust toward the experimenter, perceiving the latter as a representative of a reputable science. He has heard thousands of times that science will save us, and he is prepared to do his bit. The student would be given several questions to answer. He would then be told, regardless of his responses to the questions, "You have not performed well on this task" or "Your responses are not adequate." Sometimes the student is enticed in under the guise of getting counseling; he is given the Rorschach and then told, again regardless of his responses, "Your responses are similar to sixty percent of emotionally disturbed people" or "You show by this test that you don't have the ability to succeed at this university." The overall aim is to break down the student's self-esteem and then to record the anxiety.

A curious thing about such experiments is how young graduate psychologists are trained, assumedly by the professor supervising the study, to deceive others skillfully in making these statements. It is obviously necessary to learn to lie with a straight face to increase one's credibility in what is a grand system of pretenses.

If one identifies with the students who are the victims of these deceptions, one could imagine several reactions. The first would be the trusting student who has absorbed the lesson of his culture that one should believe everything told to him by a person in authority. His self-esteem would, as expected, take a nose-dive. (And it is the height of naïveté to believe that this can be corrected later by explaining to the student that he was deceived.) Or the student might be the sophisticated type who knows that we all survive by lying to each other anyway. He would be partially protected by his suspiciousness; he would certainly be confirmed in his cynical view of the world, and the general climate of suspiciousness in which he lives would also be confirmed. He would wonder how graduate students and professors can actually think that the subjects believe those lies anyway.

One might ask, out of a cynicism similar to this last-cited student, if they don't believe the deceit anyway, how can it harm their self-esteem? Overlooking the fact that this would void the whole experiment, we may answer that what goes on requires an understanding of the levels of consciousness and awareness in the human being. On the conscious level, the chief effect is the blow to the student's self-esteem, and this effect would be in proportion to how much he believes what he has been told. But on a deeper level of consciousness something else, I believe, happens: the awareness that this respected scientist is lying to him. These two levels may be present simultaneously. One does not need to practice psychotherapy very long to discover that, when the therapist, for some reason, lies, clients will believe it on a conscious level, for they join in the cultural conspiracy which holds you should believe what is said by respected persons in positions of authority. But it becomes clear that on an unconscious level—shown in their dreams or such things as slips of speech—they *know* what he says is untrue but they dare not let themselves *know that they know it*.

My colleague and I, reading on, found to our initial relief that there were other papers in criticism of such experimentally induced anxiety. Aha, perhaps these researchers had some ethical concerns. But no; it turned out to be, in each case, a criticism not of the deception in the experiments, but of the fact that the anxiety induced in one student, cued off by his feeling of failure and hence lowered self-esteem, could not necessarily be taken as equivalent to other students' anxiety. Another criticism was that there was no way to tell how much of the apprehension was habitual with that particular student and how much was situational, i.e., cued off by the experiment. This is surely a just criticism.

But it totally omits the major ethical issue, which is the matter of lying to the subjects and thinking the "explaining" of it afterward clears everything up. I believe that such experiments take their place with lobotomies and shock treatments as practices any profession worthy of the name should control among its members.

Whatever one's ethical stand on the above questions may be, several facts stand out clearly in any survey of psychological studies of human anxiety. One is that the most fruitful researches for illuminating this area have been those which employed clinical procedures along with experimental techniques. For example, the studies of ulcer patients and the case of Tom, reviewed in the preceding chapter.[64] This includes taking one's subjects from those populations which already have anxiety in their life situation. Irving Janis did this in studying anxiety and stress in pre-operative patients in hospitals. Other groups which illustrate life-situation anxiety are combat soldiers, unmarried mothers, parachutists, or test-anxious school children. Obviously, then one can use experimental techniques in assessing the phenomena without themselves inducing the anxiety in the subjects.

Another fact that stands out is that the experimental academic psychologists who have pertinently attacked the problem of anxiety have been those who were led to it via their increasing interest in clinical work and who adopted clinical techniques as their method, like O. Hobart Mowrer, Irving Janis, and John Mason.

The third fact which stands out clearly is that most of the significant data on anxiety comes from the psychotherapists—Freud, Rank, Adler, Sullivan, and others—whose clinical methods permit an intensive study of the subjective dynamics and whose focus of attention is by definition on the individual as a totality confronting crises in his life situation.

My other comments have to do with certain curious anxiety phenomena which have appeared in my own psychotherapeutic practice and are inexplicable on the basis of the classical psychoanalytic doctrine of anxiety. I noticed that some patients did not repress their sexual, aggressive, or "antisocial" urges (in Freud's sense) in any discernible way. Instead they repressed their needs and desires to have responsible, friendly, and charitable relations with other people. When aggressive, sexual, or other behavior in egocentric form emerged in the analysis, these patients showed no anxiety. But when the opposite needs and desires emerged—i.e. to have responsible and constructive social relations—there appeared much anxiety, accompanied by the typical reactions of patients who feel a crucial psychological strategy to be threatened. Such repression of constructive social urges occurs particularly, and understandably, with defiant, aggressive types of patients. (In Greek terms, this is repression of love in *agape*, rather than the libido, sense.)

It will no doubt be agreed that there are multitudes of these defiant, aggressive types in our culture. But they do not frequent psychoanalysts' offices because our competitive culture (in which, to a considerable extent, the individual who can aggressively exploit others without conscious guilt feeling is "successful") supports and "cushions" them to a greater extent than the opposite types. It is generally the culturally "weak" individuals who get to the psychoanalyst; for in cultural terms they have the "neurosis" and the successfully aggressive person does not. It is these non-aggressive types who repress their "defiance," along with their sexual and hostile inclinations. Perhaps these considerations help us understand why most psychoanalytic theories have emphasized repression of sex and aggression as causing anxiety. Possibly if we could analyze more of the aggressive types—those "successful" people who never get into a therapist's office—we should find that the concept of anxiety as repression of responsible impulses is true on a broad scale.

While it is true that many persons have guilt and anxiety because of fear of expressing their own individual capacities and urges, sexual or otherwise, as Freud originally indicated, it is at the same time true that many have guilt and anxiety because they have become "autonomous" without becoming "responsible."[65]

This is repression of what Alfred Adler termed "social interest." Adler's viewpoint has the merit of emphasizing a profoundly important point—namely that the needs of the human being to be a responsible social creature are as fundamental as his needs to express his individualistic, egoistic urgings. It might be argued that urgings for self-gratification are more primal than those for social interest and generosity, since the latter develop at a later stage in the child. But we are learning in recent years the implications of the facts that each human being was born in a dyad, namely he and his mother, and that the fetus was gestated in the womb for nine months. Individualism comes *after* community ties. There is the fact that the human being is bound by social ties from its fetal, *in utero* stage onward (as Sullivan points out), regardless of whether awareness of social ties and their meaning emerges into consciousness sooner or later.

This adds up to a general agreement with the idea espoused by Mowrer, that we have overlooked the function of guilt and social responsibility as a cause of anxiety in our culture. A revealing demonstration of this is found in the case of Helen (Chapter 9), who would admit none of her extensive guilt feelings about her extramarital pregnancy because such an admission would conflict with her aim of being a "rationally" emancipated person. As a consequence her strong feelings of anxiety likewise remained repressed and unamenable to therapy. It would seem that the repression of guilt feelings, with its concomitant generation of neurotic anxiety, is a prevalent characteristic of certain groups in our culture and in some ways it pervades our culture as a whole.

It is surely true, also, that many patients carry a heavy burden of irrational guilt and anxiety which is not a product of their own irresponsibility. In my experience, borderline psychotics fit this category most dramatically. This irrational guilt certainly needs to be clarified and relieved in any adequate therapy. But there are other patients with whom, when guilt feeling is reduced in therapy by the endeavors of the analyst, it eventuates that the genuine, if confused, insights of the patient into himself have been violated and obscured; and that the most valuable and objectively accurate motivation for change is lost. I have known of cases in analysis which have been unsuccessful precisely because the analyst joined the patient in diluting and depreciating guilt feelings. Temporary allaying of anxiety was achieved, of course, but the problems which underlay the anxiety were unsolved and only became buried under a more complicated system of repression.

Is it possible to overestimate the importance of guilt in therapy? The answer obviously is yes. I believe Mowrer does this in some of his later ideas. Take, for example, his commendatory use of the term "superego" and his confusing phrase "repression of the superego." This positive use of the term "superego" can give rise to impression that one is recommending simply an acceding to cultural mores, as though freedom from anxiety and personality health were best exemplified in the conventional person who follows the "rules" and never runs athwart the cultural patterns.

The difficulties to which I refer are exemplified by Ada, one of the two black young women in the study of unmarried mothers later in this book (p. 299). She had a strong superego, in Freud's sense and, I believe, also in Mowrer's. Ada (I quote from p. 300) had a "great need to measure up *but no self-chosen goals or feelings of what she wanted to measure up to.*" As a consequence, her spontaneity and inner instinctual promptings were almost entirely repressed. Her responsiveness to others gave her anxiety because she could not respond in ways that fitted her high standards. When she felt she had not lived up to her internalized expectations, a profound disorientation occurred and much neurotic anxiety ensued.

The "bind" in which she was caught consisted of the fact that she had learned to comply with authority, and when the young man by whom she was pregnant insisted on his wishes, she could not say no to *his* authority. She was not guilty because of the sex or pregnancy as such, but rather because she responded to an authority other than her mother. *This is the dilemma of the person who depends centrally on an authority external to the self, no matter how wise or good that authority happens to be; for the important point is the positing of the authority as the ultimate reference rather than one's own integrity.* It is likewise the dilemma of those whose freedom from neurotic anxiety depends upon compliance with a parent or a "superego" which is simply the parent internalized.

CHAPTER
5

Anxiety Interpreted by
the Psychotherapists

> Whereas the life fear is anxiety at going forward, becoming an individual, the death fear is anxiety at going backward, losing individuality. Between these two fear possibilities, the individual is thrown back and forth all his life.
>
> —Otto Rank

FREUD'S EVOLVING THEORIES OF ANXIETY

Sigmund Freud was a giant who, like Marx and Einstein, became a symbol for the new age. Whether we are "Freudians" or not, as I am not, we are surely all post-Freudian. He set the tone for vast changes in our culture: in literature, *vide* James Joyce and the stream of consciousness; in art, Paul Klee and Picasso in their painting of forms of which people are unaware; in poetry the works of W. H. Auden. The drama on Broadway of the twentieth century, *vide* Eugene O'Neill's *Mourning Becomes Electra,* is not understandable except as we see Freud's discoveries as its background. His theory of the unconscious was in effect a vast broadening of the minds of all of us, and the source not only of psychoanalysis, but of a new view of medicine, psychology, and ethics. No social science is free from his influence. Hence it is important for all of us, regardless of whether we agree with Freud or not, to have some familiarity with the evolution of this thought.

Freud stands in the line of those explorers of human

nature of the nineteenth century—including Kierkegaard, Nietzsche, Schopenhauer—who rediscovered the significance of the irrational, dynamic, "unconscious" elements in personality.[1] These aspects of personality had tended to be overlooked—and in many ways suppressed—by the rationalistic preoccupations of most Western thinking since the Renaissance (see Chapter 2). Though Kierkegaard, Nietzsche, and Freud attacked the rationalism of the nineteenth century for different reasons, they had in common the conviction that the traditional modes of thought omitted elements vital for the understanding of personality. The irrational springs of human behavior had been left outside the accepted area of scientific investigation or lumped under the so-called instincts. Freud's reaction against the endeavors of academic medicine of his day to explain anxiety by "describing the nerve-pathways by which the excitations travel" and his conviction that the methods of academic psychology of his day yielded little or no help in the dynamic understanding of human behavior which he sought, can be understood in this light. At the same time, Freud felt himself to be an enthusiastic champion of science in his avowed intention of making the "irrational" elements in behavior explicable in terms of his broader concept of scientific method. That he carried over into his work some of the presuppositions of nineteenth-century traditional (physical) science is illustrated in his libido theory, which we will comment on below.

Though others, like Kierkegaard, had preceded Freud in recognizing the crucial importance of the problem of anxiety in understanding human behavior, Freud was the first in the scientific tradition to see the fundamental significance of the problem. More specifically, Freud directed attention to anxiety as the basic question for the understanding of emotional and psychological disorders. Anxiety, he notes in his later essay devoted to this topic, is the "fundamental phenomenon and the central problem of neurosis."[2]

Students of dynamic psychology would no doubt agree that Freud is the pre-eminent explorer of the psychology of anxiety, that he both showed the way and gave many of the most efficacious techniques for the understanding of the problem, and that, therefore, his work is of classic importance. This is despite the fact that it is now widely believed that many of his conclusions must be qualified and reinterpreted. To study Freud on anxiety is to become aware that his thinking on the topic was in process of *evolution* throughout his life. His theories of anxiety underwent many minor changes as well as one revolutionary change. Since anxiety is so fundamental a question, it cannot be given any simple answers; and Freud significantly confesses in his last writings that he is still presenting hypotheses rather than a "final solution" to the problem.[3] Therefore, we shall endeavor in this survey not only to present Freud's central insights and his innumerable observations into the mechanics of anxiety, but also to plot the *directions* in which his concept of anxiety was evolving.

To begin with, Freud makes the customary distinction between fear and anxiety which we have already noted in the work of Goldstein and others. Freud holds that in fear the attention is directed to the object, whereas anxiety refers to the condition of the individual and "disregards the object."[4] To him the more significant distinction is between objective (what I would term "normal") and neurotic anxiety. The former, "real" anxiety, is the reaction to an external danger like death. He conceives it as a natural, rational, and useful function. This objective anxiety is an expression of the "instincts of self-preservation." "On what occasions anxiety is felt—that is to say in the face of what objects and in what situations—will of course depend to a large extent on the state of a person's knowledge and his sense of power *vis-à-vis* the external world."[5] This "anxious readiness," as Freud terms objective anxiety, is an expedient function, since it protects the individual from being surprised by sudden threats (frights) for which he is unprepared. Objective anxiety does not in itself constitute a clinical problem.

But any development of anxiety beyond the initial prompting to survey the danger and make the best preparation for flight is inexpedient. It paralyzes action. "The *preparation* for anxiety seems to me to be the expedient element in what we call anxiety and the *generation* of anxiety the inexpedient one."[6] It is, of course, this development of anxiety in amounts out of proportion to the actual danger, or even in situations where no ostensible external danger exists, which constitutes the problem of neurotic anxiety.

Anxiety and Repression

How is it possible, Freud asks in his early writing, to bring the phenomenon of neurotic anxiety into logical relationship with objective anxiety? In the endeavor to answer this question he cites his observations in clinical work. He had noticed that patients who exhibit inhibitions or symptoms of various sorts are often remarkably free from overt anxiety, a phenomenon to which we have referred in Chapter 4. In phobias, for example, the patient exhibits an intense concentration of anxiety on one point in his environment—namely, the object of his phobia—but he is free from anxiety at other points in his environment. In obsessional acts, likewise, the patient seems to be free of anxiety so long as he is permitted to carry out his act in unmolested fashion, but as soon as he is prevented from performing the obsessional act, intense anxiety appears. So Freud reasoned, understandably, that some substitutive process must be occurring—i.e., *the symptom must in some way be taking the place of the anxiety.*

He observed at the same time that his patients who experienced continual sexual excitation which was ungratified—he cites cases of coitus interruptus, for one example—also exhibited a good deal of anxiety. Hence, he concluded, the substitutive process occurring must be the interchange of anxiety, or anxiety-equivalents in the form of symptoms, for unexpressed libido. He writes, "libidinal excitation vanishes and anxiety appears in its place, whether in the form of expectant anxiety or in attacks and anxiety-equivalents."[7] Looking back from a later date on the observations which led to this theory, Freud remarks,

I found that certain sexual practices, such as coitus interruptus, frustrated excitement, enforced abstinence, give rise to outbreaks of anxiety and a general predisposition to anxiety—which may be induced whenever, therefore, sexual excitation is inhibited, frustrated, or diverted in the course of its discharge in gratification. Since sexual excitement is the expression of libidinal instinctual impulses, it did not seem rash to suppose that through the influence of such disturbances the libido became converted into anxiety."[8]

The first theory, therefore, states that when libido is repressed, it becomes transformed into anxiety, and then reappears as free-floating anxiety or as an anxiety-equivalent (a symptom). "Anxiety is therefore the universally current coinage for which *any* affective impulse is or can be exchanged if the ideational content attached to it is subjected to repression."[9] When an affect is repressed, its fate is "to be transformed into anxiety, whatever quality it may have exhibited apart from this in the normal course of events."[10] The source of the child's anxiety at missing his mother, or at the appearance of strange people (which represents the same danger situation as missing the mother, since the presence of the strange people signifies the mother's absence), lies in the fact that the child cannot then expend his libido toward the mother, and the libido is "discharged as anxiety."[11]

Recalling that objective anxiety is a flight-reaction to external danger, Freud asks what the individual is afraid of in neurotic anxiety. The latter, he answers, represents a flight from the demands of one's own libido. In neurotic anxiety the ego is attempting a flight from the demands of its libido, and is treating this internal danger as if it were an external one.

Repression corresponds to an attempt at flight by the ego from libido which is felt as a danger. A phobia may be compared to an entrenchment against an external danger which now represents the dreaded libido.[12] To summarize Freud's first theory of neurotic anxiety: *the individual experiences libidinal impulses which he interprets as dangerous, the libidinal impulses are repressed, they become automatically converted into anxiety, and they find their expression as free-floating anxiety or as symptoms which are anxiety-equivalents.*

This first endeavor of Freud's to formulate a theory of anxiety is undeniably based initially on observable clinical phenomena. Everyone has noticed that when strong and persistent desires are held in check or repressed, the person will often exhibit chronic restlessness or various forms of anxiety. But this is a phenomenological description, which is a quite different thing from a *causal explanation* of anxiety—as Freud himself was later to acknowledge. Furthermore, the phenomenon of sexual repression resulting in anxiety is by no means consistent; the frank libertine may be a very anxious person, and many well-clarified persons may bear a great deal of sexual abstinence without anxiety.

On the positive side, this first theory does have the value of emphasizing the intrapsychic locus of neurotic anxiety. But the suggested mechanism of automatic conversion of libido—an attractive concept, perhaps chiefly because it fits chemical-physiological analogies so handily—is highly dubious, as Freud himself was later to see. Some of the inadequacies of the first theory can best be seen by following the clinical observations and reasoning which led Freud to reject it.

On later analysis of patients with phobias and other anxiety symptoms, Freud found that a quite different process with respect to anxiety was occurring. A new theory was made necessary, too, by his increasing emphasis on the role of the ego, which had played only an auxiliary part in the first theory. "The division of the mental personality into a super-ego, ego and id," he writes, "has forced us to take up a new position with regard to the problem of anxiety."[13]

He demonstrates the analysis which led to the new theory with the case of Hans, the five-year-old boy who refused to go out into the street (the inhibition) because of his phobia of horses (the symptom). Hans had considerable ambivalence toward his father, which Freud explains in classical Oedipus fashion. That is, the little boy felt strong desires for the love of his mother and consequent jealousy and hatred of his father. But at the same time he was devoted to his father in so far as his mother did not enter the picture as a cause of dissension. Because of the father's strength, the impulses of jealousy and hatred—or hostility—in Hans would cue off anxiety. The hostility carries with it frightening possibilities of retaliation, and it also involves the boy in continuous ambivalence toward a father to whom he is at the same time devoted; hence the hostility and related anxiety undergo repression. These affects are then displaced upon horses. Without going into detail about the mechanism of phobia formation, we wish only to illustrate Freud's point that *the phobia of horses is a symptomatic representation of Hans's fears of his father*. Freud interprets this fear in typical castration terms: the fear of the bite of the horse is fear of having his penis bitten off. Freud writes:

This substitute formation [i.e., the phobia] has two patent advantages: first, that it avoids the conflict due to ambivalence, for the father is an object who is at the same time loved; and secondly, that it allows the ego to prevent any further development of anxiety.[14]

The crucial point in this analysis is that the *ego perceives the danger*. This perception arouses anxiety (Freud speaks of the "ego" arousing anxiety), and as an endeavor to avoid the anxiety the ego effects the repression of the impulses and desires which would lead the person into danger. *"It was not the repression that created the anxiety,"* Freud now remarks against his first theory; *"the anxiety was there earlier and created the repression."*[15] The same process holds true for other symptoms and inhibitions: the ego perceives the danger signal, and the symptoms and inhibitions are then created in the endeavor to avoid the anxiety. We may now, writes Freud, take the new view that the "ego is the real locus of anxiety, and reject the earlier conception that the cathectic energy of the repressed impulse automatically becomes converted into anxiety."[16]

A qualification is now also made by Freud in his earlier statement that the danger feared in neurotic anxiety is that simply of inner instinctual impulses. Speaking of Hans, he writes:

But what sort of anxiety can it be? It can only be *fear of a threatening external danger;* that is to say, objective anxiety. It is true that the boy is afraid of the demands of his libido, in this case of his love for his mother; so that this is really an instance of neurotic anxiety. But this being in love seems to him to be an internal danger, which he must avoid by renouncing his object, only because it involves an external danger-situation [retaliation, castration].

Though this interrelationship of external and internal factors was found by Freud in every case he investigated during this later period, he confesses "that we were not prepared to find that internal instinctual danger would turn out to be a situation of determinant and preparation for an external, real situation."[17]

Many students of anxiety feel that this second theory,

with its emphasis on the ego function, is more compatible with other psychological approaches of the problem.[18] Horney, for example, holds that whereas the first theory was essentially "physiochemical," the second is "more psychological." In any case, the second hypothesis evidences some clear and significant trends in Freud's understanding of anxiety, which will be discussed below.

Origins of Anxiety as Seen by Freud

Freud states that the capacity for anxiety is innate in the organism, that it is part of the self-preservation instinct, and that it is phylogenetically inherited. In his words, "we attribute to children a strong inclination to realistic anxiety and we should regard it as quite an expedient arrangement if this apprehensiveness were an innate heritage in them."[19] Specific anxieties, however, are taught. Of genuine "objective anxieties"—by which Freud means fear of climbing on window sills, fear of fire, etc.—the child seems to bring very little into the world. And "when in the end realistic anxiety is awakened in them, that is wholly the result of education."[20] Thus he takes maturation into account:

A certain predisposition to anxiety on the part of the infant is indubitable. It is not at its maximum immediately after birth, to diminish gradually thereafter, but first makes its appearance later on with the progress of psychic development, and persists over a certain period of childhood.

Beyond the above general statement, Freud finds the origin of anxiety in the *birth trauma* and *fear of castration*. These two concepts are interwoven and progressively reinterpreted in his writings. The *affect* which comes with anxiety, Freud holds in his early lectures, is a reproduction and repetition of some particular very significant previous experience. This he believed to be the birth experience— "an experience which involves just such a concatenation of painful feelings, of discharges and excitation, and of bodily sensations, as to have become a prototype for all occasions on which life is endangered, ever after to be reproduced again in us as the dread of 'anxiety' condition." He adds, foreshadowing his later broadening of the birth concept, *"It is very suggestive too that the first anxiety state arose on the occasion of the separation from the mother."*[21] The child's having anxiety at the appearance of strange people and its fears of darkness and loneliness (which he terms the first phobias of the child) have their origin in dread lest the child be separated from his mother.

It is an important question, in reviewing Freud's later writings, how far he was considering the birth experience as a literal source of anxiety, to be cued off by later danger situations, and how far he regarded it as a prototype in a symbolic sense—i.e., symbolic for separation from the loved object. Since he places great emphasis on castration as the specific source of anxiety underlying many neuroses, he is at pains to explain how castration and the birth experience are interrelated. We shall, therefore, now investigate how he progressively reinterprets and interrelates castration and the birth experience page by page in his chief essay on anxiety.[22]

Speaking of the danger underlying the development of phobias, conversion hysteria, and compulsion neuroses, he notes, "in all these, we assume castration anxiety as the motive force behind the struggles of the ego."[23] Even fear of death is an analogue of castration, since no one has actually experienced death but everyone has experienced a castration-like experience in the loss of the mother's breast in weaning. He then speaks of the danger of castration *"as a reaction to a loss, to a separation,"* of which the prototype is the birth experience. But he is critical of Rank's too specific deduction of anxiety and consequent neurosis from the severity of the birth trauma. In reaction against Rank, he holds that the danger situation in birth is "the loss of the loved (longed for) person," and the "most basic anxiety of all, the 'primal anxiety' of birth, arises in connection with separation from the mother."[24] Castration he now relates to the loss of the mother by Ferenczi's reasoning: the loss of the genital deprives the individual of the means of later reunion with the mother (or mother substitute). Fear of castration later develops into dread of conscience—i.e., social anxiety; now the ego is afraid of the anger, punishment, loss of love of the superego. The final transformation of this fear of the superego consists of death anxiety.[25]

Thus we are presented with a hierarchy: *fear of loss of the mother at birth, loss of the penis in the phallic period, loss of the approval of the superego (social and moral approval) in the latency period, and finally loss of life, all of which go back to the prototype, the separation from the mother.* All later anxiety occasions "signify in some sense *a separation from the mother.*"[26] This must mean that castration stands for the loss of a prized object of value in the same sense as birth stands for the loss of the mother. Another datum which impelled him to interpret castration in a nonliteral fashion was the fact that the female sex, "certainly more predisposed to neurosis," as he remarks, cannot suffer literal castration because of the absence of a penis to begin with. In the case of women, he states that anxiety arises over fear of the loss of the object (mother, husband) rather than loss of the penis.

Though one cannot be certain as to how far Freud was regarding the birth experience and castration literally and how far symbolically, we submit that the *trend in Freud's reasoning cited above is toward an increasingly symbolic interpretation.* I regard this trend as positive. With respect to castration, there may legitimately be considerable question as to whether it is literally a source of anxiety on any wide scale. I suggest that *castration is a culturally determined symbol around which neurotic anxiety may cluster.*[27]

With respect to the birth trauma, I regard Freud's increasingly symbolic interpretation also as a positive trend. It is still an open question in experimental and clinical psychology how far the severity of the birth experience is a literal source of later anxiety.[28] But even if the actual birth experience cannot be accepted as the source of anxiety in literal fashion, it would certainly be widely agreed that the infant's early relations with its mother, which so intimately condition both its biological and psychological development, are of the greatest significance for later anxiety patterns. Hence I emphasize that facet of Freud's thought which holds that *anxiety has its source, as far as a primal source is reactivated in later neurotic anxiety, in the fear of premature loss of or separation from the mother (or mother's love), and thence fear of the loss of subsequent values.* Indeed, in the development and clinical application of Freudian theory, this interpretation is widely made, often in the form of the primal source of anxiety as being rejection by the mother.[29]

Trends in Freud's Theories of Anxiety

Since we are concerned with the evolution of Freud's understanding of anxiety, we shall summarize certain directions in which his thinking was moving from his earlier to his later writings on anxiety.

Our approach—plotting the trends in Freud's thinking— is fitting in the respect that Freud's thinking was germinal; it was changing and developing through most of his life. This makes dogmatism about his views of very dubious worth; but the changing nature of his views also makes for ambiguity in his writings. For example, at times Freud writes as though he had completely rejected his first theory, but at other times as though he believed it compatible, in a subsumed position, with the second theory.

The first trend follows from the above; it is a trend *toward removing the libido theory from the primary position in his understanding of anxiety to a secondary position.* Whereas the earlier theory of anxiety was almost wholly a description of what happened to libido (it was an "exclusively economic interpretation," Freud remarks), in his later writing he states that he is now not so much interested in the fate of the libido. His second theory still presupposes the libido concept, however: the energy which becomes anxiety is still libido withdrawn from the cathexis of repressed libido. In this second theory, the ego performs its repressive functions by means of "desexualized" libido; and the danger faced (to which anxiety is the reaction) is the "economic disturbance brought about by an increase in stimuli demanding some disposition be made of them."[30] Though Freud retained the libido concept through all his writings, the trend is *from a description of anxiety as an automatic conversion of libido to a description of the individual perceiving a danger and utilizing libido (energy) in coping with this danger.* This trend accounts partially for the fact that Freud's second theory presents a more adequate description of the mechanism of anxiety. But I question whether even the secondary emphasis on the libido theory in Freud's later writings on anxiety does not confuse the problem by its emphasis on the individual as a carrier of instinctual or libidinal needs which must be gratified.[31] The view I take in the present study (see Chapter 7) involves carrying the above trend in Freud's thinking further in the respect that libido or energy factors are seen not as given economic quantities which must be expressed, but *as functions of the values or goals the individual seeks to attain as he relates himself to his world.*

A second trend is seen in Freud's conception of how anxiety symptoms are formed. This trend is shown most vividly in the reversal of his early view that repression causes anxiety to the later view that anxiety causes repression. What this shift implies is that anxiety and its symptoms are seen not as merely the outcome of a simple intrapsychic process, but *as arising out of the individual's endeavor to avoid danger situations in his world of relationships.*

A third trend, with implications similar to that above, is shown in Freud's endeavor to overcome the *dichotomy between "internal" and "external" factors* in the occasions of anxiety. Whereas in the earlier theory neurotic anxiety was viewed as arising from fear of one's own libidinous impulses, Freud later saw that the libidinous impulses are dangerous only because the expression of them would involve an external danger. The external danger was of only minor importance in the first theory when anxiety could be viewed as an automatic intrapsychic transformation of libido. But it became a pressing problem to him in the cases he was analyzing in his later periods when he saw that the internal danger—danger from one's own impulses—arose from the fact that the individual was struggling against an "external and real danger-situation."

This same trend toward seeing the anxious individual in a struggle with his environment (past or present) is indicated in the increasing prominence in Freud's later writings of the phrase "danger situation" rather than merely "danger." In his early writings we are informed that the symptom is developed to protect the individual from the demands of his own libido. But in developing his second theory he writes:

One might say, then, that symptoms are created in order to avoid the development of anxiety, but such a formulation does not go below the surface. It is more accurate to say that symptoms are created in order to avoid the *danger situation* of which anxiety sounds the alarm.[32]

Later in this same essay he notes:

> We have become convinced also that instinctual demands often become an (internal) danger only because of the fact that their gratification would bring about an external danger—because, therefore, this internal danger represents an external one."[33]

Therefore, the symptom is not merely a protection against inner impulses: "For our point of view the relationships between anxiety and symptom prove to be less close than was supposed, the result of our having interposed between the two the factor of the danger situation."[34]

It may seem at first blush that we are laboring a minor point in emphasizing this shift from "danger" to "danger situation." But I believe that it is by no means an unimportant issue or a mere question of terminology. *It involves the whole difference between seeing anxiety as a more or less exclusively intrapsychic process, on the one hand, and the view that anxiety arises out of the individual's endeavor to relate himself to his world, on the other.* In this second view intrapsychic processes are significant because they are reactions to, and means of coping with, the difficulties in the interpersonal world. The trend in Freud is toward a more *organismic* view—*organismic* being here defined as connoting a view of the person in his constellation of relationships. But it is well known that Freud never developed this trend to its logical conclusions in terms of a consistent organismic and cultural viewpoint. I believe he was prevented from doing so by both his libido theory and his topological concept of personality.

A fourth trend in Freud's thinking on anxiety is shown in his increased emphasis on the *topology of the psyche,* arising out of his division of the personality into superego, ego, and id. This makes it possible for him to center more of his attention on anxiety as being a function of the way the individual, via the ego, *perceives and interprets the danger situation.* He remarks that the phrase he employed in his earlier theory, "anxiety of the id," is infelicitous since neither id nor superego can be said to perceive anxiety.

While this trend, like the others mentioned above, makes Freud's later concepts of anxiety more adequate and more understandable psychologically, I raise the question as to whether this topology, when employed in any strict sense, does not confuse the problem of anxiety. For example, Freud speaks in his later writing of the ego "creating" repression after it perceives the danger situation. Does not repression involve unconscious ("id," in topological terms) functions as well? Indeed, any symptom formation which is effective must involve elements which are excluded from awareness, as Freud himself, despite his topology, would be the first to admit.

I suggest that repressions and symptoms can best be viewed as the organism's means of adjusting to a danger situation. While it is helpful and necessary to see in given cases that certain elements are in awareness and others are excluded from awareness, the strict application of the topology makes not only for inconsistencies in the theory but also shifts the attention away from the real locus of the problem, namely the organism and its danger situation.[35]

An application of his topology made by Freud which reveals this problem is seen in his discussion of helplessness in anxiety. He holds that in neurotic anxiety the ego is made helpless by its conflict with the id and superego. In all neurotic anxiety the individual is engaged in intrapsychic conflict. But is not this conflict, rather than being a lack of accord among ego, superego, and id, really a conflict between contradictory values and goals the individual seeks to attain in relating himself to his interpersonal world? It is to be granted that certain poles of these conflicts will be in awareness and others will be repressed, and it is also to be granted that in neurotic anxiety previous conflicts in the individual's life-history are reactivated. But to my mind *both the present and the previous conflicts are to be seen not as between different "parts" of the personality but as between mutually exclusive goals made necessary by the individual's endeavor to adapt to a danger situation.*

It is unnecessary to labor the point of Freud's far-reaching contributions to the understanding of anxiety. For our purposes here, these contributions consist chiefly in the many-sided illumination he shed upon symptom formation, in his many insights into the primal source of anxiety in the separation of the child from its mother, and in his emphasis on the subjective and intrapsychic aspects of neurotic anxiety.

Freud will go down in history as the great figure in

modern psychology, the one who correctly sensed the significance of psychology—in its form of psychotherapy—for a world in transition and turmoil. Again, whether we agree with him or not is irrelevant. His contributions to the theory of anxiety, "the nodal problem," remain in the center around which other theories congregate.

RANK: ANXIETY AND INDIVIDUATION

Otto Rank's view of anxiety stems logically from his belief that the central problem in human development is *individuation*. He conceived of the life history of a human being as an endless series of experiences of *separation*, each such experience presenting the possibility of greater autonomy for the individual. Birth is the first and most dramatic event in this continuum of separations, but the same psychological experience occurs, in greater or lesser degree, when the child is weaned, when it goes off to school, when the adult separates from his or her single state in favor of marriage, and at all steps in personality development until ultimate separation in death. Now, for Rank, *anxiety is the apprehension involved in these separations*. Anxiety is experienced in the breaking of previous situations of relative unity with, and dependence upon, the personal environment: this is anxiety in the face of the need to live as an autonomous individual. But anxiety is also experienced if the individual refuses to separate from his immediate position of security: this is anxiety lest one lose one's individual autonomy.[36]

Rank's understanding of anxiety was influenced by his celebrated studies of the birth trauma.[37] The symbol of birth has basic significance in Rank's interpretation of psychological events all through the life career of an individual, even though his belief that the infant feels anxiety at the time of parturition is debatable. He held that the "child experiences his first feeling of fear in the act of birth," an apprehension which Rank termed "fear in the face of life."[38] This primal anxiety is anxiety at being separated from the previous situation of wholeness with the mother and being projected into the radically different state of individual existence in the world.

Now, I would agree that our adult minds can imagine the birth experience to be filled with portentous possibilities, certainly enough to engender profound anxiety. But what the infant being born experiences, or whether it experiences anything which can be called a "feeling" is a different question, and in my judgment an open question. It seems more accurate to speak of "potential" anxiety at birth rather than actual, and to treat birth as a symbol. Indeed, it is clear from Rank's later writings (with the exception of such sentences as that quoted above) that he does employ the birth experience symbolically. For example, Rank rightly held that the patient goes through a birth experience at separation from the analyst in the end phases of psychotherapy.[39]

What Rank insists upon is that anxiety exists in the infant *before* any specific content attaches to it. "The individual comes to the world with fear," he remarks, "and this inner fear exists independently of outside threats, whether of a sexual or other nature." Later in the development of the child the "inner fear" becomes attached to outer experiences of threat, a process which serves to "objectify and make partial the general inner fear." This attaching of primal anxiety to specific experiences in the form of fears he describes as "therapeutic," implying that the individual can deal more effectively with specific threats.[40] Thus Rank distinguishes between the primal undifferentiated apprehension, which in this study we term "anxiety," and the later specific, objectified forms of apprehension, which we term "fears."

A confusion is presented by the fact that Rank uses the term *fear* to stand for both fear and anxiety. But it seems clear in the contexts of his writing as well as in the phrases themselves that what he refers to as "fear of life," "inner fear," and the "primal fear" of newborn infants is what other authors such as Freud, Horney, and Goldstein call anxiety. For example, he describes primal fear as the "undifferentiated feeling of insecurity," a phrase which is certainly a sound definition of early anxiety. Indeed, it seems to me clear that such general phrases as "life fear" and "death fear" have no meaning unless they refer to anxiety. One can be afraid his neighbor will shoot him, but persistent "death fear" is a different matter. The reader will make better sense of Rank's discussion in this connection if he reads "anxiety" in most cases where Rank writes "fear."

The primal anxiety present in the infant, says Rank,

takes two forms throughout the individual's life career, namely *life fear* and *death fear*. These two terms, unspecific as they seem at first glance, refer in Rank's thought to the two aspects of individuation which are shown in an infinite variety of forms in every person's experience. The life fear is the anxiety at every new possibility of autonomous activity. It is the "fear of having to live as an isolated individual."[41] Such anxiety occurs, Rank held, when a person senses creative capacities within himself. The actualization of these capacities would mean creating new constellations, not only in works of art (in the case of artists) but also in new forms of relationship with others and new integration within one's self. Thus such creative possibilities bring the threat of separation from previous forms of relationship. It is, of course, not coincidental that this concept of anxiety in creative activity is presented by the psychologist, namely Rank, who has done perhaps the most penetrating work in all depth-psychology on the psychology of the artist. It is a concept we have already seen in Kierkegaard and one which is presented in classical form in the Greek myth of Prometheus.[42]

The death fear in Rank's thought is the opposite to the above. Whereas the life fear is anxiety at "going forward," becoming an individual, the death fear is anxiety at "going backward," losing individuality. It is anxiety at being swallowed up in the whole, or in more psychological language, anxiety lest one stagnate in dependent symbiotic relationships.

Rank believed that each person experiences these two forms of anxiety in polarity:

> Between these two fear possibilities, these poles of fear, the individual is thrown back and forth all his life, which accounts for the fact that we have not been able to trace fear back to a single root, or to overcome it therapeutically.[43]

The neurotic has never been able to keep these two forms of anxiety in balance. His anxiety in the face of individual autonomy keeps him from affirming his own capacities, and his anxiety in the face of dependency on others renders him incapable of giving himself in friendship and love. Hence many neurotics are characterized by a great need to *appear independent* but at the same time to keep an actual excessive *dependence*. Because of his exaggerated anxiety, the neurotic engages in widespread constraint of his impulsive and spontaneous activity; and as a consequence of this constraint, Rank held, the neurotic experiences excessive guilt feelings. The healthy, creative individual, on the other hand, can surmount his anxiety sufficiently to affirm his individual capacities, negotiate the crises of psychological separation necessary for growth, and reunite himself with others in progressively new ways.

Though Rank's chief interest is in individuation, he is well aware that the individual can realize himself only in interaction with his culture, or, as he phrases it, in participation in "collective values." Indeed, the characteristics of the prevalent neurotic type in our culture—characteristics which he describes as "a feeling of inferiority and inadequacy, fear of responsibility and guilt feeling, in addition to a hyper-selfconsciousness"—are to be understood as products of a culture in which "collective values including religion have been overthrown and the individual has been pushed to the fore."[44] The loss of collective values in our culture (or, as I would say, the chaotic condition of social values) is not only a cause of neurotic anxiety but sets for the individual an especially difficult task in overcoming neurotic anxiety.

Many readers will find Rank's terminology and his dualistic mode of thought uncongenial. But it would be unfortunate if this kept anyone from reading him. No one has attacked more insightfully two basic aspects of the problem of anxiety—namely the relation between anxiety and individuation, and anxiety and separation.

ADLER: ANXIETY AND INFERIORITY FEELINGS

Alfred Adler does not present a systematic analysis of anxiety, partly because of the unsystematic nature of his thinking as a whole, and partly because the problem of anxiety is contained in his central and inclusive concept of *inferiority feelings*. When Adler refers to "inferiority feelings" as the basic motivation of neuroses, he is using the term as almost every other psychologist would employ the term "anxiety." Hence to discover his understanding of anxiety we must examine his concept of inferiority—a concept which is significant but unfortunately elusive.

Every human being, according to Adler, begins life in a state of biological inferiority and insecurity. Indeed, the whole human race was inferior, tooth for tooth and claw for claw, in the animal world. For Adler, civilization—the development of tools, arts, symbols—is a result of man's endeavor to compensate for his inferiority in nature.[45] Each infant begins his existence in a state of helplessness and would not survive except for the social acts of his parents. Normally the child overcomes his helplessness and achieves security through progressively affirming his social relationships—through affirming, as Adler puts it, the "multiplex bonds that bind human being to human being."[46] But normal development is jeopardized by both objective and subjective factors. The objective factors are that the infant's inferiority may be augmented by *organic weaknesses* (of which even in adulthood he may be unaware). Or by *social discrimination* (e.g., being born into a minority group, or being a woman in a culture which holds masculinity to be superior—Adler was a women's liberationist several decades before this was popular). Or by an *adverse position in the family constellation* (for Adler, being an only child was an example of this). Objective inferiority, however, can be adjusted to realistically despite the fact that it sets up hurdles to be surmounted in the individual's development.

The crucial factor for the development of the neurotic character is the *subjective attitude toward one's weaknesses* —which brings us to the important distinction Adler makes between inferiority as a fact and inferiority "feelings." It is a characteristic of the human infant, Adler holds, that he apprehends his inferiority long before he can do anything about it. His self-awareness develops in the context of comparison with older siblings and adults who have much more power than he. This may lead to a valuation of the *self* as inferior ("I *am* weak" being a different statement about one's self from "I *have* weaknesses"). Such inferiority feelings about the self, which focus on the objective inferiorities mentioned above, set the stage for the development of neurotic compensatory endeavors to gain security by achieving superiority.

This problem of the distinction between inferiority as a fact and inferiority "feelings" is, in different language, the problem of why some persons can accept weaknesses without special anxiety whereas for others weaknesses always become the fulcra for neurotic anxiety. Adler is not clear as to the determinants of these radically different ways of viewing weaknesses, beyond his helpful point that it depends on whether the valuation of the *self as weak* is made. He would certainly say that the determinants of this kind of self-valuation lie in the relations of the child with its parents, and particularly in the parents' attitude toward the child. I would go further and suggest that it lies in the nature of the parents' "love" for the child—i.e., is their "love" essentially exploitative (as is the case with parents who regard children as compensations for their own weaknesses or extensions of their own selves, etc.), in which case the child in his own self-valuation will identify himself with power, or its reverse, weakness. Or is the love of the parents based upon an appreciation of the child as a person quite apart from specific strengths or weaknesses the child may have? In such case, the child's valuation of himself will not be identified with power or weakness.

The neurotic inferiority feeling (or, as we would say, anxiety) is the driving force behind neurotic character formation. The neurotic character, writes Adler,

> is a product and instrument of a cautious psyche which strengthens its guiding principle [neurotic goal] for the purpose of ridding itself of a feeling of inferiority, an attempt which is destined to be wrecked as a consequence of inner contradictions, on the barriers of civilization or on the rights of others.[47]

By "inner contradictions" he refers to the fact that the human being is fundamentally a social creature, biologically and psychologically interdependent upon other people, and that, therefore, inferiority can be constructively overcome only by affirming and increasing social bonds. The essence of the neurotic endeavor to overcome inferiority is the drive to gain superiority and power *over* other persons, the drive to demote others in prestige and power in order to elevate one's self. Hence the neurotic endeavors actually undermine the individual's only lasting basis of security. As Horney and others have pointed out also, striving for power over other persons increases intrasocial hostility and makes the individual's own position in the long run more isolated.

Turning specifically to anxiety, Adler asks: What purpose does it serve? For the anxious individual himself, anxiety serves the purpose of blocking further activity; it is a cue to retreat to previous states of security. Hence it serves as a motivation for evading decisions and responsibility. But even more frequently emphasized by Adler is the function of anxiety as a weapon of aggression, a means of dominating others. "What appears to us as important," he holds, "is that a child will make use of anxiety in order to arrive at its goal of superiority—or *control* over the mother."[48] Adler's writings are replete with illustrations of patients employing anxiety in order to force the household to accept their regimes, of anxious wives controlling their husbands by means of a convenient attack of apprehension, and so forth.

Now no one would dispute the contention that anxiety is often used for these "secondary gains." But to imply that these are the chief motivations of anxiety is to oversimplify the problem. It is difficult to see how anyone who has experienced or witnessed genuine attacks of anxiety and comprehended the torment they involve would conclude that such panics are produced chiefly for the benefit of their effects upon others. One has the impression that Adler in these contexts is talking about *pseudo,* rather than genuine, anxiety. This impression is given support by the fact that he treats anxiety often as a "character trait"[49] rather than an emotion. All of which indicates again that he subsumes the basic, genuine forms of anxiety under his "inferiority feelings"—which he would certainly not hold to have their genesis in the fact that they may be used for controlling others.

In genuine anxiety as contrasted with pseudo anxiety, the control exercised over others is a secondary, not a primary, element; and it occurs as a result of the desperation which the patient experiences in his isolation and powerlessness. The distinction between *pseudo* and *genuine* anxiety is an important problem which has been very little clarified as yet. It is often difficult to distinguish the two because they may be intermixed in the motivations and behavior of the same person. Many anxiety neurotics, having established their neurotic patterns because of genuine anxiety, powerlessness, and helplessness in the family constellation, learn sooner or later that a strategy (façade) of weakness may be an effective means of gaining power. Hence weakness is used as a way of gaining strength. The case of Harold Brown and others in Part II of this book illustrate this point.[50]

With regard to the causes of anxiety, Adler does not yield much illumination beyond his general description of the genesis of inferiority feelings. He remarks that anxiety neurosis is always due to the individual's having been a "pampered" child. This is another example of his tendency toward oversimplification, though perhaps it is no more of an oversimplification than the early Freudian theory that anxiety neurosis was specifically due to coitus interruptus. It is true that anxiety neurotics have learned, generally in early childhood, to depend excessively on others, but this behavior would neither become so firmly entrenched or persist except as the patients are in basic conflict concerning their own capacities.[51]

Concerning methods of overcoming anxiety, Adler is very clear, albeit still general. Anxiety

can be dissolved solely by that bond which binds the individual to humanity. Only that individual can go through life without anxiety who is conscious of belonging to the fellowship of man.[52]

The "bond" is affirmed through love and socially useful work. Behind statements like these lies Adler's whole positive evaluation of the social nature of man, an emphasis radically different from Freud's and involving radically different implications for the overcoming of anxiety. Despite his oversimplifications and generalities, Adler has contributed perdurable insights, particularly in the realm of the power struggles between persons and their social implications. These insights are especially valuable because they generally occur in the areas of Freud's "blind spots."

As will be indicated later, the valuable insights of Adler have to a large extent been incorporated in more systematic and profound form as parts of the emphases of such later psychoanalysts as Horney, Fromm, and Sullivan. The influence of Adler on later analysts is no doubt both direct and indirect, with similar emphases arrived at partially independently. The influence on Sullivan may have been indirectly through William Alanson White, who was interested in Adler and wrote an introduction to one of his books.

JUNG: ANXIETY AND THE THREAT
OF THE IRRATIONAL

Only a note concerning C. G. Jung is included in this book, chiefly because Jung has never systematized his views of anxiety. So far as I can determine, the problem of anxiety is not directly and specifically attacked in Jung's writings, and a comprehensive summary of the implications of his thought for anxiety theory would require a detailed research into all his writings.

One distinctive contribution, however, will be cited here, namely, Jung's belief that *anxiety is the individual's reaction to the invasion of his conscious mind by irrational forces and images from the collective unconscious.* Anxiety is "fear of the dominants of the collective unconscious," fear of that residue of the functions of our animal ancestry and the archaic human functions which Jung conceives as still existing on subrational levels in the human personality.[53] This possible upsurging of irrational material constitutes a threat to the orderly, stable existence of the individual. If the barriers within the individual to irrational tendencies and images in the collective unconscious are thin, there is the threat of psychosis, with its concomitant anxiety. But if, on the opposite extreme, the irrational tendencies are blocked off too completely, there is the experience of futility and lack of creativity. Therefore, as Kierkegaard would say, to avoid futility one must have the courage to confront and work through anxiety.

To Jung, the threat of irrational material in the unconscious explains "why people are afraid of becoming conscious of themselves. There might really be something behind the screen—one never knows—and thus people 'prefer to take into account and to observe carefully' factors external to their consciousness." In most persons

there is a secret fear of the unknown "perils of the soul." Of course one is reluctant to admit such a ridiculous fear. But one should realize that this fear is by no means unjustifiable; on the contrary it is only too well founded.[54]

Primitive peoples are more readily aware of the "unexpected, dangerous tendencies of the unconscious," Jung holds; and they devise various ceremonies and taboos as protections. Civilized man has likewise devised his defenses against this invasion of irrational forces, which defenses often become systematized and habitual so that the "dominants of the collective unconscious" come into direct control only in such phenomena. for example, as mass panic, or into indirect control in individual psychosis or neurosis.

One of Jung's central points is that modern Western man places an excessive emphasis on "rational," intellectual functions, and he holds that in most modern Western individuals this emphasis does not lead to rational integration but rather represents the "misuse of reason and intellect for an egoistical power purpose."[55] He cites the case of his patient who was suffering from a cancer phobia. The patient had "forced everything under the inexorable law of reason, but somewhere nature escaped and came back with a vengeance in the form of perfectly unassailable nonsense, the cancer idea."[56]

In my judgment, the above-mentioned emphases of Jung have a corrective value with respect to characteristics of modern Western culture. They also reveal a common aspect of individual neurosis—namely the misuse of rationalistic functions as a defense against anxiety rather than as a means of understanding and clarifying it. But the problems appear to be that these same emphases in Jung lead to a dichotomy between the "rational" and "irrational" (e.g., his concept of the "*autonomy* of the unconscious mind"[57]). This also renders much of his thought difficult to coordinate with other theories of anxiety.

HORNEY: ANXIETY AND HOSTILITY

Important psychoanalytic developments, based on the work of Freud but presenting new elements, are those in which the problem of anxiety is seen in a sociopsychological setting. These views in essence are that anxiety arises out of disturbed interpersonal relationships, an emphasis made, though in somewhat different ways, by Karen Horney, Erich Fromm, and Harry Stack Sullivan. These therapists are often called neo-Freudian or, somewhat derogatorily, revisionists. Since these psychoanalytic developments have large areas of agreement with Freud, we are here concerned with their differences from Freud and with their special contributions to the understanding of anxiety.

This approach involves a new emphasis on culture, both in the broader sense of cultural patterns as determinants in the anxiety prevalent in a given historical period, and culture in the more limited sense of the relationship between the child and the significant persons in his environment. In this last relationship, neurotic anxiety has its source. This approach does not deny, of course, the fact of biological needs in the child or adult. But it holds that the significant psychological question is the role these needs play in interpersonal relations. Fromm, for example, points out that the "particular needs which are *relevant to understanding the personality and its difficulties* are not instinctual in character but are created out of the entirety of conditions under which we live."[58]

Anxiety thus is not specifically the reaction to the anticipation of frustration of instinctual or libidinous needs. Considerable frustration of instinctual (such as sexual) need can be borne without anxiety by the normal person. The frustration of instinctual tendencies—again sex is a good example—results in anxiety *only when this frustration threatens some value or mode of interpersonal relationship which the individual holds vital to his security.* Freud conceived of environmental influences chiefly as a factor in molding instinctual drives; the psychoanalytic developments discussed here, in contrast, make the interpersonal context (the environment, viewed psychologically) central, with instinctual factors as important to the extent that they represent vital values in this interpersonal context.[59]

To discuss Horney first, it is significant that her viewpoint places anxiety *prior to the instinctual drives.* What Freud terms instinctual drives, far from being basic, she holds, are themselves a product of anxiety. The concept of "drive" implies some compulsion from within the organism, some stringent and demanding characteristic. (Freud realized that instinctual drives are compulsive in the cases of neurotics; he assumed, however, that the "drive" is biologically determined and that it receives its compulsive strength in neurotics from the fact that they are, for constitutional reasons or because of too much libidinal gratification as infants, unable to tolerate instinctual frustration as much as "normal" persons.) But Horney holds that impulses and desires do not become "drives" except as they are motivated by anxiety.

> Compulsive drives are specifically neurotic; they are born of feelings of isolation, helplessness, fear, and hostility, and represent ways of coping with the world despite these feelings; they aim primarily not at satisfaction but at safety; their compulsive character is due to the anxiety lurking behind them.[60]

She equates Freud's "instinctual drives" with her "neurotic trends." She believes she thus makes anxiety more basic in personality disturbances than does Freud: "In spite of Freud's recognition of anxiety as 'the central problem of neuroses,' he has nevertheless not seen the all-pervasive role of anxiety as a dynamic factor driving toward certain goals."[61]

Horney agrees with the customary distinction between fears and anxiety. A fear is a reaction to a specific danger, to which the individual can make a specific adjustment. But what characterizes anxiety is the feeling of diffuseness and uncertainty and the experience of helplessness toward the threat. Anxiety is a reaction to a threat to something belonging to the "core or essence" of the personality. She is here in agreement with Goldstein's concept, described earlier, that anxiety, as inhering in the "catastrophic condition," is a reaction to a threat to some value which the individual holds essential to his existence as a personality. The question basic for the understanding of anxiety, therefore, is: What is endangered by the threat which provokes anxiety? Her answers to this question can best be understood if we outline first her conception of the origins of anxiety.

Horney takes account of the normal anxiety which is implicit in the human situation of contingency in the face of death, powers of Nature, and so forth. This is the anxiety which has been termed *Urangst* or *Angst der Kreatur* in German thought.[62] But this is to be differentiated from neurotic anxiety, in that *Urangst* does not connote hostility on the part of Nature or the conditions which make for human contingency; it does not provoke inner conflict or lead to neurotic defense measures. Neurotic anxiety and helplessness are not the result of a realistic view of inadequacy of power but arise out of an inner conflict between dependency and hostility. What is felt as the source of danger is primarily the anticipated hostility of others.

Basic anxiety is Horney's term for the anxiety which leads to the formation of neurotic defenses. Such anxiety, itself a neurotic manifestation, is "basic" in two senses: First, it is the basis for neurosis. Second, it is basic in the sense that it develops in early life out of disturbed relationships between the child and the significant individuals in his personal environment, normally his parents. "The typical conflict leading to anxiety in a child is that between dependency on the parents—enhanced by the child's feeling of being isolated and intimidated—and hostile impulses against the parents."

The hostility involved in this conflict with the parents has to be repressed because of the child's dependency on the parents. And since repressed hostility deprives the individual of the capacity to recognize and fight against real dangers, and also since the act of repression itself creates inner unconscious conflict, such repression contributes to the child's feeling of defenselessness and helplessness. Basic anxiety is "inseparably interwoven with a basic hostility."[63]

We have here one example of the reciprocal functioning of anxiety and hostility, each affect accentuating the other. In other language this would be termed the "vicious circle" of anxiety and hostility. Helplessness inheres in the very nature of basic anxiety itself. Horney is well aware that every person—the "normal" adult, for example—has to struggle against opposing forces in the culture, many of which are in fact hostile, but this in itself does not provoke neurotic anxiety. The difference she feels is that the normal adult had the bulk of his unfortunate experiences at a period when he could integrate them, whereas the child in a dependent relationship with essentially hostile parents is *in fact* helpless and can do nothing about the conflict except develop neurotic defenses. Basic anxiety is anxiety in the face of a potentially hostile world. The multifarious forms of personality disturbances are neurotic defenses created in the effort to cope with this potentially hostile world despite one's feeling of weakness and helplessness. *Neurotic trends,* in Horney's viewpoint, *are thus essentially security measures arising out of basic anxiety.*

It becomes possible, now, to answer the question: What is endangered by the threat which produces an anxiety attack? Anxiety is the reaction to the *threat to any pattern which the individual has developed upon which he feels his safety to depend.* The adult in a period of personality disturbance feels the threatening of a neurotic trend which was his only method of coping with earlier basic anxiety, and hence the prospect is one of renewed helplessness and defenselessness. In contradistinction to Freud, Horney holds that it is not the expression of instinctual drives which is threatened, but rather the neurotic trends which operate as safety devices.

Thus neurotic anxiety will be cued off in different persons by different threats; what is important is the particular neurotic trend in the given person upon which he feels his security rests. In a person characterized by masochistic dependence—i.e., a person whose basic anxiety can be allayed only by clinging indiscriminately to another —the threat of desertion by the partner will arouse an anxiety attack. In the case of a narcissistic person—for example, one whose basic anxiety as a child could be allayed only by the unqualified admiration of the parents— anxiety will arise at the prospect of being thrust into a situation in which he is unrecognized and unadmired. If a person's safety depends on being unobtrusive, anxiety will emerge when he is thrust into the limelight.

In the problem of anxiety we must, therefore, always ask the question of what vital value is being threatened; and specifically in neurotic anxiety, what neurotic trend vital to the preservation of the personality against previous helplessness is being threatened. Thus, "anything may provoke anxiety," Horney writes, "which is likely to jeopardize the individual's specific protective pursuits, his specific neurotic trends."[64] Of course, the threat may be not only ostensibly external, like desertion by the partner, but it may be any kind of intrapsychic impulse or desire which, if expressed, would threaten the security pattern. Thus certain sexual or hostile inclinations arouse anxiety not because of the anticipation of their frustration per se, but rather because the expression of the inclinations would threaten some pattern of interpersonal relationships which the individual feels vital to his existence as a personality.

The fact that one or the other of the sides of the contradiction will be either continually or at various times repressed only removes the problem to a deeper level.[65]

It will already have been noted that Horney places a

great deal of emphasis on the *reciprocal relation of hostility and anxiety*. This is her forte. She believes that by far the most common intrapsychic factor provoking anxiety is hostility. In fact, "hostile impulses of various kinds form the main source from which neurotic anxiety springs."[66] Anxiety generates hostility, and hostile impulses, in the anxious person, generate new anxiety. One is understandably hostile against those experiences and persons which threaten him and which give him the painful experience of helplessness and anxiety. But since neurotic anxiety is caused by weakness and dependence on other powerful persons, any hostile impulses toward these persons would threaten this dependency, which must be maintained at all costs. Likewise, intrapsychic impulses to attack those persons cue off fears of retaliation and counterattack, the prospects of which increase anxiety.

Noting all the reciprocal interactions of hostility and anxiety, Horney concludes that there is a "specific cause" of anxiety in "repressed hostile impulses."[67] Whether such a statement can be made as a generalization without constant reference to our culture we leave an open question. But it probably would be generally agreed that, in our culture, the interrelation of hostility and anxiety is a demonstrated clinical fact.

The contribution of Horney to anxiety theory lies in her *elucidation of the conflicting trends in personality as the sources of neurotic anxiety, and in her placing of the problem of anxiety squarely on the psychological level, with its necessary social aspects, in contrast to Freud's tendencies toward quasi-physiochemical forms of thinking.*[68]

SULLIVAN: ANXIETY AS APPREHENSION OF DISAPPROVAL

The concept of anxiety as arising in the locus of interpersonal relations has been most cogently stated by Harry Stack Sullivan. Indeed, he defined psychiatry as the "study of the biology of interpersonal relations." Though his theory of anxiety was never completely formulated, the salient points presented by him are of considerable importance for any comprehensive understanding of anxiety. Basic for his theory of anxiety is Sullivan's concept of personality as essentially an interpersonal phenomenon, developing out of the relations of the infant with the significant persons in his environment. Even in the biological beginnings of life—the fertilized ovum *in utero*—the cell and environment are unitary, are indissolubly bound. After birth the infant is in intimate relationship with its mother (or mother substitutes), which is both the prototype and the real beginning of those relationships with significant other persons out of which matrix his personality will be formed.

Sullivan divides the activities of the human organism into two classes. First, there are those activities the aim of which is to gain *satisfactions*, such as eating, drinking, and sleeping. These satisfactions pertain rather closely to the bodily organization of man. The second class is those activities which are in pursuit of *security*, and these pertain "more closely to man's cultural equipment than to his bodily organization."[69]

A central factor in this pursuit of security is, of course, the organism's feeling of ability and power. The "power motive"—by which Sullivan means the need and tendency of the organism to expand in ability and achievement—is to some extent inborn.[70] It is a "given" in the human organism *qua* organism. This second class of activities—directed toward the pursuit of security—is "ordinarily much more important in the human being than the impulses resulting from a feeling of hunger, or thirst," or as he goes on to say, of sex as it later emerges in the maturing organism.[71] These needs of the organism which are biological, in the more limited sense of that term, are really to be seen as "manifestations of the organism's efforts not merely to maintain itself in stable balance with and in its environment, but to expand, to 'reach out' to, and interact with, widening circles of the environment."[72] The growth and characteristics of personality depend largely on how this power motive, and the pursuit of security it entails, are fulfilled in interpersonal relations.

The infant is first in a state of relative powerlessness. His cry becomes an early tool in his interpersonal relations, and later there develop language and the use of symbols, both of which are powerful cultural instrumentalities in man's pursuit of security in relations with his fellow-men. But long before language or specific emotional expression or comprehension is possible for the infant, the acculturalization is proceeding apace through *empathy,* the "emotional contagion and communion" that occurs between the infant and the early significant persons, again chiefly the mother. In this interpersonal matrix, governed chiefly by the needs of the organism for security and self-expression, anxiety is born.

Anxiety, to Sullivan, *arises out of the infant's apprehension of the disapproval of the significant persons in his interpersonal world.* Anxiety is felt empathically, in a sensing of the mother's disapprobation, long before conscious awareness is possible for the infant. It is self-evident that the mother's disapproval will be very portentous for the infant. Disapproval in the present sense refers to a threatening of the relationship between the infant and its human world. This relationship is all-important to the infant in the respect that he depends upon it not only for the satisfaction of his physical needs but for his more inclusive sense of security as well.[73] Hence anxiety is felt as an all-over, a "cosmic," experience.

With the mother's approbation come rewards, and with her disapproval comes punishment. But more important, there comes the peculiar discomfort of anxiety. This system of approbation and rewards versus disapprobation and discomfort (anxiety) becomes the most powerful fulcrum on which the acculturation and education of the individual proceeds throughout life. Sullivan's summary of the importance of the mother in this system is as follows: "I have spoken of the functional interaction, in infancy and childhood, of the significant other person, the mother, as a source of satisfaction, as an agency of acculturation, and finally as a source of anxiety and insecurity in the development of social habits which is the basis of development of the self system."[74]

Anxiety serves to restrain the infant, to restrict his development to those activities of which the significant other persons approve. Sullivan presents the highly significant idea that the *self is formed out of the growing infant's necessity to deal with anxiety-creating experiences.* The self is formed out of the need to distinguish between activities which produce approval and those which result in disapprobation. "The self-dynamism is built up out of this experience of approbation and disapproval, reward and punishment."[75] The self "comes into being as a dynamism to preserve the feeling of security."[76] It is a startling idea—that *the self is formed to protect us from anxiety*. The self is a dynamic process by which the organism incorporates those experiences which produce approbation and reward, and learns to exclude those activities which have resulted in disapproval and anxiety. The limitations thus set by early experience tend to be maintained year after year "by our experiencing anxiety whenever we tend to overstep the margin."[77]

We now need to make explicit what is implied above, namely, that the limitations set by anxiety-creating experiences are not merely prohibitions of action, but are *limitations of awareness* as well. Whatever tendencies would arouse anxiety tend to be excluded from awareness, or, in Sullivan's term, *dissociated*. Sullivan summarizes as follows:

> The self comes to control awareness, to restrict one's consciousness of what is going on in one's situation very largely by the instrumentality of anxiety with, as a result, a dissociation from personal awareness of those tendencies of the personality which are not included or incorporated in the approved structure of the self.[78]

These concepts throw new light upon some of the common phenomena in anxiety. The restriction of awareness in anxiety states—an occurrence discernible in everyone's experience as well as a daily observation in clinical work—is Sullivan's reinterpretation of the classical psychoanalytic idea that anxiety leads to repression. Sullivan sheds new light on why and how this restriction of awareness takes place in his elucidation of the dynamics of interpersonal relations, especially between infant and mother, and the centrally important need of the organism to preserve security. With respect to anxiety and the formation of symptoms, it can readily be seen that, when the dissociation of strong anxiety-creating experience or impulses becomes difficult for the organism to accomplish—as in neurotic states—substitutive and compulsive symptoms develop. These are a rigid means of demarcating awareness. Hence it follows that the dissociated tendencies and experiences will remain dissociated so long as the anxiety connected with them is felt by the person to be too great to be borne.

In Sullivan's contribution there are also stimulating formulations of the relation between emotional health and anxiety. These might be phrased as follows: *Anxiety restricts growth and awareness, shrinking the area of effective living. Emotional health is equal to the degree of personal awareness. Hence clarification of anxiety makes possible expanded awareness and an expansion of the self. This last means the achieving of emotional health.*

CHAPTER
6

Anxiety Interpreted Culturally

The truth is that all history is important *because* it is contemporary and nothing is perhaps more so than those hidden parts of the past that still survive without our being aware of their daily impact.

People whose course of life has reached a crisis must confront their collective past as fully as a neurotic patient must unbury his personal life: long-forgotten traumas in history may have a disastrous effect upon millions who remain unaware of them.

—Lewis Mumford, *The Condition of Man*

We have observed in the previous chapters that cultural factors emerge at almost every point in any discussion of anxiety. Whether we are investigating children's fears, or anxiety in psychosomatic disorders, or anxiety in the various forms of individual neurosis, it is clear that the cultural milieu is always part of the warp and woof of the anxiety experience. In the last chapter we have also noted the rationale for this significance of cultural factors as presented by various investigators. Sullivan, for example, describes the indissoluble interrelation of the individual with his world at every point in development from the cell *in utero* to the adult interrelated in love and work with the other members of his society. The general importance of cultural factors in anxiety is now so widely admitted that it does not in itself require laboring.

My purposes in this chapter are, therefore, more specific. I want to show how the *occasions* of an individual's anxiety are conditioned by the standards and values of his culture. By "occasions" I mean the kinds of threats which cue off anxiety: these are largely defined by the culture in which the individual lives. I also want to show how the *quantities* of the person's anxiety are conditioned by the relative unity and stability—or lack of them—in the culture.

In primitive society, Hallowell demonstrates, the occasions of threat vary from culture to culture, as we all have known. But Hallowell goes on to conclude that the *anxiety is a function of the beliefs accepted in the culture superimposed on the actual danger situation.*[1] This valuable idea can be illustrated in our own culture by the crucial weight accorded the goal of individual competitive ambition. We have seen in the survey of anxiety in the psychosomatic studies of patients with peptic ulcer (the "disease of the striving and ambitious men of Western civilization") that the anxiety is a function of the needs of men in our society to appear strong, independent, and triumphant in the competitive struggle and to repress their dependent needs. We have seen also in the studies of children's fears that as children grow older and absorb more of the accepted attitudes of the culture, fears and anxiety related to competitive status increase. Indeed, studies of the worries of school children regularly show the most pronounced anxiety to lie in the area of competitive success, whether in school itself or in work.[2] Apparently, the weight given the goal of competitive success increases as the individual moves into adulthood: we noted that adults reporting their childhood fears gave a much larger incidence of fears related to competitive success and failure than did the children, which we interpreted as a "reading back" into childhood of the fulcra of fear and anxiety which have become important to them as adults. In my study of anxiety in unmarried mothers reported later in the present book, one might reasonably have expected that the young women's chief occasions of anxiety would be social disapproval or guilt. But no: the predominant occasion of anxiety reported by the girls was competitive ambition—i.e., whether they would measure up to cultural standards of "success." The weight placed upon the value of competitive success is so great in our culture and the anxiety occasioned by the possibility of failure to achieve this goal is so prevalent that there is reason for assuming that *individual competitive success is both the dominant goal in our culture and the most pervasive occasion for anxiety.*

Why is this so? How did individual competitive success become the chief source of anxiety in our culture? Why is the threat of failure to achieve this success so prevalent? These questions obviously cannot be answered by definitions of "normality." It may be assumed that every individual has normal needs to gain security and acceptance, but this does not explain why in our culture such security is conceived chiefly in *competitive* terms. And although it may be assumed that every individual has normal needs to expand in his achievement and to increase his capacities and power, why is it that in our society this "normal" ambition takes an individualistic form? Why is it defined chiefly in inverse relation to the community, so that the failure of others has the same relative effect *as one's own success?* Discussing the culture of the Comanche Indians, Abram Kardiner points out that there is a great deal of competition, "but it does not interfere with security or with the common goal of the society."[3] It is not hard to see that our contemporary competitiveness is bound to have a destructive effect on the community at every turn. And why does competition in our culture carry such stringent penalties and rewards, so that (as will be indicated presently) the individual's feeling of *value as a human being* so regularly depends upon his competitive triumph?

These questions indicate that a goal like competitive individual success cannot be understood as simply an "immutable attribute" of human nature, but must be seen also as a cultural product. It is the expression of a cultural pattern in which there exists a particular confluence of individualism with competitive ambition. This pattern is discernible in our culture from the time of the Renaissance, but it was almost entirely absent in the Middle Ages. The value of individual competitive success, as a prevailing occasion for anxiety, has its particular historical genesis and development, and to this we turn.

THE IMPORTANCE OF THE HISTORICAL DIMENSION

The generally accepted statement that the culture conditions anxiety must, therefore, be expanded to read: *An individual's anxiety is conditioned by the fact that he lives in a given culture at a particular point in the historical development of that culture*. This brings in the genetic, long-term, developmental background of the patterns which are the occasions of contemporaneous anxiety. In his discussion of "man as the time-binding creature," Dilthey emphasized the importance of this historical dimension. "Man is a historical being as well as a mammal," he held, and what is needed is "to relate the total personality to the various manifestations of an historically conditioned personality."[4] While there has been broad acceptance in contemporary psychology and psychoanalysis of the importance of cultural factors in the contemporaneous scene, the historical dimension has been largely neglected to date.

But there is an increasing realization on the part of students of anxiety that an investigation of anxiety, as of other aspects of personality in its cultural setting, raises questions which can only be answered in terms of seeing the individual in his historical position. Lawrence K. Frank, writing of the "growing realization among thoughtful people that our culture is sick." remarks, "the individual striving ushered in at the Renaissance now leads us into error."[5] Mannheim describes the problem in terms of the need for a psychology which will be historically relevant as well as socially relevant. a type of psychology "which could explain how particular historical types were derived from the general faculties of man." He asks, for example, "Why did the Middle Ages and the Renaissance produce entirely different types of men?"[6] In general terms, the historical is to the man-in-society what the genetic dimension is to man-as-adult. That is to say, the understanding of the historical development of modern man's character structure is as necessary for an understanding of contemporaneous anxiety as an analysis of childhood factors is to the understanding of the anxiety of a particular adult.

The historical approach which I recommend here—and which will guide the discussion throughout this chapter—does not consist of a mere garnering of historical facts. It involves the more difficult procedure of *historical con-*

sciousness—a consciousness of history as it is embodied in one's own attitudes and psychological patterns as well as in the patterns of the culture as a whole. Now, since every member of a society is to a greater or lesser extent the product of the patterns and attitudes which have been developing in the history of his culture, an awareness of the cultural past is to an extent self-awareness. The capacity for awareness of history as embodied within selfhood has been described by Kierkegaard, Cassirer, and others as one of the distinctive capacities of the human being as differentiated from infrahuman beings. We have previously discussed Mowrer's conclusion that the capacity to bring the past into the present as part of the total causal nexus is the essence of "mind" and "personality" alike. C. G. Jung puts our truth graphically when he likens the individual to a person who is standing at the top of a pyramid supported by the combined consciousness of everyone who has lived before. How absurd the conceit that history begins with one's own research or the last board meeting!

The capacity for historical consciousness is a development of the capacity for self consciousness—i.e., the ability of man to see himself as subject and object at the same time. This approach involves seeing one's own presuppositions (and the presuppositions of one's culture) as historically relative, whether those presuppositions are religious or scientific or whether they refer to a general psychological attitude like the high valuation of competitive individualism in our own culture. Some cultural analysts take certain presuppositions from modern science as an absolute base from which to study other historical periods (Kardiner, *op. cit.*, does this). But it is manifestly impossible to understand such periods as those of ancient Greece or the Middle Ages without realizing that our own presuppositions are as relative to a point in history—namely, our own—and as much products of history, as were the presuppositions in those periods.

In this historical study, a way is opened for a *dynamic* approach by which it is possible to take a corrective attitude toward cultural patterns. Thus we can avoid being merely the objects of historical determinism. The cultural past is rigidly deterministic to the extent that the individual is unaware of it. An analogy, of course, is found in any psychoanalytic treatment: the patient is rigidly determined by past experiences and previously developed patterns to the extent that he is unaware of these experiences and patterns. Through his capacity for historical consciousness man is able to achieve a measure of freedom with respect to his historical past, to modify the historical influences which come to bear upon him, and to reform his history as well as to be formed by it. "But man is not only made by history," Fromm points out,

> history is made by man. The solution of this seeming contradiction constitutes the field of social psychology. Its task is to show not only how passions, desires, anxieties change and develop as a result of the social process, but also how man's energies thus shaped into specific forms in their turn become productive forces, molding the social process.[7]

Since the total historical development of the character structure of modern man is too broad a topic for treatment, I shall limit myself to the one central aspect of that character structure which interests us—namely, competitive individual ambition. And since it is manifestly impossible to treat this problem throughout all ages of Western history, I shall begin with the Renaissance, the *formative* period of the modern age.[8] In the Renaissance, our aim will be to show the emergence and extent of individualism, how the individualism became competitive in nature, and the consequences of this competitive individualism for interpersonal isolation and anxiety.

INDIVIDUALISM IN THE RENAISSANCE

The individualistic nature of Western man's character structure can be seen as a reaction to, and a contrast with, medieval collectivism. The citizen of the Middle Ages "was conscious of himself only as a member of a race, people, party, family or corporation—only through some general category," in Burckhardt's words.[9] Each person theoretically knew his place in the economic structure of the guilds, in the psychological structure of the family and the hierarchy of feudal loyalties, and in the moral and spiritual structure of the church. Emotional expression was channeled communally, the conjunctive emotions in festivals and the aggressive emotions in such movements as the crusades. "All emotions required a rigid system of conventional forms," Huizinga remarks, "for without them passion and ferocity would have made havoc of life."[10]

But by the fourteenth and fifteenth centuries, Huizinga points out, the hierarchal forms of church and society, previously serving as ways of channeling emotions and experience, had become methods of *suppressing* individual vitality. The use of symbols was rampant in this period at the end of the Middle Ages, the symbols now having become ends in themselves. They were forms emptied of vital content and divorced from reality. The last century of the Middle Ages was pervaded by feelings of depression, melancholy, skepticism, and much anxiety. This anxiety took the form of excessive dread of death and pervasive fears of devils and sorcerers.[11] "One has only to look at pictures like those of Bosch and Grunwald," remarks Mannheim, "in order to see that the disorganization of the medieval order expressed itself in a general fear and anxiety, the symbolic expression of which was the widespread fear of the devil."[12] Renaissance individualism is partly to be understood as a reaction against this deteriorated collectivism of the closing phase of medievalism.

The new valuation of the individual and the new conception of the individual's relation to nature, which were to become the central motifs of the Renaissance, can be seen graphically in the paintings of Giotto. It is between Giotto and his master, Cimabue, that many authorities hold the new age to have begun. Giotto actually lived in the "first Italian Renaissance," which preceded the main Renaissance.[13] In contrast to the symbolic, stiff, frontal figures in medieval painting, Giotto's figures are presented in three-quarter perspective and are given *independent movement*. In contrast to the generalized, otherworldly, typed, and therefore often rigid sentiments in preceding painting, Giotto begins to portray *individual emotions*. He presents the individual sorrow, joy, passion, and surprise of simple people in everyday, concrete situations—a father kissing his daughter, a friend mourning at the grave of the deceased. The delight in natural sentiment carries over into his sympathetic portrayal of animals; and the relish with which he paints trees and rocks foreshadows the new enjoyment of natural forms for their own sakes. Retaining some of the symbolic character of medieval art, Giotto presents at the same time the emerging attitudes which are to characterize the Renaissance, namely the *new humanism* and the *new naturalism*.

In contradistinction to the medieval concept of man as a unit in the social organism, the Renaissance viewed the individual as a discrete entity and the social setting as a background against which the individual achieved eminence. The chief difference between Giotto and the Renaissance in full bloom is that for the former the simple individual was valued (the influence of St. Francis upon Giotto is important in this valuation of simple persons); but in the full development of the Renaissance it became the *powerful* individual who was valued. This phenomenon, which is basic for anxiety-creating patterns in modern culture, we now wish to trace developmentally.

The revolutionary cultural changes and expansion which characterized the Renaissance in almost every area—economic, intellectual, geographic, and political—are too well known to require description. All these cultural changes had a relationship of both cause and effect with the new confidence in the power of the free, autonomous individual. On one hand, the revolutionary changes were based upon the new view of the individual, and on the other the sociological changes placed a premium on the exercise of individual power, initiative, courage, knowledge, and shrewdness. Social motility released the individual from medieval family caste; by courageous action he could now achieve eminence regardless of the level of his birth. The riches available from expanding trade and growing capitalism gave new opportunities for enterprise and reward to the individual who was bold enough to take the risks. The new appreciation of education and learning was both an expression of intellectual freedom and released curiosity; the itinerant student, making the known world his university, is symbolic of the relation of the new learning to freedom of movement. But at the same time knowledge was valued as a means of gaining power. "Only he who has learned everything," remarked Lorenzo Ghiberti, a Renaissance artist who spoke for his time, "can fearlessly despise the changes of fortune."[14]

The political ferment of the Renaissance, when the rule of cities rapidly passed from the hands of one despot to another, likewise placed a premium on the free exercise of power. It was often a case of each man for himself, and the individual of courage and ability could gain and hold a position of eminence.

> The impulse to the free play of ambitious individuality which this state of things communicated was enormous. Capacity might raise the meanest monk to the chair of St. Peter's, the meanest soldier to the duchy of Milan. Audacity, vigour, unscrupulous crime were the chief requisites for success.[15]

Speaking of the violence connected with the expression of individuality in this period, Burckhardt remarks, "The fundamental vice of the character was at the same time a condition of its greatness, namely, excessive individualism. . . . The sight of victorious egoism in others drives him [the individual] to defend his own right by his own arm."[16]

The high valuation of the individual in the Renaissance was not a valuation of persons as such. Rather, as mentioned above, it referred to the *strong* individual. It was presupposed that the weak could be exploited and manipulated by the strong without remorse or regret. It is important to remember that, though in many respects the Renaissance set the principles which were to be unconsciously assimilated by large segments of modern society in succeeding centuries, it was a movement not of masses of people but of a handful of strong, creative individuals.

Virtu in the Renaissance was conceived largely in terms of courage and other characteristics which made for success. "Success was the standard by which acts were judged; and the man who could help his friends, intimidate his enemies, and carve a way to fortune for himself by any means he chose, was regarded as a hero. Machiavelli's use of the term 'virtu' . . . retains only so much of the Roman 'virtus' as is applicable to the courage, intellectual ability, and personal prowess of one who has achieved his purpose, be that what it may."[17] *We note here the confluence of individualism and competitiveness.* Granted the apotheosis of the strong individual, who regarded the community chiefly as the arena in which he battled for eminence, the concept of success was bound to be competitive. The whole cultural constellation placed a premium on self-realization by means of excelling and triumphing *over* other persons.

This confidence in the power of the free individual was an entirely conscious attitude on the part of the strong men and women of the Renaissance. Leon Alberti, one of those towering personalities who excelled at everything from gymnastics to mathematics, formulated what may be considered the motto of these strong individuals: "Men can do all things if they will."[18] But nowhere is the attitude of the Renaissance better articulated than in Pico della Mirandola, who wrote twelve books to prove that man is master of his own fate. In his notable *Oration on the dignity of man,* he pictures the Creator saying to Adam,

> Neither a fixed abode, nor a form in thine own like-
> ness . . . have we given thee. . . . Thou, restrained by
> no narrow bounds, according to thine own free will,
> in whose power I have placed thee, shall define thy
> nature for thyself. I have set thee midmost in the
> world, that thence thou mightest the more convenient-
> ly survey whatsoever is in the world. Nor have we
> made thee either heavenly or earthly, mortal or im-
> mortal, to the end that thou, being, as it were, thy
> own free maker and moulder, shouldst fashion thyself
> in what form may like thee best. Thou shalt have
> power to decline into the lower or brute creatures.
> Thou shalt have power to be born into higher, or
> divine, according to the sentence of thy intellect.

This sweeping conception of man's power and his vast free-dom to move into any realm he chooses—which is to be accomplished by the power of his intellect—is described by Symonds as the "epiphany of the modern spirit."[19] There were no boundaries to human creativity if, as Michelangelo put it, the individual could but "trust him-self." The conscious ideal was *l'uomo universale,* the fully developed, many-sided individual.

But where is the negative side of this "brave new world"? Our clinical experience teaches us that such con-fidence must be balanced by some opposite attitudes. In the Renaissance we find, on a less conscious level, beneath this optimism and confidence, an *undercurrent of despair with nascent feelings of anxiety.* This undercurrent, com-ing to the surface only toward the end of the Renaissance. can be vividly seen in Michelangelo. Consciously Michel-angelo gloried in the individualistic struggle, defiantly accepting the isolation it involved. "I have no friend of any kind, and I do not want any," he wrote. "Whoever follows others will never go forward, and whoever does not know how to create by his own abilities can gain no profit from the works of other men."[20] There is nothing here of Auden's insight,

> . . . for the ego is a dream
> Till a neighbor's need create it.

But in Michelangelo's paintings can be seen the tension and conflict which were the underlying psychological counterpart of the excessive individualism of the period. His figures on the Sistine ceiling exhibit a continuous restlessness and perturbation. The human form in Michelangelo, Symonds points out, "is turbid with a strange and awful sense of inbreathed agitation." The men of the Renaissance felt they were renewing the spirit of classical Greece, but the essential difference, Symonds indicates, can be seen in the "sedate serenity" of Phidias contrasted with this agitation in Michelangelo.[21]

Almost all of Michelangelo's human beings, powerful and triumphant as they appear at first glance, present on closer inspection the *dilated eyes which are a tell-tale sign of anxiety.* One would expect an expression of intense apprehension on the faces of the figures in his painting "The Damned Frightened by Their Fall," but the remarkable point is that the same frightened expression in less intense form is present in the other figures in the Sistine Chapel as well. As if to demonstrate that he is expressing the inner tensions not only of his age but of himself as a member of his age, Michelangelo in his self-portrait paints eyes which are again pronouncedly distended in the way typical of apprehension. By and large the conscious ideal covered over the nascent anxiety in the bulk of the Renaissance artists (*vide* the harmonious human beings in Raphael). But Michelangelo's long life carried him beyond the youthful confidence of the Renaissance at its height. By his genius and profundity he brought the goals of his period into actuality to a greater extent than the earlier representatives. Thus he brought the undercurrents of the period into more overt expression. The figures of Michelangelo may be taken as symbols both of the conscious ideal and the psychological undercurrent of the Renaissance—triumphant, strong, fully developed human beings, who are at the same moment tense, agitated, and anxious.

It is significant that the undercurrent of tension and despair is to be found in those persons who, like Michelangelo, actually were *successful* in the individualistic struggle. Thus the nascent anxiety is not due to any frustration of the goal of individual success. Rather, I submit, it is due to the state of *psychological isolation and the lack of the positive value of community, both results of excessive individualism.*

These two characteristics of the strong individuals of the Renaissance are described by Fromm: "It seems that the new freedom brought two things to them: an increased feeling of strength and at the same time an increased isolation, doubt, scepticism, and—resulting from all these —anxiety."[22] An outstanding symptom of the psychological undercurrent was the "morbid craving for fame," as Burckhardt phrases it. Sometimes the driving desire for fame was so great that the individual committed assassination or other flagrantly antisocial acts in the hope that he might thereby be remembered by posterity.[23] This bespeaks considerable isolation and frustration in the individual's relatedness to others and a powerful need to gain some recognition from one's fellows even by way of aggression against them. Whether one was remembered for villainous or constructive deeds seems not to have been the point. This suggests an aspect of individualism which is present in competitive economic striving of the present day—namely, that aggression against one's fellows is accepted as the way to gain recognition from them. This reminds us of the fact that an isolated child will commit delinquencies in order to gain at least an inverted form of concern and recognition.

The competitive individualistic ambition had important psychological repercussions on *the individual's relation to himself.* By an understandable psychological process, a person's attitudes toward others become his attitudes toward himself. Alienation from others leads sooner or later to self-alienation. As a result of the manipulation of others for purposes of increasing wealth and power (as exemplified in the nobles and burghers), the "successful individual's relation to his own self, his sense of security and confidence were poisoned too. His own self became as much an object of manipulation to him as other persons had become."[24] Moreover the individual's own *self-valuation* depended upon his achieving competitive success. In the unconditioned weight then given success—"unconditioned" in the sense that both one's social esteem and one's self-esteem depended upon it—we see the beginning of the *stringent drive for competitive success which characterizes contemporaneous individuals*. Kardiner describes the problem this sets for modern man:

> The anxieties of Western man are therefore concerned with success as a form of self-realization in the same way that salvation was in the Middle Ages. But in comparison with the individual who merely sought salvation, the psychological task for modern man is much more arduous. It is a responsibility, and failure brings with it less social censure and contempt than it does self-contempt, a feeling of inferiority and hopelessness. Success is a goal without a satiation point, and the desire for it, instead of abating, increases with achievement. The use made of success is largely power over others.[25]

As an explanation for the emergence of the new concern for individual success, Kardiner emphasizes the shift from the "other-worldly," post-mortem rewards and punishments of the Middle Ages to the concern in the Renaissance with rewards and punishments here and now. I agree that the Renaissance was marked by a new appreciation of the values and possibilities for satisfactions in the present world. This is evidenced as far back as Boccaccio and in the humanism and naturalism appearing in Giotto. But what impresses me is that whereas rewards in the Middle Ages were gained by virtue of one's participation in a corporate body—family, feudal group, or church—the rewards in the Renaissance always were gained by virtue of the striving of the separated individual in competition with his group. The driving desire for fame in the Renaissance is a seeking of post-mortem reward in the *present* world. But what is significant is the highly *individualistic character* of this reward: one gains fame, or remembrance by posterity, by excelling, standing *out from* one's fellows.

Kardiner's viewpoint is that the post-mortem rewards and punishments of medieval ecclesiasticism kept aggressions under control and gave validation to the self. As the power of post-mortem rewards and punishments diminished, there developed an increasing emphasis on rewards here and now and an increased concern for social well-being (prestige, success). The self, no longer validated by post-mortem rewards, then found validation in present success. In my judgment, Kardiner's point is partially accurate—specifically in the new concern for present rewards in the Renaissance and the modern development since. But the distinction between *when* rewards and punishments are received—post-mortem in the Middle Ages or here and now in the modern period—easily lends itself to oversimplification, and covers only one aspect of a complex picture. For one example, Boccaccio lauds the pursuit of present satisfactions, in the spirit of the Renaissance; but he also holds that a suprapersonal force, *fortuna,* seeks to block man in his pursuit of pleasure. The important point, however, is that Boccaccio holds that the bold individual has the power to outwit *fortuna. It is this confidence that rewards are gained through individual power which strikes me as the essential characteristic of the Renaissance.* To approach the same problems from a different angle: the tendency to make the distinction between post-mortem and present rewards central as an explanation of the modern concern with success is an oversimplification in the respect that post-mortem religious rewards were presupposed throughout most of the modern period. Immortality was not widely questioned until the nineteenth century (Tillich). But again, the significant aspect of the modern period is not *when* the rewards are received, but *the relation between rewards and the individual's own striving.* The good deeds for which one was rewarded in immortality were the same deeds as made for individual economic success, namely industrious work and conforming to bourgeois morality.

The positive aspects of the individualism emerging at the Renaissance, especially in respect to the new possibilities for individual self-realization, do not require laboring since they have become an integral part of the conscious and unconscious assumptions of modern culture. But the negative aspects, which have not been so widely recognized, are pertinent to our present study. They are (1) the essentially competitive nature of this individualism, (2) the emphasis placed on individual power as against communal values, (3) the beginnings of the unconditional weight placed in modern culture on the goal of individual competitive success, and (4) the psychological concomitants of these developments, present in the Renaissance but to reemerge in the nineteenth and twentieth centuries in more serious form. These psychological concomitants are *interpersonal isolation and anxiety*.

I have used the term "nascent" anxiety in the Renaissance because the consequences of the individualistic pattern in overt, conscious anxiety were largely avoided at the time. Anxiety is discernible in the Renaissance chiefly in symptomatic form. We have seen in the case of Michelangelo that, although he defiantly admitted isolation, he made no conscious admission of anxiety. In this respect there is a sharp difference between the isolated individuals of the fifteenth and sixteenth centuries and those of the nineteenth and twentieth centuries, who, like Kierkegaard, were *consciously aware of the anxiety resulting from individual isolation*. The great expansiveness of the period caused the full implications of interpersonal isolation to be evaded and consequently the full impact of conscious anxiety was avoided. New areas were always available into which the individual could direct his striving if he were frustrated at any one point. This is one way of emphasizing that it was the *beginning*, rather than the end, of a historical period.

The problem for modern Western culture, with respect to anxiety, was thus set in the Renaissance: *How is interpersonal community (psychological, economic, ethical, etc.) to be developed and integrated with the values of individual self-realization, thus freeing the members of the society from the sense of isolation and concomitant anxiety inhering in excessive individualism?*

COMPETITIVE INDIVIDUALISM IN WORK AND WEALTH

The competitive tendencies of the individual in our society have been greatly abetted and reinforced by economic developments since the Renaissance. The breakdown of the medieval guild (in which competition was impossible) opened the door for intensive individual economic competition. This is a central characteristic of modern capitalism and industrialism. Hence it is particularly important to inquire how individual competitive ambition in modern man's character structure is intertwined with these economic developments. We will here follow Richard Tawney's discussion of economic developments in the centuries since the Renaissance, with particular reference to the psychological implications of industrialism and capitalism. In this section we are concerned with the application and working out of the principles which we have described in their emergent form in the Renaissance.

Modern industrialism and capitalism were conditioned by many factors, but on the psychological side the new view of the power of the free individual was of central importance. The rationale for modern industrialism and capitalism was given by the emphasis on the "right" of the individual to amass wealth and employ it as power. Tawney points out that the individual's self-interest and "natural instinct" for aggrandizement were apotheosized as the accepted economic motivations. Industrialism, especially in the last two centuries, is based upon *"the repudiation of any authority [such as social value and function] superior to individual reason."*[26] This "left men free to follow their own interests or ambitions or appetites, untrammeled by subordination to any common center of allegiance."[27] In this respect modern *"industrialism is the perversion of individualism."*[28]

This "economic egotism," as Tawney calls it, was based on the assumption that the free pursuit of individual self-interest would automatically lead to economic harmony in society at large. This assumption served to allay anxieties arising from the intrasocial isolation and hostility in economic competition. The competitive individual could believe that the community was enhanced by his strivings for aggrandizement. During the major part of the modern period this assumption was pragmatically true. It was dramatically substantiated in the respect that the growth of industrialism did greatly increase the means of satisfying everyone's material needs. But in other respects, especially in the later development of monopoly capitalism, the individualistic economic developments here discussed were to have a damaging and disintegrative effect upon the individual's relation to himself, as well as to his fellow men.

The full psychological implications and results of economic individualism were not to emerge until the middle of the nineteenth century. One of the psychological results of industrialism, especially in its recent phases, is that for the majority of people *work has lost its intrinsic meaning*. Work has become a "job," in which the criterion of value is not the productive activity itself but the relatively fortuitous results of labor—wages or salary. This shifts the basis of both social esteem and self-esteem from the creative activity itself (the satisfactions from which genuinely increase the individual's feeling of self-strength and thereby realistically decrease anxiety) to the acquisition of wealth.

The value placed highest in the industrial system is the aggrandizement of wealth. Thus another of the psychological results of industrialism is that *wealth becomes the accepted criterion of prestige and success*, "the foundation of public esteem," in Tawney's phrase. The aggrandizement of wealth is by its very nature competitive; success consists of having more wealth than one's neighbors; others going down the scale is the same as one's self going up. Tawney sees from the economic point of view what we will later point out from the psychological viewpoint—namely, that success defined as the acquisition of wealth involves a vicious circle. One can never be certain one's neighbors and competitors will not gain more wealth; one can never be sure one has attained a position of unassailable security, and hence *one is driven by the need always to increase his wealth*. In their chapter "Why do they work so hard?" the Lynds, in their first study of Middletown, note that "both business men and working men seem to be running for dear life in this business of making the money they earn keep pace with the even more rapid growth of their subjective wants."[29] It is fair to infer that these "subjective wants" are largely competitive in motivation—i.e., "keeping up with the Joneses."

It is important to note that the acquisition of wealth, as the accepted standard of success, does not refer to increasing material goods for sustenance purposes, or even for the purpose of increasing enjoyment. It refers rather to wealth as a sign of individual power, a proof of achievement and self-worth.

Modern economic individualism, though based on belief in the power of the free individual, has resulted in the phenomenon that increasingly larger numbers of people have to work on the property (capital) of a few powerful owners. It is not surprising that such a situation should lead to widespread insecurity, for not only is the individual faced with a criterion of success over which he has only partial control but also his opportunities for a job are in considerable measure out of his control. Tawney writes that the "need for security is fundamental, and almost the gravest indictment of our civilization is that the mass of mankind are without it."[30] *Thus the actual economic developments, particularly in the monopolistic phase of capitalism, work directly against the assumption of freedom for individual endeavor upon which industrialism and capitalism are based.*

But, as Tawney points out, the individualistic assumptions are implanted so firmly in our culture that great numbers of people cling to these assumptions despite their contradiction with the reality situation. When anxiety is experienced by members of the middle and lower middle classes, they redouble their efforts to gain security on the basis of the same cultural assumption of individual (property) rights—e.g., saving, investing in property, annuities, etc. *Anxiety in members of these classes often becomes an added motivation for their endeavor to defend the individualistic assumptions which are part of the cause of their insecurity.*[31] The "hunger for security is so imperious that those who suffer most from the abuses of property [and the assumptions of individual rights upon which property rights are based] . . . will tolerate and even defend them, for fear lest the knife which trims dead matter should cut into the quick."[32]

Tawney also makes the highly significant point that the revolutions which served to better the conditions of the middle and lower classes (as in the eighteenth century) were based upon the same assumptions as the ruling classes held, namely the sovereignty of individual rights and the derivative assumption of property rights. These revolutions did have valuable results in extending the base of individual rights. But for Tawney they rested on the same fallacious assumption, that individual freedom for aggrandizement is sovereign over social function. This point is of fundamental importance for the question we shall later ask: Is there an essential difference between the revolutions and social changes which have occurred in the previous centuries of the modern period and the revolutions and upheavals which at present confront our contemporaneous culture?

What is lacking in the individualism which has characterized economic developments since the Renaissance is, in Tawney's view, a sense of the *social function of work and property*. The individualistic assumption "cannot unite men, for what unites them is the bond of service to a common purpose, and that bond it repudiates, since its very essence is the maintenance of rights irrespective of service."[33] This is in accord with the hypothesis of this book that *competitive individualism militates against the experience of community, and that lack of community is a centrally important factor in contemporaneous anxiety*.

Tawney gives several explanations for the fact that the contradictions in modern industrial development were largely held in check in the modern period until the nineteenth and twentieth centuries. One reason was that industrialism seemed capable of infinite expansion. Another reason was that the motivations of hunger and fear on the part of the workers kept the system working with some efficiency. But when it became manifest that capitalism in its monopolistic phases contradicts the very assumptions of individual freedom on which it is based; and when in the nineteenth and twentieth centuries the threats of fear and hunger had been mitigated by the growth of the labor unions, the contradictions inherent in individualistic economic development became overt.

FROMM: INDIVIDUAL ISOLATION IN MODERN CULTURE

We now turn to two writers who interpret the psychological and cultural meaning of these developments: Erich Fromm and Abram Kardiner. Fromm's central concern is with the psychological isolation of modern man which has accompanied the individual freedom emerging at the Renaissance.[34] His discussion is particularly cogent in respect to the interrelationship of this isolation with economic developments. He shows that "certain factors in the modern industrial system in general and in its monopolistic phase in particular make for the development of a personality which feels powerless and alone, anxious and insecure."[35] It is self-evident that the experience of isolation is first cousin to anxiety. More specifically, psychological isolation beyond a certain point always results in anxiety. Since the human being develops as an individual in a social matrix, the problem Fromm confronts is how the individual, with his freedom, is able or unable to relate himself to his interpersonal world. This is like Kierkegaard in the nineteenth century, who also saw the problem of anxiety in terms of individuality, freedom, and isolation.

It is necessary first to note Fromm's concept of the *dialectical* nature of freedom. Freedom always has two aspects: in its negative aspect it is freedom *from* restraints and authority, but in its positive aspect it always involves the question of whether this freedom will be used *for* new relatedness. Mere negative freedom results in the isolation of the individual.

This dialectical nature of freedom can be seen in the genesis of the individual child as well as in the phylogenesis of character structure in a culture like that of Western man since the Renaissance. The child begins life bound to parents by "primary ties." His growth involves an increasing freedom from dependence on parents—the process called individuation. But individuation brings with it threats, potential or actual; it involves a progressive breaking of the original unity of the primary ties; the child becomes aware of being a separate entity, of being alone.

> This separation from a world which in comparison with one's own individual existence is overwhelmingly strong and powerful, and often threatening and dangerous, creates a feeling of powerlessness and anxiety. As long as one was an integral part of that world, unaware of the possibilities and responsibilities of individual action, one did not need to be afraid of it.[36]

This sense of isolation and concomitant anxiety cannot be tolerated indefinitely. Ideally, one expects the child to develop new and positive relatedness on the basis of his growing strength as an individual, a relatedness which is expressed as he becomes an adult by means of love and productive work. But actually the problem is never solved ideally or simply; individual freedom involves a persistent dialectic at every point of growth. How will the issue be met? By new positive relatedness on one hand, or by surrendering freedom in order to avoid isolation and anxiety; by developing new dependencies, or by the formation of the innumerable compromise solutions which allay anxiety (the "neurotic patterns") on the other hand? The answer to this will be decisive for the development of personality.

The same dialectic of freedom can be observed on the cultural level. The emergence of individuality at the Renaissance brought freedom *from* medieval authority and regulation—freedom from ecclesiastical, economic, social, and political restraints. But simultaneously the freedom meant a severing of those ties which had afforded security and the sense of belonging. This severance, in Fromm's terms, was "bound to create a deep feeling of insecurity, powerlessness, doubt, aloneness and anxiety."[37]

The freedom from medieval restraints in the economic area—the freeing of the markets from guild regulation, the lifting of the proscriptions on usury and the accumulation of wealth—was both an expression of the new individualism and a powerful incentive for it. One could now devote one's self to economic aggrandizement to the extent of one's abilities (and luck). But this economic freedom involved increasing tendencies toward individual isolation and subjection to new powers. The individual is now

> threatened by powerful suprapersonal forces, capital and the market. His relationship to his fellow-men, with everyone a potential competitor, has become hostile and estranged; he is free—that is, alone, isolated, threatened from all sides.[38]

It is particularly important to observe the effect of these developments on the middle class, not only because this class was to become increasingly dominant in the modern period, but also because there is some reason for hypothesizing that neurotic anxiety in modern culture is especially a middle-class problem. At first chiefly the concern of a few powerful capitalists of the Renaissance, the accumulation of wealth became an increasingly dominant concern of the urban middle classes. In the sixteenth century the middle class was caught between the very rich, who made considerable exhibition of their luxury and power, and the very poor. Though threatened by the rising capitalists, the members of the middle class were concerned with preserving law and order. It might be added that they accepted the assumptions underlying the new capitalism. Hence the hostility which members of the middle class experienced in their threatened situation was not expressed in open rebellion as was the case with the peasants in Central Europe. Middle-class hostility was largely repressed and took the form of indignation and resentment. It is a known phenomenon that repressed hostility generates more anxiety,[39] and hence an intrapsychic dynamic served to increase middle-class anxiety.

One means of allaying anxiety is frantic activity.[40] The anxiety arising out of the dilemma of powerlessness in the face of suprapersonal economic forces on one hand, but theoretical belief in the efficacy of individual effort on the other, was symptomized partly by excessive activism. Indeed, the great emphasis in the sixteenth and subsequent centuries on work had as one of its psychodynamics the allaying of anxiety. Work became a virtue in itself, quite apart from the creative and social values emerging from work. (In Calvinism, successful work, though not a means of gaining salvation, is a visible sign that one is among the chosen.) A high valuation on the importance of time and regularity accompanied this emphasis on work. "The drive for relentless work," Fromm writes of the sixteenth century, "was one of the fundamental productive forces, no less important for the development of our industrial system than steam and electricity.[41]

Anxiety and the Market Place

The consequences of these developments for the character structure of Western man are, of course, profound. Since the values of the market were the highest criteria, persons also became valued as commodities which could be bought and sold. A person's worth is then his salable market value, whether it is skill or "personality" that is up for sale. This commercial valuing (or, more accurately, devaluing) of persons and its consequences in our culture has been vividly and penetratingly described by W. H. Auden in his poem, *The Age of Anxiety*. When a young man in that poem wonders whether he can find a useful vocation, another character answers:

> . . . Well, you will soon
> Not bother but acknowledge yourself
> As market-made, a commodity
> Whose value varies, a vendor who has
> To obey his buyer. . . .[42]

The market value, then, becomes the individual's valuation of himself, so that self-confidence and "self-feeling" (one's experience of identity with one's self) are largely reflections of what others think of one, in this case the "others" being those who represent the market. Thus contemporary economic processes have contributed not only to an alienation of man from man, but likewise to "self-alienation"—an alienation of the individual from himself. Feelings of isolation and anxiety consequently occur not only because the individual is set in competition with his fellows, but also because he is thrown into conflict about his inner valuation of himself. As Fromm very well summarizes the point:

> Since modern man experiences himself both as the seller and as the commodity to be sold on the market, his self-esteem depends on conditions beyond his control. If he is "successful," he is valuable; if he is not, he is worthless. The degree of insecurity which results from this orientation can hardly be overestimated. If one feels that one's own value is not constituted primarily by the human qualities one possesses, but by one's success on a competitive market with ever-changing conditions, one's self-esteem is bound to be shaky and in constant need of confirmation by others.[43]

In such a situation one is driven to strive relentlessly for "success"; this is the chief way to validate one's self and to allay anxiety. And any failure in the competitive struggle is a threat to the quasi-esteem for one's self—which, quasi though it be, is all one has in such a situation. This obviously leads to powerful feelings of helplessness and inferiority.

Fromm points out that in the more recent developments of monopoly capitalism, the tendencies toward devaluation of persons have been accelerated. Not only workers, but middle-sized businessmen, white-collar workers, and even consumers as well, play an increasingly *impersonal* role. The function of each is, by and large, to be a cog in a technical machine too vast for the ordinary individual to understand, let alone to influence. There exists the theoretical freedom to change one's job or buy a different kind of product, but this generally is a negative freedom in that one changes from being one cog to being another. The "market" continues to operate on the basis of suprapersonal forces over which the ordinary individual has little if any control. To be sure, such movements as labor unions and consumer co-operatives have made headway against these developments, but it would probably be generally agreed that their influence has been so far to mitigate the impersonality of economic life rather than to overcome it.

Mechanisms of Escape

It is to be expected that certain "mechanisms of escape" from the situation of isolation and anxiety should have developed. The mechanism most frequently employed in our culture, Fromm believes, is that of *automation conformity*. An individual "adopts entirely the kind of personality offered to him by cultural patterns; and he therefore becomes exactly as all others are and as they expect him to be."[44] This conformity proceeds on the assumption that the "person who gives up his individual self and becomes an automaton, identical with millions of other automatons around him, need not feel alone and anxious any more."[45] Such conformity can be understood again in terms of Fromm's idea of the dialectical nature of freedom. There has been much progress in our culture in regard to the negative aspect of freedom, e.g., freedom from outward authority over individual belief, faith, opinion, but this has resulted to a great extent in a psychological and spiritual vacuum. Since the isolation involved in mere freedom from authority cannot long be maintained, there develop new inner substitutes for the rejected authority, which Fromm terms the "anonymous authorities" like public opinion and common sense.

One phase of modern freedom has been the right of each individual to worship as he chooses. But, adds Fromm, "we do not sufficiently recognize that while it is a victory against those powers of Church and State which did not allow man to worship according to his own conscience, the modern individual has lost to a great extent the inner capacity to have faith in anything which is not provable by the methods of the natural sciences."[46] The "inner restraints, compulsions, fears" which fill the vacuum left by

mere negative freedom provide strong motivations for
automaton conformity. Though this conformity is acquired
by the individual as a means of avoiding isolation and anxiety, it actually works the other way: the individual con-
forms at the price of renouncing his autonomous strength,
and hence he becomes more helpless, powerless, and insecure.

Other mechanisms of escape from individual isolation
which Fromm describes are sado-masochism and destructiveness. Though sadism and masochism may have as one
of their expressions the desire to inflict pain or have pain
inflicted on one's self, they are more basically forms of
symbiosis in which an individual endeavors to overcome
isolation by becoming absorbed in the existence of another
person or persons. "The different forms which the masochistic strivings assume have one aim: *to get rid of the
individual self, to lose one's self; in other words, to get rid
of the burden of freedom.*"[47] In masochism we also find
the individual endeavoring to compensate for helplessness
by becoming part of the "bigger" power. Destructiveness—
a phenomenon much evidenced in recent sociopolitical developments like fascism—is likewise related to the need to
escape from unbearable feelings of powerlessness and isolation. The rationale for this can be seen in the relation of
anxiety (in this context, anxiety arising from isolation) to
hostility. Anxiety creates hostility, as we pointed out
earlier; and destructiveness is one of the overt forms of this
hostility.

Fascism was a complex socioeconomic phenomenon, but
certainly on its psychological side it could not be understood without reference to anxiety. Of particular importance are these phases of anxiety—namely, the feelings of
isolation, insignificance, and powerlessness of the individual. It is accepted that fascism began chiefly as a lower-
middle-class phenomenon. In analyzing the origins of the
German form of fascism, Fromm described the powerlessness experienced especially by the middle class after World
War I and after the depression of 1929. "The vast majority
of the population was seized with the feeling of individual
insignificance and powerlessness which we have described
as typical for monopolistic capitalism in general."[48] This
class was not only economically, but also psychologically,
insecure; it had lost its previous centers of authority, the

monarchy and the family. The fascist authoritarianism, characterized by sado-masochism and destructiveness, had a function which is comparable psychologically to a neurotic symptom—namely, fascism compensated for powerlessness and individual isolation and protected the individual from the anxiety-creating situations.[49] If one can compare fascism to a neurotic symptom, it can be said that fascism is a neurotic form of community.

In criticism of Fromm, my main point is that he underestimates the biological side of human development or gives it only lip service. An example of this is his statement, "Man's nature, his passions, and anxieties are a cultural product. . . ." I find myself responding, "No, man's nature and passions and anxiety are not produced by culture, but are the products of *both* biological equipment, which is the source of the capacities for human aggression, hostility, anxiety, etc., *and* culture, which directs and mitigates the expression of these given capacities." In this sense the critics of Fromm (chiefly Marcuse) are right in branding him a revisionist. But these points should not obscure the fact that his early books represent a seminally important contribution and had an influence on American thinking equivalent to their importance. Hence, I refer in the above pages chiefly to *Escape from Freedom. Man for Himself,* though derivative from Heidegger, also seems to me to be a genuine contribution, and is used partially in the references above.

KARDINER: WESTERN MAN'S GROWTH PATTERN

Kardiner's psychodynamic analysis of Plainville, an American Midwestern rural village, and his outline of the psychological growth pattern of Western man, furnish an approach to the problem of the cultural sources of modern anxiety different from Fromm's. Kardiner's focus is on the *basic personality structure* of Western man, which he feels has changed very little in the last 2,000 years, whereas Fromm's concern is with the *particular character structure* of Western man in the modern period. Using Plainville as his base, Kardiner outlines the personality growth pattern out of which anxiety arises, and he briefly suggests how this growth pattern and its anxieties are manifested in the historical development of Western man.[50]

In Plainville Kardiner finds a great deal of anxiety and much intrasocial hostility. Social-prestige goals are dominant among the citizens. In the competition for achieving these goals the individual person finds his self-validation on the one hand or his loss of self-esteem and feelings of inferiority and failure on the other. How the social-prestige goals become dominant, why the striving for them is characterized by such compulsive competitiveness, and how anxiety and hostility are thereby aroused are questions Kardiner asks. Answering, then, requires some explanation of the psychological growth pattern of the individual in Plainville.

The pattern of individual growth in Plainville and in Western man, Kardiner extrapolates, is characterized first of all by a strong affective relation with the mother. Compared to primitive cultures, the maternal care, affective satisfaction, and protection given the baby in Plainville are very good. This lays the groundwork in the child for a high valuation of himself. Such good early affective development makes for the building of both a strong ego and a strong superego, which involves idealization of parents. Though this close affective relationship with the mother may open the way for passivity and excessive affective dependence on the part of the individual as he confronts later crises, its effect is normally very constructive in that it lays a solid base for personality development.

But the second characteristic of the growth pattern is the *introduction of taboos* via parental discipline. Kardiner sees these taboos as relating chiefly to sex and toilet training. This considerably distorts the psychological growth which has begun so constructively. Doubt arises in the child's mind concerning the continuation of parental care and the satisfaction of his affective needs which have been cultivated by this care. The child's pleasure patterns, which Kardiner calls the relaxor function, become blocked. The ensuing conflict may have several results. *Hostility* may develop as one result of the blocked pleasure patterns. This hostility may be directed toward parents—in which case, in proportion to the severity of the hostility, it tends to be repressed. Or the hostility may be directed toward siblings, who are rivals in the striving for the affective support the child has learned to expect but now sees threatened. Since the satisfaction of affective needs was originally associated with parents (especially the mother), the anxiety arising from blocked pleasure patterns may lead the child to increased dependence on the mother. Or, with lesser probability, on the father. Parents may thus occupy an inflated position as relievers of anxiety. Finally, and of considerable significance in this growth pattern, the concept of *obedience* is greatly inflated. Special force attaches to *allaying anxiety by obedience*, and, conversely, special force is given to guilt feeling and concomitant anxiety cued off by disobedience.

The personality growing up with this pattern will be characterized by considerable "emotional potential," as Kardiner phrases it, but also by an incapacity for direct expression of this emotional potential because of the blocked action patterns. This has its positive aspect in the high degree of productivity of which Western man is capable. But its negative aspect lies in the fact that it makes Western man vulnerable to considerable anxiety.

How do the particular occasions of anxiety in Plainville and in Western man, such as anxiety related to success, competition for social prestige, and so forth, arise out of this growth pattern? Kardiner, like Tawney and Fromm earlier, is concerned about the great importance given to *success*.

> [The] socially approved goal of success is made the vehicle of compensation for all other shortcomings in pleasure and relaxor functions. As long as the individual can pretend to some goal of success or security, he can claim some self-esteem.[51]

The extensive capacities for self-expression which the personality in such a culture has developed are channeled in the direction of achieving social prestige, or wealth as a symbol of prestige. "The struggle for success becomes such a powerful force because it is the equivalent of self-preservation and self-esteem."[52] The personality produced by the above growth pattern has strong needs for validation of his self-esteem and at the same time experiences considerable frustration of that self-esteem. Hence it is understandable that, whenever anxiety arises in a person in such a culture, his tendency would be to endeavor to allay the anxiety and re-establish his self-esteem by striving for new success.

The intrasocial hostility is also an added motivation for competitive striving. Kardiner describes this intrasocial hostility as again arising chiefly from blocked pleasure drives. The hostility tends to be self-increasing in the society, since when one is prohibited from pleasures himself, he joins with the group in prohibiting others (e.g., gossip). The intrasocial hostility can then be expressed in socially approved aggressive competition, generally in competitive work. But such hostility and aggression prevent the individual from establishing friendly relations with his fellows, and hence his feeling of isolation tends to increase. The personality in Plainville and in Western society generally has a firm base set for community, and strong needs for community, by virtue of the good early affective relationships. The adult citizen joins the Rotary Club, the Lions, or the Optimists. But community tends to be blocked by these other factors in the constellation, we have seen—e.g., the intrasocial hostility leading to aggression and competition.

The values in Kardiner's analysis of the psychological growth pattern are self-evident. A question is raised here, however, in line with the viewpoint expressed previously in this book: *Is it the blocking of pleasure patterns through taboos which accounts for the conflict, anxiety, and hostility arising in this growth pattern, or are these taboos, rather, the* locus *in which the control and domination of the child by parents and consequent limitation of the normal requirements for expansion of the child's personality take place? The emphasis in this book is the latter.*

The fact of control and suppression of development of the child, I propose, and the arbitrary uses made of parental discipline are the important elements in the growth pattern, and sexual and toilet taboos are one form (in some phases of our culture, such as Plainville, the most prominent form) in which the parent-child struggle occurs. To me what seems most crucial as the psychological source of later anxiety are the *inconsistencies* in the child-training in Western culture as Kardiner describes it. This is borne out by Kardiner's analysis of the Alorese society, in which the parental behavior toward children is marked by irregularity, deceit, and undependability and the child typically grows up to be isolated, mistrustful, and anxious.

How did competitive social prestige emerge as the dominant goal in the historical trajectory of Western man? As we remarked above, Kardiner holds that there has been very little change in the basic personality structure of Western man from the time of Job and Sophocles to the modern citizen of New York. The good early parental care, the subsequent extensive taboos and systems of impulse control, and the hostility and aggression arising from these taboos and control have been fairly constant throughout Western history, according to Kardiner. There has normally been a strong system of parental obedience, with rewards and punishments to keep the system of taboos and concomitant aggressions under control. Kardiner's view is that this control was maintained in the Middle Ages by the immobile family constellation, by the protection and power of the lord in feudalism, and by the religious system of postmortem rewards and punishments. Obedience could be obtained and anxiety allayed by family, feudal lord, and church.

When the power of these sources of control radically diminished in the Renaissance, the concern with social well-being (success, prestige) was substituted. This concern with social success was greatly facilitated by the development of science and capitalism. The self now found its validation in social prestige; tensions and anxiety were allayed by success in terms of social well-being. Intrasocial hostility and aggression, no longer held in check by ecclesiastical, family, and feudal controls, now became motivations for self-validation *via* competitive striving.

I would raise a question about the implications of Kardiner's statement that there has been very little change from Job to a modern John Doe. It may be true that the citizens of Greece in the fifth century B.C. and those of modern New York exhibit great similarities in basic personality structure when both are compared to the Eskimo. But the crucial practical problem historically is how differences occurred between different periods in our own culture. In the words of Mannheim, to which we have referred above, "Why did the Middle Ages and the Renaissance produce entirely different types of men?" It may be that "basic personality structure" is a concept which does not lend itself to an illumination of the changes of character structure which produce different types in different periods. But the main consideration is that Kardiner fails to see the historical relativity of all presuppositions, including the presuppositions upon which our contemporaneous psychological science is based. I have indicated above that this sense of historical relativity is necessary for a genuine historical consciousness.

CHAPTER 7

Summary and Synthesis of Theories of Anxiety

I speak purposely of "hypotheses." This [formulating of hypotheses on anxiety] is the most difficult task that has been set us, but the difficulty does not lie in the incompleteness of our observations, for it is actually the commonest and most familiar phenomena that present us with such riddles; nor does it lie in the remoteness of the speculations to which these phenomena give rise, for speculation hardly comes into the picture in this connection. No, it is genuinely a question of hypotheses; that is to say, of the introduction of the right abstract ideas, and of their application to the raw material of observation so as to bring order and lucidity into it.

—Sigmund Freud, "Anxiety,"
New Introductory Lectures

In this chapter our purpose is to synthesize the theories and data on anxiety presented in the preceding chapters. In Freud's words, our aim is to try, through "introduction of the right abstract ideas," to bring some "order and lucidity" into the field. Our purpose is to construct a comprehensive theory of anxiety so far as this is possible and, where integration is impossible, to point out the crucial areas of difference among the various theories. My own viewpoint will be discernible both implicitly and explicitly in this synthesis.

THE NATURE OF ANXIETY

It is agreed by students of anxiety—Freud, Goldstein, Horney, to mention only three—that anxiety is a *diffuse* apprehension, and that the central difference between fear and anxiety is that fear is a reaction to a specific danger while anxiety is unspecific, "vague," "objectless." The special characteristics of anxiety are the feelings of *uncertainty* and *helplessness* in the face of the danger. The nature of anxiety can be understood when we ask *what* is threatened in the experience which produces anxiety.

Let us say that I am a college student walking to the dentist's office to have a tooth pulled. On the way I meet a revered professor whose class I have been in this term and whom I have seen in his office. He does not speak to me nor nod nor give me any greeting whatever. After I pass him I feel a diffuse gnawing "in my breast." *Am I not worth noticing? Am I nobody—nothing?* When the dentist picks up his pincers to pull my tooth, I feel a fear much more intense than the anxiety on the street. But the fear is forgotten as soon as I'm out of the dentist's chair. The anxiety, with its gnawing, stays with me all day long and may even appear in my dreams that night.

The threat, thus, in anxiety is not necessarily more intense than fear. Rather, it attacks us on a deeper level. The threat must be to something in the "core" or "essence" of the personality. My self-esteem, my experience of myself as a person, my feeling of being of worth—all of these are imperfect descriptions of what is threatened.

I propose the following definition: *Anxiety is the apprehension cued off by a threat to some value that the individual holds essential to his existence as a personality.* The threat may be to physical life (the threat of death), or to psychological existence (the loss of freedom, meaninglessness). Or the threat may be to some other value which one identifies with one's existence (patriotism, the love of another person, "success," etc.). Nancy, whom we will discuss below (p. 251), illustrates the identification of the love of another person with her existence when she said, speaking of her fiancé, "If anything went wrong with his love for me, I'd break down completely." Her security as a self depended upon this other person's love and acceptance of her.

The identification of a value with one's existence as a personality is dramatized in the remark of Tom[1] in his anxiety over whether he would be retained in his job or be forced to resort again to government relief: "If I couldn't support my family, I'd as soon jump off the end of the dock." He thus tells us that if he could not preserve the self-respecting position of being the responsible wage-earner, his whole life would have no meaning and he might as well not exist. This he would confirm by snuffing out his own life—committing suicide. The occasions of anxiety will vary with different people as widely as the values on which they depend vary. But what will always be true in anxiety is that the threat is to a value held by that particular individual to be essential to his existence and, consequently, to his security as a personality.

The terms "diffuse" and "vague," so often used to describe anxiety, do not mean that anxiety is less painful than other affects. Indeed, other things being equal, anxiety may be more painful than fear. Nor do these terms refer merely to the generalized, "over-all" psychophysical quality of anxiety. Other emotions, like fear, anger, and hostility, also permeate the whole organism. Rather, the diffuse and undifferentiated quality of anxiety refers to the *level* in the personality on which the threat is experienced. An individual experiences various fears on the basis of a security pattern he has developed; *but in anxiety it is this security pattern itself which is threatened.* However uncomfortable a fear may be, it is experienced as a threat which can be located spatially and to which an adjustment can, at least in theory, be made. The relation of the organism to a given object is what is important, and if that object can be removed, either by reassurance or appropriate flight, the apprehension disappears. But since anxiety attacks the foundation (core, essence) of the personality, the individual cannot "stand outside" the threat, cannot objectify it. Thereby, one is powerless to take steps to confront it. One cannot fight what one does not know. In common parlance, one feels caught, or if the anxiety is severe, overwhelmed; one is afraid but uncertain of what one is afraid. The fact that anxiety is a threat to the essential, rather than to the peripheral, security of the person has led some authors like Freud and Sullivan to describe it as a "cosmic" experience. It *is* "cosmic" in that it invades us totally, penetrating our whole subjective universe. We cannot stand outside it to objectify it. We cannot see it separately from ourselves, for the very perception with which we look will also be invaded by anxiety.

These considerations help us to understand why anxiety appears as a subjective, objectless experience. When Kierkegaard emphasizes that anxiety refers to an inner state and Freud holds that in anxiety the object is "ignored," it is not meant (or *ought* not to be meant) that the danger situation which cues off the anxiety is unimportant. Nor does the term "objectless" refer only to the fact that the danger causing the anxiety, in the case of neurotic anxiety, has been repressed into unconsciousness. Rather, *anxiety is objectless because it strikes at that basis of the psychological structure on which the perception of one's self as distinct from the world of objects occurs.*

Sullivan has remarked that the self-dynamism is developed in order to protect the individual from anxiety. The converse is as true—that mounting anxiety reduces self-awareness. In proportion to the increase in anxiety, the awareness of one's self as a subject related to objects in the external world is obscured. Awareness of one's self is simply a correlate of awareness of objects in the external world. It is precisely this differentiation between subjectivity and objectivity which breaks down in proportion to the severity of the anxiety experienced. Hence the expression that anxiety "attacks from the rear," or from all sides at once. In anxiety, the individual is proportionately less able to see himself in relation to stimuli and hence less able to make adequate evaluation of the stimuli. In various languages the usual expressions, accurately enough, are "One *has* a fear" but "One *is* anxious." Thus in severe clinical cases anxiety is experienced as a "dissolution of the self."

Harold Brown (p. 313) illustrates this when he states that he is "afraid of losing my mind"—a phrase often used by patients to describe this feared imminent "dissolution." Brown also stated that he had no "clear or distinct feelings, even of sex," and that the emotional vacuum was "excruciatingly uncomfortable." (One wonders whether the great preoccupation with sex in this country and in the Western world nowadays is a grasping at the easiest way to get distinct feelings to shore the self up against the anxiety of disintegrating society.) It is very difficult to appreciate from the outside what a person in severe anxiety is experiencing. Brown rightly remarked about his friends "imploring a drowning man [me] to swim when they don't know that under the water his hands and feet are tied."

To summarize: the objectless nature of anxiety arises from the fact that *the security base of the individual is threatened, and since it is in terms of this security base that the individual has been able to experience himself as a self in relation to objects, the distinction between subject and object also breaks down.*

Since anxiety threatens the basis of selfhood, it is described on the philosophical level as the realization that one may cease to exist as a self. This is phrased by Tillich as the threat of "nonbeing." One is a being, a self; but there is at any moment the possibility of "not being." Death, fatigue, illness, destructive aggression, etc., are all illustrations of nonbeing. The normal anxiety associated in the minds of most people with death is, of course, the most universal form of this anxiety. But the dissolution of the self may consist not simply of physical death. It may consist also of the loss of psychological or spiritual meaning which is identified with one's existence as a self—i.e., the threat of meaninglessness. Hence Kierkegaard's statement that anxiety is the "fear of nothingness" means in this context the fear of becoming nothing. As will be seen later, the courageous and constructive confronting and working through of this anxiety connected with the threat of dissolution of the self actually results in the strengthening of one's sense of distinction from objects and nonbeing. This is a strengthening of the experience of being a self.

NORMAL AND NEUROTIC ANXIETY

The phenomenological description of anxiety given in the above several pages is applicable to different kinds of anxiety, not only to neurotic anxiety. It can be applied, for example, to the reaction to the catastrophic condition seen in Goldstein's brain-injured patients. It is also applicable, making allowance for differences in the intensity of the reaction, to normal anxiety experienced by all kinds of people in all kinds of situations.

As an example of normal anxiety, let us consider an illustration which is pieced together from what persons who lived under totalitarian governments have reported to me.

A prominent Socialist was living in Germany when Hitler came into power. Over a period of some months he knew that some of his colleagues were being imprisoned in concentration camps or taken off to other unknown fates. During this period he lived in the perpetual awareness that he himself was in danger, but he never could be certain *if* he would be apprehended, or, if he were, *when* the Gestapo would come, or, finally, *what* would happen to him if he were arrested. Throughout this period he experienced the diffuse, painful, and persistent feelings of uncertainty and helplessness which we have described above as characteristic of anxiety. And the threat confronting him was not merely that of possible death or the pain and humiliation of the concentration camp; it was a threat to the meaning of his existence as a person, since the freedom to work for his beliefs was a value which he identified with his existence. This man's reactions to threat had all the essential characteristics of anxiety, yet it was proportionate to the actual threat and could not be termed neurotic.

Normal anxiety is that reaction which (1) is not disproportionate to the objective threat, (2) does not involve repression or other mechanisms of intrapsychic conflict, and, as a corollary to the second point, (3) does not require neurotic defense mechanisms for its management. It (4) can be confronted constructively on the level of conscious awareness *or* can be relieved if the objective situation is altered. The undifferentiated and diffuse reactions of the very young infant to threats— such as falling or not being fed—fall in the category of normal anxiety. These threats occur before the infant is mature enough for the intrapsychic processes of repression and conflict involved in neurotic anxiety. Also, so far as we know, the threats may be experienced by the infant in its state of relative helplessness as objectively real dangers to its existence.

Normal anxiety continues throughout life in the form of what Freud termed "objective anxiety." The signs of the presence of such normal anxiety may be only a general restiveness, wariness, a glancing about alertly even though there is no stalking enemy outside. Howard Liddell has said (Chapters 3 and 4) that anxiety accompanies intellect like its shadow. Lawrence Kubie similarly makes anxiety the bridge between the early startle pattern and later rationality in human beings. Alfred Adler believed that civilization itself is a product of man's capacity to be aware of his inadequacies, which is another expression of anxiety. I cite these ideas to demonstrate the importance of normal anxiety in everyday life.

The existence of normal anxiety in adults is frequently overlooked because the intensity of the experience is often so much less than that of neurotic anxiety. And, since one characteristic of normal anxiety is that it can be managed constructively, it does not show itself in "panic" or in other dramatic forms. But the *quantity* of reaction should not be confused with its *quality*. The intensity of the reaction is important as a distinction between neurotic and normal anxiety only when we are considering the question of whether the reaction is proportionate to the objective threat. Every individual experiences greater or lesser threats to his existence and to values he identifies with his existence in the course of his normal development as a human being. But the human being normally confronts these experiences constructively, uses them as "learning experiences" (in the broad and profound meaning of that term), and moves on in his development.

One common form of normal anxiety is that inhering in man's contingency—i.e., the human being's vulnerability to the powers of Nature, to sickness and fatigue, and to eventual death. This is termed *Urangst*[2] or *Angst der Kreatur* in German philosophical thought, and is referred to by contemporary students of anxiety such as Horney and Mowrer. This kind of anxiety is distinguished from neurotic anxiety in that *Urangst* does not imply the hostility of Nature. Furthermore, *Urangst* does not lead to defense mechanisms, except as human contingency becomes the *symbol or focus for other conflicts and problems* within the individual.

Practically speaking, it is often very difficult to distinguish the normal from the neurotic elements in anxiety connected with death, for example, or with other aspects of the contingency of the human situation. In most persons the two kinds of anxiety are intermingled. It is certainly true that much anxiety about death falls in the neurotic category—for example, the excessive concern with death in periods of adolescent melancholy. In our culture, whatever neurotic conflicts the individual has in adolescence, old age, or any other period of development may cluster around the symbols of human helplessness and powerlessness in the face of eventual death.[3] Hence I do not wish to open the way for the rationalization of neurotic anxiety under the façade of normal anxiety about human contingency. As a practical measure in clinical work, it may be that, whenever concern about death arises, it is best to work first on the assumption that neurotic elements may be present and to endeavor to ferret them out. But scientific concern with neurotic elements in such anxiety should not be permitted to obscure the fact that death can be, and should be, admitted and confronted as an objective fact.

At points like this, the work of the poets and writers who, as Sophocles put it, seek to "see life steadily and see it whole," may be a useful corrective to the constrictive tendencies in our scientific preoccupation with the neurotic forms of behavior. Death is a concern in poetry of all sorts, and one certainly would not presume to lump all the poets under the category of neurotics. A person of poetic imagination, for example, may contemplate the ocean from a rocky promontory and "consider the brief span of my life, swallowed up in the eternity before and behind it, the small space that I fill, or even see, engulfed in the infinite immensity of spaces which I know not, and which know not me," and he may "wonder to see myself here rather than there . . . now rather than then" (Pascal). Such feelings are terror that he may drown, and retreats from the visual experience and the contemplation. Both are anxiety, but the former is normal and the latter neurotic. On the contrary, the poetic feelings of the immensity of time and space and the brevity of one individual's existence (together, of course, with the realization that man is the mammal who can transcend this brevity in the respect that he *knows* it, as other animals do not, and that man is the mammal who can *wonder*)—these feelings can highlight the value and significance of the individual's present experience and his creative possibilities, whether in the aesthetic, scientific, or any other realm.

The normal anxiety associated with death does not at all imply depression or melancholy. Like any normal anxiety it can be used constructively. The realization that we shall be eventually separated from our fellows can be a motivation for achieving closer bonds to other human beings now. The normal anxiety inherent in the realization that our activity and creativity will eventually be cut off can be a motivation—like death itself—for the more responsible, zestful, and purposeful use of the time in which we do live.

Another common form of normal anxiety is that related to the fact that each human being develops as an individual in a social matrix, a world of other individuals. As seen most clearly in the development of the child, this growth in a context of social relationships involves a progressive breaking of dependent ties with parents, which in turn involves greater or lesser crises and clashes with parents. This source of anxiety has been discussed by Kierkegaard and Otto Rank, among others. Normal anxiety, Rank held, inheres in all experiences of "separation" throughout the individual's life career, beginning with separation from the mother when the umbilical cord is cut, and ending with the separation from human existence in death. If these potentially anxiety-creating experiences are negotiated successfully, they lead not only to greater independence on the part of the child or adolescent but to the reestablishment of relations with parents and other persons on new and more mature levels. The anxiety in such cases should then be described as "normal" rather than "neurotic."

In the above examples of normal anxiety, it will be seen that in each case the anxiety is proportionate to an objective threat. It does not involve repression or intrapsychic conflict, and can be met by constructive development and increasing employment of the person's own courage and powers rather than retrenchment into neurotic defense mechanisms. Some persons might wish to call these situations of normal anxiety *"potentially* anxiety-creating situations."* They would feel that, when the individual is not overwhelmed or does not exhibit the anxiety in any pronounced ways, the term "potential" is more accurate. In one sense this is pedagogically useful. But strictly speaking, I do not believe that the distinction has meaning beyond its useful connotation; *potential anxiety is still anxiety*. If a person is aware that a situation confronting him *may* involve anxiety, he is already experiencing anxiety; and he will presumably take steps to meet the situation in such a way that he will not be overwhelmed or defeated by it.

It may be useful to note in greater detail why the subjective aspect is essential to the understanding of neurotic anxiety. If one were merely to phrase the problem of anxiety objectively—i.e., in terms of the relative capacity of the individual to cope adequately with threatening situations—it surely could justifiably be argued that there is no logical need to distinguish between neurotic and normal anxiety. All one could say is that anxious individuals are less able than other individuals to cope with threats. In the cases, for example, of feeble-minded persons, or of Goldstein's brain-injured patients, one cannot term the frequent vulnerability to threats "neurotic." To one of the compulsively orderly brain-injured patients, finding the objects in his closet in disarray *might* be an objective threat and plenty of cause for the profound anxiety which ensues, since because of his curtailed capacities he could not then orient himself to the objects. So far as we know, the threats which cue off the frequent and severe anxiety of Goldstein's patients are for them objectively real threats. As we have indicated above, the same would be true for young infants and might very well be true in many cases for children or others who are in fact relatively weak and powerless.

But, as is obvious to any observer, many people are thrown into anxiety by situations which are not objectively threatening either in kind or degree. The person may very often state himself that the occasion of his anxiety is a relatively minor event, that his apprehension is "silly," and he may be angry with himself for letting such a minor thing bother him; but he still feels it. Sometimes persons who respond to relatively minor threats as though they were catastrophic are described as persons who "carry" an "inordinate quantity" of anxiety within themselves. This, however, is a misleading description. Actually these are persons who are extremely vulnerable to threats. The problem is why they are so vulnerable.

Neurotic anxiety, on the other hand, is the reverse of our definition of normal. It is a reaction to threat which is (1) disproportionate to the objective danger, (2) involves repression (dissociation) and other forms of intrapsychic conflict, and as a corollary (3) is managed by means of various forms of retrenchment of activity and awareness, such as inhibitions, the development of symptoms, and the varied neurotic defense mechanisms.[4] Generally, when the term "anxiety" is used in scientific literature, "neurotic anxiety" is meant.[5] It will be noted that these characteristics are related to each other: *the reaction is disproportionate to the objective danger because some intrapsychic conflict is involved.* Thus the reaction is never dispropor-

tionate to the subjective threat. It will likewise be noted
that each of the above characteristics involves a subjective
reference. Thus the definition of neurotic anxiety can be
made only when the subjective approach to the problem
—i.e., based on what is going on intrapsychically within
the individual—is included.

It was largely through Freud's genius that scientific attention was focused on the inner psychological patterns
and conflicts which render the individual unable to cope
with a relatively minor objective threat. Harold Brown
hears of the slight accident his mother had to her arm; this
sets in motion a train of associations which leads him to
dream of being killed and to conflicts which are indeed
catastrophic. Thus the problem of understanding neurotic
anxiety boils down to the question of understanding the
subjective inner psychological patterns which underlie that
particular person's excessive vulnerability to threats. The
distinction made in Freud's early writing—a viewpoint
carried through his work with only slight modification—
is that objective anxiety refers to "real," external threats
and neurotic anxiety is a fear of one's own instinctual
"impulse claims." This distinction has the merit of under-
lining the subjective locale of neurotic anxiety. But it is
not strictly accurate in the respect that an impulse arising
within the individual constitutes a threat only if its expression would result in a "real" danger, such as punishment or disapproval by other persons. Though Freud
modified his earlier view to some extent in this direction
(Chapter 4 above), he did not fully carry through the implications of this insight to ask the question: *What is involved in the relationship between the individual and
other persons to bring it about that a given impulse, if
expressed, should constitute a threat?*[6]

Neurotic anxiety, therefore, is that which occurs when
the incapacity for coping adequately with threats is not
objective but subjective—i.e., is due not to objective weakness but to inner psychological patterns and conflicts which
prevent the individual from using his powers.[7] These conflicts generally have their genesis (as will be discussed
more fully in succeeding sections) in the situation in early
childhood, when the child was not able objectively to
meet the problems of a threatening interpersonal situation.
At the same time the child cannot consciously admit the
source of the threat (as, for example, in the awareness

"My parents don't love me or want me"). Hence repression of the object of the anxiety is a central feature of his or her neurotic anxiety.

Though the repression generally begins in the child's relations with his or her parents, it continues in the form of repression of similar threats as they occur throughout life. This could be illustrated in practically any clinical case: see especially the cases of Nancy, Frances, and Brown.[8] Repression of fear of the threat results in the individual's being unaware of the source of his apprehension; thus in neurotic anxiety there is a specific reason why the affect is "objectless," in addition to the general source mentioned earlier of the objectless nature of all anxiety. The repression (dissociation, blocking off of awareness) which occurs in neurotic anxiety in itself renders the individual more vulnerable to threats and thus increases neurotic anxiety. First, repression sets up inner contradictions within the personality, thus making for a shaky psychological equilibrium, which is bound to be continually threatened in the course of everyday life. Second, because of the repression the individual is less able to distinguish and fight against real dangers as they occur. For example, the person who represses a good deal of aggression and hostility may at the same time assume a compliant and passive attitude toward others, which in turn increases the likelihood that he will be exploited by other people, which in turn gives him more aggression and hostility to repress. Finally, *repression increases the individual's feeling of helplessness in that it involves a curtailing of his own autonomy, an inner retrenchment and shelving of his own power.*

We have presented this brief discussion of neurotic anxiety as an aid to defining what we mean by the term. More complete discussion of the dynamics and sources of such anxiety appears in succeeding sections.

ORIGINS OF ANXIETY

Normal anxiety is an expression of the capacity of the organism to react to threats; this capacity is innate and has its inherited neurophysiological system. Freud remarks that the "tendency toward objective anxiety" is inherent in the child; he believed that it is an expression of the self-preservation instinct and has an obvious biological utility. The particular forms this capacity to react to threats will assume in a given individual are conditioned by the nature of the threats (environment) and by how the individual has learned to deal with them (past and present experience).

This problem of the origin of anxiety raises the question of *whether and to what extent anxiety and fears are learned.* In past decades this question has been approached by means of debates on which fears are inherited and which are not. I believe that these debates were based on a confused statement of the problem and, therefore, have largely been beside the point. The accepting of a list of "inherited" fears, as did Stanley Hall, had both practical and theoretical weaknesses. The practical weakness was that assuming certain fears and foci of anxiety to be inherited implied that little or nothing could be done to correct or alleviate them. The theoretical weakness was that these so-called instinctual fears could be easily disproved, as in the case of the "innate fears" described by John B. Watson.

Given the fact that very few protective responses are present in the new-born infant, it does not follow that all later responses are due solely to learning.[9] With respect to the problem of the "inheritance" of anxiety or fear, I submit that the only assumption necessary is that *the human organism has the capacity to react to threats, a capacity which its ancestors possessed likewise.*

But the question of *which* particular events will have threat value for an individual depends upon learning. These events are the "conditioned stimuli." This is especially clear in the matter of fears: they are conditioned responses to particular events which the individual has learned are a threat to him. The same is true for particular foci of anxiety. In a personal communication to me, Hobart Mowrer had the following to say on the problem:

I would put it this way: we are so constructed that traumatic (painful) experiences produce the emergency reaction of Cannon. Objects and events associated with trauma take on threat value, i.e., become capable of producing the emergency reaction. When this reaction thus occurs, as a conditioned response, it is fear. The capacity to react to threats then means (a) the capacity to *learn* to do so, or (b) the actual end-results of learning.[10]

One general comment may be added. At the present time the different approaches to the problem of whether anxiety is learned not only involve the question of definition—i.e., whether the author is talking about normal or neurotic anxiety or fears—but also the protagonists have divergent emphases. The tendency is for learning psychologists, observing that each particular fear or focus of anxiety is demonstrably closely related to the given individual's experience, to state simply that anxiety is learned. On the other hand, neurophysiologists such as Cannon, centering their attention on the given capacities of the organism, have tended to assume that anxiety is not learned. I believe that there does not need to be a conflict between these two emphases.

I here suggest that the capacity for anxiety is not learned, but the quantities and forms of anxiety in a given individual are learned. This means that normal anxiety is a function of the organism *qua* organism; every human being would experience anxiety in situations of threat to its vital values. (And every animal would experience vigilance in such a situation.) But *what* the individual regards as a situation of threat to vital values *is* largely due to learning. Particular fears and foci of anxiety are the expression of patterns which develop out of the interrelation of the individual's capacities for reacting to threat with his environment and conditioning. The matrix in which these patterns develop is the family situation in particular. This, in turn, is part of the larger general culture in which the individual lives.

With regard to the specific sources of neurotic anxiety, Freud centers his attention chiefly on the *birth trauma* and on the fear of *castration*. In his early writings he treats the birth trauma as a literal source of anxiety, later anxiety being a "repetition" of affect which originally occurred with the birth trauma. It has been pointed out (Mowrer) that the "repetition of affect" is a dubious concept; a threat must continue to be present or the affect would not be present. Later, Freud tended to employ the birth experience more symbolically; it stood for "separation from the mother." This is more understandable, for although there is no way of knowing on the basis of present data whether the difficulty of one's birth predisposes to later anxiety, the symbol of early anxiety as dread of separation from the mother does have meaning. Rankians and some Freudians speak of birth as breaking one set of ties and moving into a new and strange situation, a symbol which is similar to Kierkegaard's concept of anxiety as arising at every new possibility in one's experience. In any case, if separation from the mother is seen as the origin of anxiety, the crucial question for understanding the development of patterns which underlie later anxiety is the *meaning* of this separation—i.e., what particular values are involved in the relation of the child to its mother which are threatened by the separation? In the case studies of unmarried mothers in this book, separation from their mothers in infancy and childhood meant something different to the middle-class young women than to the proletarians. To the former it meant a confusion of values, a double-bind, an inability to orient one's self; to the latter, it meant simply going out on the street and making new friends.

With regard to castration, again Freud's position is ambiguous. At times he treats castration as a literal source of anxiety (Hans is afraid the horse will bite his penis off). At other times he uses the term symbolically, castration standing for the loss of a prized object or value. There would not be radical disagreement with the contention that castration is often a symbol in our culture for the child's being deprived of individual power at the hands of stronger adults, power here referring not only to sexual activity but to work or any sort of individual creative activity. If fear of the loss of the penis is seen as the origin of anxiety, the crucial question again is the *meaning* of this loss—i.e., what is the nature of the relation between the child and its parents that the child should feel threatened, and what particular *values* significant for the child are threatened?[11]

Since anxiety is a reaction to a threat to values held essential to the existence of the personality, and since the human organism owes its existence to its relation to certain significant persons in its infancy, *the essential values are originally the security patterns existing between the infant and these significant persons*. Hence there is considerable agreement that the relation between the child and its parents is crucial for the origins of anxiety (Sullivan, Horney etc.) In Sullivan's concept of anxiety, the mother occupies the significant position. The mother is not only the source of the satisfaction of the infant's physical needs; she is the source of its over-all emotional security as well. Whatever would endanger that relationship would be a threat to the infant's total status in his interpersonal world. Hence Sullivan holds that anxiety has its origin in the infant's apprehension of disapproval by its mother. This apprehension occurs via empathy between infant and mother long before the infant is sufficiently mature to be consciously aware of approval or disapproval. For Horney, basic anxiety has its origin in the child's conflict between his dependency on his parents and his hostility toward them. Several writers hold that anxiety has its origin in the conflicts in the developing individuality of the child and the need to relate to other persons in its community (Fromm, Kierkegaard).

It will be noted that the term "conflict" emerges in the above two statements. Further understanding of the origins of neurotic anxiety requires an exploration of the nature and sources of the conflicts which underlie it. This we shall consider below on page 200.

MATURATION OF THE CAPACITY FOR ANXIETY

In preceding chapters we have considered three types of response to danger which are exhibited by the developing human organism: first, the *startle pattern,* a pre-emotional, innate reflective reaction; second, *anxiety,* the undifferentiated emotional response; and third, *fear,* a differentiated emotional reaction. We noted that the infant very early exhibits the startle pattern—as early as the first month of life. We recall that emotions which can be called anxiety came only later: Gesell's infant confined to the pen showed mild apprehension at five months, one sign of which was persistent head-turning. I earlier remarked that this head-turning seemed to me a significant picture of anxiety: the infant feels some threat is imminent but cannot know where it comes from nor how to relate himself to it spatially. Only several months later, as we also saw, the same infant in response to the same stimulus exhibited reactions marked by crying, which Gesell terms "fear." This progression is *maturation,* a development from a less differentiated toward a more differentiated type of response.

In an earlier chapter I mentioned the "eighth month anxiety" described by René Spitz. The child's maturation proceeds to the point where he can recognize his mother and the environment in which she fits. Thus he is thrown into anxiety when a stranger appears where the mother ought to be.

How does maturing neurologically affect anxiety and fear? At birth the infant's perceptive and discriminative capacities are not sufficiently developed to permit him adequately to identify and localize dangers. Maturing neurologically means not only an increasing capacity to locate possible threats visually, for example, but it also means increasing capacity for cortical interpretation of stimuli. The behavior correlates of this maturing process are a decreasing reliance on simple reflexive behavior and an increasing amount of emotional behavior. This, in turn, involves an increasing degree of discrimination of stimuli and the voluntary control of responses. In other words, some neurological maturation is presupposed before the infant can respond to threatening stimuli with undifferentiated emotion—i.e., experience anxiety. Greater maturation is necessary before the infant can differentiate between various stimuli, objectivate the danger, and respond to it as a fear. An interesting converse of this order is seen in the behavior of the soldiers studied by Grinker and Spiegel. Under severe stress the tendency of the men in combat was to respond to the threat by means of diffuse, undifferentiated behavior. Grinker and Spiegel remark that this is equivalent to behavior on a level of lessened cortical differentiation and control—i.e., a level closer to that of the infant.

It is clear that the factor of maturation must be taken into account in understanding the child's protective reactions. Freud noted this when he remarked that the capacity for anxiety is not at its maximum at birth, but emerges and develops in the maturing infant to a high point which he believed occurred in early childhood. Goldstein holds that anxiety may be observable in the new-born infant in some situations, but that the capacity to respond with specific fears is a later development. Agreeing, therefore, that maturation must be taken into account, we proceed to the more controversial problem—and the problem which has very important implications for anxiety theory—of *whether anxiety or fear appears first*.

It is widely agreed that the infant may exhibit anxiety responses in its very early days. Lauretta Bender remarks that clear anxiety responses can be observed as early as the eighth or ninth day of the infant's life. But whereas responses which can be called fear are described in infants in later months, I have never come across descriptions of behavior in these first weeks of the infant's life which could be termed fear. Or when very early responses are called fear—as by Watson in his theory of the "two original fears"—it seems clear that what is being described is the diffuse, undifferentiated apprehension properly to be termed anxiety. To me it seems a curious phenomenon that many writers in the field of anxiety and fear speak of the "early fears" of the infant but no one, as indicated above, identifies these so-called early fears. For example, Symonds speaks of anxiety as growing out of "primitive fear states" and as a corollary he employs fear as the more inclusive, generic term and anxiety as the derived emotion.[12] But the apprehensive behavior Symonds describes in the very young infant seems certainly to be anxiety—as he, in fact, terms it. He actually describes no reactions which he calls fears in these earliest experiences of the infant. It seems to me that there is a general uncriticized assumption in much psychological literature that somehow fears must be the first to emerge and anxiety must be a later development. Perhaps that assumption is due partially to the fact that the study of anxiety has chiefly dealt with *neurotic* anxiety—which is certainly a complex affect and does not appear before the development of the capacity for self-awareness and other complicated psychological processes in the child. Perhaps, also, the uncriticized tendency to employ fear as the generic term is partially a product of the tendency in our culture (discussed in Chapters 2 and 4) to be preoccupied with the specific items of behavior which traditionally have fitted the methods of the dominant form of thought in our period, mathematical rationalism.

My knowledge and experience of anxiety and fear leads me to summarize their origin in the following way. After the first reflexive protective reactions, there emerge *the diffuse, undifferentiated emotional responses to threat—namely, anxiety; and last to emerge in maturation are the differentiated emotional responses to specific, localized dangers—namely, fears.* This order is also discernible in an adult's reaction to a danger stimulus—let us say to the sudden blast of a gunshot. First, the adult responds with startle. Second, as he becomes aware of the threat but is unable to localize the source of the shooting or to tell whether it is aimed at him, he is in the state of anxiety. Third, as he is able to spot the source of the gunshot and to take steps to get out of the way, he is in the state of fear.

ANXIETY AND FEAR

Until recent years the distinction between fears and anxiety has been frequently overlooked in psychological studies, or the two affects have been lumped together on the assumption that they have the same neurophysiological base. But this failure to make a differentiation confuses the understanding of both fears and anxiety. The reactions of an organism in times of fear and of anxiety may be radically different, due to the fact that these reactions occur on different psychological levels of the personality.

This difference may be clearly seen in the psychosomatic studies of gastrointestinal activities in states of fear and anxiety. When Tom, the person with the fistula into his stomach (as discussed in Chapter 3), was confronted with a specific danger—e.g., that the irate doctor would discover the mistake he had made—Tom's gastric activity was suspended and his psychological and physiological state was that of the familiar pattern of mobilization for flight. Clearly, this was fear. But when Tom had lain awake at night distressed about how long his employment at the hospital would last, his neurophysiological reactions were the exact opposite: gastric activity was accelerated and sympathetic ("flight") activity was at a minimum. This was anxiety. The difference in these two reactions may be described as follows: in the fear Tom knew what he was afraid of, and a specific adaptation in one direction was possible—namely, flight. In the anxiety, though the tension was occasioned by an apparently specific danger, the threat cued off in Tom an internal conflict on whether he could be a self-supporting man or would have to return to government relief. Detection by the doctor in the instance of fear would have been uncomfortable but not catastrophic. But *the threat in the second instance was to values Tom held essential to his existence as a self-respecting personality*. The point emphasized here is not only that the reactions in fear and in anxiety may be quite different, but that fear and anxiety represent threats to different levels in the personality.

In studies of children's fears it is highly significant that a large proportion of the fears are "irrational"—i.e., have no direct relation to the misfortunes which had actually befallen the children. The "shifting," "unpredictable" quality of children's fears in these studies is also a datum of considerable significance. Both of these data suggest that some affect is present underlying the so-called fears. Indeed, the phrase "irrational fear" is strictly speaking a contradiction in terms; if a fear cannot be understood as a flight from a danger that one has learned in experience is painful or harmful, then something else is involved in the reactions of the person toward the threat.

It may be countered that "irrational fear" is not a contradiction in terms, since Freud and others speak of "neurotic fears"—i.e., fears which are irrational in the respect that they are out of proportion to the reality situation. But Freud cites various phobias as examples of neurotic fears, and phobias are by definition forms of anxiety localized on one object. I propose that *it is the anxiety underlying the neurotic fear which lends it its unrealistic, "irrational" quality*. The study of fears points toward a process of reaction more basic than the specific fears themselves.

It is now possible to solve the problem of the relation between anxiety and fears. The capacity of the organism to react to threats to its existence and to its values is, in its general and original form, anxiety. Later, as the organism becomes mature enough neurologically and psychologically to differentiate specific objects of danger, the protective reactions can likewise become specific; such differentiated reactions to specific dangers are fears. *Thus anxiety is the basic, underlying reaction—the generic term; and fear is the expression of the same capacity in its specific, objectivated form.* This relation between anxiety and fear holds for the neurotic as well as for the normal forms of these affects. A neurotic fear is a specific, differentiated, objectivated expression of underlying neurotic anxiety. In other words, neurotic fears bear the same relation to neurotic anxiety as normal fears do to normal anxiety. I believe anxiety is "primal" rather than "derived." If one is to speak of either emotion as derived, it is fear that is derived rather than anxiety. In any case, the customary procedure of subsuming the study of anxiety under the study of fear, or trying to make anxiety intelligible through a study of fear, is, I am convinced, illogical. The understanding of fears hinges upon the understanding of the prior problem of anxiety.

We speak of anxiety as "basic" not only in the sense that it is the general, original response to threat, but also because it is a response to threat on the basic level of the personality. It is a response to a threat to the "core" or "essence" of the personality rather than to a peripheral danger. Fears are the responses to threats before they get to the basic level. By reacting adequately to the various specific dangers which threaten him (i.e., by reacting adequately on the level of fears), the individual avoids having his essential values threatened, avoids being threatened at the "inner citadel" of his security system. This is what Goldstein meant when he defined fear as "fear of the onset of anxiety."

If, however, one cannot cope with dangers in their specific forms, one will be threatened on the deeper level which we call the "core" or "essence" of personality. Using a military analogy, battles on various segments of the front lines represent specific threats; so long as the battle can be fought out on the periphery, so long as the dangers can be warded off in the area of the outer fortifications, the vital areas are not threatened. But when the enemy breaks through into the capital of the country, when the inner lines of communication are broken and the battle is no longer localized; when, that is, the enemy attacks from all directions and the defending soldiers do not know which way to march or where to take a stand, we have the threat of being overwhelmed, with its corollaries, panic and frantic behavior. The latter is analogous to a threat to the basic values, the "inner citadel" of the personality; and *in individual psychological terms it is the threat responded to as anxiety.*

Thus, figuratively speaking, we may describe fear as the armor against anxiety. The phrase "fear of fear," employed by President Franklin D. Roosevelt as well as by several other previous figures in history, refers to the apprehension that one will not be able to cope with dangers as they arise and will thereby be thrown into a catastrophic situation. "Fear of fear," thus, really means anxiety.

ANXIETY AND CONFLICT

Neurotic anxiety always involves inner conflict. There is often a reciprocal relation between the two: a state of persistent unresolved conflict may lead eventually to the person's repressing one side of the conflict, which then produces neurotic anxiety. And anxiety, in turn, brings in its train feelings of helplessness, impotence, and a paralysis of action which tend to cause or increase psychological conflict. The descriptions of this state of conflict range from Stekel's summary statement, "anxiety *is* psychic conflict," to the systematic endeavors of Freud, Kierkegaard, Horney, et al., to discover the nature of this conflict.

The view that the conflict underlying anxiety is between instinctual needs within the individual and social prohibitions stems from Freud. His topological description is that the ego is caught between id (instinctual urges chiefly of a libidinous character) on one hand and superego (cultural requirements) on the other. Though Freud modified his first theory that anxiety was simply converted repressed libido to the theory that the ego perceives the danger situation and then represses the libido, the content of the conflict and concomitant anxiety has been asked by numerous students cannot be gratified. The threat which cues off anxiety is seen in Freud as the threat of frustration of libido or, what amounts to the same thing, the threat of punishment if the libido is gratified.

This question of whether frustration of libido per se causes conflict and concomitant anxiety has been asked by numerous students of anxiety after Freud (Horney, Sullivan, Mowrer, etc.). The consensus of these investigators is that frustration itself does not cause conflict. The relevant question is, rather: What essential value is threatened by the frustration? This may be illustrated in the area of sex. Some persons have a great deal of sexual expression (i.e., suffer no frustration) and still have much anxiety. Other persons bear considerable sexual privation and are not prey to excessive anxiety. Still others, significantly, *are thrown into conflict and anxiety when their sexual desires are frustrated by one possible partner but not when the same desires are frustrated by another person.* Thus something more than the need for mere sexual gratification is occurring.

The problem is not the frustration in itself, but whether the frustration threatens some mode of interpersonal relationship which the individual holds vital to his security and self-esteem. In our culture sexual activity is generally identified by the individual with his sense of power, esteem, and prestige; in such an individual the threat of sexual frustration is very likely to cause conflict and anxiety. Our disagreement is not with Freud's phenomenological description of the frequent relation between sexual repression and anxiety in his Victorian culture. It is due to the fact that sexual prohibitions are very frequently the modus in our culture of authoritative constraint of the child by his parents and later by society. These constraints result in a suppression of the child's development and expansion. Sexual impulses will then involve a conflict with these authorities (usually parents) and will arouse the prospect of punishment by and alienation from the authorities. This conflict will certainly in many cases produce anxiety. But that does not mean that the libidinal frustration itself causes the conflict and anxiety. The threat of frustration of a biological urge does not cause conflict and anxiety unless that urge is identified with some value essential to the existence of the personality. When Sullivan states that the activities directed toward the pursuit of security are ordinarily more important to the human being than those directed toward physical satisfactions like hunger and sex, he does not mean to discount the biological aspect of behavior. He means, rather, to indicate that the physical needs are subsumed under the more comprehensive need of the organism to maintain and extend its total security and power.

Kardiner sees the conflict underlying anxiety in Western man as caused by the introduction of taboos early in the child's development which block relaxor pleasure patterns. While similar to Freud in his emphasis on the biological content of this conflict, Kardiner goes on to state that the severity of the conflict is due to the fact that in the psychological growth pattern of Western culture the introduction of taboos occurs after the parents have cultivated strong affective needs and expectations in the infant. Thus the anxiety is due not merely to frustration of pleasure patterns as such but to the child's experience of the undependability and inconsistency of his parents in their failure to fulfill the expectations which they have engendered in him.

Is there any common denominator of these conflicts? I believe that the common denominator can be found in *the dialectical relation of the individual and his community*.[13] On one hand the human being develops as an individual; the fact of individuality is a given datum in the respect that each person is unique and to an extent discrete from other individuals. Actions, no matter how much conditioned by social factors, are still actions by an individual. At the point in development at which self-awareness emerges, there also emerges a measure of freedom and responsibility in each individual action. But, on the other hand, this individual develops at every moment as a member of a social nexus upon which he is dependent not only for the early meeting of his biological needs but also for his emotional security. It is only in interaction with other individuals in a social nexus that the development of a "self" and the development of personality are understandable.

The infant's and child's existence consists of a progressive differentiation of himself from his parents. When he is viewed from the individual aspect of the dialectical relationship, his growth consists of decreasing dependence on parents and increasing reliance upon and use of his own powers. When he is viewed from the social aspect, the child's growth consists of his progressive relating to the parent on new levels. *Blockage of development at either pole in this dialectic engenders psychological conflict, the end result of which is anxiety.* Where there is "freedom from" without corresponding interrelationship, there is the anxiety of the defiant and isolated individual. Where there is dependence without freedom, there is the anxiety of the clinging person who cannot live outside a symbiosis. When one lacks the capacity to act on the basis of one's own powers, he or she sets him- or herself up to be threatened by every new situation which requires autonomous action.

To the extent that development is blocked at either pole, inner mechanisms will also be set in operation within the individual that increase the conflict and anxiety. In the individual who is characterized by independence without corresponding relatedness, there will develop hostility toward those whom he believes to be the occasion of his isolation. In the individual who is symbiotically dependent, there will develop hostility toward those whom he regards as instrumental in the suppression of his capacities and freedom. In each case, the hostility increases the conflict and hence the anxiety.

Another mechanism will also be present—namely repression. The unutilized capacities and the unfulfilled needs are not lost but repressed. The phenomenon is often observed clinically that the defiantly independent, isolated individual is repressing considerable need and desire to make affirmative relationships with other people, and the symbiotically dependent person is repressing need and desire to act independently. It is well known, as has already been pointed out, that the mechanism of repression itself decreases autonomy and increases helplessness and conflict.

In this discussion it is not meant to imply that the conflict is *between* the individual and society, either in the Freudian negative usage of the term "society" or in the opposite Adlerian positive sense. The point, rather, is that a failure of development at either pole in the dialectical relationship of individual-in-community results in a conflict which affects both poles. For example, if a person avoids autonomous individual decisions, he retrenches to a shut-in condition (Kierkegaard) and his possibilities of communicating with others are sacrificed along with his autonomy as an individual. The shut-in condition is a result of the endeavor to avoid conflict, but it actually results later in greater conflict—i.e., neurotic conflict and neurotic anxiety.

This description of the basic conflict underlying anxiety in terms of individual-in-community has the problem of generality, but it has the merit of emphasizing both sides of the development that is necessary for the overcoming of conflict and anxiety. It also has the merit of providing a frame of reference for the divergent theories of conflict presented in the literature of anxiety. The various emphases on the origin of conflict in early childhood (Freud, Horney, etc.) are understandable since this is the first arena in which the conflicts relating to individual-in-community are fought out. Sex may express individual-in-community or may be distorted into egocentricity (pseudo-individuality, or the exploitative Don Juan) or into symbiotic dependence (pseudo-community, the cling-ing-vine type).

The theories of conflict which hold that persistent re-straint of individual impulses will sooner or later result in conflict and anxiety (Freud) are true but incomplete. The theories which emphasize the social pole in the dialectic (Sullivan, Adler) present another phase of the picture as well as provide a corrective to overemphasis on the ex-pression of individual impulses per se. Hence Mowrer and others can argue that anxiety and conflict are often caused by guilt feeling which arises from the failure of the indi-vidual to relate himself maturely and responsibly to his social group. It seems safe to conclude, on the basis of the various analyses of the conflict underlying anxiety, that the constructive solution of the conflict involves *the in-dividual's progressive actualization of his capacities in expanding community.*

ANXIETY AND HOSTILITY

Anxiety and hostility are interrelated; one usually gen-erates the other. *First, anxiety gives rise to hostility.* This can be understood in its simplest form in the fact that anx-iety, with its concomitant feelings of helplessness, isolation, and conflict, is an exceedingly painful experience. One tends to be angry and resentful toward those responsible for placing him in such a situation of pain. Clinical ex-perience yields many examples like the following: A dependent person, finding himself in a situation of respon-sibility with which he feels he cannot cope, reacts with hostility both toward those who have placed him in the situation and toward those (usually parents) who caused him to be unable to cope with it. Or he feels hostility to-ward his therapist, whom he believes should bail him out, as Brown did toward me (below, page 229).

Second, hostility in anxious persons gives rise to in-creased anxiety. In Freud's example, Hans was hostile toward his father because he stood in the way of the gratification of Hans's excessive libidinal needs for his mother. But if Hans were to express this hostility, the result would be retaliation by the stronger father, the prospect of which would increase Hans's anxiety. Another example is presented by Kardiner in his study of Plainville:

the intrasocial hostility in the village, arising chiefly out of reciprocal blocking of pleasure patterns (e.g., by gossip), served to increase the individual's feeling of isolation and hence to increase his anxiety.

Granted the interrelation between hostility and anxiety, which affect is generally basic? There is ground for believing that, even though hostility may be the specific affect present in many situations, anxiety is often present below the hostility. This is especially observable in cases that show repressed hostility. Tom, we recall, "had a fear of his mother like a fear of the Lord," and since one does not talk back to the Lord one fears so much, we can conclude that whatever hostility he had would be repressed. In some of the psychosomatic studies of patients with hypertension (a somatic symptom generally associated with repressed hostility) it has been found that the reason the patients repressed their hostility in the first place was that they were anxious and dependent. The rationale of such patterns can be broadened to cover many situations in which repressed hostility and anxiety are interrelated: *The hostility would not have to be repressed in the first place except that the individual is anxious and fears counterhostility or alienation.* I do not mean to subsume all hostility under the problem of anxiety; it is certainly true that normal hostility may arise whenever an individual's activity is constrained. We are speaking here specifically of *repressed* hostility.

In neurotic patterns, including the special group of these patterns termed psychosomatic illnesses, anxiety is the primary etiological phenomenon. In this sense anxiety is the *psychic* common denominator of all disease as well as of all behavior disturbances.

CULTURE AND COMMUNITY

I have discussed in the last chapter the genetic background of a pattern which is the *occasion* for much anxiety in contemporaneous culture—namely, individual competitive ambition. It remains to summarize the status of the personality in our society with respect to this pattern and then to consider particularly the *quantity* of contemporaneous anxiety in relation to the historical stage of development of modern culture.

To recapitulate briefly, social prestige goals are dominant in our culture, social prestige being defined as success, this success in turn being defined chiefly in economic terms. The acquisition of wealth is accepted as proof and symbol of individual power. Since success is measured against the status of others, the striving for success is essentially competitive: one is successful if one excels and triumphs over others. The goal of competitive success not only arose by virtue of an emphasis on individual power set over against the community in the Renaissance, but as this goal persists it tends always to increase the juxtaposition of the individual and the community. Being the dominant cultural value, competitive success is likewise the dominant criterion of self-valuation; it is accepted as the means of validating the self in one's own eyes as well as in the eyes of others. *Whatever threatens this goal is, therefore, the occasion for profound anxiety for the individual in our culture because the threat is to values held essential to one's existence as a personality—i.e., essential to one's worth and prestige as a personality.*

The dominant goal of competitive success, though defined chiefly in economic terms, carries over to become the individual's goal in his personal relationships as well. Horney has excellently described this phenomenon in our culture:

It must be emphasized that competitiveness, and the potential hostility that accompanies it, pervades all human relationships. Competitiveness is one of the predominant factors in social relationships. It pervades the relationships between men and men, between women and women, and whether the point of competition be popularity, competence, attractiveness, or any other social value, it greatly impairs the possibilities of reliable friendship. It also as already indicated disturbs the relations between men and women, not only in the choice of the partner but in the entire struggle with him for superiority. It pervades school life. And perhaps most important of all, it pervades the family situation, so that as a rule the child is inoculated with this germ from the very beginning.[14]

Thus love, for example, instead of being a constructive means of overcoming individual isolation, is often a means of self-aggrandizement. One uses love for competitive purposes in the rivalry over winning a socially desirable and enviable mate; it is a proof of one's social competence; the mate is viewed as an acquisition in much the same way as one would view winning profits on the stock market. Another common example is valuing one's children because they win prizes in college or in other ways add to the competitive status of the family name. In our culture love is frequently sought as a means of allaying anxiety, but when it occurs in a competitive, depersonalized framework, it increases feelings of isolation and hostility and thereby increases anxiety.

Anxiety arises as a result of the individualistic competitive pattern here discussed not simply when the individual finds his possibilities for success threatened but in many more subtle ways. Anxiety arises out of the *interpersonal isolation and alienation from others that inheres in a pattern in which self-validation depends on triumphing over others*. This anxiety was already discernible in many of the powerful and successful individuals of the Renaissance (we noted it in Michelangelo). Anxiety likewise arises out of the *intrasocial hostility* produced by competitive individualism. Finally, anxiety arises out of the self-alienation resulting from *viewing one's self as an object* of the market, or making one's feeling of self-strength dependent on extrinsic wealth rather than intrinsic capacity and productivity. We are a "commodity . . . who has to obey his buyer," in Auden's terms. These attitudes not only distort one's relation to one's self, but to the extent that they make one's criterion of self-worth contingent upon a kind of success which can be threatened every day by one's neighbors' counter-success, they augment one's feelings of vulnerability, helplessness, and powerlessness.

Moreover, "vicious circle" mechanisms operate in the individualistic competitive pattern which tend to make anxiety self-increasing. The culturally accepted method of allaying anxiety is redoubling one's efforts to achieve success. Since intrasocial hostility and aggression can be expressed in the socially approved method of competition, the anxious individual increases his competitive striving. But the more competitive, aggressive striving, the more isolation, hostility, and anxiety. This vicious circle may be graphed as follows: competitive individual striving→ intrasocial hostility→ isolation→ anxiety→ increased competitive striving. *Thus the methods most generally used to dispel anxiety in such a constellation actually increase anxiety in the long run.*

We now turn to the problem of the relation between the quantity of anxiety experienced by contemporaneous individuals and the present state of our culture. The conviction that Western civilization in the twentieth century is permeated by considerable quantities of anxiety (or anxiety-like states) has been expressed in different ways by Tawney, Tillich, Mumford, Fromm, Horney, Mannheim, Cassirer, Riezler, and others. Each presents the evidence and the explanation for the situation from the particular viewpoint of his or her own explorations. The common agreement is that underlying this anxiety are profound cultural changes, which are described in varying terms like "the crisis in man's view of himself," or the "disintegration" of traditional cultural forms, and so forth.

In the second half of the nineteenth and the early twentieth centuries, the belief in pre-existent harmony—that which, in one way or another, had held people in some kind of community despite their competition against each other—had also disintegrated. Penetrating thinkers, like Karl Marx, realized that individual competitive ambition does not result automatically in the advance of social wellbeing. On the contrary, it was then producing feelings of powerlessness and isolation and increasing "dehumanization" (Marx), estrangement of people from each other (Paul Tillich), and increasing self-estrangement. The ideals and social "faith" which had *dispelled* anxiety now no longer did so; they only worked to *allay* anxiety in those willing to cling to the illusion which their old "faith" had become.[15]

Hence the cultural disunity which is described by almost every explorer of the contemporary scene. Mannheim, from the sociological viewpoint, spoke of the "phase of disintegration" through which Western society is passing. Cassirer, from the philosophical viewpoint, derived the disunity from the "loss of conceptual unity." And Riezler, from the viewpoint of social psychology, derives the disunity from the "lack of a universe of discourse" in our culture.

The disunity, or contradiction, from the psychological side can be seen by anyone who looks seriously at contemporaneous culture. Horney phrases the contradiction as between

> the alleged freedom of the individual and all his factual limitations. The individual is told by society that he is free, independent, can decide his life according to his own free will; "the great game of life" is open to him, and he can get what he wants if he is efficient and energetic. In actual fact, for the majority of people all these possibilities are limited. . . . The result for the individual is a *wavering between a feeling of boundless power in determining his own fate and a feeling of entire helplessness.*[16]

There is the contradiction between the accepted theory that each individual is free to gain economic success by his own efforts and merit and the actuality that he is to a great extent dependent upon suprapersonal technical forces (e.g., the market) over which he has little or no control. Kardiner noted that the people in Plainville "subscribe in the main to the American credo of vertical mobility and believe that a man can become anything he wants to. Actually, opportunities are very limited for them . . . even if they go away."[17]

Another contradiction is between the accepted individualistic rationalism ("each individual can decide on the basis of the facts") and the actuality that most decisions of the individual are based on motivations quite beyond conscious rational appraisal of the situation. The psychological helplessness arising out of this contradiction often leads the individual to cling to the illusion of rational power under the "anonymous authorities of public opinion," "science," and so forth. Kurt Riezler wrote:

> To the rational man of the industrial age everything has a "natural cause"; no demons interfere. Yet in times of crisis, he too can be gripped by indefinite fear. . . . Rational man is the heir of a long period of relative security in which he accumulated a great many matters of course to be taken for granted. This dubious training may be partly responsible for his vulnerability. His scheme of order is rational only in theory.[18]

The illusion of rationality temporarily allays anxiety by suppressing the contradictions. This has special point for the problem of anxiety since the confronting of anxiety is often avoided because of its "irrational" nature. We shall observe this in the case of Helen (p. 240 ff.), who tried to suppress the fact that she was pregnant and used all kinds of "scientific" data in the service of her illusion. The tendency throughout our culture is to "rationalize" anxiety into specific fears, which the individual may then believe he confronts in a rational way. But this involves a suppression of the real source of the anxiety. And, in most people, the illusion sooner or later breaks down.

Contradictions and inconsistencies in a culture, of course, make the member of the society more vulnerable to anxiety because they increase the number of situations in which he is unable to decide on any approved course of action. We recall the Lynds' statement that the individual in Middletown is frequently "caught in a chaos of conflicting patterns, none of them wholly condemned, but no one of them clearly approved and free from confusion." Now when the individual's values and goals are threatened, he cannot orient himself by reference to consistent systems of value within his culture. The threat the individual experiences is, therefore, not just to his possibility of attaining his goal, but almost any threat may likewise raise doubts as to whether the goal is worth attaining—i.e., *the threat becomes a threat to the goal itself. The reader will recall that I pointed out that fear changes into the more profound and pervasive state of anxiety when the threat ceases to be peripheral but becomes a threat to the standard of value itself. This is what leads to the feeling of the "dissolution of the self."* I believe this is what is going on in our society. Thus what might objectively appear to be only a minor threat to an individual's values may in our culture throw the individual into panic and profound disorientation.

In a similar vein, Mannheim holds that "it is important to remember that our society is faced, not with brief unrest, *but with a radical change of structure.*"[19] In periods of unemployment, for example, anxiety arises not simply because of the temporary threat to subsistence:

For man, however, the catastrophe [of unemployment] lies not merely in the disappearance of external opportunities for work but also in the fact that his elaborate emotional system, intricately connected as it is with the smooth working of social institutions, now loses its object-fixation. The petty aims towards which almost all his strivings are directed suddenly disappear, and, not merely does he now lack a place to work, a daily task, and an opportunity for using the integrated labor attitudes formed through long training, but his habitual desires and impulses remain ungratified. Even if the immediate needs of life are satisfied, by means of unemployment relief, the whole life-organization and the family hopes and expectations are annihilated.[20]

Then Mannheim proceeds to the point which seems to me of crucial significance:

The panic reaches its height when the individual comes to realize that his insecurity is not simply a personal one, but is common to masses of his fellows, and it becomes clear to him that there is no longer any social authority to set unquestioned standards and determine his behavior. *Herein lies the difference between individual unemployment and general insecurity.* If in normal times an individual loses his job, he may indeed despair, but his reactions are more or less prescribed and he follows a general pattern in his distress.[21]

In other words, in individual unemployment the person can still believe in the validity of the cultural values and goals, despite the fact that his achieving the goals himself is at the time threatened. But in mass unemployment and insecurity the individual cannot even believe in the values and goals basic to his culture.

I here propose that the *quantity of anxiety prevalent in the present period arises from the fact that the values and standards underlying modern culture are themselves threatened.*[22] The distinction, like Mannheim's, is between a peripheral threat—i.e., a threat which members of the society can meet on the basis of the assumptions of their culture—and a threat on a deeper level—namely, a threat to the underlying assumptions, the "charter"[23] of the culture itself. We recall Tawney's argument that the previous revolutions in the modern period occurred on the accepted cultural assumption of the sovereignty of individual rights; the revolutions sought and obtained a broadening of the base of individual rights. But this underlying assumption of the culture was itself unquestioned and unthreatened. I believe the situation now is different. *The threats involved in the present social changes are not threats which can be met on the basis of the assumptions of the culture but rather are threats to those underlying assumptions themselves.*

Only thus can we understand the profound anxiety which occurs in many an individual in our society at the prospect of some minor economic change, an anxiety entirely out of proportion to the actual threat. The threat is experienced not as a threat to subsistence, nor even chiefly to the prestige of the individual concerned, but is rather *a threat to basic assumptions which have been identified with the existence of the culture, and which the individual, as a participant in the culture, has identified with his own existence.*

The basic assumptions threatened in our present culture include those connected with the pattern of competitive individualistic ambition which has been central in our society since the Renaissance. In this respect, what is threatened is the individual's "faith"—a faith which we have described as confidence in the efficacy of competitive individualistic ambition. The individualistic assumptions are threatened because in the present phases of social development they destroy the individual's experience of community. Totalitarianism is a cultural neurotic symptom of the need for community—a symptom in the respect that it is grasped as a means of allaying anxiety resulting from the feelings of powerlessness and helplessness of the isolated, alienated individuals produced in a society in which competitive individualism has been the dominant goal. Totalitarianism is the substitution of collectivism for community, as Tillich has pointed out. I submit that one of the central requirements for the constructive overcoming of anxiety in our society is the development of adequate forms of community.

The term "community," as used here, implies a positive quality of relatedness of the individual to the other persons in his social environment. In this sense it is to be differentiated from the neutral term "society." Everyone belongs to a society whether he wishes it or not, whether he chooses it or not, whether he contributes constructively to its development or does the reverse. Community, on the contrary, implies one's relating one's self to others affirmatively and responsibly. Community in the economic sense implies an emphasis on the social values and functions of work. Community in the psychological sense involves the individual's relating himself to others in love as well as creativity.

PART

II

CLINICAL ANALYSIS
OF ANXIETY

CHAPTER
8

Case Studies
Demonstrating Anxiety

Anxiety is the dynamic center of neuroses and thus we shall have to deal with it all the time.

—Karen Horney, *The Neurotic Personality of Our Time*

How are we to study anxiety in human beings? In a previous section we discussed the grave problems in inducing anxiety in human beings in the laboratory. We also pointed out that we need to know how the individual, in his fantasy or imagination, *symbolically interprets* the situation. Indeed, we need to know a good deal both objectively and subjectively about the individual we are studying before we can even tell *whether* his reaction is anxiety, let alone understand it.

A chief reason the experience of anxiety in human beings is so complex is that its determinants are often unconscious. As illustrated in such cases as those of Brown and Helen in the following pages, the person in severe anxiety may actually be driven to *deny* the existence of the apprehension—not by caprice or by any uncooperativeness, but simply as a function of the severity of the anxiety itself. The subject can protect himself from the overwhelming effects of anxiety only by persuading himself that he is not afraid. This phenomenon is not at all limited to the consulting room; it is a common human experience, as everyone knows. *Vide* the whistling-in-the-dark strategy, and the war experience of many soldiers. Small wonder, then, that check-lists on which the subject reports conscious data about his "anxieties" are of such minor value (as I was myself to discover in the study reported later in this book). Some students of anxiety hold that it is in understanding *fantasy* that we come to the "heart of the anxiety problem." That is to say, a method is needed which will make accessible the subjective and unconscious forms of motivation as well as motivation in its conscious manifestations. Anxiety has an "inner locus," as Kierkegaard and Freud insisted, and to the extent that we cannot get at that, the essential meaning of anxiety in human beings will elude us.

There are two phases of this problem. The first is the question of whether the individual-in-a-life-situation is to be taken as the unit of study. I answer this emphatically in the affirmative. Today many sociologists and social psychologists report studies in "life-event crises" such as war, accidents, death.[1] The second phase is the more specific one of determining what particular methods within the dynamic field are to be employed. Until the advent of psychoanalysis there was no technique of ascertaining the subjective meanings of an experience like anxiety except the insightful self-observation and intuitive understanding of others by gifted individuals like Pascal and Kierkegaard. But if the term "clinical" is used to refer to method, it must be interpreted broadly to include all those methods which illuminate unconscious motivations.[2] The projective technique of the Rorschach, giving what the subject will not or cannot tell, was invaluable in the following studies for yielding keys to the dynamics and underlying patterns in the individual's behavior, which were later corroborated by a multitude of other data.

WHAT WE SEEK TO DISCOVER

The following case studies are presented to illustrate the summary and synthesis of anxiety theory given in the preceding chapter. Obviously no clinical case can be placed on the Procrustean bed of our expectation that it answer certain questions and not others. Each case must be taken on its own merits and should be approached in the open-minded mood typified by the inquiry: What has this particular person to teach us about anxiety? But our keeping certain more specific questions in mind as we investigate each case makes for greater clarity and concreteness. I shall, therefore, list some crucial questions for the theory of anxiety which I was asking myself in the following case studies.

Concerning the nature of anxiety and its relation to fears, I asked: *Can we ascertain whether specific fears are the foci of underlying anxiety?* If neurotic fears are the expression in specific form of neurotic anxiety and if, as I have indicated, the latter arises from basic conflicts within the individual, it should be true that the neurotic fears will focus now on this object and now on that, but that the underlying pattern of anxiety will remain fairly constant. Hence, *can we ascertain whether neurotic fears shift as the issues and problems the individual confronts shift, while the underlying neurotic anxiety remains relatively constant?*

In the preceding chapter it was held that neurotic anxiety always has some *psychological conflict* at its source and that the conflict originally occurs in the child's relation to its parents. Two questions emerge from this aspect of anxiety theory: (a) *Can it be shown in the following cases that subjective, inner conflict is always present as the dynamic source of neurotic anxiety?* (b) *Can it be shown that individuals who have experienced rejection by their parents (especially by the mother) have a greater predisposition for neurotic anxiety?* This is one way of stating the classical hypothesis, propounded in various ways by Freud, Horney, Sullivan, *et al.*, and widely accepted in the field of clinical psychology and psychoanalysis, that the origin of psychological patterns which predispose to neurotic anxiety are in the child's early relations with its parents, especially with its mother.

The interrelation of the subject's anxiety to his or her culture should be demonstrable at almost every turn in the following cases. Out of this complex area, we select one question: *Does the individual's socioeconomic status in the society (e.g., middle-class, proletarian) appear to have significant bearing on the kinds and quantities of his or her anxiety?*

Concerning anxiety and hostility, *Can it be shown that anxiety is related to hostile feelings, that the more anxious a person is, the greater the tendency to have feelings of*

*hostility? And when the anxiety subsides, do the hostile
feelings abate likewise?*

In every person there are a number of rule of thumb
ways of dealing with anxiety learned over the years. *Can
we discover whether, when an individual is confronted
with an anxiety-creating situation, characteristic behavioral
strategies are called into play (defenses, symptoms, etc.),
and that these serve to protect the individual from the
anxiety-creating situation?*

Finally, I shall approach the problem of anxiety and
the development of the self from its reverse side in the
first two of the following three questions, seeking to determine whether the presence of anxiety tends to retard
the development of the self. *Can it be shown that the
presence of severe neurotic anxiety impoverishes the personality? Does the acceptance of impoverishment on the
part of the individual serve as a defense against the anxiety-
creating situation? Can we discover whether the more
creative and productive the individual, the more he is
confronted with anxiety-creating situations?*

HAROLD BROWN: CONFLICT UNDERLYING
SEVERE ANXIETY

This first case is that of a young man of thirty-two who
was diagnosed as suffering from what is called an anxiety
neurosis.[3] Whatever diagnostic terms one may use to describe his problems, there is no doubt that he experienced
a great amount of anxiety which threatened continually
to overwhelm him.

Harold Brown was my first patient in the course of my
psychoanalytic training. He is presented here on the hypothesis that certain aspects of the problem of anxiety—
such as unconscious conflicts—can best be illustrated by
the comprehensive subjective data which this method
yields. Though the major parts of what transpired have
to be omitted, I hope enough is presented here concerning his anxiety to make sense to readers. I saw Brown for
more than three hundred hours under the supervision of
Erich Fromm, whose help I wish to acknowledge.

It was only after the following material was written up
that I realized how well Brown illustrates Kierkegaard's
main points about subjective conflict underlying all anxi-

ety. For me, Harold Brown cast new light on Kierke-gaard's statements, "Anxiety is afraid, yet it maintains a sly intercourse with its object, cannot look away from it, indeed will not. . . ." Anxiety "is a desire for what one dreads, a sympathetic antipathy. Anxiety is an alien power which lays hold of an individual, and yet one cannot tear oneself away, nor has a will to do so; for one fears, but what one fears one desires. Anxiety then makes the individual impotent."[4]

This young man had been suffering for the preceding nine years from a severe, recurring anxiety condition. On graduation from college, where he had received high academic honors, he had entered medical school. After two months he had felt increasingly inadequate and helpless in the face of his assignment. The first anxiety state then developed, the symptoms of which were inability to sleep or work, difficulty in making the simplest decisions, and fear that he was "losing his mind." The anxiety state was relieved by his discontinuing medical school.

During the next years he tried several different vocations, only to have to discontinue each on the recurrence of anxiety attacks. The anxiety states, generally lasting several months (or until he dropped the particular work he was doing), were accompanied by profound depression and suicidal thoughts. In two of the more severe anxiety spells he had committed himself to mental hospitals for periods of one and eleven months. He had finally enrolled in another graduate school, a theological seminary, and when, in his third and final year, another developing anxiety state incapacitated him for work, he applied for psychoanalytic treatment.

During the early sessions of his work with me, Harold Brown's mood oscillated between lethargy and inertia on one hand and intense anxiety on the other, the one seeming to be a prelude to the other. In the passive states he characterized himself as "like a dog lying in the sun hoping somebody will feed it." In this stage he had many "blissful" memories of the care he had received as a child. In the subsequent anxiety states he exhibited great tension and talked very rapidly, as though driven to get out a torrent of words. He described his feelings in anxiety as having a general emotional vagueness and a "blurred" quality. When in anxiety it was *difficult or impossible for him to have any clear and distinct feelings,* whether of a sexual nature or otherwise. This state of emotional "vacuum" was excruciatingly uncomfortable for him. He would often go to movies or try to become engrossed in a novel, for, as he phrased it, if he could gain "empathy" with other persons, if he could feel something which other people were feeling, he would to that extent find relief from his anxiety. He is apparently here describing the *state of diminished awareness of one's self which characterizes severe anxiety.* I think it a significant insight on his part that if he could become aware on a feeling level of the reality of other persons, he would to that extent become aware of himself as a subject differentiated from objects.

The chief features of Harold Brown's first Rorschach, which was given to him at the beginning of his analysis when he was in a relatively severe anxiety state, were the great predominance of vague, unelaborated whole responses, the low degree of the responsiveness and productivity, the general banality, and the complete absence of any originality.[5] The "blurred" relation to reality which characterized this first Rorschach corresponds to Brown's testimony that in severe anxiety he could not experience "distinct feelings." It is as though the inner, subjective vagueness involved in the anxiety carried over into a general vagueness in his manner of evaluating outside, objective stimuli as well. This is an illustration of the thesis advanced earlier that severe anxiety breaks down the capacity to experience the self in relation to objects and is, correspondingly, an experience of "dissolution" of the self. Brown's endeavor to overcome his anxiety by becoming aware of other people's feelings is insightful in the respect that he could then become aware of himself in relation to other people and to this extent overcome the state which we term the "dissolution" of self.

He had been born in India, the son of American missionaries. While his mother was pregnant with him, the only two other children in the family died in a plague. In his childhood he felt he had been "coddled," not only by his mother but by the native women servants, who insisted on dressing him until he was seven. Three girl siblings were born later, with one of whom he engaged in very severe and violent competition for the favor of his parents. "I wanted to be the baby," he phrased it; and when his parents would adjudicate a dispute in the sister's favor, he would feel deeply incensed and threatened. When the patient was in his teens, his father broke down in what was diagnosed as manic-depressive psychosis and the family returned to this country, where his father was hospitalized. Several years later his father committed suicide.[6]

The pattern that seemed crucial to Brown's anxiety was his very dependent, symbiotic relationship with his mother. Two significant memories illuminate the early relationship. First, when he was five, his mother, while nursing one of the babies, had offered him her breast with the remark, "Do you want a drink too?" The intense humiliation he had felt at this implication that he was still a baby came up repeatedly in the therapy in many different contexts of his relations with his mother. Second, when he had engaged in a prank at the age of eight, his mother had punished him by making him whip her. The traumatic experience of his being forced to punish his mother, became the focus for his later feeling that he could never hold any opinion or exercise any judgment independently of his mother, for she would then assume a martyr role and "my hands would be tied." He was dominated by the mother under the formula, "If you go against my authority, you do not love me."

At the time of this therapy he was being supported by his mother, as he had been during his previous periods of incapacitation. Both he and his mother were worried about how he would be supported when she died. Even at his present age his mother's letters addressed him as "my darling boy," after receiving which he often had anxiety dreams of "someone trying to kill me" or, in one illuminating example, of "Russia trying to converge on a small country." In one of the letters he received from his mother during the analysis, she stated that if *she* had sufficient faith in God, he would be cured of his illnesses through *her* faith. He was understandably resentful at her implication that he could do nothing whatever, religiously or psychologically, to help himself apart from her. The origins of Brown's anxiety pattern can be understood in the context of his having to deal from the time of birth onward with a dominating, sado-masochistic mother, who exercised her tyranny at one moment by an assumption of strength but at other times by the more effective—and, for

Harold, more confusing—strategy of cloaking the tyranny under a pretense of her weakness.

This conflict underlying his anxiety was shown in two dreams during the first months of therapy:

> I was in bed enjoying a close physical embrace with a woman. It became apparent that it was my mother. My penis was erect, and I was embarrassed. As I tried to pull away, she said, "You've got to grant me some satisfaction." So I fondled her breasts. Then an emission of semen came from her breasts, as from a male genital.

We note in this dream that the mother *commands* him to devote himself to her satisfactions, and that he imputes to her the sexual functions of the male. Several weeks later he received word that his mother had hurt her arm, which news so perturbed him that he had immediately phoned her in the distant city where she lived. That night he had the following dream:

> A rotting, putrid arm had reached out from a hole in a rock and grabbed my penis, pulling it away from me. I was mad, and I reached in the hole to grab the hand, pull it out, and make it let go of my penis. Then I felt someone punch me in the back with a knife or pistol, to force me to let go. It seemed to be another person, an accomplice of the hand, who was going to kill me if I didn't let go. I awoke in great fright.

His associations with penis—"strength," "power," "my own penis is small"—indicated that the word for him, as for many persons in our culture, stood for his own individual power. Since the arm obviously is his mother's, the dream seems to say in the easiest way possible that his mother has taken his individual power away from him, and if he tries to regain it he will be killed. In both dreams he sees his mother as possessing great power, including masculine power, and himself as the victim of her demands.

His conflict may be stated: *If he tries to use his own power, to produce and achieve independently of his mother, he will be killed. But the opposite path, namely remain-*

*ing dependent upon her, can be pursued only at the price
of continued feelings of inadequacy and helplessness.* The
latter way out of the conflict requires a renunciation of
his individual autonomy and strength, but, in symbolic
language, it is better to be castrated than to be dead.

These dreams might be interpreted in the classical mode
of Oedipus, incest and castration. But in my judgment, the
meaning of the symbols is significant rather than the sexual
content per se. From this viewpoint the essential point
about the first dream is not simply that the subject has
sexual contact with the mother, but that the mother commands it. In the second dream it is his mother who cas-
trates Brown, not his father.

There are, of course, bound to be many incest references
in a case of this sort. The significant point is illustrated
in the following dream: "I was secretly married to an
older woman. *I didn't want to be, so I had myself committed to an institution.*" This is an eloquent statement of
his struggle to get away from his mother—even to the
point of having himself committed to a mental hospital
(which suggests, also, that his psychological illness has
some function of protection against his mother). One
might hypothesize that his not wanting to be married to
her and his having himself incarcerated are the result of
guilt feelings arising from the incest desires; but it does
not seem necessary to make that interpretation. The dream
can be understood more simply and directly as saying that
he knows what marriage to his mother really means—i.e.,
to be enslaved by a tyrant—and being incarcerated is
preferable if that is the only way one can avoid such a
relationship. In the present study I treat incest phenomena as indicative of excessively dependent relations of the
person upon the parent, beyond which the person has
been unable to "grow up."

The above dreams indicate *how severe the conflict underlying neurotic anxiety may be.* It is scarcely surprising
that such a conflict should have such thoroughly paralyzing and incapacitating effects upon Harold Brown. Much
of the superficial material in this case could be interpreted
in Adlerian fashion—e.g., as anxiety used as a strategy for
remaining under the care of the mother and mother substitutes. But if such an interpretation is made, we must
not overlook the crippling conflict which underlies the
anxiety. It is comprehensible why this person should de-

scribe his feelings during anxiety as "like fighting something in the dark, when you don't know what it is." When he received letters of moralistic advice from his friends, he reacted with a surprisingly insightful analogy: "They [the friends] are like people calling to a drowning man to swim, when they don't know that under the water his hands and feet are tied."

We turn now to the question of the *occasions* which cued off anxiety in Harold Brown. In spells of acute anxiety, which generally lasted from three days to a week, it was almost impossible to discover at the time what situation in his present experience had cued off the panic. When I would urge him to inquire into the occasion of the present anxiety spell or "what" he was then afraid of, he would insist that the occasion had nothing whatever to do with the anxiety and assert, "I'm afraid of everything, I'm afraid of life." He was aware only of intense, paralyzing conflict. Despite the fact that the event or experience which cued off that particular anxiety spell could often be recovered in retrospect after the panic was over, there is logic in his feeling that the occasion was of secondary importance. I do not refer simply to the fact that his severe anxiety rendered him incapable of surveying his reality situation objectively. I refer, rather, to the fact that the *occasion* was not the *cause* of his anxiety. Whatever had cued the conflict off, it was none the less the conflict which caused his anxiety—i.e., produced his paralysis and helplessness. If we are to interpret his "logic," it would be that the particular event or experience which activated the conflict might be objectively a relatively minor event, but it had its subjective significance in the fact that it served to cue off the conflict, and it receded in objective importance as the conflict became more severe.[7]

In less severe anxiety attacks, it was possible to discover the occasions of his anxiety with fair accuracy. These occasions, together with the occasions reconstructed in retrospect after severe panics, fall into three main categories. First, anxiety was obviously occasioned by *situations in which he had to assume individual responsibility.* For one example, in a period just before our therapeutic work had to be suspended for the summer, he experienced a great deal of tension and spewed out a torrent of words about his dread that he might have cancer. This cancer fear was associated with an anxiety panic in childhood when he feared that he might have leprosy and would have to be separated from his family. It goes without saying that a person with such pronounced feelings of inadequacy would profoundly dread separation and isolation from those upon whom he depended. The fear of cancer vanished on this occasion when the anxiety at separation from me, his therapist, was clarified. Another example of anxiety at having to assume responsibility occurred when, after a year of analysis, he re-enrolled for his final year of study for his graduate degree. Several severe anxiety attacks ensued, during which he was overwhelmed with feelings of helplessness and inadequacy at the prospect of having to produce papers and write examinations. He felt that he "would not measure up," would "lose out in the race," would "lose face," etc. Since he subsequently did accomplish these dreaded academic assignments successfully, with no intervening factor except a reduction in anxiety, it is clear that the anxiety arose not from a realistic appraisal of inadequacy in the face of tasks (i.e., the occasion) but rather from the neurotic conflict which facing these tasks activated.

The second category of occasions of his anxiety was *situations of competition.* These occasions were not only major events such as academic examinations, but also relatively minor events like bridge games or discussions with his colleagues. This anxiety in competition was generally associated with his severe rivalry with his sister during childhood. The prototype for this anxiety, therefore, seems to be the threat to his excessive needs to be in an approved and favored position with his mother. In such matters as academic examinations, this approval could be gained by his being successful in competition. But on a level quite below his feeling of lack of personal power to achieve, he is faced with the dilemma that if he does achieve—i.e., does use his own power—he will be met with death at the hands of his mother. It is understandable, therefore, that the most minor competitive situation would thus activate a major subjective conflict.

But most significant of all is the third group of occasions of anxiety—namely, *anxiety after achieving success.* During his final year of graduate study he was invited to preside at a meeting of an important professional society, an event which represented considerable achievement to him. Some undercurrent of tension which he experienced before this event was clarified, and he discharged his responsibility successfully, receiving compliments from persons who had status in his eyes. The next day began one of his most severe attacks of anxiety and depression. This is understandable on the basis of the conflict outlined above, since using his own powers raises the threat of being killed. His general practice was to refuse to admit any achievement, such as wearing his Phi Beta Kappa key, for, as he phrased it, "When I'm succeeding, I'm afraid it will be a barrier between me and others." If he awoke in the morning feeling rested and strong, he reported apprehension lest he be "separated from other people." He felt he could overcome anxiety spells by crying in the therapy sessions, by "showing my weakness." This use of weakness alleviated his conflict in at least two respects: first, by being weak he would be accepted, "loved"—prototypically by his mother—while being strong would mean isolation and separation from his mother; and second, being weak and unsuccessful avoided the threat of being killed.

We have referred to the *cause* of the anxiety as the neurotic conflict, and the *occasions* of it as the experiences or events which activated that conflict. It can be noted that the more severe Brown's anxiety, the more the conflict predominated and the more the occasion receded in importance in his experience. In this respect the significance of the occasion lay in its subjective function of cuing off the conflict. We have also noted that the occasions always bore a logical and consistent relationship to the particular nature of his conflict—e.g., it was not fortuitous that occasions of responsibility, competition, and achieving success cued off this particular patient's conflict. The occasion always involved some anticipated threat (defeat in competition, "loss of face," etc.). But what I wish to emphasize is that when the conflict was activated, Harold Brown was faced with threats whichever way he turned. *The anxiety was, therefore, due not just to the anticipation of threat inhering in the occasion* (e.g., he might fail in an examination), *but rather was due to the experience of being in a dilemma in which he was threatened from both sides at once.* If he achieved some success, he was threatened with death by his mother; if he failed to achieve the success and remained dependent, he was threatened with continued feelings of helplessness and inadequacy.

The *regular pattern of progression assumed by most of his anxiety spells* is revealing. First, he would report a fear that he had cancer, or that he had recently experienced a momentary spell of dizziness as "though someone had struck me in the back of the neck." He spoke of this several times as a "rabbit punch," a blow at the back of the neck with which you kill a rabbit. This implies that he is the rabbit. This latter symptom, associated with some electric shock treatments he had received several years earlier, was felt by him to indicate that he had some organic brain injury.[8] Both the fear of cancer and the dizziness were presented by Brown as entirely rational, with supporting evidence from the daily papers, for example, about the contemporary high incidence of deaths from cancer.[9] When I suggested that the psychological meaning of the fears be explored, he would show offense and insist he felt no conscious anxiety whatever.

The second stage would follow a day or so later: the fears associated with cancer and the dizziness would be forgotten, but *anxiety dreams would appear, generally about his mother.* Still there would be no conscious admission of anxiety. In the third stage he would exhibit increased dependence on me, insisting that authoritative guidance be given, with increasing covert or overt hostility if these demands were not met.

The final, fourth step in the progression, again appearing a day or two later, would be *the emergence of a conscious anxiety attack,* with concomitant severe tension, discouragement, and eventual depression.

It seems to me that we have in these steps the progressive emergence of anxiety into conscious awareness, the anxiety assumedly occasioned by some experience or event just prior to the reporting of the original dizzy spell or the fear of cancer.

From the dreams and other material so far related it is evident that the patient had much repressed hostility against his mother. Indeed, from the standpoint of almost any form of psychology it would be impossible to conceive of a human being existing in such a dilemma without his experiencing great hostility. During therapy, his hostility was manifested in two opposite forms. First, he exhibited hostility whenever he felt he was not being allowed to remain in a dependent state. This is hostility as a *reaction to anxiety at having to assume the independent responsibility for which he felt inadequate.* When he felt that being analyzed required too much effort and responsibility on his part, he would demand that the analyst give him specific advice and authoritative directions for his behavior, as he felt a minister would give him "specific moral and religious instruction" or a physician would tell him exactly what was wrong and exactly what he should do without his having to assume any self-direction whatever. The psychosomatic symptom often accompanying this hostility at having to assume independent responsibility was diarrhea. This was illustrated in a remark, "I feel all plugged up; if I could just have a big bowel movement— if I could just get mad!"

The other form of hostility emerged whenever he was placed in a dependent, helpless position. Most of the repressed hostility toward the mother falls in this category. We have noted the evidence for this hostility as early as the fifth year, when he was humiliated by his mother's implication that he was still a baby in proffering him milk from her breast.

His difficulty in admitting overt hostility was present in his relation with me as well as with all other persons, and was particularly in evidence when he was anxious. Generally, his hostility took the forms of general resentment, occasional hostile dreams, or displacement on other persons. During his anxious periods, he saw everybody as hostile to him.

It will be noted that these occasions of hostility are really contradictory and that they correspond to the two aspects of Brown's fundamental conflict. In other words, hostility was a reaction to the exacerbation of either side of his conflict. There was a direct relation between the arousing of the conflict and hostility since the more anxiety he felt, the more hostility (covert or overt) was present. When his anxiety abated his hostility did likewise. It was almost impossible for him to admit overt hostility toward his mother, despite the presence of this hostility in dreams and its evidence as a general undercurrent of resentment toward her and specific annoyance at her letters. The hostility had to be in large measure repressed, lest the great dependence upon his mother be threatened. Two secondary gains of his recurring psychological illness, revealed in his associations, were that since his mother was then required to support him, he could both remain dependent upon her and at the same time get even with her.

A second Rorschach, given to Brown after ten months of analysis when he was relatively free from anxiety, showed a remarkably different picture.[10] He now had fifty responses, compared to eighteen on the first record, three original responses compared to none on the first, and a much greater capacity to relate to concrete, specific realities. The banality of the first record was gone; we now see the picture of a productive and effective personality. No matter to what one attributes the change—to the year of psychoanalysis, to the transference situation, etc.—the fact remains that at the time of the first record he was in an anxiety state, and at the time of the second he was not. It seems necessary to conclude that we have in these two records the contrasting pictures of the same individual's behavior and personality when in a state of severe anxiety and when he is relatively free from anxiety. We have in the first Rorschach an individual whose anxiety blocks his capacity to relate to concrete reality, renders reality "blurred" and vague, and undermines both his feeling and thinking capacities. It is the picture of an individual who cannot let himself be aware of other people or respond to them, a "shut-up," unfree, and thus impoverished personality. In the second, we see a radically freer person able to see and relate to the world around him, to be aware of others and correlatively of himself, a person with his previous banality gone and in its place some genuine originality.

CONCLUSIONS

The study of Harold Brown demonstrates a number of significant aspects of the dynamics of anxiety, several of which I shall here summarize. In all summaries, the problems seem simpler than they actually are. In the following conclusions, anxiety may sound again like an abnormal condition affecting only unfortunate individuals. I would like to emphasize again that anxiety is a life-long challenge. The tragedy of Brown is that his anxiety, which was severe enough at times to remove almost all possibilities from his existence, is mainly destructive and paralyzing rather than challenging and enlivening. I hope the reader will keep in mind the *essential humanness* of anxiety.

(1) *Relation between Fears and Anxiety*

How anxiety relates to fear is illustrated in the phenomenon of the cancer dread. This appeared as a specific, "realistic" fear, clung to by Brown with all sorts of arguments. But it was later demonstrated to be an objectivated manifestation of underlying neurotic anxiety.[11]

(2) *Conflict Underlying Neurotic Anxiety*

I have proposed that his anxiety rose out of his symbiotic relation with his mother. This relationship was characterized by a conflict between his own needs to achieve some autonomy and use of his own powers and the conviction that if he *did* appropriate his own power he would be subject to the dire threat of being killed by his mother. Consequently his behavior was characterized by passivity, a subordination of himself to others (prototypically his mother), and a need to have others take care of him. At the same time he experienced overwhelming feelings of inadequacy and helplessness. Severe anxiety ensued whenever this conflict was activated.

In theory one might assume that there would be no conflict if he simply subordinated himself to his mother's power and forgot about his own autonomy. Such a prospect only increased his feelings of worthlessness and inadequacy. Whether any human being could permanently surrender his own autonomy to someone else and thus avoid conflict is very much open to doubt.

It might be added that the progress of this patient toward overcoming his anxiety neurosis was characterized by development on three flanks: (1) a gradual clarification of the previously unconscious mother relation; (2) a renunciation of the excessive aspects of his ambition (which had previously shown themselves in perfectionistic academic striving); and (3) a gradual growth in, and experiencing of, his capacity to use his own strength without thereafter feeling threatened. This account of the direction of his development is grossly oversimplified, but at least it may illustrate how the two sides of his conflict were relieved more or less simultaneously.

(3) *Relation between Hostility and Anxiety*

This relation is illustrated in that the above conflict (and concomitant anxiety) was greatly abetted by his repressed hostility toward his mother. Speaking more specifically, we noted the relation between hostility and anxiety in the fact that when Brown was in relatively greater anxiety, he exhibited increased hostility (covert or overt); and when his anxiety abated, his hostile feelings did likewise.

(4) *Symptoms and Anxiety*

The symptom of dizziness (a psychosomatic symptom) and the fear of cancer (a psychological symptom) appeared as the first step in the progression of unconscious anxiety into awareness. These symptoms disappeared as the anxiety became conscious. This is in accord with the contention advanced earlier in this study that the presence of symptoms bears an inverse relation to conscious anxiety. The function of these symptoms is *to protect the person from the anxiety-creating situation—i.e., any situation which will cue off his conflict.* This can be seen when we consider that if this young man really *had* cancer or an organic injury, his conflict would be relieved in several respects: (a) he could remain in a dependent role (such as being hospitalized) without guilt feelings; (b) he could avoid having to undertake tasks for which he felt inadequate; and (c) he could get even with his mother by requiring her to support him during the illness.

(5) *Severe Anxiety and Impoverishment of Personality*

This relation is seen in a comparison of the two Rorschachs, which I wish briefly to repeat. The one taken when Harold Brown was in anxiety is characterized by meager productivity, vagueness, no originality, and a blockage both of "inner" activity and the capacity to respond to emotional stimuli from the outside. The Rorschach taken when Brown was relatively free from anxiety shows much greater productivity, radically increased capacity to deal with concrete realities, a fair degree of originality, and greatly increased "inner" activity as well as increased emotional responsiveness to things and persons in his world.[12]

CHAPTER
9

The Study of
Unmarried Mothers

It is very suggestive too that the first anxiety state arose on the occasion of the separation from the mother.

—Sigmund Freud

These thirteen cases comprise a study, made by myself, of anxiety as found in unmarried mothers at Walnut House, a shelter in New York City.[1] I chose that particular group because I wanted to study persons who were in a *crisis situation*. My presupposition was that, when an individual is in a crisis situation, the dynamics of individual behavior are more accessible to study than in so-called "normal" situations.

Since I believe there may be damaging effects in inducing anxiety in the experimental laboratory, I took what may be called "nature's experiments" for study. The condition of extramarital pregnancy was presumably an anxiety-creating situation in that period in our society.

Furthermore, I believed that it would be useful to study a group of which all the members were in the same anxiety-creating situation. The possibility, which I considered, of presenting a number of cases from my own therapeutic practice, like that of Brown, I therefore rejected in favor of investigating a group of persons all presumably in the same crisis situation.

It should be emphasized that I am *not* concerned in this study with investigating the relation between extramarital pregnancy and anxiety.[2] In theory, another anxiety-creating situation might have served my purpose just as well. The Russian psychologist A. R. Luria selected criminals in jail and students at the time of crucial examinations for his study of psychological conflict. The important point is that it be a crisis situation sufficient to bring the person's buried patterns into the open. Furthermore, I am accepting the presupposition that when an individual is in an anxiety-creating situation, his or her anxiety reactions are not only specifically related to that particular situation but also reveal a pattern which is characteristic of that particular individual and would be revealed by him or her in other anxiety-creating situations. As will be seen in the actual case studies, the data that emerge in the study of these young women have to do with *anxiety and competitive ambition, anxiety in phobial patterns, anxiety related to hostility and aggression, anxiety connected with various inner conflicts,* and other forms of anxiety which have very little, if anything, to do specifically with the condition of extramarital pregnancy as such. Most of these patterns of anxiety could be as applicable to businessmen, university professors, students, housewives, and other groups in our society.

I am assuming that the more intensively we study a given individual, the more we tend to uncover patterns which this individual holds in common with other persons in other groups in the society. That is to say, the more intensively we study one man or woman, the more we arrive at data which lie below individual differences and the more, therefore, we arrive at data which are applicable to human beings in general.[3]

METHODS USED

A variety of techniques of collecting data were employed in the case studies of unmarried mothers. The methods of gaining information directly from the young women consisted of personal interviews, Rorschachs (one Rorschach was given to every girl before parturition, and second Rorschachs were administered to five girls after parturition), and anxiety check-lists. I had from four to eight one-hour personal interviews with each young woman. The social workers had from a score to two score of personal interviews with each one. While these interviews were not geared specifically to the purposes of this study, they yielded a wealth of pertinent data concerning the young woman's attitudes, behavior, and background.[4] Three check-lists—to be checked by the young woman— were employed. The first was designed to elicit the foci of anxiety which the girl remembered from her childhood, the second to elicit foci of anxiety in her present state of pregnancy, and the third (administered after parturition) to elicit foci of anxiety as she faced her problems after the birth of the baby.[5] Observations of the young woman's behavior in Walnut House were contributed by the nurses and other personnel of the house as well as by the social workers. A great amount of collateral data was also available, such as the report of the medical examinations of each woman, psychometric examinations where deemed necessary, reports from her school or college, and, in most of the cases, objective data on her home background gained through other social agencies. In more than half the cases, the parents and relatives of the young woman were also interviewed by the social workers at Walnut House.

The *scoring* of each Rorschach, done originally by me, was checked independently by a Rorschach specialist. My *interpretation* (as distinguished from scoring) of each Rorschach was checked by Dr. Bruno Klopfer, who also rated each Rorschach according to *depth* and *width* of anxiety, as well as to the effectiveness of the subject's *handling* of the anxiety.[6] One purpose of the check-lists was to gain additional data on the amount of the young woman's anxiety (i.e., number of items checked). In the purely quantitative ranking, a check in the "often" column (indicating the girl believed she "often" had that item of anxiety) was given double the weight of a check in the "sometimes" column. But a second purpose (and, as it turned out, the more useful one) of the check-lists was to gain information on the *kinds* (or *areas*) of anxiety the girl experienced. For this purpose the items of the check-lists were classified in five categories: (1) apprehensions of a phobial nature; (2) the girl's anxiety about what her family thought of her; (3) anxiety about what her peers thought of her; (4) anxiety in the area of ambition—e.g., success or failure in work or school; (5) miscellaneous.[7] An almost unlimited number of data are available in each case study of this sort, data which are neither quantitatively nor qualitatively parallel. In the light of all the data in each case, I endeavored to see each young woman in three dimensions: *structurally*, chiefly by means of the Rorschach; *behaviorally*, or the person's present behavior; and *genetically*, or the developmental dimension, an important aspect of which was the childhood background. Using these three dimensions, I sought to arrive at a conceptualization of each case, or a *picture of the constellation* of each personality. The quantities and qualities of anxiety in each case are integral parts of this constellation. It was necessary, then, to relate the anxiety in each case to other elements in the constellation, such as the rejection each young woman experienced in her relation with her parents. To expedite this interrelating process, each subject was ranked by me as to the degree of anxiety and the degree of rejection in one of four categories: high, moderately high, moderately low, and low. These rankings are based on all the data available and also upon the judgments, independently arrived at, of the investigator and the social workers.[8]

The central criterion of the validity of the conceptualization of each case, as well as a sound estimate and understanding of the anxiety, is *internal consistency*.[9] I continually asked, for example: Do the data arrived at by the various methods (interviews, Rorschachs, check-lists) exhibit *inner consistency within the framework of the conceptualization of the case?* And is inner consistency shown in the conceptualization from the structural, behavioral, and genetic aspects of each case? Likewise, if the anxiety has been correctly assessed, it should show inner consistency with the other elements in the constellation of each personality.

I may say that in my judgment the data from the different sources did, by and large, make a consistent picture, with the one exception of the quantities of anxiety on the check-lists. The reasons that this item was at times at odds with an otherwise consistent picture are noted in the case discussions.

Some of the following cases, through which it was desired to illustrate or demonstrate only one or two points, are presented only briefly. As frequently as practicable, the subject's own words are given. In the face of the great mass of data about each person, some selection in presentation was obviously necessary. I hope that enough of each case is presented to make evident the conceptualization of the case and to clarify the points we desire to illustrate. Although the Rorschach numerical scores are given, it is understood that the configuration in each Rorschach is more crucial for its interpretation than the numerical scoring. Unless otherwise stated, the parents in each case were white, American, and Protestant.

HELEN: INTELLECTUALIZING AS A DEFENSE AGAINST ANXIETY

On arrival at Walnut House, Helen walked into the office smoking a cigarette, appearing poised and nonchalant. Somewhat attractive, she exuded the vitality of a person who cultivates her spontaneity. The impression she created in the first interview was a snapshot of aspects of her behavior which later proved to be of considerable significance.

On her own initiative she stated immediately that she had no guilt feeling whatever about her pregnancy. She volunteered the information that she had lived with two different men since arriving in New York, asserting in the same breath that "only priggish people have any feelings about such matters." But there were indications of anxiety and tension beneath her ostensibly friendly and free manner of talking—during her frequent breezy laughter, her eyes remained dilated, giving the appearance of some fright even while she laughed. Helen created the immediate impression both to the social worker in her interview and me that she was employing her evasive, laugh-it-off techniques in order to cover over some anxiety, the nature of which was not yet apparent.

She was the twenty-two-year-old daughter of middle-class, Catholic parents, her father being of Italian extraction. Because of her father's erratic work habits during her childhood, the family had alternated between being well off and enduring straitened financial conditions. Helen had attended parochial schools and a Catholic college for two years, but at the present time she felt she had emancipated herself from the religious aspects of her background. There were two siblings, a brother a year older and a sister two years younger, with whom Helen had close and affectionate relationships. She informed me that the three children had learned to stick together because their parents quarreled so much. Her parents had been divorced when she was eleven and had both remarried. She had lived intermittently with one and then the other, having to leave the father at one time because her stepmother was "jealous of my being more attractive," and having to leave the mother because the stepfather, and later the mother's lovers, made advances to her.

Her two years at college had been on a scholarship, where she had done brilliant but erratic academic work. Since leaving college she had held routine jobs such as operating mimeograph machines. Because of boredom she would quit her job every two or three months, "and then is when I would get into difficulty"—i.e., she would live with a man. Her hope was to write radio scripts. The sample scripts she had written which she showed me seemed to be very good technically but artificial in content and lacking in genuine feeling.

Two years earlier she had come to New York with an unmarried aunt two years her senior, with whom she had a very affectionate relationship. The aunt was also now pregnant and had gone to another city. Helen commented, "She has made a mess of her life too." The father of Helen's baby, the second man with whom she had shared an apartment since coming to New York, was a member of the merchant marine. Though she described him as an intelligent person whom she had liked, she had experienced a profound revulsion toward him after she discovered she was pregnant and had broken off all contact with him. Helen's medical examination was negative; she was described as "nervous and high-strung" and was placed by the psychiatrist on a daily dose of phenobarbital.

The most immediate focus of Helen's anxiety seemed to be her pregnancy and impending parturition. This, with its related defenses of intellectualizing, laughing-it-off, and evasion, was evidenced not only in our interviews with her but in her behavior with the other young women in the house. She regularly refused to discuss her pregnancy with the social worker, insisting, "It just seems to me I'm not pregnant, and until the baby is born I refuse to give it a thought." But it was observed that she spent a great deal of time discussing pregnancy in an intellectualized, quasi-scientific manner with the others in the house. She described to them the fetus at various stages in its development as though she were talking from a scientific manual. One day she received a letter from her aunt, telling of the latter's having gone to the hospital for parturition; Helen reacted with a fit of hysterical weeping. It was evident that she displaced much of her own anxiety about parturition on the aunt, but when the social worker pointed this out, Helen still refused to talk about her own pregnancy.

When I indicated that her Rorschach suggested she felt anxious about going to the hospital for the birth, Helen replied:

> No, I haven't the slightest fear. In the event of death or making provision for the baby to be taken care of, I just think, "how dramatic!" But the girls around here are always telling hideous stories of births. They tell of doctors standing over them in the hospital and all the details. They tell terrible stories of women screaming. They tell of Caesarean and forceps births, and they say, "You're just the one to have one." They tell a lot of old wives' tales about every heart-throb giving the baby a mark. They go around feeling each other's stomachs; they want to feel mine but I won't let them. I won't even feel it myself. (Her hands had been folded on her abdomen; at this point she violently jerked them away.) I guess the fact that I'm not afraid shows in the fact that I'm so impatient to go to the hospital. I'm willing to suffer the punishments of the damned to get it over quickly.

The reader will agree, I assume, that this speech, combining emphases on catastrophe and urgency, reveals a very frightened person. It suggests the typical picture of someone whistling in the dark, putting up a front of dramatic bravado toward the prospect she dreads most. This reminds us of the observation of R. R. Grinker and S. P. Spiegel in *Men under Stress*, that the anxious airman would be the first to get himself into the air and into a situation of danger, the danger itself being less painful than the anticipation of it.

Helen's bravado and laughing-it-off techniques of allaying anxiety were so well developed that they were carried right up to parturition itself: on departing for the hospital she left a note for me, "I'm off to get myself a new figure."

The obstetrician reported that her last words before going under ether were, "This has got to be adoptable material."

The chief facts that stood out in Helen's description of her childhood were the violent quarrels of her parents, the frequent periods of upheaval in the family group (parental divorce, conflict with stepparents, etc.), and Helen's testimony to her considerable loneliness as a child. There was evidence for much outright rejection of her, as well as of the other children, by her father. She recalled that his regular practice was to deposit the children at the movies all day while he played golf. He would then come home drunk, and a quarrel between the parents would ensue.

Her present attitude toward her mother was one of pity, with resentment at her mother's "disloyalty" toward her. This "loyalty" had been felt by Helen since she was fifteen, when she and her mother had begun to quarrel violently. Her reasons for thinking her mother disloyal were (a) the mother's ill-considered love affairs; (b) the fact that the mother now permitted the sister to have more influence over her than Helen; and (c) the fact that her mother had served a short prison sentence for involvement in some minor crime. This is another aspect of the contradiction in Helen over guilt feeling and moral standards: she held her mother responsible for infractions which apparently have a moral character despite her protest that she and her mother were entirely emancipated from moral standards.

It is difficult to determine with any clarity Helen's attitude toward her mother during early childhood. She speaks of being "excessively devoted" to her mother as a child, but it was my impression that this "devotion" was really a construct from the fact that at that age Helen was considered the favorite child by the mother. Definite indications of hostility and resentment toward both parents, and especially the mother, were present in Helen's Rorschach and in the interviews. One such response on the Rorschach was "children scaring their parents to death," and another was "Brownies with round bellies laughing with great pleasure because they have just pulled a hot joke, messing up the housewife's floor." This last response suggests that her pregnancy is associated with aggression against her mother. The hostile, aggressive elements in both these responses were omitted in the Rorschach after parturition, the Brownies now specifically described by Helen as *"wistful, not malicious."* Likewise the aggression and hostility toward her parents, especially toward her mother, diminished after parturition. Several hypotheses suggest themselves: she was more anxious before parturition and, therefore, felt more hostility and aggression, or she employed the pregnancy as a weapon against the parents and after birth this weapon could be discarded. Finally, she may have held them in some way responsible for her being in this difficult state of pregnancy.

The above motif of "disloyalty," quite apart from its content, implies strong disappointment with, and resentment toward, her mother. Since the objective data indicate that her mother was a very unstable, inconsistent, and emotionally immature person, the hypothesis is justified that Helen experienced considerable rejection in her early as well as her later relations with her mother. This rejection probably was all the more painful and psychologically significant for Helen because of her having been at the same time the "favorite" child. We placed Helen in the *moderately high* category with respect to rejection by her parents.

Helen's Rorschach indicated superior intellectual capacity but uneven performance, much originality and variety of interest, much emotional responsiveness but of an impulse variety and unintegrated with her intellectual functions.[10] Her emotional responsiveness was regularly experienced as disturbing and upsetting to her rational control. Her response to several of the colored cards, "muddy, turbid waters," was an apt description of how she viewed her emotional responsiveness when she could not control it intellectually. Anxiety signs were slight shading shock (connected in part with sexual problems), a large number of diffusion responses, and intermittent vagueness and evasiveness. The Whole compulsion (66 per cent) in this record is not only indicative of evasiveness as a symptom of anxiety, but also of intellectual ambition. It was the record of a "bright" person who must breeze through everything.

I find three main centers of anxiety in the content. First, social disapproval and guilt feeling; second, competitive ambition; and third, her pregnancy and impending trip to the hospital for parturition. Her anxiety was, in general, of the unsystematized, intermittent kind. It was deeply disturbing, but she was able to recover from it quickly. Her chief methods of dealing with this dread were intellectualizing, "laughing-it-off," denial, and evasion.[11] We rated her with respect to anxiety on the Rorschach: depth 4, width 2, handling 2. This placed her in the *moderately high* category of anxiety in rank with the other girls. Her childhood anxiety check-list ranks in the high category with respect to quantity of anxiety, the chief areas of anxiety being *ambition,* and what *her friends* and *her family* thought of her, in that order.

Let us first discuss Helen's anxiety as it focused on her *pregnancy and impending trip to the hospital* for the birth of the baby. She showed considerable anxiety in six responses of "X-rays" and "medical illustrations" on her Rorschach. We may conclude that this is anxiety attached to her anticipation of parturition since in her second Rorschach, after parturition, these responses are almost entirely omitted and since she herself makes the association of these responses with her pregnancy. She apologized after three of these responses with the phrase, "Sorry, it must be my condition." One such response was associated with an erupting volcano (presumably a birth symbol), which so disturbed her that the following response was markedly distorted. It is important to note that these anxiety responses are intellectualized—i.e., given a "scientific" content. The responses were regularly accompanied by forced, tense laughter and remarks of evasion and denial ("I shouldn't know about these—I never read medical books").

With respect to the problem of defining Helen's "fear" of parturition, it might be argued that it was a "real" fear, or normal anxiety, since her anticipated labor might involve suffering. But several things argue against this easy conclusion. One is that her apprehension was greatly out of proportion to that of the other girls in similar situations. Certainly, the reports from the girls returning from the hospitals, where parturition was handled with modern expertness, gave no basis for such intense apprehension or for her emphasis on the possible horrors of birth in her speech quoted above. Another is that this fear was consciously denied.[12] We recall the opening sentences of her first speech, "No, I haven't the slightest fear. In the event of death or making provision for the baby to be taken care of, I just think, 'how dramatic!'" This conscious denial removes it from the category of real fears. I here term it a *neurotic fear*. We shall discuss below the evidence for believing that this fear was a focus for neurotic anxiety. What the meaning of this fear was, and why her anxiety should be attached to this particular focal point and not another, are questions which can be answered only on the basis of further understanding of other aspects of Helen's anxiety pattern; they will be discussed below.

Another prominent area of Helen's anxiety, which we mentioned earlier, was *social disapproval and guilt feeling*. We are immediately struck by her contradictory statements with regard to guilt feeling: her interviews were filled both with indications of strong guilt feeling and with verbal denials of this very guilt feeling. She felt that people on the street were looking at her as if to say, "Go home, don't have your baby in public." She would like to "crawl into a hole till after the baby comes." A newspaperman friend wished to visit her at Walnut House, but she couldn't "bear to have him see me in my shame." But at the same time she made strenuous efforts to cover up this guilt feeling. This was evidenced in the very first interview, when without the question being raised Helen needed to state emphatically that she had no guilt feelings whatever, which suggests the mechanism described in Shakespeare's words, "The lady doth protest too much, methinks."

On the Rorschach some of the guilt feeling was connected with sex: on Card VI, which generally elicits a sexual response, there was more nervous laughter than usual, and she paused for long periods after each response saying, "It looks like something else I can't get." The final response in this card was a vista of a woman in an idolatrous shrine, which suggests that Helen was not as emancipated from her religious background as she would believe. But most of her guilt feeling and concomitant anxiety seemed to be connected with what people thought of her: after a response "two old maids pointing and gossiping about the pretty widow," she gave one of her typical anxiety responses related to her pregnancy. On the childhood anxiety check-list, anxiety related to disapproval by her peers was second, and anxiety related to disapproval by her family was third in quantity. The same mechanisms which she employed to allay anxiety were used for allaying guilt feelings: a blasé, laugh-it-off attitude and an endeavor to intellectualize and depersonalize the issue of guilt (e.g., "My mother and I are *un*moral, not immoral").

Helen's anxiety about social disapproval and guilt merged into her competitive feelings. Often her remarks indicated an association between being disapproved of, being guilty, and losing her competitive standing and power with family and friends. She was adamant that her family not know of her pregnancy, for inasmuch as they had held such high hopes for her, they would be hurt and humiliated. In the next breath, however, she explained that she did not want them to have the "satisfaction of knowing that this had happened to her"; she wanted them to continue thinking she was a big success in New York, and she wished to buy a "splendid outfit" and go home and surprise them (which suggests competitive feelings). This same connection between guilt and loss of power and prestige was evidenced in her attitudes toward her friends. The father of the baby must not know of her pregnancy, for he would take fiendish delight in telling all her friends and humiliating her. On her childhood anxiety check-list she indicated strong anxiety lest people ridicule or make fun of her. Underlying her fear of ridicule in these varied contexts seems to be a formulation like the following: "If others have cause for disapproving of me, they will humiliate [demote] me and I will lose my power and prestige."

A similar merging of guilt and competitive feelings was evidenced in her numerous remarks of self-deprecation in the interviews. At the outset of the Rorschach she coyly warned that she never did well on tests; then she proceeded to throw herself into the endeavor to produce a superior record. On the whole, the many self-deprecatory remarks of Helen were partly an expression of guilt, and partly a way of disarming others and covering up her competitive striving so that her eventual success would be the more noticeable.

We now consider *competitive ambition* as such, the final and in many respects the most pronounced area of Helen's anxiety. In contrast to her denial of apprehension in the areas of parturition and feeling, Helen consciously admitted that competitive ambition was a source of pronounced anxiety for her. The highest score on her childhood anxiety check-list was for anxiety in the area of success and failure in school and work. She was unwilling merely to check "often" for her anxiety about "failing a

test in school" or "not being a success," but added several
exclamation points for special emphasis. Competitive ambition in intellectualized form was shown in the Rorschach
not only in the "whole compulsion" but also in her strain-
ing herself to the limit, which she rationalized by misinter-
preting my directions ("You told me to give all I could").
Other evidence of this competitive ambition, in the social
worker's judgment, is that Helen sought to impress her
with the high intellectual talent of the groups in which
she moved in the city.

Helen was aware that her intense anxiety about competitive status inhibited her productivity: "I'm always worried about success," she remarked, "that's why I failed the
newspaper typing test last night." Though her competitiveness chiefly assumed an intellectual expression, it carried
over into the area of physical attractiveness. The only
young woman in the house with whom Helen had difficulty
in relationship, a difficulty largely caused by rivalry, was
the one (Agnes) who by common consent was prettier than
Helen. But it is consistent with Helen's pattern that she
always hid this rivalry under a façade of casual poise (in
itself a subtle way of asserting superiority).

It is not difficult to see why Helen chose an intellectual
sphere as the chief area for the exercise of her competitive
ambition. As a child she was precocious in school; her
family had rewarded her with considerable prestige for
her academic successes. In periods of emotional insecurity
in the family—caused chiefly by violent quarrels between
the parents—Helen was able, even as a child, to assume
leadership and exercise control over her parents because
they recognized her as the "bright one" in the family. Apparently from her early childhood onward her intellectual
capacities had been rewarded not only as a method of gaining competitive prestige but also specifically as a means
of controlling and ameliorating anxiety-creating situations.

In a person as competitive as Helen, we should expect
to find strong needs to remain independent and detached
from other people; one has to remain detached in order
to triumph *over* others, and to be absorbed in a close
relationship would, therefore, be a threat to a security device. There was evidence that Helen had this need for
detachment. She regarded marriage as a "ball and chain,"
and asked rhetorically, "What is the matter with me that

I feel repelled by a man as soon as he proposes marriage?"
She felt the present man would interpret the pregnancy,
if he should hear of it, as a sign that he had "caught" her
and use it as an additional argument for marriage. Another indication of her strong needs to appear independent
and not beholden to anyone is seen in the fact that she
refused to accept money from Walnut House for her personal necessities, even though she let it be known that
she was in need.

Our over-all ranking for Helen's degree of anxiety was
moderately high. Her ranking for rejection by her parents
was likewise *moderately high*.

The *methods of avoiding anxiety* illustrated in the case
of Helen deserve further discussion. We have seen that
these methods included laughing-it-off behavior, evasion
and outright denial, which might be termed an "ostrich"
pattern of behavior toward anxiety, and intellectualizing.
If these are Helen's chief methods of avoiding anxiety,
two conditions should be demonstrable. First, it should
be true that when her anxiety is relatively greater, these
avoidance forms of behavior should be more in evidence;
and second, when the anxiety subsides, the avoidance behavior mechanisms should abate. In other words, the
more the subject experiences anxiety, the more the mechanisms for avoiding are called into play, and vice versa.

Both of these conditions were demonstrable in Helen.
We have observed above that at the points in the first
Rorschach where Helen showed anxiety, she also exhibited
more forced laughter, evasion, and intellectualization. In
the second, post-parturition Rorschach, in which there
was less anxiety largely because the anxiety responses related to parturition were almost entirely omitted,[13] the
behavior mechanisms for avoiding anxiety abated accord-
ingly. Intellectualizing and forced laughter were considerably lessened in the second record. The whole compulsion
was reduced from 66 per cent to 47 per cent, and the responses to specific details were considerably increased,
indicating less evasiveness. This relaxing of the whole compulsion also may be taken to indicate that she is now less
pushed to exercise her intellectual ambition. This suggests
that her intellectual ambition takes a compulsive form,
that it is used for purposes of allaying anxiety ("If I can

be intellectually successful, I will not be anxious"), and therefore it abates when the anxiety does.

It is fascinating to note that Helen's techniques of denying anxiety and at the same time intellectualizing it are logically contradictory. Helen's pattern, as shown especially in her valiant endeavor to avoid the anxiety focusing on pregnancy and parturition, might be formulated as follows: "If I deny the anxiety, it will not be there," and at the same time, "If I wave the wand of 'scientific' knowledge, the anxiety will vanish." The former was an outright endeavor to repress the anxiety. As Sullivan has pointed out, individuals have varying levels of awareness, of which conscious awareness is only one, albeit the most complete kind of awareness. In studying patients with anxiety, a phenomenon like Helen's is often observable; the persons do not consciously admit the anxiety, but *behave* in all sorts of ways as though they were aware of it, which must mean they are aware of it on levels other than consciousness. On this "deeper" level Helen was aware of the anxiety, and this level was the base of the intellectualizing method of warding off anxiety (such as the "scientific" Rorschach responses and the quasi-scientific discussions with the young women). What both the outright denial and the intellectualizing had in common was evasion of an emotional reality.

Helen's methods of avoiding anxiety are *typical of a trend in our culture*. To me, Helen's pattern is illustrative of what has previously been discussed in this book (Chapter 2) as a dominant pattern in modern Western culture with respect to both sources of anxiety and methods of avoiding anxiety. We have noted in Helen a dichotomy between emotion and intellectual functions, with an endeavor to control her emotions intellectually; and when this control was ineffective (e.g., when she became emotionally involved in her Rorschach responses), she became upset. It is a curious training formula in our culture—to be involved is to be upset. We have earlier discussed the tendency in our society to deny anxiety because it seems to be "irrational." It is highly significant, in this regard, that the two most important aspects of her emotions—anxiety and guilt feeling—she emphatically denied. The denial and the intellectualizing were both parts of the same pattern with Helen, as we have submitted they are in our culture; if the anxiety and guilt cannot be denied, it must be rationalized; and to the extent that it cannot be rationalized, it must be denied.[14] The admission of anxiety about parturition would be both a confession of failure for Helen (the scientific "wand" should be able to dispel the anxiety) and would also be a severe threat to a security device. Likewise the admission of guilt feelings about pregnancy would imply to Helen a failure to have become intellectually "emancipated." The earlier discussions in this study have been concerned with the repression and denial of anxiety because of its seeming irrationality. I now propose that the repression of guilt feeling falls in the same category and is likewise a tendency in our culture.

Helen is also typical of our culture in that the one area of anxiety which she could consciously and freely admit was that of success and failure. Apparently she had learned, in her school experience among other places, that it is acceptable and respectable to compete and to admit one's anxiety about the outcome of that competition.

We now raise the interesting question: Why was Helen afraid of parturition? I submit that *this neurotic fear is a focus for anxiety which arose from her repressed guilt feeling about the pregnancy.* Her phrases such as "suffering the punishments of the damned" in childbirth and the association of "dying" with parturition, bring into the picture both her guilt feeling (being "damned") and the anticipation of punishment. It is as though a formulation, "I have done wrong, I will be punished," is in operation. It is well known that repressed guilt feeling gives rise to anxiety. I believe it is plausible to conclude that it is this anxiety in Helen which emerges in the exaggerated fear of parturition.

But why did her anxiety focus on parturition and not elsewhere? I propose that anxiety clustered around parturition because that was the point at which her habitual anxiety defenses were unavailing. Despite her endeavors to think that she was not even pregnant ("It seems to me I am not pregnant until the baby is born"), one's fat stomach—to go back to her Brownies—cannot be wholly denied short of more serious psychological deterioration than Helen's state. It was clear, even to her, that her abdomen was enlarged whether she would permit herself to feel it or not. Birth is an experience in which there is bound to be feeling and emotion; and hence parturition was a point at which her intellectualizing and suppressing feeling would not be effective, and her defenses would dramatically collapse in a heap.

NANCY: EXPECTATIONS AT WAR WITH REALITY

The mother of Nancy (age nineteen) had divorced her father, a chauffeur, when Nancy was two, and two years later had married a musician whom Nancy described as "very intelligent, like my mother." Until the age of twelve Nancy had lived with her mother and stepfather in an upper-middle-class suburb, the cultural level of which, as well as the "good home we had and the good upbringing I received during that period," were greatly prized by Nancy. When she was sixteen, her mother separated from the stepfather, which unstable behavior Nancy described as "too much for me." She then left her mother and school, having completed the ninth grade, and went to work as a clerk, then as a cashier, and later as a milliner. Nancy's friends, her work, and that part of her background with which she identifies place her in the middle class.

Because of her loneliness in living in New York rather than "love" or sexual interest, she explained, she had accepted the relationship with the young man who was the baby's father. Through him she had met another young man with whom she had fallen in love and to whom she was now engaged. The college education and good family standing of her fiancé, his father being a member of a university faculty, were very important to Nancy. The fiancé knew of her pregnancy and apparently accepted it with understanding, expressing his willingness that they keep the baby as their own after their marriage. Nancy, however, had decided to give the baby up for adoption.

Nancy impressed almost everyone at Walnut House as a well-adjusted, very responsible, conscientious, and considerate person, with a marked capacity for avoiding conflict in her personal relations. She was described by a social worker as "one of the nicest girls we have ever had at Walnut House." Physically and socially attractive, she had cultivated an educated bearing, and in the first interviews she seemed poised and uninhibited, with no apparent indications of the pervasive anxiety we were later to discover.

It became clear in Nancy's behavior and in my interviews with her that her security, and consequently her ability to keep anxiety at bay, depended almost entirely on whether she could convince herself that other people accepted her. She was intensely worried about whether her fiancé's parents would continue to like her, and tried constantly to reassure herself by the fact that they seemed to like her now. Her continual reference to them, as to most people she admired, was, "They are such nice people, and they like me." She searched the letters from her fiancé for assurances that he still loved her. It was only by the security she found in him, she emphasized, that she could go through her present difficulties: "If anything went wrong with his love for me, I'd break down completely." The criterion of whether the fiancé, or anyone else for that matter, loved her was whether he could be *depended upon,* as her mother and her first boy friend could not be, but as she believed her fiancé could be.

Though Nancy had amicable relations with everyone, she stated that she was very cautious in choosing real girl friends, for "most girls can't be depended upon to help you." She never brought up any references to her own feelings which would indicate affective, outgoing responses to these other people who were so important to her. Her own emotional response, even to her fiancé, seemed not to enter the picture, her only reference being the general statement that she loved him. The important point for her was not how she felt toward the other but whether the other person "loved" *her*—by which she meant a condition in which the other would not reject her. *Thus "love" for Nancy was essentially a security device by which she could keep anxiety at bay.*

Her behavior was a revelation of expertly devised means of placating others and keeping them in a benevolent attitude toward her. She apologized effusively when she was late for an interview and showed excessive gratitude when anyone helped her. In one interview with the social worker, Nancy, in trying to avoid discussing her childhood, made a remark that was only in the most minor way aggressive: but she made a special visit to the social worker's office the next day in considerable anxiety to ask whether the social worker had been offended. She never permitted herself outbursts toward other people, even toward her stepfather, who apparently had often given her just cause. "You have to live with people" was Nancy's formula, "so you might as well get along with them."

Her repeated statements that loneliness was her motivation for making love and having sexual relations with the first boy friend now make sense in the respect that sexual activity was a way of placating him and thereby holding him. She was upset by the need to deceive anyone. She stated several times that she hoped she could some day tell her prospective mother-in-law about the pregnancy—though this was certainly not an objective problem at the moment—because she hated to have that deceit between them. As an adolescent she had often been given money by her stepfather for her personal needs; she could never keep this fact from her mother despite the fact that she knew her mother would then take the money from her to spend on liquor. All of the above indications give us a picture of Nancy as a person to whom any rejection is a profound threat, and who must, therefore, placate other people at all costs. Her interpersonal security was so tenuous that the slightest ill will, aggression, discord, or deceit, however justified, would destroy it, and unmanageable anxiety would ensue.

Her conscientiousness in her work, as we shall see, on her Rorschach, was a method of buying acceptance. Though Nancy had never had any problems in getting and retaining jobs in the workaday world, she had always been anxious about her work, feeling she would be discharged if she did not keep constantly alert. "There's always someone to take your place if you don't keep on your toes." This repeated phrase "keeping on your toes" is a very apt expression for this type of anxiety, in which the individual feels that disaster can be avoided only by remaining perpetually in a state of tense balance.

We now inquire into the sources of this anxiety pattern in Nancy's childhood. The following memories piece together a picture of a child who was clung to by the mother but at the same time severely rejected. Nancy reported (on the basis of information she had received from an aunt) that it had been the mother's practice frequently to leave her alone in the house before the divorce, when Nancy was two, as well as after the separation from Nancy's father. One of Nancy's earliest memories, dating from about the age of three, was of her father kidnapping her from her mother's house when she had been left alone. In the ensuing taxi ride to the father's house, Nancy had cried violently for her mother. Later, the mother came with a policeman to get her back. Nancy related a variety of other early memories all of which had these elements: (a) the mother had left Nancy alone; (b) not having proper supervision, Nancy would get hurt (e.g., fall down the cellar steps); and (c) the mother would come home but be "unconcerned." Nancy's explanation was, "My mother cared more about going out to bars than having children."

Apparently this rejection of the child continued, though on a somewhat diminished scale, after the mother remarried. The subsequent period, when "we had a good home in the suburbs," is emphasized by Nancy as a kind of Garden of Eden period of happy childhood. In her interpretation of her background, she dates her real misfortunes from the time of their losing this house when she was twelve.

> After that my mother became unsteady, and she and my stepfather began to go out to bars all the time. They'd take me sometimes, but I didn't like that. Sometimes they wouldn't come home all night. They'd leave a girl with me, of course, but I'd wake up in the morning and not find them there. That's not right. . . . I'd worry for fear something had happened to them. Then, when I got to be sixteen, my mother really did go bad.

Nancy was not condemning toward her mother in a moral sense, but only in the sense that the mother could not then be depended upon. Nancy would not tell what the "going bad" consisted of. At that point in the interview she reverted to reminiscence, "But she was such a *good* mother in the suburbs."

Nancy intensely disliked talking about her childhood, a discomfort which was shown in inordinate smoking and in her stating that such conversation made her "nervous," which embarrassed her. She remarked that she could remember the events but not the feelings and added, "That's strange—the way I seemed to want my mother as a child, you'd think I would remember the feelings about her." She exhibited a need not only to block off the affect connected with these childhood rejections themselves but also to block off the immediate affect in telling about the events. The fact that she had shown emotional involvement, "nervousness," in telling of these childhood rejections very much upset her. During the subsequent two interviews she remained carefully poised and exhibited an unspoken determination not to display any emotional involvement again.

It will already be evident to the reader that there was a patent contradiction in Nancy's description of her childhood. This contradiction, consisting of conflicting attitudes toward her mother, was of fundamental importance. On one hand there was the actual fact that Nancy felt, with considerable basis in reality, that she was rejected as a child, and that this rejection was exceedingly painful to her. But on the other hand there was her tendency to idealize her mother and parts of her background. In her recounting these memories, there emerged time and again the refrain about the "good home in the suburbs, with a little brown road leading up to it," and the accompanying assertion, "My mother was *such* a good mother then." I take the romanticized references to the "good home in the suburbs" as one symbol of her idealization of her relationship with her mother. When Nancy would approach some aspect of her childhood which was repugnant to her, she would interpolate as a vague but intense hope, "But my mother *could* have been such a good mother." This phrase sounded like the talisman of a primitive, an incantation with magical properties, an amulet to ward off evil.

So far as could be determined, her mother had left Nancy alone a good deal even during the period in the suburbs, though perhaps not as much as during the later and earlier periods. In any case, the supposition that her mother was "good" (in the sense of "stable") part of the time and "bad" the rest of the time does not make objective sense: that statement itself suggests profound inconsistency in the behavior of her mother. The conclusion seems justified that this motif of the "good" mother and the "happy" childhood period was brought in by Nancy because she could not bear to face the reality of her rejection by her mother and her feelings toward her mother. The fact that the recurrent refrain that the mother *could* have been good came up in the interviews whenever Nancy found the discussion of her early rejection too painful to continue supports the conclusion her idealization of her mother was used to cover up the reality of their actual relationship.

Nancy approached the Rorschach with the same over-conscientiousness, an attitude seeming to me to be an effort to buy acceptance. Her record showed an intelligent, original person with a marked anxiety neurosis of the type in which the "anxious attitude" toward life is accepted and so well systematized that it gives her the outward appearance of "success" in her personal relations.[15] The outstanding feature of the Rorschach was the very high proportion of responses using the tiny details (36). Indeed, her regular procedure was to go around the circumference of the blot, responding to each small detail as she went, but being careful to cling to the edge and avoiding any threat of losing her bearings by going into the larger areas of the blot itself. Figuratively, this is the picture of an individual who believes herself to be perpetually walking on the edge of a precipice and, therefore, must step very cautiously from stone to stone lest she fall. Nancy's behavior in the Rorschach corresponds to the behavior of Goldstein's patients who, in a much more pathological degree than Nancy, would write their names only in the very corner of the paper, any venture away from clear boundaries being too severe a threat. The content of these responses was chiefly faces, which suggests again that Nancy's anxiety was connected with a great concern with other people looking at her and what they thought of her.

The record indicated an isolated personality, with an almost complete absence of outgoing, affective response to other people. Though much "inner" activity was present, the instinctual aspects of inner promptings were subordinated. The Rorschach thus corroborated her statement that the motives for her sexual relations leading to the pregnancy were something other than "love" or sexual interest. In the few responses in the Rorschach in which she did become emotionally involved, the pattern of clinging to tiny details "lest she fall" was broken and considerable anxiety ensued. Thus one of the functions of the emotional constriction was to protect her from the anxiety-creating situation of emotional involvement with other persons. With the appearance of bright color in Card II, she is shocked into making one of her few whole responses, but it is a severely disturbed response, and she drops the card immediately for the next. A similar reaction, though not quite so pronounced, occurs with the appearance of the totally colored cards (VIII).

Much ambition was shown in the record, taking the form of compulsions to produce in quantity, to get everything in (as though she must cover all of experience by including every tiny detail), to produce perfectly, and to show originality. The perfectionism was partly a way of gaining security by sticking to details in which she could be meticulously accurate, but it was also an endeavor to gain acceptance and reassurance from the tester. Her ambition was not to gain power over others (like Helen's) but rather served as a way of getting acceptance—e.g., "If I do well, if I am 'interesting,' I will not be rejected." Her rating for anxiety on the Rorschach was: depth 3, width 5, handling, 1, which placed her highest among all the young women in this study.

Nancy filled out the anxiety check-lists with the same meticulous care for accuracy, pondering each item ("I don't like to check them unless I'm sure"), and returning to reconsider items and revise her checking. In quantity, she ranked in the high category on the childhood list, moderately high on the present list, and low on the future list. All three lists showed the chief areas of anxiety to be success and failure in work and what her peers thought of her.

A curious phenomenon was evidenced in her behavior in checking the lists, which may partially explain why the "future" anxiety list shows less quantity of anxiety than the other two. Every item of anxiety suggested on the lists threw Nancy into a dilemma, which she verbalized by saying she had thought a lot about the item in point. *It was very difficult for her to separate herself enough from her anxiety to know whether she was anxious about a given item or not.* Her criterion seemed to be: if she had been able to manage the suggested item of anxiety, she checked it as not a source of anxiety, despite the fact that her way of managing it generally involved obvious anxiety. The "future" anxieties had not yet proved unmanageable, and hence they would be less frequently checked.

As an over-all rating, we found in Nancy a *high* degree of anxiety. She illustrates one type of anxiety neurosis, characterized by the adoption of the "anxious attitude" toward life, so that practically everything she thought or did was motivated by anxiety. The goal of her behavior was not to *avoid* anxiety; rather, it was *to keep anxiety at bay*. She was characterized by continual foreboding and a constant endeavor to keep herself precariously balanced in her relations with people lest catastrophe (in Nancy's sense, rejection) should occur. *We can say that this is not a case of the person having anxiety, but of "anxiety having the person."*

It may seem confusing to make this distinction between *avoiding* anxiety and *keeping anxiety at bay*. But a real distinction is referred to—namely, the fact that in this type of anxiety neurosis the anxious attitude is so intimately a part of the individual's method of evaluating stimuli, of orienting herself or himself to every experience, that he or she cannot separate him- or herself enough from anxiety to comprehend the goal of avoidance of, or freedom from, anxiety. What Nancy sought was to be able to step cautiously from rock to rock without falling; the idea or possibility of not being on a precipice at all did not occur to her.

Her well-systematized methods of keeping anxiety at bay were, on the objective level, placating others, avoiding all discord, and doing conscientious work. The goals of these methods were to be accepted and to be "loved," in which state she was temporarily secure. These methods were eminently successful in the sense that she did get herself universally liked; but the security she achieved was very tentative, and she persistently expected that tomorrow she might be rejected.

On the subjective level, Nancy's methods of keeping anxiety at bay were to avoid emotional entanglements, to suppress the affect connected with her childhood rejection and anxiety, and to idealize anxiety-creating situations.[16] The method of avoiding emotional entanglements was not successful for Nancy, however, since she depended almost entirely for her security on what other people thought of her. This is a contradiction: you cannot avoid emotional entanglements on one hand and depend entirely on what other people think of you on the other.[17]

When all is said, it is notable that Nancy *had no effective subjective protections against anxiety-creating situations.* Her only protection against anxiety was to be anxious —i.e., to live continually "on her toes," and in a state of constant preparedness.

We find *a high degree of rejection by her mother* simultaneously present in Nancy with a high degree of anxiety. This rejection by her mother was not accepted as an objective reality. Rather, it was continually held in juxtaposition with idealized expectation about her mother, which we could see in the amulets Nancy repeated whenever she found herself in an anxiety-creating situation. Hence the rejection led to subjective conflict. The feelings of rejection and the idealization of the mother, opposites though they seem to be, reinforced each other. Feeling rejected, she yearned more strongly for an idealized acceptance by the mother; and having the idealized picture of what her mother "could" have been, her rejection was experienced as all the more painful. The feelings connected with her rejection then tended to be repressed and, therefore, increased.

Nancy's case is an illustration of the fact that what is significant about rejection, as a source of neurotic anxiety, is how it is interpreted by the child. In impact upon the child, there is a radical difference between rejection as an *objective* experience (which does not necessarily result in subjective conflict for the child), and rejection as a subjective experience. The important question psychologically is whether the child *felt himself or herself* rejected. That Nancy did feel herself greatly rejected is clear, though in actual fact she was objectively less rejected than some of the other girls discussed below (Louise, Bessie) who were not nearly so concerned subjectively about their rejection. My contention is that Nancy's *idealization of her mother is the essential element in understanding why she gave such a pronounced subjective weight to her rejection.*

The conflict underlying Nancy's neurotic anxiety may be described as arising from a *hiatus between expectations and reality.* The conflict was perpetuated in the form of an excessive need on one hand to depend on others (specifically, on their accepting, liking her) as her security device; but an underlying conviction on the other hand that other people were not dependable and would reject her. We have observed this conflict in its original form in her attitudes toward her mother, and in its present form in her attitudes toward her fiancé as well as toward other contemporaries.

A more specific formulation of Nancy's conflict would require psychoanalytic knowledge of her unconscious patterns—data which the above methods do not yield. It is certainly a justified hypothesis, however, that a great deal of hostility would be present in a pattern in which the individual is so dependent on other people but believes these others to be undependable; and it is entirely understandable that such hostility, in a person as anxious as Nancy, would be radically repressed.

AGNES: ANXIETY RELATED TO HOSTILITY AND AGGRESSION

Agnes, now eighteen, had been a night club dancer since leaving her father at the age of fourteen. On the day she was to have her first interview with me, she had apparently spent hours making herself up, and I was somewhat taken aback. She had long black curls and very blue eyes which gave her an exotic look. But her facial expression belied her appearance: she seemed, in this first interview with me, as well as the one with the social worker, to be in pronounced, though well-controlled, terror. Her eyes were dilated, her gestures sharp and nervous, and though she occasionally laughed metallically, she never smiled.

It appeared in these first interviews that Agnes was expecting, consciously or unconsciously, some attack. This same expectation of aggression against her appeared in forms of phobic anxiety in her behavior at Walnut House; whenever she was given an aspirin by the nurse, she would look at it carefully with the expectation that she was being poisoned. Later, in telling me about this and other phobic feelings, Agnes realized their irrationality. She stated that she often had "claustrophobia" in her room at Walnut House and on the subways, which she associated with a traumatic experience as a child when her stepmother, who after "she got tired slapping me, locked me in a closet."

Agnes' real mother had died when she was one year old. She had lived with her father and stepmother, both

Catholic, until the latter died when she was thirteen. After keeping house for her father for a year, she left him because of his excessive drinking and his attitude, as she expressed it, of "complete lack of concern for me." There was some doubt in her mind as to whether her father and mother had been her real parents; this doubt was also shared by the social workers at Walnut House on the basis of the scanty legal birth data available. She had no siblings. Her father and stepmother had adopted a boy when Agnes was eight, but she had objected so strongly that they had returned the boy to the orphanage. Her Wassermann test at entrance to Walnut House was +4, considered by the physician as congenital syphilis.

It is difficult to place Agnes accurately with respect to socioeconomic class; her father had frequently changed his occupation, at this time being a cook in a restaurant. Her vocational aims at the time of her stay at Walnut House were to leave show business, attend art school, and then become a commercial artist. On the basis of her aims, as well as the socioeconomic status of her friends, we think of her as in the middle class.

She was pregnant by a married man considerably older than herself, whom she had met as a fellow performer in show business. Because she "loved" him, she stated, she had entered willingly into the relationship, which lasted about half a year.

Her relations to the other young women at Walnut House were marked by much open hostility and some contempt on her part, with no effort whatever to be friendly. As a consequence, the other girls were hostile toward her and teased her frequently, which Agnes affected to meet with disdain. Her general mood at the house was characterized by brooding on one hand and temper tantrums on the other.

There were many evidences that Agnes was engaged in continual struggles for power—getting the upper hand— over other people. She stated that she greatly admired strength, especially in men. She felt contempt for her father because of what she called his weakness in drinking, and contempt for the men in night clubs who "pulled the line of my-wife-doesn't-understand-me." Her attitude toward Bob, the man by whom she was pregnant, was generally aggressive: she would "get a lawyer and ruin him" if he did not support her through her pregnancy. When she had direct contact with him, however, this aggression was usually masked behind a strategy of feminine weakness; with entirely conscious premeditation, she would weep over the telephone to convince him of her "helplessness" and play what she called her "martyr act" ("look how much I am suffering"). But when he did periodically send her a check, she would be temporarily filled with affectionate feelings toward him and say she had misjudged him. She employed her exotic, feminine attractiveness likewise for aggressive purposes: when she was to meet Bob for lunch (or, for that matter, on the days she was to have interviews with me) she would spend hours getting herself made up as attractively as possible. This procedure seemed strangely like preparation for war. After parturition, she enjoyed considerable feelings of triumph from creating a "sensation" in stores by her stunning appearance. These particular evidences of her aggressive struggle to gain power over other people fit the sado-masochistic pattern which will also be seen in her Rorschach.

At first, Agnes refused to accept her pregnancy as a realistic fact. Apparently, it made her feel weak and victimized, and prevented her from using her attractiveness as a weapon of aggression. But she soon was able to work the expected baby into her sado-masochistic pattern: she began to talk continually of her responsibility as a mother. (In this connection the other young women referred to her as the "madonna.") She treated the baby after its arrival as a "toy," an extension of herself, and emphasized that now at long last she had someone to belong to. These attitudes toward the baby were accompanied by a complete absence of realistic planning for the baby's future. The baby also now served her as an aggressive weapon against Bob; she stated that the baby was something to "fight for."

It was clear that Agnes felt a high degree of rejection by her parents. Beyond the doubt as to whether they were her real parents (which is significant symbolically as well as possibly true in fact), considerable factual data indicated that she had had a cold and reciprocally hostile relationship with her stepmother. Her father's attitude toward her had always been one of indifference to her and to her abilities. Even at the present time, Agnes was engaged in trying to break down his indifference. After parturition she made a trip to a nearby city to see him, ostensibly to get factual data about her birth records but actually to get him at long last to show some concern for her. This concern was to be expressed in symbolic terms by her hope that he would give her a little money. I say the money was a "symbol" because Agnes was not particularly in need at the time, and, furthermore, the sum she suggested (five dollars) would have made very little realistic difference. She expressed the conviction before the trip that he would not "materialize"—i.e., give her material proof of his concern. After the trip she reported that he had enjoyed showing his colleagues what an attractive daughter he had, but beyond that had, as always, exhibited complete indifference to her. In her interviews at Walnut House, Agnes continually talked of her loneliness—"I never belonged to anyone." Making allowance for her need to dramatize this loneliness, there is still adequate ground for concluding that she had always been a very isolated person. We place her in the *high* category of rejection by parents.

The chief feature of her Rorschach was the large amount of aggression and hostility.[18] Almost every response having to do with human beings consisted of people fighting or of semihuman monsters. The monsters were seen in sexual contexts; she assumedly associated sex with brutal aggression against her. Though her inner promptings of an imaginative sort were given much expression, her instinctual promptings were suppressed, the sexual promptings being suppressed in order for her to avoid becoming the victim of aggression. The Rorschach indicated that she felt driven by her extensive hostile and aggressive tendencies (both potential and actual) and that if these were not at least partially suppressed, they would be uncontrollable for her. There was a good deal of emotional excitability, particularly of a narcissistic form.

On the whole, her Rorschach showed a sado-masochistic pattern. She endeavored to avoid her aggression and hostility by retreats into fancy, abstraction, and moralism—e.g., the aggression was seen as a struggle between "good and evil." Her good intellectual capacities were used for purposes of aggressive ambition—gaining control over others. The hostility and aggression in this record involved much anxiety, cued off largely by her expecting others' aggression and hostility against her, which, in turn, was to a considerable extent a projection of her aggressive and hostile feelings toward them. Her chief way of trying to manage the anxiety was by retaliatory aggression and hostility.

Her rating on anxiety in the Rorschach was: depth 2½, width 4½, handling 4½, which placed her in the *high* category of anxiety in comparison to the other girls. On the childhood anxiety check-list Agnes ranked moderately low, and on the future check-list moderately high. The predominant areas of anxiety were *ambition* and *phobic* apprehension.

The interrelation of anxiety with her hostility and aggression seems to be the chief thing the study of Agnes has to teach us. First, her anxiety was a reaction to situations which she interpreted in terms of the threat of outright attack upon her by others. This seemed to be a prominent source of her terror in the first interviews at Walnut House. It is entirely understandable that the anxiety reaction to such threats would be accompanied by counter-hostility and aggression on Agnes' part—which at Walnut House she did not express against the social workers or me but displaced on the other young women there. Second, her anxiety was a reaction to the threat of being rejected, made lonely. Her hostility and aggression connected with this anxiety reaction is the familiar pattern of being angry at those who cause one the pain of isolation and anxiety.

But a third and less common aspect of the interrelationship of anxiety with hostility and aggression is demonstrated in Agnes' case—namely, *she uses hostility and aggression as a method of avoiding the anxiety-creating situation*. This is not the usual behavior: we have seen that other girls try to avoid anxiety by withdrawing or by placating or by being compliant to others. In most cases the periods when they are anxious are precisely the times when they are *least* aggressive in order not to alienate the persons on whom they are dependent. Agnes, however, operates on the formula that by attacking others she can force them not to reject her, not to make her anxious.

This can be seen more clearly by inquiring further into her behavior toward the father of her baby. Her general attitude toward him was: "He rejects me; therefore, he, like all men, is a welcher." Whenever he did reject her (e.g., fail to send her a check), she reacted with anxiety and great anger, the chief content of which was: "He must not be allowed to welch on me." But, when, in response to her determined long-distance telephone calls, he did send her money, she felt relieved of her anxiety and satisfied despite the fact that the sum of money was so paltry as to make very little objective difference. *The issue was not the money itself* (Agnes could have gotten that from Walnut House) *but that he must be made to show concern for her.* The fact that the symbol of concern, in Agnes' struggles with Bob and her father, is money is interesting in itself. In her mind "love" consists of giving up something, and her power to make others "concerned" for her consists of taking away something from them.

The case of Agnes may throw light on anxiety phenomena in sado-masochistic cases in general—namely, *relief from anxiety comes not only from keeping the other persons tied to one's self in a symbiotic relationship, but also in gaining control, triumphing over, or bending the other person to one's own will.* If one cannot gain relief from anxiety except by bending the other to fit one's own goals, one's method of allaying anxiety is bound to be essentially aggressive.

In Agnes' case we have seen a *high degree of anxiety* together with a *high degree of rejection by parents.* The relation of her present anxiety pattern to her early relations with her parents was shown in a number of ways, one of them being her association of her phobial anxiety with her early relation of reciprocal hostility and aggression with her stepmother. Another was the fact that the anxiety-creating pattern of relationship with the father of her baby followed very closely her relationship with her own father. It is to be emphasized that Agnes, like Nancy and Helen, did not accept rejection by her father as a realistic fact. Through thick and thin she clung to a contradictory position with her father—the contradiction between her subjective expectations and what she knew to be the realistic situation in her relation with her father. This is the hiatus between expectation and reality, discussed later. It was shown most clearly in her journey to see him to force him to show concern for her, despite the fact that she knew realistically that he would not change.

Agnes also demonstrates the *interrelation of anxiety with feelings of aggression and hostility.* Agnes was made anxious by her expectations of others' hostility and aggression against her (e.g., the phobial crystallizations), which, in turn, were related through the mechanism of projection with her own hostility and aggression against others. This pattern can assume an endless number of subtle forms. The hostility and aggression were expressions in Agnes of a sado-masochistic character structure, which involved her interpreting anxiety-creating situations as her being victimized by others. As a corollary, she employed her own hostility and aggression as a means of escape, a way of avoiding being victimized. In her life as well as in the world the escape never works.

Thus Agnes' chief defenses against the anxiety-creating situation were hostility and aggression—a striving to triumph over the other person, to become the victor rather than the victimized. In this respect she interpreted others' rejection of her as *their* victory over her and her capacity to keep them in a symbiotic relationship as her triumph over them, her bending them to *her* will. It is clear that such a pattern would generate great quantities of anxiety, for she would always expect that other people were doing to her what she was trying to do to them. This great quantity of anxiety was illustrated in her terror in the first interviews, and in her phobia at Walnut House.

A further question arises: *Can any specific causal elements* be discovered in Agnes' case which determine her use of aggression and hostility as methods of avoiding the anxiety-creating situation? Why would a person unconsciously select these weapons? I suggest that such methods in Agnes' case point toward the presence of a *level of overprotection in her early background.* Her considerable degree of narcissism would fit such a hypothesis. The hypothesis is likewise supported by her father's behavior in taking pride in her attractive appearance but rejecting her in all other respects. It is, of course, not at all uncommon that parents overprotect children and at the same time reject them, or direct excessive affect toward them on some levels and reject them on other levels. The overprotection and rejection are sometimes reactions to each other—e.g., if the parent really rejects the child, he may "spoil" it on a different level in order to make up for his rejection.

There are evidences that she did wield power in her family situation as a child: her objections forced the parents to relinquish the adopted boy. If such a hypothesis is true, it would explain why the aggressive method of forcing others not to reject her and bending them to her will was to some extent successful and, therefore, reinforced, in her relations with her parents. This hypothesis would also explain why Agnes interpreted rejection as an attack upon her, as though if others did not fulfill her expectations of directing affect toward her, they were "welching on agreements." She had learned to expect this attention as her "right," and others were, therefore, exploiting her when they did not give it to her.

The official judgment at Walnut House was that Agnes' personality pattern was so firmly crystallized that very little therapy could at that time be accomplished. Her second Rorschach, taken three weeks after parturition and, therefore, when she was relieved of the particular feelings of helplessness which attended her inability to use her feminine attractiveness as a source of power, shows some relaxing of the feeling that she is the victim of aggression. Hence it also shows some relaxing of the stringency of her pattern. But it was still essentially a sado-masochistic character structure characterized by strong feelings of aggression and hostility.

The last we heard of Agnes (from a letter written a month after her leaving Walnut House), she was being supported by a man much older than herself and bringing up her baby on Bach and Beethoven.

LOUISE: REJECTION BY MOTHER WITHOUT ANXIETY

Louise, the twenty-four-year-old daughter of proletarian parents, was a domestic servant, an occupation she had followed since her mother's death when she was twelve. Her father, who had been a laborer in a steel foundry, had died when Louise was thirteen. The only sibling, a sister, had died before Louise was old enough to know her. Louise was pregnant by a man eleven years her senior, the only man with whom she had ever felt herself to be in love or with whom she had ever had sexual relations. When she had been informed by her doctor that she was three months pregnant, she had had momentary thoughts of suicide but had later made the simple adjustment of calling a telephone operator and asking where a girl should go "in a fix like mine."

Louise's childhood history indicated an extreme rejection, expressed in cruel punishment, at the hands of her mother. In her words:

My mother beat me all the time. Even my father would ask her why she did it, and then she would beat me all the more. . . . She beat me with everything she had. She broke my elbow, she broke my back and nose. The neighbors next door used to want to call the police, but they didn't want to interfere. My mother would say, "Come here, or I'll kill you." Sometimes I was so banged up I would feel all right if somebody ran a knife through me. . . . My aunt and uncle wanted to take me, but she wouldn't let them. I don't understand why, seeing she hated me, that she didn't get rid of me.

Louise related these incidents of childhood punishment without much affect or change in expression. I had the impression that she had probably told the story frequently (possibly to the women for whom she worked as a domestic) and that there may be some exaggeration for effect upon the listener (e.g., the details surrounding the "breaking" of the elbow and back did not sound convincing). But granted this possibility of some exaggeration, there still is every indication 'hat she was the victim of physical cruelty and severe rejection as a child. While there was obviously great objective trauma in these childhood experiences, the significant fact is that Louise was able to avoid subjective trauma, both as a child and now as an adult. Her relation to her father, toward whom she felt friendly, was apparently a mitigating influence but on a superficial rather than profound level (e.g., she sees no men in the Rorschach).

It does not seem a tenable hypothesis that Louise was simply repressing all affect connected with this mother relationship; at other points in the interviews, she did express considerable emotion—she cried when she told of her hatred for her mother. But the hatred was stated as a simple fact, without indication of accompanying psychological conflict and without evidence of pervasive underlying resentment of the mother.

As a child Louise's chief concerns—beyond the understandable desire to escape the pain of the beatings—were a fear that other people might hate her because her mother did, and a perplexity as to why her mother was so hostile toward her. In her childhood thoughts she had hypothesized that perhaps she was not really her mother's own daughter. In her behavior toward her mother Louise made no pretense or endeavor to cover up the reality of their relationship. When company was present, the mother would demand that Louise show her affection, but Louise always refused to do this even though she knew she would be punished for it on the morrow. Louise's own subjective attitude toward her childhood rejection and punishment is shown in her lumping of these experiences under the heading of "hard luck." In short, Louise seems to have accepted rejection at the hands of her mother realistically, as an objective and somewhat impersonal fact.

Her Rorschach showed a relatively undifferentiated personality, with average intelligence and some originality.[19] There were no movement responses in the record, indicating both a meagerness of intratensive activity and a repression of instinctual promptings. She showed an easy, ready adaptation to stimuli from the outside, but this was a somewhat *pseudo* form of responsiveness and suggested a superficial adjustment to relations with other people. It is significant that she saw no human beings in the cards (which is frequently the case with persons who have had bad relations with parents). The closest Louise got to a human being was the "back of a woman's head," which she implied was saying that "women turn away from me." In this response she placed the woman's head not in the blot itself but in the space, which suggested her own oppositional tendencies toward women. It is a sound inference that both of these ways of relating to women referred prototypically to her relations with her mother.

Practically no overt anxiety was shown in the Rorschach. Some underlying anxiety may be inferred from the lack of movement responses: whereas this absence of inner promptings was partly a mark of an undifferentiated personality in Louise's case, it was also partly due to a blocking off of instinctual urges, particularly with respect to sexual contact with men, to make herself less vulnerable. We rated her for anxiety on the Rorschach: depth 3, width 2, handling 1. This placed her in the *moderately low* category of anxiety in relation to the other young women. Louise was able to avoid personal relationships which might arouse anxiety, and the avoidance system did not seem to present her with any deep conflicts.

While filling out the childhood anxiety check-list, Louise significantly remarked, "You don't worry as a child. You just take things as they come, you don't suffer." Though the number of items she checked placed her in the *high* category of anxiety on this childhood list, her ranking for anxiety on the *present* check-list was the *lowest* among all the young women.[20] She stated while filling out the latter list, "I practically never worry about anything." The chief kinds of anxiety in the check-lists were disapproval by her peers and phobial apprehensions. With respect to anxiety related to competitive ambition, she ranked lowest among all the girls.

Louise's behavior and attitude toward the psychologist and social workers and me were always deferential, with apologies for taking their time and some indications that she felt it unusual that they should be interested in her. In the interviews she talked freely but gave the impression (particularly in the fact that her facial expression was generally characterized by narrowed eyelids) that she was prepared to be rebuked. She showed considerable desire to please her "superiors" and performed her duties at the house with conspicuous conscientiousness. The opposite side to this compliant behavior seemed to be expressed in some defiance of the other young women: she was critical of them to the housemother and consequently was disliked by them. This did not seem to bother her: she stated that when she didn't get along with other people, "I just keep out of their way." Her only amusement was taking long daily walks by herself, which served the purposes, in addition to her enjoyment, of keeping her out of the way of the other girls and helping her to go to sleep at night rather than "lie awake with the blues," as she put it.

There was never any question in Louise's mind about her wanting to keep her baby, and she made realistic plans about placing it in a foster home until she had earned enough to establish her own home or had married. How much her own baby would have meant to her was shown in her great pleasure in taking care of the other girls' babies before her own parturition.

When her own baby was stillborn, Louise was inconsolable. She wept profusely the first days in the hospital, and could talk of nothing else during her three weeks of convalescence at Walnut House. She then went to a convalescent home in the country, where she made a good recovery from her depression and grief. The final data concerning Louise were the long, endearment-filled letters which she continued to write to the nurse at Walnut House, with whom she had established a close and affectionate relationship.

Our over-all rating for Louise was *low* in anxiety and *high* in rejection by her mother. This immediately presents a problem of a person who experienced severe rejection but did not exhibit consequent neurotic anxiety. It goes directly against my hypothesis that maternal rejection is the origin of neurotic anxiety.

Is this lack of anxiety to be explained by her lack of differentiation as a personality or by repression of affect? This question must be answered in its two phases. To some extent it may be said that Louise was a relatively simple, undifferentiated personality in the "normal" sense (i.e., the lack of differentiation was not due to present subjective conflicts). The repression of inner promptings in the Rorschach referred to her sexual promptings toward men and did not in itself explain the lack of neurotic anxiety from her rejection by her mother. To what extent her meagerness in responsiveness to relations with other people was a result of the lack of affection in her relation with her mother it is not possible to state beyond the obvious point that there would be an important relation between these two factors. But her lack of neurotic anxiety could not be explained as a lack or suppression of all affect. This is shown in (a) the fact that she did exhibit affect in talking of her hatred for her mother, (b) she had very great feelings for her hoped-for baby, and (c) she was able to establish an affectionate relationship with the nurse at Walnut House.

Louise accepted her mother's rejection as a realistic fact rather than as a source of subjective conflict. To me this seems the essential point in her freedom from neurotic anxiety. Her mother's hatred and punishment of her were taken as objective and relatively impersonal—as "hard luck." Her own statement that children accept things as they come without suffering (in the sense of experiencing neurotic anxiety) seems to be a fairly accurate description of her understanding of herself. That the rejection and punishment caused objective trauma and great pain is clear, but subjective trauma and conflict with respect to her relations with her mother was not present. Her mother's hatred is met with direct hatred and does not become a reason for persistent resentment in Louise.

It is significant that Louise entertained no pretense about her mother: in radical distinction from the case of Nancy, for example, Louise did not live in expectation that her mother could or would change into a "good" mother. Likewise, Louise's behavior toward her mother was not influenced by pretension, as witness her refusal to show hypocritical affection for her mother when company was present despite the surety of being beaten for this self-assertion. In contrast to a number of other women in this study (Nancy, Helen, Agnes, etc.), *Louise did not have a cleavage between her expectations and the reality situation with respect to the parent.* Her case demonstrates that neurotic anxiety is not produced by rejection if the individual is free from subjective contradictions in her attitudes toward her parents.

Some elements in this case, if they should appear in a more extreme form than we have observed in Louise, would suggest psychopathic developments. The psychopathic personality, produced by such complete rejection in the family that the child has no basis for future relatedness, does not exhibit neurotic anxiety (see footnote re Lauretta Bender's viewpoint, page 406). But I believe it is clear that Louise cannot be classed as psychopathic.

It has been noted that Louise's adaptation to traumatic situations of all sorts was characterized not by neurotic conflict but by seeing the problem as objective and "keeping out of the way." This can be seen in her desire to get away from her mother as well as in her adaptation to difficulties with the girls at the house. It is true that this "keeping out of the way" might take pathological forms with Louise if she were confronted with an insupportable trauma; on learning of her pregnancy, though she later made a simple objective adjustment, there were the first thoughts of suicide. There were likewise thoughts of suicide in her childhood as the only way out, if the pain of her mother's beatings were to become insupportable. It is my impression, which I cannot substantiate in detail, that an insupportable trauma in Louise's experience would result in psychotic developments rather than deep neurotic conflicts. I believe this point does not, however, qualify our above statements as to her freedom from neurotic anxiety.

BESSIE: REJECTION BY PARENTS WITHOUT ANXIETY

Bessie, the one case of incest pregnancy in this study, was the fifteen-year-old daughter in a proletarian family. Her father was employed on a river barge that plied up and down the Hudson from Albany to New York. There were eight siblings, four older than Bessie; the living conditions in the home had been poor and crowded. At the time of her pregnancy, Bessie was in the second year of a vocational high school in which she was learning the trade of textile machine operating.

She had been impregnated by her father during the preceding summer. It had been the mother's practice to insist that the children spend the summer on the barge to lessen her work in the house. Since Bessie knew that an older sister had been forced by the father to submit to sexual relations (and was herself pregnant by the father at this time), Bessie protested violently against going on the barge—a protest which went to the extent of her drinking some iodine. But she eventually had to give in to her mother's demand. On the barge Bessie occupied a bed with a brother and her father. During the summer she was forced three times by the father to submit to intercourse with him, he threatening to kill her if she refused his demands or if she told anyone.

When her mother subsequently learned of Bessie's pregnancy by the father, she placed all the blame on Bessie, beat her severely, and threatened to kill her if she remained in the house. Bessie was housed temporarily at the Society for the Prevention of Cruelty to Children and was later removed to Walnut House. During her confinement her , the father was brought to trial on the charge of rape by the older sister and was sentenced to the penitentiary.

Though it was difficult for Bessie to talk of the particular events leading to her pregnancy, she was responsive and open, albeit somewhat restless and bashful. In the interviews she impressed social workers and myself alike as an outgoing, cooperative, and responsible young woman.

Her mother not only exhibited an attitude of severe rejection toward Bessie, but also she consistently sought to make Bessie's problems in the pregnancy as difficult as possible. At first the mother insisted that she wanted no responsibility whatever for Bessie, but when Bessie had decided to have the baby adopted, the mother began to insist that Bessie keep it and bring it home. Since it was "Bessie's fault," she should be made to take care of the baby; and the mother rationalized her desire to have Bessie and the baby under her control by saying that since her husband was the father, the baby was her own flesh and blood. But it was obvious, as an older sister pointed out to the social worker, that the mother's real motives were punitive; she wished to have Bessie and the baby home in order that she could forever berate Bessie for the pregnancy. Whenever Bessie had decided on a plan of her own, the mother would aggressively attack her with a contrary plan. She strongly opposed Bessie's first decision to make her home with an older sister after parturition and also her later plan to live in a foster home. These indications all form a picture of the mother as definitely sadistic.

It was not easy for Bessie to take a stand against her mother, as it was likewise difficult for her to verbalize hostility toward her mother. But the significant point is that in each issue, Bessie arrived at a realistic decision independently of her mother's demands or pressure. Bessie's attitude, in her own words, was "My mother is just that way—I just have to pay no attention to what she says." During her visits to her family, when her mother would begin the familiar berating of her, Bessie would simply remark, "I came here on pleasure, not business," and walk out of the house.

Bessie's Rorschach showed an averagely intelligent, restless, self-assertive (in the constructive sense of "independent") person, but with a meagerness and somewhat emaciated quality of personality.[21] By "emaciated" I refer to the indications in the record that her meagerness was not entirely a result of lack of capacity for differentiation; it was also due to her slight tendency to keep herself at a relatively simple level of emotional development in order to avoid difficulties (i.e., complications) in her relations with other persons. The human beings in the responses were frequently skeletons or pictures, a fact which, coupled with the fact that her record showed her able to respond directly and easily to people, suggests that she sought to keep her dynamic, vital impulses out of her interpersonal relations. The only overt anxiety shown in the record was in three vista *(FK)* responses; but these, in the relatively balanced proportion in which they appeared in the record, indicated a fairly adequate and direct method of handling conflicts.

The particular conflicts which arose in the Rorschach, and to which these direct methods of handling were applied, were sexual and seemed to refer directly to her problem with her father and indirectly to her difficulties with her mother. Two of these vista responses were scenes in parks, a fact which makes sense in view of Bessie's remark that it had been her practice to escape into a park near her home when her parents were abusive toward her. There was some latent schizoid possibility in the record (suggested in the bland use of color). It was not pronounced and is significant here chiefly in its indication of the form Bessie's development would take in the face of insupportable stresses. While the anxiety in the Rorschach was in general not at all severe, there was an indication of some deeply encapsulated anxiety which would become overt in Bessie's case only in a very severe crisis. Her Rorschach rating was: depth 3, width 2, handling 1, which placed her in the moderately low category of anxiety in comparison to the other girls.

Both Bessie's *childhood* and *present* check-lists showed very little anxiety. She ranked lowest of all the girls in quantity on the former, and third from the lowest on the latter.[22] The areas of anxiety were success or failure in work, what her family thought of her, and what her peers thought of her (though this determination of kinds should not be given much weight because of the small number of items checked in each area).

Bessie had warm and affectionate relations with her brothers and sisters. Apparently some of Bessie's difficulty in standing against her mother was related to the power the mother derived from the fact that she happened to be the head of a family which—by virtue of the siblings—meant a great deal to Bessie. I wish to make it clear, however, that Bessie's difficulty in standing against her mother was realistic and not neurotic. In each issue which occurred during her months at Walnut House and the later foster home, Bessie did not capitulate either subjectively or objectively to her mother's demands.

The siblings had had during childhood, and likewise now had, their own constellation of affection quite apart from the parents. There was no competition among them for a love from parents which they apparently knew would not be forthcoming anyway. It seems that these brothers and sisters viewed their parents as the dominating and punitive persons they actually were. That Bessie was able to have these affectionate relations with siblings, in the face of parental rejection, undoubtedly is basically connected with her relative freedom from neurotic anxiety.

Bessie's rejection by her father, already obvious from his treatment of her in the rape, has an illuminating prelude in the stories she related about her childhood. Whenever the father was romping with the other children and Bessie would approach, the father would immediately stop his playing. Bessie had always wondered about his behavior in these instances and had ascribed it to the fact that he had wanted another boy when she was born. But what is significant is that on these occasions Bessie would not withdraw from the group in a pout. "I just went ahead," she remarked, entering into the play with the siblings regardless of the father's withdrawal. Apparently his rejection of her was accepted by Bessie as an objective fact and neither led to subjective conflict and resentment nor changed her behavior.

While at Walnut House the anxiety Bessie exhibited was always connected with realistic situations. She was very much afraid of going to court in the instance of her father's trial, and also in the later instance of the court hearing to permit her to stay at a foster home rather than at her mother's. In the first instance she feared meeting her father; and in the second she was apprehensive about taking the stand before judges to testify.[23] She experienced a realistic conflict about giving up her baby but came to the conclusion that she could take care of her married sister's baby in place of her own. It was the judgment of social workers and psychologist that Bessie's anxiety in these instances was situational rather than neurotic—i.e., was not the result of subjective conflict—and was handled by her with objectivity and responsibility.

Her relations with both the other young women and personnel at Walnut House were uniformly good. She laughingly spoke of herself as the "house tease," but her teasing was all of the amicable kind and was accepted as such by the others. She received much spontaneous pleasure from taking care of the other girls' babies, and apparently was stating a fact when she said, "All the children I've minded in my life like me, and I like them." In her placement in the foster home after leaving Walnut House, she stated that she was very happy and she was described by the foster mother as a dependable girl with a very good disposition.

Bessie exhibited a *moderately low* degree of anxiety. Her conflicts were chiefly situational, and she handled them with a relatively high degree of realism and responsibility. There was an understandable tendency to withdraw from stresses which could not otherwise be managed. This withdrawal generally took a realistic (in this sense "normal") form—e.g., in her going into the park to get away from her parents' abuse. There was the latent possibility of schizoid behavior if stresses should become insupportable. But the fact that no such extreme tendency entered into her behavior in the face of the severe crisis of an incest pregnancy indicated that this latent tendency should not militate against the conclusion that she was prey to relatively little neurotic anxiety and that what anxiety she did have was handled in a relatively healthy way.

Bessie experienced a *high degree of rejection* by both parents. This, again, like the case of Louise, presents us with a distinct problem. Why did severe parental rejection not lead to the development of neurotic anxiety? In Bessie's case it seems clear that the parental rejection did not engender internal, subjective conflicts. The problems with her parents were not introjected, either as a source of self-condemnation or as a source of persistent resentment. She accepted her parents' rejection as an objective, realistic fact, an acceptance which was based on her realistic appraisal of her father; and (though her mother still had the power to make decisions difficult for her) her appraisal of her mother was likewise realistic. Thus the rejection was dealt with on the level of conscious awareness; it did not become confused with expectations that the parents might or could be different. The rejection did not basically pervert her own behavior: in the interesting childhood vignette, she continued her plan of playing with the other children despite her father's flagrant rejection on her approach. She was able to develop affectionate relationships with siblings, peers, and other persons of all ages.

I tentatively suggest this principle: *The adjustment to her rejection without internal conflict—i.e., without a rift between subjective expectations and objective reality—is the essential element in Bessie's relative freedom from neurotic anxiety.*

DOLORES: ANXIETY PANIC WHILE UNDER SEVERE THREAT

Dolores was a fourteen-year-old Puerto Rican, white, Catholic girl who had come to the United States three years before the present interviews. She was proletarian, her father being an unskilled factory laborer in Puerto Rico. Dolores was partially crippled from tuberculosis of the leg bone in childhood. There were four siblings, two older brothers, an older sister, and a younger brother, all in Puerto Rico. When Dolores was five, her mother was taken sick, and Dolores was required to remain home from school for six years to take care of her.

On the mother's death, Dolores was brought to the United States by an aunt who was childless. The impression given by this aunt in her interviews with the social workers at Walnut House was that she had wanted Dolores in order to fill her own emotional needs. Affectionate toward Dolores for the first few months, the aunt had then abruptly changed to treating the girl with complete coldness, beating her frequently, and ostentatiously rejecting her in favor of the children of a relative who lived nearby.

All we could learn from Dolores was that an unknown man had pushed her into a cellar and had raped her. For over six weeks, during the preliminary interviews for her entrance to Walnut House and in the first weeks in the house, Dolores had clung tenaciously to this explanation of her pregnancy. We knew nothing except that her story was vague and unconvincing. During this period Dolores was very subservient and resigned, answering questions in the manner of one who dutifully obeys authorities but in every other way was markedly withdrawn. It was observed that she seemed alert when she thought she was unnoticed, but as soon as she felt anyone was watching her she assumed a hunched-over position and an "encased" attitude. This case is significant because it reveals the anxiety panic and psychological immobilization of an individual under a strong, persistent threat.

In her first Rorschach she gave only three responses, rejecting seven of the ten cards. The record clearly shows some very severe disturbance. She had a headache at the time scheduled for her Rorschach but at the last moment decided to take it anyway. Since headaches are often a psychosomatic symptom of conflict, hers was later seen to fit plausibly into her situation at the time. Her behavior during the test was marked by silent but very strenuous effort; she would hold on to each card for periods of three to five minutes, studying the card, then looking silently at the tester or up at the ceiling. It was evident that a strong subjective struggle was occurring. A diagnosis of psychosis was precluded by the fact that the three responses she did give are the most obvious ones in the test.[24]

There was indication in her behavior in the test that she tended to impute great power to authority (one aspect of which was the marked suspicion with which she regarded the tester's taking notes on her responses). But she submitted to authority at the same time. We could only hypothesize that Dolores was in an exceedingly severe emotional conflict, which resulted in her being psychologically paralyzed on the test. The content of the conflict we could not determine at the time beyond the indications that it had something to do with the above-mentioned power she imputed to authorities. Her anxiety rating on this Rorschach was: depth 5, width 5, handling 3.

During this same first month she was taken three times to a clinic for the routine gynecological examination preparatory to parturition. The first two times, after having made no previous objection, Dolores became immobile at the clinic and refused to permit any examination. When it was later explained to her that the house could take no responsibility unless she cooperated, she finally agreed to go through with the examination, but when she again arrived at the clinic and was on the examination table she became hysterical and so muscularly rigid that the doctors could not proceed. We then hypothesized that her conflict had to do with the circumstances under which she had become pregnant. In the next two interviews with the social worker, during which Dolores was assured she would be protected from her aunt, she disclosed the whole account of her pregnancy.

Dolores was pregnant by her uncle, the aunt's husband. He had come into her bed while she was sleeping, and the act had been completed before she could resist. Dolores had told her aunt, who then added continual threats to her punitive behavior, one threat being that if Dolores ever told anyone the truth about the origin of her pregnancy she would be sent to an institution where she would be beaten daily.

It was now clear that the extreme block on being examined—apparently Dolores had viewed the Rorschach in the same category as the gynecological examination—was due to the profound terror that the origin of her pregnancy might in some way be discovered. She would then be subject to her aunt's threats; i.e., be killed or placed in a punitive institution. The conflict itself took the form of the authority of the social workers, Rorschach tester, and doctors on one side and the authority of her aunt on the other—with her aunt's authority having the additional weight of specific punitive threats. It will have been observed that she readily subjected herself to the "authority" of the psychologist, social workers, and doctors—e.g., she came to take the Rorschach, and she made the trips to the clinic without objection—until her subjection to these "authorities" came into immediate conflict with the power of her aunt.

After this conflict was relieved, Dolores' attitudes and behavior underwent a radical change. She became outgoing and friendly in her relations to the other young women as well as to the personnel at Walnut House, and in contrast to the previous severely subservient behavior she now showed considerable independence in initiating projects in the house and developing her own hobbies. During the latter part of Dolores' stay at the house, a minor problem began to develop in her defiant and at times aggressive attitude toward some of the girls. I take this behavior to be the opposite side of her compliant, subservient behavior toward authority, which was so predominant in her early attitude toward social workers and myself. It may be assumed that a compliant-defiant pattern, particularly related to her belief in authority, is a prominent part of Dolores' character structure.

The second Rorschach, taken several months after the clarification of the conflict, also exhibits a radical change.[25] The pathological blockage had disappeared.[26] The Rorschach presented the picture not of overwhelming conflict but of an averagely intelligent, relatively undifferentiated personality with a very healthy core. There was some indication of a need to protect herself from emotional involvement with other persons, and of problems in the area of sex—e.g., she saw no men in the cards; Card IV, the top portion of which often elicits the response of a "man's penis," she termed a "gorilla." The avoidance of men, and the association of sex with possible aggression, are understandable in view of her own recent traumatic sexual experience. It is fascinating that she first rejected Card VI (the card which also often elicits sexual responses) but in the inquiry she used it as a "parrot which can talk." This makes us think immediately of the fact that she had been able to talk about her sexual problem and the origin of her pregnancy. The rating on anxiety in this second Rorschach was: depth 2½, width 2½, handling 2. This places her in the *moderately low* category in relation to the other young women.

Dolores ranked moderately high in quantity of anxiety on the *childhood* check-list, and high on both the *present* and *future* lists. Since the last was taken after the relief from her conflict, the high quantity of anxiety is not to be explained as a result of that conflict. I believe her relatively large number of items checked on these lists was due—as has been pointed out in cases above which represent the same character structure—to her being a compliant type in relation to authority and her feeling that she must diligently check every item which she could conceivably ever have worried about.[27] The phobial forms of anxiety were the predominant area.

With respect to Dolores' rejection by parental figures, we receive different pictures as we consider her relation to her aunt, to her mother, and to her father. It is clear that her aunt subjected her to extreme rejection. But the data concerning the more crucial early relations with her mother are less clear and must be largely inferred. Dolores stated in very general terms that she had had a warm relation with her mother. But the fact that the mother had been sick since Dolores was five, and that it devolved upon Dolores to remain home (at the price of missing schooling which she had greatly desired) to take care of the mother, despite the presence of two older brothers and an older sister in the family, gives a hint that there may have been some discrimination against Dolores and more rejection than she admits.

Her rejection at the hands of her father is indicated more clearly in her recital of childhood events. Since the onset of her mother's illness, the father had lived with another woman, returning home only infrequently. On questioning, Dolores stated that her father had never played with her as a child, though he did play with her younger brother. When I asked Dolores whether she had regretted that her father never played with her, she looked up in considerable surprise, as though such a question had never entered her head. To me, her subsequent answer of "no" is even less impressive than the significant phenomenon that it not only had never occurred to her as a subjective problem but she was amazed that anyone else would raise it as such.

We rate Dolores' rejection by her father as *moderately high*. Because of the paucity of data, especially with respect to the mother, we make our over-all rating of *moderately high* rejection tentative for Dolores, with the realization that she might perhaps as plausibly be placed in the *moderately low* category.

Dolores' case demonstrated *severe conflict while under threat, resulting in anxiety which approached the intensity of panic, characterized by extreme withdrawal and partial psychological paralysis.* She illustrates how a person can literally be scared stiff. The conflict was situational and vanished when Dolores, freed from the power of her aunt's threats, was able to disclose the truth about her pregnancy. But while she was under the conflict, its power carried over to everything she felt might lead to discovering the secret which she must kept hidden. In this respect, it appears that an irrational, "magical" power to reveal the truth about the origin of her pregnancy was imputed to the gynecological examination.

The fact that Dolores' character structure includes a marked attitude of power over her imputed to authorities and a corresponding tendency to subordinate herself to these powers is important for understanding why her conflict was so severe. For example, it could be hypothesized that the conflict would not have been so marked, and the manufactured story would not have been clung to so persistently and tenaciously, if she had not believed that the aunt had the power to enforce the threats and she herself had no power. And on the other side, the conflict would similarly have been less severe if Dolores had not imputed such power to social workers and the doctors. One could conceive, on this hypothesis, of her then holding to the dissimulation about the pregnancy with less feeling of being "trapped." While in the conflict, Dolores' anxiety was very high; after the conflict was relieved, her anxiety was rated as *moderately low*.[28]

We have tentatively rated Dolores as *moderately high* in rejection. The significant point, however, is that Dolores —like Louise and Bessie—*did not interpret rejection as a subjective problem*. The clearest example of this was her amazement at the question of whether she was sorry her father had never played with her. Rejection was accepted as a realistic fact, not as a cause of subjective questioning and conflict. On the basis of this reasoning, it is probable that even if there had been a high degree of rejection of her by her mother, Dolores would neither have interpreted it nor reported it as such.

PHYLLIS: ABSENCE OF ANXIETY IN AN IMPOVERISHED PERSONALITY

Phyllis, age twenty-three, was the oldest daughter in a middle-class family. She had two siblings, sisters of seventeen and twelve. Her father was Protestant and her mother Catholic; Phyllis had been brought up in conformity with her mother's religion. At the time of her pregnancy she was employed as a bookkeeper in a bank. In school and business college (as, indeed, in the other phases of her life) she had always been known as quiet, studious, efficient, and meticulous. This last quality was shown at Walnut House in her excessively careful grooming whenever she came for an interview. The father of her baby was a physician in the army, whom she had met when she served as a USO hostess. His profession and rank of major were points of considerable pride to both Phyllis and her mother. Phyllis' relationship with this man was marked by naïveté on her part and much idealization of him, her repeated remarks being that he was "brilliant" and "without flaw."

Phyllis described her childhood as one in which she was "never unhappy" and in which she regularly acceded to the advice of her father ("whom we would never go against") and to the will of her mother, who was a very dominating person. During the interviews at Walnut House at which her mother was present, Phyllis would always sit placidly by while her mother endeavored to deliver the decisions for Phyllis concerning the baby. Only once during her childhood could Phyllis remember having talked back to her parents; this was on an auto trip when she was eight. After her doing so, her parents had promptly put her out of the car and temporarily left her beside the road. Apparently she learned never again to take a stand against her parents. Phyllis had no friends of her own age, but this caused her no regret for, so far as her peers were concerned, she felt she could "have a good time without needing anybody else." She preferred the company of older people; her "ideal of a good time," never yet realized, was to be invited to join the ladies in her mother's bridge club.

The great concern of Phyllis and her mother was that she have expert medical care during her pregnancy. She repeatedly emphasized that she was to go to the best women's hospital in the city, and was now under the care of the head obstetrician at this clinic. The experiences at this clinic which Phyllis related to me illuminate the dynamics underlying her great emphasis on expert medical care. During a visit to this clinic preparatory to parturition, an assistant obstetrician had remarked that a Caesarian section might be necessary. Phyllis reported that the head obstetrician had then taken the assistant aside to caution him "against telling me anything that would make me nervous." Whenever Phyllis had asked the chief obstetrician about her case, she reported that he always remarked, "You're all right; we don't talk to patients."

Phyllis *smiled contentedly* when relating this; it seemed clear that being in the hands of an authority and *not knowing anything about her condition herself* seemed to her an ideal situation. This "ostrich policy," or *positive valuation placed upon not knowing,* had its motivation, I assume, in the fact that it was a means of obviating any concern, conflict, or anxiety on her part. Once during the week preceding parturition, Phyllis was seized by a momentary anxiety that she might die. She immediately put this out of her mind by saying to herself, "It's all science, there is no need for worry." She emphasized that she believed "implicitly in science, and only in science."

Phyllis' Rorschach indicated a highly constricted, compartmentalized, "flat" personality, with very little inner activity or use of capacity for emotional relatedness with others.[29] She exhibited excessive caution, confining her responses to details in which she could be meticulously accurate and successfully held herself aloof from emotional involvements with other people. Practically no conflicts or tensions were shown in the record, and very little anxiety. Evidently the constricted and cautious behavior had been so well ingrained in her that she accepted such impoverished modes of reaction without any particular subjective problems. Her anxiety rating on the Rorschach was: depth 2, width 2, handling 2, which placed her in the low category of anxiety in relation to the other young women. On the childhood anxiety check-list she ranked moderately low in quantity, with anxiety highest in the areas of the attitude of her peers toward her, success or failure in work, and the attitude of her family toward her. On the present anxiety check-list she ranked high, anxiety about the imminent parturition accounting for the increase.

Though Phyllis did have some anxiety about the prospective parturition (apprehension which focused around the fact that the birth was expected to be Caesarian), there is some suspicion that the markedly higher quantity of anxiety on this check-list represents at least partially her mother's great anxiety about the parturition rather than her own. This hypothesis is in accord with the fact that Phyllis regularly adopted her mother's attitudes in almost everything. In any case, the high quantity of anxiety on this check-list stands alone, all other criteria indicating that Phyllis had very little anxiety.

Only the slightest indications of rebellion against her mother ever emerged in the interviews. One was her interest in horseback riding, which prior to her pregnancy she had pursued despite her mother's apprehension and mild disapproval. But in every major matter, such as in the plans for the baby, Phyllis acceded to her mother's will. It was her mother's eventual decision that they should keep the baby and raise it as their own. The question arises as to whether Phyllis' extramarital pregnancy was in some way a rebellion against the mother, specifically a rebellion against the thwarting, suppressive influence of her mother upon her. No data emerged to confirm such a hypothesis. The data available—e.g., Phyllis' naiveté in her sexual relations and her idealization of the man—suggest that the pregnancy was a product of her conforming, compliant pattern (that is, she engaged in sexual relations out of compliance to the desires of the man) rather than a rebellion against this pattern.

Phyllis expressed the desire to go home after parturition and never leave again. Just prior to parturition, the domination of the mother approached the point of cruelty: she made a practice of watching outside Phyllis' door in the evening at Walnut House until ejected by the nurse and vented her extreme anxiety in the form of outbursts of rage at Phyllis. But all of this behavior by the mother was accepted by Phyllis placidly.

Two weeks after parturition Phyllis and her mother took the baby home, where it shortly died of pneumonia. In her subsequent visits to Walnut House, Phyllis was always dressed in black. She exhibited a large colored painting she and her mother had ordered made of the baby in its coffin; but beyond these ways of dramatizing the death of the baby, she exhibited no particular affect. In the follow-up interviews, Phyllis stated that she had given up horseback riding and was refusing dates with men on the pretext that she was married. The social worker reported that Phyllis seemed like a dignified, dependent little girl, operating almost entirely on the theory "mother knows best."

In Phyllis, a person of a *low* degree of anxiety, we have observed a conforming, compliant personality. She remained free from emotional entanglements by means of affective impoverishment and submitted to her mother without subjective struggle at the price of surrender of her own individual autonomy. She had been "successfully" constricted by a dominating mother. The constriction was "successful" in the mother's sense in that Phyllis did not rebel; and it was "successful" in Phyllis' sense in that by means of capitulating to the mother and curtailing her own development she avoided conflicts, tensions, and anxiety. Phyllis reported no rejection (except the child-hood incident, which was to her the exception that proves the rule). She never went against her mother enough to elicit outright rejection; and the covert rejection (e.g., in the mother's hostility and rage just before parturition) was not interpreted in that light by Phyllis. Presumably Phyllis' pattern of constriction had its genesis as a strategy in her childhood of avoiding the anxiety-creating situation of con-flict with her mother. Phyllis' present practice was to sur-render herself to authorities—the mother, the idealized sexual partner, the expert medical care—and thus to avoid concern, conflict, and anxiety. What we have termed the "ostrich policy," the desire not to know about her condi-tion, the irrational faith shown in the use of the phrase "it's all science, there is no need for worry" were all in-tegral parts of her constriction.

I speak of irrational faith in science not with reference to the medical care itself (which in other persons may obviously be related to rational methods of coping with anxiety) but rather to the use Phyllis makes of what she terms "science" but I would call "scientism." With Phyllis, belief in "scientism" is clearly a way of avoiding facing her anxiety, which in the instance of the momentary anxi-ety about death, might have had any one of many origins quite other than apprehension about death itself. This kind of "faith in science" is a superstition, falling in the same psychological category as a magical incantation or the use of a prayer-wheel, and serves the same psycho-logical function for Phyllis as her submission to her mother's authority. *This case demonstrates that it is pos-sible to avoid anxiety-creating situations by means of im-poverishment of personality. But the price for such avoid-ance is loss of individual autonomy, personal responsibility, and the capacity for meaningful emotional relatedness to other persons.*

Phyllis is an illuminating demonstration of the varying theories of Kierkegaard, Goldstein, and others that since anxiety arises as the person confronts possibilities for individual development and expansion, anxiety-creating situations may be avoided if the individual refuses to con-front these possibilities. But the opportunities for psycho-logical growth and expansion are lost at the same time. I may remark psychotherapeutically that the emergence of anxiety would be the most positive prognostic sign in the personality of Phyllis.

Of course, the most interesting question of all is, What will happen to Phyllis in the long run? Is it possible for a person to remain constricted as severely as she is without ultimately going into a depression or a radical revolt?[30] Though each of us would answer that question on the basis of his or her own presuppositions about human nature, I would definitely say no. I believe that sooner or later this "perfect" adjustment will collapse. It may take the form, of course, of a resignation into a chronic depression which will then be called "normality." This question bears upon the dynamics of "conformism," adjustment to social norms, and what happens when authority is accepted not wisely but too well.

FRANCES: CONSTRICTION VERSUS THE CREATIVE IMPULSE

Frances, a twenty-one-year-old professional tap-dancer, was the adopted only child of a middle-class family. The case is interesting in the respect that Frances tried to constrict her personality in order to avoid anxiety but (in contrast to Phyllis) was not able to effect constriction successfully. At the points where the constrictive pattern broke down, anxiety emerged.

Her description of her relationships to her father and mother was marked by idealization. She stated that her childhood was "completely contented"; her father was "perfect" and her mother was "sweet" and always responded to her needs and wishes. But these references were regularly summed up in some general, evasive remark, such as, "You know how a mother and daughter talk understandingly with each other," and there were no trustworthy indications that the affirmative relationship with her parents was more than superficial. When she was a child her mother had told her about her being adopted in the form of a "fairy-tale," just as she told her other fairy-tales at bedtime. In later years the mother had suggested that Frances inquire into her real parentage through the adoption agency, but Frances had refused this advice because she "wanted to leave it as a fairy-tale." Some indication appeared in dreams she happened to relate during the in-

terviews that, underneath her ostensibly affirmative relation with her parents, she had pronounced feelings of
isolation and hostility arising from the fact that she did
not have her own parents. It seems a sound inference
that the fairy-tale motif and the idealization of the parents
served, as did the idealization of her boy friend, to cover
up her hostility toward her parents.

Frances was pregnant by a young man whom she had
idealized during the four years of their close friendship
because he was a "gentleman and very dependable." When,
at her pregnancy, he did not propose marriage and even
refused to contribute to her preparturition support, her
attitude toward him abruptly changed to one of hatred.
She verbalized this attitude freely, adding that she now
"hated all men." Presumably her idealization of the man
had served as a defense against the underlying suspicion
of, and her own repressed hostility toward, him; the sudden shift to antagonism suggests that this attitude, in repressed form, was there all the time. What both the idealization and complete antagonism have in common was the
pattern to be indicated in the Rorschach, namely that she
needed to avoid a realistic appraisal of human relations.
After parturition, her attitude toward men (as shown in
both interviews and the second Rorschach) changed from
avoiding contact with men to avoiding involvement. She
phrased it, "I no longer hate men; I'm afraid of them";
her plan was to renew contacts with men, especially in
her church groups, but never to become involved.

The Rorschach showed a relatively high degree of
rigidity and constriction of personality on the surface,
but the variety and originality in the record, the presence
of some color shock, and the fact that the constriction
often collapsed in the course of the test indicate that the
constriction was not the mark of an impoverished personality.[31] The need to constrict herself was particularly
called into play when she was confronted by emotional
involvement with other people, who she felt were malicious and hostile toward her. There was present hostility
within herself toward others, but this was repressed. The
chief technique by which she endeavored to constrict herself was a strong effort to keep her reactions on the level
of "common sense," "practicality," and "realism." When
this device broke down in the Rorschach, as it did several
times, anxiety came out. She sought to suppress her sen-

sual promptings, at which again she was only irregularly successful.

A very interesting indication in the Rorschach was that her originality tended to destroy her constrictive pattern. *There were indications that when she could suppress her originality, she was able to avoid much of her anxiety; but when her originality did emerge, it broke the pattern of constriction, and anxiety occurred.* This Rorschach presented the general picture of an individual who tried to constrict herself as a protection against anxiety-creating situations, but the constrictive strategy continually broke down, and anxiety, generally of the free-floating variety, then ensued. The Rorschach anxiety rating was: depth 4, width 3½, handling 2, which placed her in the *high* category in relation to the other young women. Her childhood, present, and future anxiety check-lists showed *moderately low, moderately high,* and *high* quantities of anxiety respectively, with ambition being the chief area of anxiety in each case.

In the interviews with both the social workers and the psychologist she always confined her talk to "practical," "realistic" topics and continually refused to deal with underlying emotional problems. It seemed that the great emphasis on "realism" was a means of covering up her real feelings. She had a slight awareness of the protective nature of the "practicality," admitting that she felt it was dangerous to express her real feelings or her originality, one of her reasons being that people would think she was "silly." Thus in the interviews, in contrast to the Rorschach, she was able to hold to her constrictive pattern successfully and avoid most topics which entailed anxiety. Her relations with the other young women in the house were characterized by directness and facility in superficial relationship on one hand, but on the other a recurrent suspicion of and hostility toward them, which constituted at times a considerable problem in the house.

In rating Frances' feeling of rejection, we confront the difficulty in the contradiction between surface statements —in which she would deny experiencing rejection—and the underlying indications. Since Frances' constrictive pattern and her strategies of avoidance of her problems could not be broken through in the interviews, and since there was ample evidence (e.g., the idealization of her parents and the fairy-tale motif) for assuming that her verbalizations about her relation to her parents were untrustworthy, we based our judgment of her rejection on the underlying indications. From her failure to see people in the Rorschach, her underlying suspicion of and hostility toward other people, and her strong need to avoid contact and involvement with them, we assumed a *moderately high* degree of rejection.

We find in Frances a *moderately high degree of anxiety. She is a demonstration of anxiety emerging in a pattern of unsuccessful constriction.* She tried to constrict herself as a means of avoiding anxiety-creating situations, particularly situations of involvement with other people. Two prominent mechanisms for this constriction were her endeavor to keep all her reactions on a very "realistic," "practical" level and to idealize the other persons. Since she was actually not an impoverished personality, since considerable hostility toward others underlay the idealization, and since, indeed, the "realism" and idealization were contradictory, her constrictive pattern regularly broke down. One cannot hold contradictory beliefs at the same time; such a contradiction is bound, sooner or later, to disintegrate. It was at these points that Frances exhibited anxiety. The suppression of sexual and hostile impulses, as well as the suppression of originality, was part of the constrictive endeavor.

It is highly significant that when originality did come out in the Rorschach, anxiety did also. We have noted in the case of Phyllis that successful constriction obviates anxiety. A similar demonstration of the relationship between constriction and avoidance of anxiety is found in this case; when Frances was able to constrict herself, she did not experience anxiety, but when she was unsuccessful in her constrictive endeavors, considerable anxiety emerged.

CHARLOTTE: PSYCHOTIC DEVELOPMENTS AS AN ESCAPE FROM ANXIETY

Charlotte was a twenty-one-year-old daughter of middle-class parents in an agricultural community. Her siblings were a brother a year older than Charlotte and two younger brothers of seventeen and twelve. Her medical examination showed congenital syphilis and recently contracted gonorrhea.

Both her behavior at Walnut House and her Rorschach showed distinct, though mild, psychotic trends. The Rorschach contained several rationally distorted responses and was marked by shading shock, a long time average per response, and a great deal of blocking.[32] She made much effort on the test, making frequent apologies with her responses, but her effort was ineffectual and without much affect. Some blandness was present, though not of the extreme sort characteristic of severe psychosis. During the Rorschach her behavior was marked by frequent ingratiating but vacant smiles at me, accompanied by an expressionless quality in her eyes. Diagnostically, the Rorschach indicated a mildly schizophrenic state, possibly of a hebephrenic nature. Very little anxiety was present, though her handling of her anxiety was by definition poor. The rating on the Rorschach was: depth 1½, width 3, handling 4, which placed her in the *low* category of anxiety with relation to the other young women.

At Walnut House, Charlotte was generally gracious, bland, and genial, but these attitudes were periodically interrupted by outbursts of intense rage. The fact of pregnancy made very little impression on her, and, correspondingly, she showed a pronounced lack of realistic planning for parturition and the baby.

Her background likewise suggests some severe psychological disturbance. In her community she was known as a person who part of the time was very respectable and faithful in church frequently becoming what was known in the town as "boy-crazy," and part of the time was given to impulsive, defiant and socially "wild" acts. At the age of twenty she impulsively married a rigid, overconscientious young man to "compensate for my lacks," she put it. The marriage may have been an attempt to avoid a psychotic episode, to hold herself together. He subsequently suffered a psychoneurotic breakdown in the army. She visited him in the army camp at this time, and they agreed their marriage had been a mistake and decided to have it annulled. She described herself at this time as being "so mixed up I didn't care about anything."

There followed a period of promiscuous sexual activity, during which the pregnancy occurred. The act of intercourse which she assumed accounted for the pregnancy—

with an army officer whose last name she did not know—
she described as an experience she had not agreed to, but
"I couldn't do anything about it." Possibly the behavior
surrounding her becoming pregnant represents a mildly
schizophrenic state (or the onset of the state) at that
time.

Though Charlotte would talk freely about her childhood in the interviews, she would never talk about any
present worries. No present problems seemed to exist for
her; and when topics referring to possible present sources
of anxiety emerged, she would assume a gay attitude or
retreat, with vacant facial expression, into long periods
of silence. Some minor remarks suggest a great deal of
buried guilt feeling—e.g., "I made a mistake and have to
pay for it"—but she showed no affect about guilt. Her
childhood anxiety check-list showed a *moderately high*
quantity of anxiety, with significant emphasis on "fear
of the dark" ("because it represents the unknown") and
other apprehensions of a phobic character. But her present
and future anxiety check-list showed *moderately low* and
low quantities of anxiety respectively. To the extent that
the quantities of anxiety shown on these check-lists can
be taken at face value, they would support the supposition that in her prepsychotic state she experienced a great
deal of anxiety, as we would expect following our discussion of anxiety and psychosis above (Chapter 3). But
that anxiety was now covered over by the mildly schizophrenic condition.

Charlotte's low degree of anxiety illustrates that psychotic developments of this kind effectively cover up the
individual's anxiety. With respect to the problem of anxiety, many forms of psychosis are to be understood as the
end result of conflicts and anxiety which are too great
for the individual to bear and at the same time are insoluble on any other level. In such cases great anxiety is
generally found just before the onset of the psychotic
state. That period may be represented in Charlotte just
after she agreed to have her marriage annulled. The
psychotic development itself may be characterized as a
means of obviating otherwise insoluble conflicts and
anxiety, at the price, in cases like Charlotte's, of the surrender of some aspect of adjustment to reality. What the
genesis of Charlotte's psychotic trend was we do not know;

but it is clear in her case that anxiety and conflict are to a considerable extent "covered over" or "lost" in the psychotic state.[33]

HESTER: ANXIETY, DEFIANCE, AND REBELLION

Hester, seventeen years old, was the only girl in a middle-class family. Two of her brothers were two and four years older respectively, and one was five years younger than she. Her father, an interior decorator, had drowned after a period of excessive drinking when she was seven. She had attended an upper-middle-class private denominational girls' boarding school for her secondary education, where she was known as rebellious, given to temper tantrums, intellectually well endowed but "lazy." She was pregnant by a sailor with whom she had had only a casual friendship.

Her Rorschach showed a good deal of emotional impulsiveness and infantilism, some tendencies toward exhibitionism, and prominent tendencies to be defiant toward those in authority over her.[34] Her sexual impulses were used largely in the service of this defiance. The only human being seen in the Rorschach was a clown. The anxiety in the Rorschach emerged especially at the points of her guilt feeling, this, in turn, being a product of her defiance, particularly her use of sexual impulsiveness as a form of defiance. The rating of anxiety in her Rorschach was: depth 3, width 3, handling 3, which placed her in the *moderately high* category in relation to the other young women. On the childhood and present anxiety check-lists she showed a *high degree* of anxiety, her chief areas of anxiety being what her peers thought of her, phobial apprehensions, and anxiety about competitive status in school and work.

The family atmosphere in her childhood had been marked by much teasing, some of it of a sadistic intensity, on the part of the father and brothers. The mother had been particularly the butt of this teasing, although Hester herself had received a considerable share. She felt she had had a fairly close relationship with her father as a small child, but some of the stories she related suggested that his teasing had pained her more than she admitted and that his behavior involved some definite rejection of her. For example, she had been out fishing with him as a child; on their way back to the car she had gotten caught on the barbed wire of the fence. He (ostensibly in "teasing") had gotten in the car and driven around the block, leaving her hanging there. Hester laid her rebellious behavior to the fact that her father died when she was young. "If I had had a father to talk with, all these messes [including the pregnancy] would not have happened." Her mother, interviewed at Walnut House, appeared to be a passive individual. Beyond the fact that she had always regarded Hester as a problem and had been forced to show some concern about Hester's predicaments at school and elsewhere, she seemed never to have shown much interest in or understanding of her daughter.

An adult relative who apparently had a fairly thorough understanding of the family was interviewed at Walnut House. She stated that the mother had been so occupied with preserving material and social advantages for her children that she had not paid attention to them personally and that she had given attention to Hester only in the girl's most severe predicaments. It is interesting that this relative thought it would have been better if the mother had been more "authoritative." To the extent that this would mean her being more responsive to Hester, more of a real and immediate person in Hester's environment, even at the price of occasional punishment of her, there is ground for the hypothesis that Hester would have received some very needed psychological orientation in her family. Her extensive rebellious behavior, designed, as we shall hypothesize below, to commandeer her mother's concern, would have been less necessary. Though Hester felt that she admired her mother, she also stated that her mother was remote and uncompanionable; she had frequently invited her mother, she asserted, to go to games with her, but the mother had always refused. According to Hester's description, the mother would take the part of the boys when, during childhood, there were quarrels between the siblings.

Hester's defiance and rebelliousness seemed covertly and overtly to be directed against her mother, and there were indications in the interviews (bearing out the Rorschach data) that the sexual impulsiveness fell in this category. Her first sexual experience had occurred when, at the age of thirteen, she had run away from home, hitchhiking to a distant city and back again. There were indications that her pregnancy served both as defiance and as a means of forcing her mother to take an interest in her. Hester's most frequent method of allaying anxiety was to laugh it off—a form of behavior which, in this context, may also be viewed as defiance (e.g., "I don't care").

We find in Hester a *moderately high* degree of anxiety and a *moderately high* degree of rejection. Her present anxiety arose out of her guilt feelings over her defiant and rebellious behavior, her sexual impulses (and probably the pregnancy) being employed in the service of such behavior. The rejection consisted centrally of the mother's lack of concern or interest in her, and Hester's defiance and rebelliousness seem to have been motivated chiefly by the need to force her mother to show some concern. The genetic source of her anxiety presumably lay in original feelings of isolation from her mother, with the father's death contributing to this isolation in a significant but probably subsidiary way. In Hester, thus, there was a vicious circle: she sought to overcome the original anxiety (isolation) by methods—defiance and rebelliousness—which produced more anxiety.

SARAH AND ADA: ABSENCE AND PRESENCE OF ANXIETY IN TWO BLACK WOMEN

Sarah

Sarah, a twenty-year-old proletarian black woman, had been born in a Southern state, where her father was a miner and her mother a domestic. At the age of four, Sarah went to live with an aunt and paternal uncle (also a miner) in a borderline Southern state, for the reason that they liked children but had none of their own. Of her five siblings, two others had lived with her at the home of the aunt and uncle. After graduation from high school, Sarah had come to New York and at the time of her pregnancy was working as a welder in a factory.

Sarah impressed the social workers and me alike as a stable, well-adjusted, independent person who accepted and dealt with her problems objectively. She planned realistically for the birth and care of her baby (and after its birth eventually succeeded in the relatively difficult task of keeping it and supporting it herself). She was certain she wished not to accept financial assistance from the city welfare department but to pay for her care at Walnut House out of her own savings. She had been very fond of the young man who was the father of her baby, having at one time considered marriage with him. But after she became pregnant, his attitude and behavior became increasingly unreliable. At the time of her stay at Walnut House, she wished neither to marry him nor to receive financial assistance from him, but she did make considerable effort to get him to permit his name to be used by the baby. When he consistently refused, Sarah was disappointed but accepted and adjusted to the fact realistically.

Sarah's ambition (which came out prominently on her check-lists) did not take an aggressively competitive form. In fact, while in school, she had worked out an ideal of "not being at the top, nor at the bottom, but somewhere in the middle."[35] She received much satisfaction from her work, and apparently her employers had a very high opinion of her, for they reserved her job for her till she could return after her parturition.

The only situation which presented a problem in Sarah's behavior at Walnut House arose from the fact that her independence sometimes took a defiant form, largely around the racial issue. Since she and Ada were the only two blacks living with a group of whites, and since several of the white women expressed some racial prejudice, Sarah at first made a practice of remaining aloof and staying much of the time in her room. "If you stay away from groups, you avoid trouble" was her formula. She exhibited outright defiance against one of the staff who, she felt, was "bossy." She reported that she had disliked remaining in the South when she visited her parents because there were "too many rules and restrictions, and you have to say ma'am to somebody no older than yourself." Sarah's defiance was sometimes more extreme than the situation warranted (she admitted that she sensed some affronts where none was intended). But at the same time it was not indiscriminate defiance; it arose only where she felt the racial issue was present in the other person's attitudes. On the whole, however, it would seem that her special sensitivity and defiant independence are understandable for a black living in an intimate situation with a group of whites in a condition (pregnancy) in which many of them were apt to be especially defensive. In this sense, I consider Sarah's defiant tendency as largely a mode of conscious adjustment rather than as the expression of a neurotic pattern. It would seem to be an entirely tenable hypothesis that this conscious defiance served a positive function—i.e., it had been developed by Sarah as a technique for adjusting to the racial issue without the impoverishment of her capacities or the surrender of her psychological freedom.

Sarah's Rorschach showed an original, somewhat naïve, genuinely extroverted person with higher-than-average intelligence.[36] There was some compliance and much capacity for caution in her relations with people, but neither of these characteristics was in neurotic form—i.e., the caution and compliance were conscious ways of adapting to situations rather than mechanisms of self-repression. A fairly high degree of independence was shown, with definite indications that she knew what she wanted and did not want. She employed a technique of not taking life too seriously, preserving a somewhat happy-go-lucky attitude, avoiding complications by avoiding depth in her relations; but these traits again did not appear in severe form and did not involve impoverishment of her capacities. On the whole, it was the picture of a differentiated but uncomplicated personality. Almost no conflicts or indications of neurotic problems were present. Her rating on anxiety in the Rorschach was: depth 1, width 1, handling 1, which placed her in the *low* category in relation to the other girls. Correspondingly, her childhood and present anxiety checklists placed her in the *low* and *moderately low* categories respectively for quantity of anxiety. The chief areas of anxiety were ambition and what her friends and family thought of her.

There were no definite signs of rejection in Sarah's background. She reported a happy childhood in her own family and in her life with the aunt and uncle, and her attitudes toward her aunt and uncle and her siblings were, like her attitudes toward her parents, affectionate. A report from the social service agency in the home city of the parents reported them to be hard-working, responsible, sympathetic persons, and all that could be deduced was that Sarah had had a relatively healthy background within her two families as a child. She did not wish her parents or her aunt and uncle to know about the pregnancy until after parturition, for she felt they would want to help her financially even though they could not afford to. Through an accident in social agency channels, Sarah's parents were informed of her pregnancy before parturition; Sarah was angry that this should have happened against her expressed wish (recall her defiance, cited above, at people who are "bossy" or go over her head). But the ensuing letters from her parents showed understanding and no condemnation of her whatever.

Sarah ranked *low* in degree of anxiety, and at the same time exhibited no discernible experience of rejection. Her problems were objective and realistic, managed without subjective conflict, with the one possible exception of the special sensitivity to racial discrimination and resulting defiance. But this, likewise, may be termed a "normal" rather than neurotic reaction in view of her realistic cultural situation as a black woman. It may be concluded that Sarah's relative lack of neurotic anxiety was related to the fact that she *did not experience psychological rejection within her family circles,* either as a child or in the present situation. But a cultural factor emerged in the case of Sarah (as of Ada, the other black woman): extramarital pregnancy is not as much of an anxiety-creating situation in the black communities from which Sarah and Ada came as in the cultural milieux of the white women. It may be, thus, that we did not have Sarah in a genuinely anxiety-creating situation. This factor, though it could account for *less* presence of anxiety, could not account for the *absence* of neurotic anxiety in Sarah. The Rorschach would assumedly reveal neurotic anxiety if it were present, whether the subject were in an objective anxiety-creating situation or not.

Ada

The other black in this study is Ada, age nineteen, Catholic, who had lived most of her life in a suburb of New York. Since her father's death when she was four, she and her brother (two years younger) had been supported by her mother with some help from the department of welfare. Ada had attended a Catholic primary school, but a public high school. After her graduation from high school at seventeen, her mother had had a "nervous breakdown from overwork" and had gone to live with relatives in the South. Ada and her brother moved to New York to live with an aunt.

Ada's original vocational aim was nursing, but with the occurrence of the pregnancy she decided that she would become a factory worker in order to support the baby. It was difficult to place Ada accurately with respect to socioeconomic class: there were proletarian elements in her background, but her original aim of being a nurse and many of her attitudes (discussed below) seemed to be middle-class. We describe her as on the borderline between proletarian and middle-class.

She was pregnant by a young man her own age with whom she had had a close relationship since the middle of her high-school career. According to her description, he had always been very "possessive" of her and jealous of her other friends, and she had apparently submitted to his dominating tendencies. Though admitting paternity, he had refused to marry her, at which she reported she had "put him out of my mind." Her medical diagnosis revealed syphilis, contracted from this young man.

Ada's Rorschach showed a very stereotyped, acquiescent, compliant person with no originality and with average intelligence.[37] The chief feature of the record was the fact that she set high standards for herself, but the standards were empty of positive content. It was as though she had *a great need to measure up but no self-chosen goals or feelings of what she wanted to measure up to.* It was the picture, in conventional terms, of an individual with a strong superego. The motivation for holding the high standards was that she could thereby comply with others' expectations of her and with her own introjected expectations. As a consequence her spontaneity and inner instinctual promptings (sex and hostility) were almost entirely repressed. There was considerable potentiality for sensual and other forms of responsiveness to other persons, but such responsiveness gave her anxiety because she could not respond in ways that fitted her high standards. We recall that her motivations for the sexual relations were never stated by her. From the Rorschach picture we hypothesized that the motivations were both her own sexual promptings and her *need to comply with the expectations of the young man*. The latter motivation was probably more significant in the respect that it would be necessary for Ada to have her compliant tendencies on the side of the sexual relationship in order to overcome her strong sexual repression.

When a response occurred (Card VII) associated with vaginal examination at the hospital, a general disturbance was cued off which lasted through all the remaining cards in the test, amounting almost to a confabulatory tendency. This would indicate that if she failed to live up to her standards (the pregnancy being associated with such a failure), she was deeply disoriented in her relation to herself as well as to others, and much anxiety arose. Anxiety rating on the Rorschach was: depth 2½, width 4½, handling 3, which placed her in the *high* category of anxiety in relation to the other young women.

Ada ranked *moderately high* in the childhood anxiety check-list and *moderately low* in both the present and future check-lists. Her chief areas of anxiety were success and failure in work and what her family and parental surrogates thought of her, anxiety about her teacher or mother scolding her being prominent.

In her behavior at Walnut House as well as in the interviews, Ada continually exhibited the above-described combination of compliance and high standards. She answered all questions conscientiously but never volunteered spontaneous expression of thoughts or feelings. She could always be depended upon to run errands at the house and to cooperate in other ways which did not require initiative. Since she had neither the independence nor the defiant tendencies of Sarah, she got along well with the white women. In her school career she had always obtained very high grades. She expressed satisfaction that in her schools "everything was drilled into you—you learn more that way."

The genesis of Ada's need to hold rigid standards for herself could be seen in her description of her mother and their relationship, and, to a lesser extent, her relation with her aunt. Though Ada remarked in blanket terms that her mother had been a "happy" person during Ada's childhood, the fact that the chief symptom of the mother's

present "breakdown" was her "worrying about everything" suggested that she was probably a tense and rigid
person. A clearer indication of the mother's rigidity was
seen in the fact that she was very strict with the children;
Ada reported that the mother frequently whipped the
son "because he didn't come exactly when she called."
Ada herself had not been punished often, according to her
reports; in fact, she felt her mother had been too lenient
with her. This statement, however, may have been an
expression of Ada's own rigid standards (i.e., she felt she
should have been punished more often) rather than an
objective description of the childhood situation. As a child
Ada was always obedient, and always conformed to her
mother's wishes, with only occasional and slight feelings
of hostility toward her mother. Ada reported that she had
learned to go off by herself and "get over" this anger.
The mother and aunt with whom Ada later lived were
faithfully practicing Catholics, as Ada likewise had always
been.

Ada described the aunt as also very strict. In an interview at Walnut House, the aunt explained that she had
made a conscious effort to inculcate high standards in
Ada, that she had been very proud of her; and although
she did not feel punitive toward Ada because of the pregnancy as such, she did not wish to accept Ada back into
her apartment after she became pregnant because it would
be a sign of the relaxing of the standards she had trained
in her own two children. If we may take the aunt's attitudes as representative of the family constellation in
which Ada was brought up, we have a graphic expression
of the formula of the adults which presumably underlay
Ada's psychological pattern: (1) these adults sought to
inculcate "high standards" in her; (2) they were proud of
her to the extent that she complied with these standards;
and (3) they threatened her with rejection if she did not
comply with these standards.

It was impossible to find overt feelings in Ada of rejection by her mother, with whom Ada felt she had had a
friendly, though somewhat distant, relationship until she
was an adolescent. It seemed clear that from childhood
onward Ada had so well accepted and complied with the
"high standards" of her mother and the environment that
the mother was never given cause to reject her overtly.

While at Walnut House, Ada could never bring herself to let her brother know about her pregnancy, since she was certain he would reject her; and she hesitated for several months before writing her mother about her situation. When she did finally inform her mother, the mother apparently accepted the fact of the baby and suggested plans for their keeping it together.

In Ada we find a *moderately high* degree of anxiety. Her degree of rejection varied as it was viewed in different aspects: she was rejected in a moderately high degree by her aunt; she expected a high degree of rejection by her brother; and although the rejection was difficult to assess in her relation with her mother because of her previous complete compliance with her mother's wishes, there were indications that Ada had considerable fear of rejection by her mother. We could, therefore, assume that rejection was present potentially in the relationship.

But the essential point for the understanding of the dynamics of Ada's anxiety is *the rejection she felt in the face of her "high standards."* These standards were not indigenous, self-chosen values, but were introjections of the formal expectations of her mother and the family environment. Hence the significant form of her present rejection was self-rejection, the self having taken over the authority of the parent. When Ada felt that she had not lived up to these internalized expectations, a profound psychological disorientation occurred (most graphically illustrated in the Rorschach), and subjective conflict and much anxiety ensued.

The fact that the mother accepted the expected baby should not be taken as an argument against the mother's potential and covert rejection of Ada. Indeed, as stated in the comments on Sarah, the problem of the occasion for rejection must be viewed differently in the cases of these black young women from the others at Walnut House. There were numerous indications in the case of Ada, as well as that of Sarah, that having a baby out of wedlock was not in itself as serious or opprobrious a situation in the black communities from which they came as it was for the white women. It does not seem that rejection in Ada's case—e.g., the aunt's not wishing her to stay at her apartment, Ada's fear of her brother's rejection, and Ada's rejection of herself—arose from the fact that she was going to have a baby out of wedlock, but rather from the acts that led up to the pregnancy. What was disapproved of in these acts is again hard to define specifically, since the "standards" that were violated are mere forms rather than having a specific content. It seems to me that the rejection facing Ada, and the psychological disorientation underlying her anxiety, had their source in the fact that Ada complied with an authority and with expectations (i.e., the young man's expectations and her own sexual impulses) other than those of her mother or the mother surrogates. Corroborating data for this statement are suggested by the fact that Ada did not exhibit any pronounced guilt feeling about the sexual relations or the pregnancy as such. The anxiety appeared to come directly out of a psychological disorientation that arose, in turn, out of her not complying with her mother's expectations.

We have pointed out in previous cases in this study that the conflict underlying neurotic anxiety may be described as a hiatus within the person between expectations and reality, originally with respect to parental attitudes. In Ada's case a clear hiatus was present underlying her anxiety, but it took a somewhat different form; it was a hiatus between her introjected expectations of herself and the reality situation.[38] *The anxiety in Ada's case did not arise out of guilt feeling because of the sexual relations or pregnancy as such, but rather arose directly out of the psychological disorientation which she experienced because of her having complied with authority and expectations other than those of her mother.*

One might make the assumption that Ada could be free of anxiety if she complied with her mother's expectations, albeit in their introjected form. But the ineffectualness of such protection from anxiety is amply demonstrated in Ada's case. To gain and preserve freedom from anxiety on this basis she could never follow her own desires, nor could she ever comply with anyone other than the mother; but since her way of relating to all other persons was to comply, her psychological patterns were bound to be continually jeopardized. The case illustrates the dilemma of the person whose freedom from anxiety depends on compliance with an authority that is not rooted in his own autonomy.

A comparison of Sarah and Ada highlights the above-described dynamic of neurotic anxiety. For both black women, the fact of illegitimate pregnancy did not present as much of an anxiety-creating situation as it did for the white women. Both showed compliance: in Sarah compliance was a conscious method of adjusting, particularly to the racial issue, but her autonomy and self-feeling were protected by conscious defiance whenever she felt that to comply would threaten her independence. But for Ada compliance was an unconscious pattern as well as conscious, her self-feeling and self-acceptance depending on how well she complied, prototypically with her mother's expectations. In Sarah, there was very little or no feeling of rejection by her parents; in Ada there was considerable feeling of rejection, in the form of rejection of herself in the face of her introjected standards. In Sarah there was very little subjective conflict and very little anxiety. In Ada there was *strong subjective conflict* between her introjected expectations and her reality situation, leading to pronounced psychological disorientation and a moderately high degree of anxiety.

IRENE: ANXIETY, OVERCONSCIENTIOUSNESS, AND SHYNESS

Irene was the nineteen-year-old adopted daughter of relatively old middle-class parents. The family had always lived in the country, and since there were no siblings, Irene's life had been relatively solitary until high school. She was pregnant by her fiancé, with whom she had had a close relationship during her high-school years. Irene stated that her parents had not overtly opposed her engagement but had not approved of her fiancé because his parents ran a liquor store. The several sexual relations she had had with the fiancé occurred after her graduation from high school and just before they planned to marry.

The chief features of Irene's Rorschach were very great conscientiousness, pronounced contact shyness and with-drawal tendencies, overrefined control, and a tendency toward stereotype of interest (presumably related to her solitary background), with a fairly high degree of originality at the same time.[39] Her very long pauses, during which she studied the cards industriously as though silently considering and rejecting possible responses, seemed to be partly due to her cultural difficulty in self-expression, but also were evidences of her compulsive conscientiousness. This latter compulsion to do well involved so much effort that it markedly inhibited her productivity.

Though her intratensive promptings were easily accepted by her, she exhibited very much caution in responding to emotional stimuli in her relations with other people. The shyness, withdrawal, and caution could be partially understood as cultural difficulties in expression and responsiveness—she herself related these traits to the fact that "I'm just a country girl." But on a deeper level the caution was a protection against anxiety-creating emotional involvements, the anxiety showing itself chiefly in her overconscientiousness. It is as though she felt she could not relate to people except by means of the compulsion to be perfect, to fulfill some very high standards. When, however, she was able to break through her shyness and caution and respond to outside stimuli on the Rorschach, both her anxiety and overconscientiousness diminished. This would imply that the overconscientiousness was a defense against the anxiety-creating situation. Anxiety rating on the Rorschach was: depth 4½, width 2, handling 2, which placed her in the *moderately high* category in relation to the other young women.

Both her childhood and present anxiety check-lists fell in the *low category* in quantity, but this was undoubtedly due to her block in expression as shown on the Rorschach. On the former list, anxiety concerning success and failure in work was the markedly predominant area, with phobic apprehensions second; on the present anxiety list, the chief area of anxiety was again success and failure in work, and the second what her family thought of her.

Apparently Irene's compulsive conscientiousness had been a character trait all through her life. She related that by dint of very great effort she had graduated at the head of her high-school class and then suffered a temporary "nervous breakdown." For another example, she said she had always been very careful not to select her friends from a "lower social class" than her own. In the interviews she also showed cautiousness and a considerable desire to please, but this behavior seemed not so much for the purpose of gaining my approval as for the purpose of living up to certain standards of behavior of her own.

Her parents were very conservative, religiously and morally, not believing in dancing, smoking, or going to the movies. They had, however, overtly granted her freedom in these respects. Irene had joined a more liberal church and participated in the above-mentioned recreations without overt conflict with her parents but—as we shall see below—probably with considerable covert conflict. She characterized her mother as having always "worried a good deal." In an interview at Walnut House the mother referred to Irene as "mother's little girl," and it was admitted by both Irene and her that she had always sought to overprotect and "coddle" the daughter. The parents had been hurt and surprised by the pregnancy but had accepted it and cooperated with Irene in her plans. Again, however, their attitude was that of adults taking care of a child.

The home background was characterized overtly by an emotional vacuum: the parents had scruples against quarreling, either between themselves or with Irene. Their practice had been never to spank her but rather, when she committed some infringement as a child, to reason with her and then to make her sit quietly in a chair—"during which I would boil," Irene remarked. It is plausible that this lack of emotional give and take and the absence of any emotional outlet as a child, together with the parents' belief in rigid standards, set the stage for the development of considerable guilt feelings in Irene. It is also plausible that these guilt feelings were an important motivation in Irene's overconscientiousness. She stated that she had always been very lonely as a child. Apologizing for saying so, she asserted that she had been closer to her two dogs than to her parents. She had never felt any bond of understanding between herself and her mother, and had never been able to talk intimately to her mother.

Her engagement and sexual relations with a boy of whom the parents did not approve seemed to be motivated both by her repressed hostility toward her parents, especially toward her mother, and by her need to compensate for the lack of warmth and understanding in her relationships at home. In her later interviews at Walnut House, Irene expressed considerable hostility and resentment against her mother, focusing chiefly on the facts that her mother had coddled her and had had so little understanding of or faith in her.

Irene was able to use the therapeutic opportunities at Walnut House very constructively. The follow-up data several months later indicated that she was making a very good and enthusiastic adjustment at college.

Although there was no physical rejection (e.g., punishment) of Irene, there were sound evidences that she experienced a good deal of emotional rejection and very much loneliness; hence we rated her as *moderately high* in rejection by her parents. On the basis of her well-defined symptoms of anxiety—overconscientiousness, withdrawal, cautiousness, and shyness—our over-all rating for her anxiety was also *moderately high*.

Though superficially these behavior traits were related to her solitary background, on a deeper level the withdrawal, conscientiousness, and caution seem to represent endeavors to adjust to the anxiety-creating situation of her relation with her parents. The withdrawal and contact shyness seemed to be protections against the emotionally cold milieu of the family, and the overconscientiousness I see as an endeavor to adjust to the fact that she could not be accepted unless she lived up to her parents' rigid standards. The emotional vacuum and unreality in the family likewise gave the context for the subjective conflict which underlay Irene's anxiety. The parents not only patently repressed their own aggression, but likewise gave her no opportunity to react against them (e.g., the "reasoning" with her and placing her in a chair amounting to an authoritative suppression of her resentment and hostility). I have indicated above that, though the parents ostensibly permitted her to make her own liberal choices, there were evidences that in making these choices, as well as in her state of suppressed hostility, Irene experienced considerable guilt feelings. The compulsive conscientiousness could be seen, on one side, as motivated by this guilt feeling.

It may be observed parenthetically that Irene's subjective conflict and guilt feeling was all the stronger psychologically because she was never permitted to feel conscious hostility against her parents. In contrast to Louise and Bessie, who suffered outright punishment at the hands of their parents, Irene thus could find no objective focus for her guilt feelings.

CHAPTER
10

Gleanings from the Case Studies

The threat of irrational material in the unconscious explains why people are afraid of becoming conscious of themselves. There might really be something behind the screen—one never knows—and thus people "prefer to take into account and to observe carefully" factors external to their consciousness.

—Carl Jung

What crucial issues are touched upon in the case studies in the last two chapters? What ideas can we get from them which will aid us in the understanding of anxiety?

ANXIETY UNDERLYING FEAR

It was observed in the first case above that Brown's fear that he had cancer was presented by him as a "realistic" and "rational" fear. He denied that it was in any way related to any underlying anxiety. But we noted that this cancer fear appeared regularly as the first step in a progression toward an anxiety spell. We noted also that as long as the cancer fear remained as the focus of his attention, conscious anxiety did not appear, but that when anxiety dreams and conscious anxiety did emerge (as they regularly did after several days), the cancer fear vanished. We cannot avoid the conclusion that the cancer fear was thus both the first form of an emerging anxiety spell and also a means of covering the underlying anxiety by displacement on a threat which could be called rational and realistic.

The anxiety spell, of which, as we have said, the cancer fear was the initial sign, was regularly related to some aspect of the conflict which underlay Brown's neurotic anxiety—namely, his conflict with his mother. If he had been able to hold consistently to his cancer fear (or if, to put the matter hypothetically, he really *had* had cancer), his underlying conflict and anxiety would have been obviated. For he would have been able to remain in a hospital and be taken care of without feeling guilty about it, and he would also have gotten even with his mother since she would have had to support him. Thus, despite superficial and apparent differences in content between the cancer fear and the conflict with his mother, I propose that a logical and subjectively consistent relationship existed between the former (the neurotic fear) and the latter (the underlying neurotic anxiety). For was not this mother problem, in a symbolic sense, a "cancer" for Harold Brown?

In the case of Helen we hypothesized that the fear of parturition was an objectification of her underlying anxiety arising from repressed guilt feeling associated with her pregnancy. In my judgment this was borne out. So long as her apprehension could be attached to the possible sufferings in childbirth—a focus of fear which could easily be construed by Helen as "rational"—she was not faced with the much more difficult problem of confronting the underlying guilt feelings. Even the admission of these guilt feelings would have threatened her whole structure of psychological protective strategies and thrown her into profound conflict.

These cases illustrate that *fears are the objectified, particularized foci of underlying anxiety.* A neurotic fear has its exaggerated quality by virtue of the neurotic anxiety underlying it. It is also to be noted that (a) *the content of the particular neurotic fear is not fortuitously or accidentally selected by the subject, but bears a consistent and subjectively logical relation to that particular subject's pattern of underlying conflict and neurotic anxiety; and (b) the neurotic fear performs the function of covering up the underlying conflict of anxiety.*

At the outset of the study of unmarried mothers, I proposed that neurotic fears would shift, as the practical issues and problems confronting the individual shifted, but that the neurotic anxiety would remain relatively constant. As stated earlier, one of the purposes of the second Rorschach and the anxiety check-lists after parturition was to determine if possible the shifts in the foci of anxiety after the birth of the baby. Some few data emerged bearing on this hypothesis. In the cases—Helen, Agnes, Charlotte, Frances, Dolores—in which it was possible to continue the study and administer a second Rorschach after parturition, the results indicated that (a) the neurotic anxiety had decreased slightly, but (b) the particular anxiety pattern remained the same. Some slight change of foci was evidenced—e.g., Helen's focus of anxiety on parturition had largely vanished, and there was a slight increase of anxiety about her relations with men over that in the preparturition Rorschach. In Frances there was a shift from a rigid defense (constriction) against the anxiety-creating situation of relations with men to a greater acceptance of the possibilities of these relations, with more overt signs of anxiety. But the data in the present study bearing on this hypothesis are scanty.

The case of Brown throws some light on why it was not possible in the study of unmarried mothers (in addition to the fact that we could not study a very large number of the women after parturition) to get more data on the shifts of foci of neurotic anxiety. In his case, studied over a period of two and one-half years, the shifts of foci of anxiety were very evident, and the above hypothesis could be clearly demonstrated. An interesting phenomenon, however, was noticed: after his severe anxiety attacks, a respite from anxiety often occurred for a week or several weeks, despite the fact that his underlying conflicts were not radically nearer solution than at the time of the anxiety.

This phenomenon—that after a period of severe anxiety there is a respite for a time, despite the fact that the underlying conflict is not radically clarified—obviously raises a perplexing problem. One explanation which suggests itself is based upon the guilt feeling involved in the anxiety. It is my observation that there is generally a considerable amount of guilt feeling, often very subtle but generally pervasive, involved in the inner conflict which underlies neurotic anxiety. In Brown's case it was clearly evident that he experienced much *guilt toward his mother in the instances when the occasion for his anxiety was his own achievement, and much guilt toward himself when the occasion was his dependency.* Now, perhaps this guilt feeling is temporarily allayed by the person's having endured the painful experience of anxiety. And hence the anxiety which was caused by the guilt feeling would also be temporarily allayed. It was as though the person were saying, "I've paid the price; now I've earned a little peace."

After this respite period the neurotic anxiety then re-emerged, generally around new foci. It would seem, therefore, that the study of the group of unmarried mothers did not continue long enough after the parturition to discover the new foci of anxiety which presumably would emerge, let us say, when the young woman got into a work situation or initiated relations with a new man friend. We can conclude that the data in the present study point toward an affirmation of the hypothesis that the foci of neurotic fears will shift while the underlying pattern of neurotic anxiety remains constant. But the data are not definite enough for this hypothesis to be termed demonstrated.

It has been illustrated in the cases in this study that *anxiety and hostility (covert and overt) rise and fall together.* When the subjects (say, Brown and Agnes) were relatively more anxious, more covert or overt hostility was evidenced, and when the anxiety abated, the hostility did likewise.

We have seen that one reason for this interrelation is that the intense pain and helplessness of the experience of anxiety arouses hostility toward those other persons whom the individual holds responsible for placing him in such a state. We have observed that another reason underlying this interrelation is that hostility (particularly repressed hostility) leads to anxiety. Brown's repressed hostility toward his mother, if expressed, would alienate the very person he is dependent upon, and hence its existence generates more anxiety. Thus, when hostility arises in persons with neurotic anxiety, *the hostility is generally repressed and may take the reactive form of an increased striving to please and placate other people.* This can be seen most vividly in the situation of Nancy, the most anxious woman in this study, who had trained her personality in great detail to please and placate other people.

One case, however, was presented (Agnes, whose character structure was sado-masochistic) in which hostility and aggression were employed as defenses against the anxiety-creating situation. By hostile and aggressive behavior she endeavored to force her boy friend not to make her more anxious by abandoning her.

CONFLICT: SOURCE OF ANXIETY

Whenever neurotic anxiety was found in the above cases, subjective conflict was likewise found.[1] On the surface this seems a relationship easy enough to see and demonstrate. In the cases in which neurotic anxiety was not found in any pronounced degree—Bessie, Louise, Sarah, Phyllis, Charlotte—subjective conflict in any pronounced form was not present either. But the more interesting question is, "What is the conflict about?"

The conflict took many different forms, depending on the individual case. To cite only three examples, the subjective conflict in the case of Brown lay in his need to achieve some autonomy and use of his own powers on one hand, but in his conviction at the same time that if he did appropriate his own power he would be killed by his mother. Hence his behavior was characterized by great dependence on his mother (and mother surrogates) and hostility toward her at the same time. Whenever this conflict was activated, profound and extensive feelings of inadequacy, helplessness, and concomitant anxiety occurred, with paralysis of capacity for acting. For Helen, the conflict lay between guilt feelings on one hand and the need (upon the achieving of which her self-esteem depended) to appear amoral and intellectually sophisticated. In Nancy the conflict appeared in the need to depend entirely upon others for her security, while at the same time she believed all others to be undependable.

The situations which cued off this conflict in the case of each person—e.g., for Brown, situations of dependency on one hand or occasions of his individual success on the other; for Helen, the guilt associated with her pregnancy; for Nancy, her relation to her fiancé—these were the anxiety-creating situations. In these studies, *inner conflict was always present with pronounced anxiety, and it was the activation of this conflict which cued off the neurotic anxiety.*

The question arises, moreover, as to the relation between the threat the individual anticipates and the conflict. The commonly accepted statement that anxiety—both normal and neurotic—always involves some anticipated threat is not contradicted by the data in the present study. In normal anxiety and fear, *the description of the threat may account relatively inclusively for the existence of the apprehension.* Anxiety about death is one example. It will be recalled that we made the distinction between anxiety and fear: when the threat is to an essential value, the reaction is anxiety; when the threat is to a peripheral value, the reaction is fear.

But in neurotic anxiety, two conditions are necessary: (1) *the threat must be to a vital value;* and (2) *the threat must be present in juxtaposition with another threat* so that the individual cannot avoid one threat without being confronted by another. In patterns of neurotic anxiety, the values held essential to the individual's existence as a personality are in contradiction with each other. If Brown uses his powers, he is threatened with death, but he can remain dependent upon his mother only at the price of continued feelings of worthlessness and complete helplessness, which is a threat almost as serious as being killed. For another example, Nancy confronted the threat of being rejected by the others (mother and fiancé) whom she believed to be undependable, but her incapacity to exist without the care of these other persons confronted her with an opposite threat. *The essence of the "trapped" feeling in neurotic anxiety is that the individual is threatened whichever way he turns.* Thus an inquiry into the nature of the threat anticipated by an individual in neurotic anxiety reveals the fact that threat is present on both sides of the conflict.

A corollary problem has also been raised and illustrated in the above cases—namely the distinction between the *occasion* and the *cause* in neurotic anxiety. (The term "occasion" is here used to mean the event which precipitated the anxiety.) It was observed that the occasions of Brown's neurotic anxiety were frequently situations which he could and did handle adequately, such as performing his academic assignments. Thus the occasion in those instances could not be identified with the cause of the anxiety. We also recall that the more severe his anxiety, the more he insisted that the occasion had nothing to do with it, that he was "afraid of everything," "afraid of life." While it is true that the particular occasion which cued off the anxiety spell could in retrospect be shown to have a psychologically consistent relation to the anxiety, there is none the less some logic in his insistence on the distinction between occasion and cause. In neurotic anxiety, *the occasion is significant in the respect that it cues off the underlying conflict, but the cause of the anxiety is the conflict.* As was demonstrated by Harold Brown, the occasions, no matter how significant they may seem to be objectively, always bear a subjectively logical relation to the particular inner conflict in the given individual. That is to say, the occasions are significant for the anxiety of the subject because they, and not other occasions, cue off his particular neurotic conflict.

It seems to me that a hypothesis may be formulated as follows: *The more nearly normal an experience of anxiety is, the more the occasion (precipitating event) and the cause of the anxiety are identical; but the more neurotic the anxiety, the more the occasion and the cause can be distinguished.* For example, a passenger on a ship in submarine-infested waters is anxious lest his ship be torpedoed. Such anxiety may be realistic and proportionate to the situation, and the occasion—the threat of being torpedoed—may conceivably be a relatively sufficient explanation of the anxiety. But at the other extreme, persons with severely neurotic anxiety may be precipitated into an anxiety spell by a chance word from an acquaintance, a lack of greeting from someone on the street, or a fleeting memory. Thus the more neurotic the anxiety, the less adequate becomes the objective occasion as an explanation, and the more we are driven to understand how the person interprets the situation to find the adequate cause of the anxiety. This is generally described as anxiety which is disproportionate to the situation. It *is* disproportionate to the occasion, but it is *not* disproportionate to the cause— namely, the inner conflict which the occasion has activated. In my experience in dealing with cases of the most severe anxiety—borderline psychotics for one example—the occasion, viewed objectively, is almost entirely inadequate as an explanation for the degree of anxiety, and the cause may be almost entirely subjective.

I have been speaking above chiefly about neurotic anxiety and the conflicts behind it. But are we not at the point where we can no longer make the distinction between normal and neurotic? Do we not all have these conflicts, in greater or lesser degree? And do not all conflicts move into contradiction at some point? When all is said and done, all anxiety arises from conflicts, with its origin in the conflict between being and nonbeing, between one's existence and that which threatens it. All of us, no matter how "neurotic" or "normal," experience the gap between our expectations and reality. This distinction becomes less important, and I believe we must look at all anxiety, preferably without special labels, as part of the human condition.

REJECTION BY PARENTS AND ANXIETY

This question is considered in the light of the study of the thirteen unmarried mothers. In these interviews particular emphasis was placed on inquiring into the relationship of the degree of rejection the young woman experienced at the hands of her parents (especially her mother) and the degree of her present neurotic anxiety. The parallel tables of the rankings according to degrees of anxiety and rejection by parents present immediately two phenomena: (1) *For the majority of the girls there is a clear correspondence between rejection and anxiety; but* (2) *for several girls there is no correspondence whatever.*

In nine cases—Nancy, Agnes, Helen, Hester, Frances, Irene, Ada, Phyllis, Sarah—the degree of anxiety falls in the same category as that of rejection. In this group, whenever there was evidenced rejection by parents, there was present neurotic anxiety, and in a roughly corresponding degree. The indications in these cases are on the side of the classical hypothesis: rejection by parents (especially by the mother) predisposes the individual to neurotic anxiety. But in two cases—Louise and Bessie—a radically different picture was presented. These two young women experienced profound and extensive parental rejection, and yet they did not have a corresponding degree of anxiety. Dolores falls in this group, though the rejection she received was not as severe and unrelieved as that which the other two experienced.

RANKING ACCORDING TO DEGREE OF ANXIETY		RANKING ACCORDING TO DEGREE OF REJECTION	
Nancy Agnes	} high	Nancy Agnes Bessie Louise	} high
Helen Hester France Irene Ada	} moderately high	Helen Hester Frances Irene Ada Dolores	} moderately high
Dolores Bessie	} moderately low	Phyllis Sarah	} low
Louise Phyllis Sarah	} low		

The key to this perplexing but fascinating problem is to be found by inquiring into the *psychological meaning of the rejection*. We shall, therefore, ask, with reference first to the cases of the young women in whom rejection was found with anxiety and then to the cases in which it was not: *How did the person subjectively interpret her rejection?* And what was the relation between her expectations of life and reality?

The chief characteristic of those who fit the hypothesis is that they always *interpreted the rejection against the background of high expectations of their parents*. They exhibited what I term a *contradiction between expectations and reality* in their attitudes toward their parents. They were never able to accept the rejection as a realistic, objective fact. In one breath Nancy described how her mother flagrantly left her alone, caring "more for going out to bars than for her child," but in the next breath she added, "She *could* have been such a good mother." Similarly, Nancy needed constantly to repeat that the mother was "good" at certain special periods in her childhood, despite the objective indications that the mother was consistently unstable and irresponsible in her relations with the child. In Nancy, a point was also demonstrated that may presumably hold for the other cases as well—namely, that the *idealized expectations on one hand and the feel-*

ings of rejection on the other reinforce each other. One specific function of the idealization in Nancy's case (as in others) was to cover up the reality of the rejection, but in the light of her idealized expectations her feelings of rejection became the more painful.

We see the same contradiction between expectations and reality in the other young women as well. Helen spoke of her mother's "disloyalty" to her, implying the expectation that the mother could and should have been different. Frances idealized her parents by describing them as "wonderful" and "sweet," preserved the idealization under the "fairy-tale" motif, and endeavored to suppress her considerable feelings of hostility toward them and her feelings of isolation as an adopted child. These young women exhibited, furthermore, what might be termed a nostalgia about their relations with their parents, dwelling on pictures of what "might have been" if their parents had been different. *This nostalgia seemed both to be part of the idealized expectations toward the parent and a way of avoiding the reality situation of their relations with their parents.* Hester exhibited a nostalgia in a somewhat different form, "If my father had not died, I wouldn't have gotten into these difficulties."

These young women, moreover, still cherished hopes and expectations of changing the parent, utterly unrealistic as this would appear to be. Hester was engaged continually in rebellious behavior designed to force her mother to pay attention to her. Though Agnes knew that her father had never showed genuine concern for her in the past, she nonetheless at her present age made another trip to see him in some vague hope that he might be different. These young women seemed to be still fighting old battles with their parents.

To summarize: in these cases which fit the classical hypothesis, where rejection is present with neurotic anxiety, we found a certain constellation always present: *The rejection was never accepted as an objective fact, but was held in juxtaposition with idealized expectations about the parent. The young woman was unable to appraise the parent realistically, but always confused the reality situation with expectations of what the parent should have been or might yet become.*[2]

We now ask, What is the genesis of this subjective conflict? We have seen, for example, that Nancy's anxiety appeared in the form of a conflict between her need to depend utterly on the love of her fiancé and her ever-present doubt as to whether his love was dependable. This is the same conflict which occurred in early years in her relation with her mother. We have seen that Frances viewed her boy friend with the same combination of idealization and repressed hostility which she exhibited in her relations with her parents. Without citing more examples here, we note that *the conflict which appeared in later excessive anxiety was the same general conflict which was and is existent in the young woman's relation with her parents.*[3]

In these cases the original conflict with parents became introjected, internalized (i.e., became *subjective conflict*), resulting in inner trauma and a fundamental *psychological disorientation of the young woman in her attitude toward herself and toward other people.* It not only remained as the source of persistent resentment toward the parents, but was the source likewise of persistent self-condemnation. This is not to say merely that it is the original conflict with parents which is reactivated in the young woman's later anxiety. It is to say, more inclusively and more accurately, that the original conflict in relating to the parents sets the character structure of the individual with regard to interpersonal relations and that the individual meets future situations on the basis of this same character structure. For example, it is clear that *a confusion of reality and expectations in relating to the parents* would render *the individual unprepared to appraise her future relations with other people realistically.* She would, therefore, be subject to recurrent subjective conflict and concomitant anxiety.

A sharply contrasting constellation—indeed, the reverse —is seen in those young women who experienced rejection but did not exhibit any pronounced neurotic anxiety— namely Bessie, Louise, and, in some respects, Dolores. The difference between the reactions of these young women to rejection and those of the former group is shown graphically in Dolores' surprise that the psychologist would raise the question of whether she had regretted as a child that her father never played with her. For any of the young women in the first group, such a question would have made entire sense, and would in most cases have been

used by her as a springboard for getting out he.
ment toward the parent. For Dolores, however,
question had apparently never entered her head. .
young women did not entertain idealized expectations about
their parents; they appraised their parents realistically.
Louise and Bessie accepted their mothers as the punitive,
hating persons they actually were. Neither girl cherished
any illusions that the parent had been "good" at some
particular date, or that the parent might become loving
the next day. Louise and Bessie accepted rejection as an
objective fact; Louise impersonally termed it "hard luck,"
and Bessie took steps to obtain her affection in relations
with persons other than her parents. *Neither girl permitted
the parental rejection to change her behavior.* Bessie went
ahead playing with the siblings, in the childhood example,
despite her father's flagrant rejection at her approach, and
Louise refused to engage in hypocritical expressions of
affection to a mother she did not love.

In these young women *there was no gap, no contradiction between expectation and reality* in their relations
with their parents. The conflicts these women experienced
in their relations to others as well as their parents were
on a conscious, objective basis. *The essential point in their
freedom from neurotic anxiety was that their rejection
was not internalized; it was not made a source of subjective conflict, and it therefore did not psychologically dis-
orient them in their self-appraisal or appraisal of others.*

CLEAVAGE BETWEEN EXPECTATIONS AND REALITY

While the present study supports the hypothesis that
the conflict underlying neurotic anxiety has its origin in
the individual's relation to his parents, it does not support
the statement that rejection as such predisposes to neurotic
anxiety. Rather, *the origin of the predisposition to neurotic
anxiety lies in that particular constellation in the child's
relation to the parent in which the child cannot appraise
the parent's attitude realistically and cannot accept the
rejection objectively. Neurotic anxiety arises not out of
the fact of having had a "bad" mother, to use Sullivan's
phrase, but out of the fact that the child is never sure
whether the mother is "good" or "bad."*[4]
What causes the conflict underlying neurotic anxiety,

looking at the parent's behavior toward the child, is *rejection covered over with pretenses of love and concern.* In the cases of Louise and Bessie, the parents—punitive and cruel as they were—at least did not endeavor to cover up their hatred for their children. Contemporary psychoanalyst Melitta Schmideberg asks why it is that children of modern parents, who obviously are more lenient toward them, still have as much or more anxiety than children of the stern, severe, Victorian parents. She believes the reason is that modern parents do not permit the child to be afraid of them, and, therefore, the child must displace his fear and hostility and suffer consequent anxiety. If parents cannot refrain from punishing the child, she adds, at least they should give the child the right to be afraid of them (see her Anxiety states, *Psychoanal. Rev.,* 1940, 27:4, 439–49). Without going into the historical question of the relative anxiety in these different periods or the complicated reasons for it, we nonetheless feel that Dr. Schmideberg's emphasis on permitting the child to appraise the relation realistically is sound. Louise and Bessie could, therefore, accept the rejection at face value —and, as illustrated in Bessie's case, seek love and affirmative relations elsewhere. Thus, when the mothers of Louise and Bessie rejected them in later childhood and adolescence, *no vital essential value was threatened;* they had not expected anything better from the parents anyway. Louise's statement, "As a child you don't suffer, you take things as they come" may be taken to mean that you don't suffer in the most basic way—i.e., experiencing a threat to your vital values—if you can, as she did, call the attitude of the mother by its right name. But in the cases of the young women with subjective conflict, the rejection tended to be covered over by idealized expectations (presumably existent in the parent's earlier pretenses to the child), and hence the child never could adjust to it as a reality.[5]

In the light of these observations, one could roughly differentiate three types of parental relationships. First, the parent rejects the child but the rejection is in the open and admitted on both sides. Second, the parent rejects the child, but covers up the rejection with pretenses of love. Third, the parent loves the child and behaves toward him or her on that basis. The data in this study affirm that it

is the *second* kind of relationship which pr...
neurotic anxiety.[6]

The point we are here discussing is so signific...
I wish to quote some remarkably similar findings ...
the studies of children by Anna Hartoch Schachtel. Describing one child whose mother rejected her but pretended
love and exhibited possessive jealousy of the child's love
for the grandmother, Mrs. Schachtel states: "This child
lives in a make-believe situation; she has to avoid facing
the real situation of not being loved; she lives in a wishful
expectancy and bases her whole interests, fears, expectations and wishes on this shaky basis." This child corresponds very closely to the young women in the first
group we have been describing. Mrs. Schachtel describes
another child who was fatherless, was frequently beaten
at home and told what a nuisance she was. "To her it
is a fact that she is not loved, but this in no way impairs
her own capacity to love." She was an independent, rather
tough, aggressive, cooperative, and reliable child who
"does not minimize or beautify inhuman and hostile things
that happen to her." This child seems to me to be remarkably like Bessie. As was the case with Bessie, this
child found love in friends and siblings despite the parental rejection. Mrs. Schachtel points out that *"not being
loved is better than the experience of a pseudo-love for a
child."* The findings of the present study would indicate
that this is very true with respect to the predisposition to
anxiety.[7]

Can anxiety in general be described in the form in
which we have discovered it in the relations of these
young women to their parents—namely as a *subjective disorientation arising from a fundamental contradiction between expectations and reality? Is it a fundamental disorientation, an inability to orient one's self to the world,
an incapacity to see the world as it is?*

These questions would lead beyond the scope of this
immediate discussion. But I suggest them as fruitful hypotheses, having both psychological and philosophical promise. Donald MacKinnon has presented a description of
anxiety which, apart from its topological features (which
may be open to question), is similar to the above hypothesis:

A person troubled by anxiety . . . simultaneously sees things as both *better* and *worse* than they are. . . . His positive irreality distorts the structure of his level of reality in accordance with his *hopes,* while at the same time his negative irreality distorts it in accordance with his *fears.* . . . This means that psychologically the individual stands on unfirm ground, for the level of reality of his life space lacks clear cognitive structure since it has simultaneously the conflicting meanings of probable success and probable failure."[8]

NEUROTIC ANXIETY AND THE MIDDLE CLASS

A final question arises from the fact that the young women in the first group—i.e., with neurotic anxiety—*were all from the middle class,* and those in the second group, who were rejected but accepted it without neurotic anxiety, *were all from the proletarian class.* Indeed, of the four proletarians in this study—Bessie, Louise, Sarah, and Dolores—not one exhibits any pronounced neurotic anxiety. It may be noted that the child Mrs. Schachtel described as accepting rejection as a realistic fact was also proletarian.

This raises the important problem of whether, in our culture, the contradiction between expectations and reality underlying the predisposition to neurotic anxiety is especially a characteristic of the middle class and, likewise, whether *neurotic anxiety is predominantly a middle-class phenomenon.* The classical hypothesis concerning rejection and predisposition to neurotic anxiety is based upon clinical and psychoanalytic work with subjects who are almost exclusively of the middle or upper middle class. This is true of the patients of Freud and of most all the patients of psychoanalysts in private practice since. Perhaps the hypothesis is true for the middle classes but not for other classes.

There is much *a priori* reason, and some *a posteriori* data, for the contention that neurotic anxiety is especially a middle-class phenomenon in our culture. The cleavage between reality and expectations is particularly in evidence, psychologically as well as economically, in the middle class. Karl Marx described the proletarian class as the class which had no expectations short of revolution. It has earlier been indicated (Chapter 4) that individual competitive ambition, a trait in our culture intimately associated with contemporaneous anxiety, is chiefly a middle-class trait. The proletarian women in this study showed definitely less competitive ambition than the middle-class women. Sarah had worked out an ingenious system by which her ambition would not be competitive, "I arrange to be not on the top, or not on the bottom, but in the middle." Fascism, a prominent cultural anxiety symptom in our day, begins as a lower-middle-class movement. Totalitarianism, a prominent cultural anxiety symptom in our day, begins as a lower-middle-class movement. The burden of anxiety falls most heavily on the middle class, caught as its members are, between difficult standards of behavior and the awareness that the values supporting the standards are defunct. This is surely an enticing topic for both sociologists and psychologists to explore.

PART

III

THE MANAGEMENT
OF ANXIETY

CHAPTER
11

Methods of Dealing
with Anxiety

Only that individual can go through life without anxiety
who is conscious of belonging to the fellowship of man.

—Alfred Adler

Anxiety has a purpose. Originally the purpose was to protect the existence of the caveman from wild beasts and savage neighbors. Nowadays the occasions for anxiety are very different—we are afraid of losing out in the competition, feeling unwanted, isolated, and ostracized. But the purpose of anxiety is still to protect us from dangers that threaten the same things: our existence or values that we identify with our existence. This normal anxiety of life cannot be avoided except at the price of apathy or the numbing of one's sensibilities and imagination.

The omnipresence of anxiety arises from the fact that, when all is said and done, anxiety is our human awareness of the fact that each of us is a *being confronted with nonbeing*. Nonbeing is that which would destroy being, such as death, severe illness, interpersonal hostility, too sudden change which destroys our psychological rootedness. In any case, anxiety is the reaction when a person faces some kind of destruction of his existence or that which he identifies with it.

I am not here concerned with listing all the various methods of coping with such apprehension. I seek rather to clarify the basic principles people have found valuable in confronting anxiety.

Anxiety cannot be avoided, but it can be reduced. *The problem of the management of anxiety is that of reducing the anxiety to normal levels, and then to use this normal anxiety as stimulation to increase one's awareness, vigilance, zest for living.*

Another way of putting the matter is that anxiety is a signal that something is wrong in one's personality and one's human relationships. Anxiety may be viewed as an inward cry for the resolution of the problem. What is wrong may, of course, vary infinitely. It may be the result of some misunderstanding between one's employer and one's self, or between friends and lovers, which often can be resolved by authentic communication with the other person. Open communication, as Harry Stack Sullivan stated with a new eloquence, can resolve a surprisingly large number of problem situations. In the following verse William Blake was speaking about anger, but he could have similarly referred to anxiety:

> I was angry with my foe,
> I hid my wrath, my wrath did grow.
> I was angry with my friend,
> I told my wrath, my wrath did end.

Or what is wrong may be some expectation of one's self that, at this stage in one's development, cannot realistically be achieved. As is often the case when children are apprehensive, the anxiety can be resolved only by the maturation of their abilities. At such a time the anxiety can at least be experienced as a sense of adventure as new possibilities unfold before the young person. Or what is wrong may have to be accepted as part of the nature of life itself: for example, "that morbidity," as some humorist has remarked, "with which we are all afflicted, death." Or the anxiety may be cued off by an awareness of the limitations of human life—limitations of one's intelligence or vitality or unavoidable loneliness, or some other aspect of human creatureliness. In these latter cases, anxiety may take the form of mild or great dread. The intensity of these situations can, of course, vary: dread may be simply an undercurrent of apprehension, or the imagining of another war with hydrogen bombs, or the fantasy of the approach of our own death.

In these occasions for anxiety, what is felt to be wrong

may be simply some aspect of human destiny which every person must accept as part of the human condition. Camus' essay, "Sisyphus," is an interpretation of the unavoidable limits to which everyone who is human is condemned. The constructive way of dealing with anxiety in this sense consists of learning to live with it, accepting it as a "teacher," to borrow Kierkegaard's phrase, to school us in confronting our human destiny. Pascal has put this beautifully:

> Man is only a reed, the feeblest reed in nature, but he is a thinking reed. There is no need for the entire universe to arm itself in order to annihilate him: a vapor, a drop of water, suffices to kill him. But were the universe to crush him, man would yet be more noble than that which slays him, *because he knows that he dies,* and the advantage the universe has over him; of this the universe knows nothing.[1]

The confronting of these limitations can inspire us to create works of art, as it inspired primitive man to seize a coal from his spent fire and draw those fantastic bison and reindeer on the walls of his cave. Poetry, drama, science, and other expressions of human civilization are also the product, in part, of our recognition of our limitations. *The yearning to give form to life arises out of our human anxiety about our own death.* This it is which sharpens our need to create and enlivens our imagination.

Most people would be surprised to learn how much of their daily behavior is motivated by the need to lessen or allay their anxiety. Magazine advertisements and TV commercials—which present what the masses of people *want* to believe about themselves and life—uniformly show confident, smiling human beings who give the appearance of not having a care in the world or, more accurately, of having gotten over all their worries because they have purchased this or that product. To illustrate everyday anxiety-allaying behavior, we do not need to resort to such crass examples as our walking down the other side of the street to avoid meeting someone who reduces our self-esteem. In all sorts of subtle ways, the manner in which people talk, joke, argue with each other demonstrates their need to establish their security by proving they are in control of the situation, avoiding what would otherwise be anxiety-creating situations. The quiet despair under which Thoreau believed most people live is largely covered over by our culturally accepted ways of allaying anxiety.

Such avoidance of anxiety is the purpose of many behavior traits which are called "normal," and can be termed "neurotic" only in their extreme, compulsive forms. "Gallows humor" comes to the fore particularly in times of anxiety; and, like all humor, it gives people a welcomed distance from the threat. Human beings do not often say outright, "We laugh that we may not cry"; but they much more often feel that way. The ubiquitous joking in the army and on the battle field are examples of the function of humor to keep one from being overcome by anxiety. The public speaker tells a joke to start his speech, fully aware that the laughter will relieve the tension with which people confront him as he stands at the podium, a tension which could otherwise lead to anxiety-motivated resistance to the message he is trying to communicate.

IN EXTREME SITUATIONS

Some ways of meeting anxiety are vividly illustrated in a study of anxiety and stress made of a team of twelve Green Beret combat soldiers in Vietnam.[2] These soldiers were posted in an isolated camp near the Cambodian border. All the men had had past combat experience and all were trained in special skills such as demolition and radio operating. They all demonstrated an unusually high level of dedication to their job. The camp was located in territory controlled by the Viet Cong, for the purpose of obstructing the flow of arms down the Ho Chi Minh trail and training the local personnel.

The threat of attack by an overwhelmingly superior force was always present, but was considerably increased at the monsoon season early in May, 1966. On May 10 the camp was notified by radio that an attack was imminent between May 18 and May 22, and most probably on the night of May 19. Although this attack failed to materialize, there was mounting anxiety caused by the realistic stress until May 19, after which it tapered off.

How these men defended themselves against their anxiety is highly instructive. First, there was their great confidence, their "self-reliance to the point of omnipotence."

Their faith in their own invulnerability bordered on a feeling of immortality. Second, they threw themselves into their work. "Their response to the environmental threat was to engage in a furor of activity which rapidly dissipated the developing tension."[3] In the third place, their faith and trust in their leaders was of course very important. It is clear also that religious faith played an important role as a defense against anxiety. To quote directly from the publication of the study:

> One subject in the present group was a very religious individual who would drive many miles in a jeep over dangerous jungle roads so that a Vietnamese Catholic priest who spoke little or no English could hear his confession. By making this hazardous journey with sufficient frequency the man was able to maintain his strong belief in divine protection, and felt he had little to fear in combat.[4]

It is significant that the two officers of the group could not avail themselves of these defenses, nor could they handle the additional stresses as easily as did the enlisted men. They were in constant contact with the base forty miles away, and hence knew more about what might happen. Also they were generally younger men who were under the temptation to take risks in order to earn the right of leadership of their men. Most of all, they had the responsibility for the safety and the lives of the men under them. This responsibility, like that of a father with his children, extends the perimeter of possible threats.

To summarize, the defenses of the team against anxiety were self-esteem, work, belief in leaders, and religious faith.

In a parallel study of the *Pueblo,* the U.S. gunboat crew that was captured by the North Koreans and incarcerated, the conclusions were similar. Namely, the men defended themselves against unbearable anxiety by their faith in their leaders, by their faith in their cause, and by their religious trust. One person in this group reported to a friend of mine that he had a faith in his captain which was like his faith in God.

It is clear that in such extreme situations human beings need defenses against anxiety. Can these defenses exist without illusions, such as the soldiers' belief in their own invulnerability? Does hope require such illusions? I ask these questions without intending to endeavor to answer them. What is very clear is that a human being can no more live without defenses against such dread in extreme situations than he can live an anxiety-free existence the whole of his life.

DESTRUCTIVE WAYS

The negative methods of dealing with anxiety range all the way from simple behavior traits like excessive shyness through the gamut of neuroses and psychosomatic illnesses to the extreme of psychosis. And in very serious conflict situations—such as "voodoo death"—anxiety can be dealt with only by the surrendering of life itself. These negative methods consist of allaying or avoiding the anxiety without resolving the conflict which underlies it. Or, in other words, evading the danger situation rather than resolving it.

The line between "normal" and "neurotic" begins to appear when any activity becomes compulsive—that is, when the person feels pushed to perform the act because it habitually allays his anxiety rather than because of any intrinsic wish to perform the act. Alcoholism and compulsive sexual activity are examples of this. The motivation then is no longer the activity itself but the external effect of it. In the drama *Peer Gynt*, Ibsen illustrates both compulsive sexuality and compulsive drinking. Experiencing the battering of his self-esteem, Peer hides behind the bushes on the way to the wedding and soliloquizes:

People always snigger behind your back,
And whisper so that it burns right through you.
If only I had a dram of something strong.
Or could go unnoticed. (If only they didn't know me.)
A drink'd be best. Then the laughter doesn't bite.[5]

Later Peer brags to three girls he meets:

PEER: (takes a sudden leap into their midst). I'm a three-headed troll, and a boy for three girls!
GIRLS: Three? Could you, lad?
PEER: Try me and see![6]

The compulsive aspect of an act is shown in the fact that more or less severe anxiety appears when the person is prohibited from performing the act. In our society sexual activity is often used as a way of avoiding the anxiety of death. But then what happens when, like Hemingway, one arrives at the point of sexual impotence?

Frantic activity of all sorts may serve to relieve the tension mobilized in the organism by anxiety. Compulsive work is perhaps the most common way in America of allaying anxiety; it can be called in this country a "normal neurosis." This is generally a combination of a sound reaction to anxiety—work *is* one of the handiest ways of relieving the tension caused by anxiety. But it can easily become compulsive. This latter is comparable to Harold Brown's very rapid talking when anxious, and is only pseudo-productive.

Frantic activity, as everyone on some level knows, is generally neither productive of one's best efforts nor authentically creative. Nor is it directed toward solving the problem which causes the tension. The significant question is whether the activity pursued permits the *release of tension without resolving the underlying conflict*. If so, the conflict still remains, and hence the activity must be engaged in repeatedly. We then may have the beginning of compulsion neurosis. This is oversimplified, to be sure; my purpose here is only to illustrate a crucial difference between the constructive and destructive methods of allaying anxiety.

Rigidity of thinking is another borderline characteristic. As it may be observed in religious or scientific dogmatism, rigidity is a way of armoring the self so that one is protected from threat. Kierkegaard tells the story of a professor who could demonstrate a theorem perfectly when the letters were *A B C,* but not when they were *D E F.* Rigid thinking can give temporary security, but at the price of the loss of the possibilities of discovering new truth, the exclusion of new learning, and the stunting of capacities to adapt to new situations. Especially in times of transition like the present, the person is then left marooned on his rock as evolution passes him by. Kierkegaard adds that the belief in fate or necessity, like the belief in superstition, is a method of avoiding full responsibility for one's conflicts. One can thus circumvent anxiety but at the price of loss of creativity. When the values the individual needs to protect are especially vulnerable to threat (often because of their own inner contradictions) and one is relatively less able to adapt to new situations, rigidity of thinking and behavior may also take the form of compulsion neurosis.

In the case studies in this book, we have seen many ways of avoiding the anxiety-creating situation. These vary from relatively realistic adaptations to a difficult situation, such as Bessie's escaping into the park to avoid her mother's abuse, to Irene's excessive shyness, to the more complicated denial of Helen's "No, I don't feel any guilt —I'm willing to suffer the tortures of the damned to get it [the birth] over with." As these methods become more complex, they involve repression and symptom-formation. Without endeavoring to catalog these protective patterns, I wish to summarize some of their common features.

We have seen that these behavior patterns were called into play when the person was confronted by an anxiety-creating situation. In Helen's case, we noted that the more anxiety was present in certain responses in her Rorschach, the more she exhibited her particular defenses of forced laughter, denial, and intellectualization. Similarly, in the case of Agnes, the more she was made anxious by her male friend's neglect, the more she exhibited her particular protective behavior—namely aggression and hostility. We saw, moreover, that when the anxiety abated, the defensive behavior likewise abated. The rationale behind these phenomena is obvious: when an anxiety-creating situation confronts the individual, the defenses against it are called into action. Thus there was a *direct relation between the presence of anxiety and the presence of behavior patterns for avoiding the anxiety-creating situation.*

But when the behavior pattern has been structured in the form of a psychological symptom, the anxiety-creating conflict is overcome before it reaches the level of conscious awareness. In this sense, a symptom may be defined as an inner, structuralized defense mechanism which obviates the conflict by automatic psychological processes. In Brown's situation, for example, as long as he felt the fear of cancer and was preoccupied with the psychosomatic symptom of dizziness, he could not or would not admit any conscious conflict or neurotic anxiety. But when the conflict and anxiety emerged into his consciousness, the symptoms vanished. Hence (and this is not contradictory to the previous statement), *there is an inverse relation between conscious anxiety and the presence of the symptoms.*

We would agree—although I do not know whether Brown would have—that he was in a "healthier" state when his conflict did become conscious. I put "healthier" in quotation marks because this state was certainly more painful, less comfortable for Brown than when he had his symptoms. But now the situation could be resolved, whereas before he was encased in rigid symptoms. To generalize this implication: *conscious anxiety is more painful but it is available also to use in the service of integration of the self.* When Brown confronted his anxiety directly, he was relieved of his fear of cancer; but he could now no longer escape having to face the dilemma arising from his neurotic dependency on his mother. This point bears on the maxim taught to psychoanalysts and therapists, that a person with a phobia must sooner or later do precisely what he has the phobia of doing if he is ever to get over it. To put it anthropomorphically, the anxiety must be challenged in its lair. We would hope the patient could gradually overcome a good deal of the neurotic anxiety in his sessions with the therapist so that the outright confrontation is not such a shock when it does occur.

It follows, therefore, that in neurotic anxiety the purpose of the defense mechanisms, symptoms, etc., is to keep the inner conflict from being activated. To the extent that these mechanisms are successful, the individual is able to avoid confronting his conflict. If Nancy could have kept everyone in her environment benevolently disposed toward her, the conflict involved in her needing to depend entirely on others but believing at the same time that they are undependable would never have arisen. If Helen could have successfully denied or intellectualized her guilt feelings, her conflict could be avoided. In the more complicated symptoms of Brown, this same purpose can be discerned: if he really *had* cancer or neurological brain damage (or could successfully believe he had), he could enter a hospital, submit himself to authorities, and be taken care of without guilt feeling. Then he would be relieved of the necessity of trying to do responsible work for which he felt inadequate, and get even with his mother by virtue of the fact that she would be forced to support him in his illness. Thus the three main elements in his conflict—his *passivity,* his need *to submit himself to au-*

thorities, and the need *to be relieved from guilt*—would have been taken care of in one fell swoop.

Inasmuch as the conflict in neurotic anxiety is subjective, the mechanism for obviating it *always involves some form of repression,* or *dissociation,* of some reality or attitude. In contrast to Bessie's objective behavior in running out of the house and into the park, the person with neurotic anxiety endeavors to run away from some elements within herself or himself. This can be accomplished only by dissociating these elements, which sets up inner contradictions. While Helen attempts on one hand to deny outright the existence of her guilt feelings, at the same time she goes to considerable lengths to intellectualize these feelings. These two methods of obviating the guilt feelings are contradictory: if she really believed she had no guilt feelings, she would not need to intellectualize it. It is as though a general were to declare on one hand that there is no war going on, and on the other simultaneously call up his troops and rush them into battle. Specifically, the pattern involved in a person like Helen is outright denial in the endeavor to repress her feeling. On a deeper level she is aware of the deception involved in this repression, so another mechanism is called into play—namely, intellectualization. The dissociation which is necessary in the endeavor to reduce the subjective conflict involves the setting up of inner contradictions, which is one explanation of the fact that the behavior patterns which allay neurotic anxiety yield only a security which is continually in jeopardy. These behavior patterns are never lastingly successful in avoiding the conflict.

One pattern for protecting the individual from anxiety-creating situations has been discussed in the above cases which, so far as I know, has not yet been dealt with in the literature on anxiety. This is the use of *anxiety itself as a defense,* a mechanism best seen in the case of Nancy. This young woman had no effective defenses against anxiety except to be continually cautious and alert—in other words, to behave anxiously and to show others how anxious she was. Her endeavor to keep others always benevolently disposed toward her (which would avoid her conflicts) was implemented by showing them how much she needed them, how much she would be hurt if they were unfriendly to her. This behavior may be summed up as a method of saying to others, "See how anxious I already am—do not make me more anxious." In cases in which being anxious and showing anxiety is a defense against more anxiety, the individual often seeks to avoid conflict by assuming an appearance of weakness, as though she believed that others would not attack her, forsake her, or expect too much of her if they saw that she was anxious. I would term the anxiety which is thus employed defensively as *pseudo-anxiety*. Alfred Adler saw this method of using anxiety, but instead of describing it as a defense or pseudo-anxiety, he placed all anxiety in this category. But such a defensive use of anxiety would not have developed except as the person was experiencing genuine anxiety on a deeper level.

The distinguishing of anxiety which is used as a defense from genuine anxiety is particularly important in psychotherapy. For the defensive pseudo-anxiety constitutes an exception to the generally accepted principle that anxiety must be relieved before the defenses against it can be relinquished by the patient. When such anxiety is honored or taken at its face value in psychotherapy, the underlying conflict is not clarified, for the anxiety (like any other defense) serves to cover up the conflict. Wilhelm Reich's discussion of the necessity in therapy for attacking the patient's defenses despite the eruption of his anxiety is significant at this point.[7]

CONSTRUCTIVE WAYS

We have stated above that anxiety can be treated constructively by accepting it as a challenge and a stimulus to clarify and, as far as possible, resolve the underlying problem. Anxiety indicates the presence of a contradiction within a person's value system. As long as there is conflict a positive solution is within the realm of possibility.

In this respect anxiety has been said to have the prognostic value of a fever: it is a sign of struggle going on within the personality and an indication that serious disintegration has not yet occurred. We saw in the case of Charlotte that when a person goes into psychosis, the anxiety may vanish. The presence of anxiety indicates that this has not yet happened.

In regard to the methods of resolving the problem causing the anxiety, two processes are held in common by the various schools of psychotherapy. These have a logical relation to our study of anxiety. One is *an expansion of awareness:* the person sees what value is threatened, and becomes aware of the conflicts between his goals and how these conflicts developed. The second is *re-education:* the person restructures his goals, makes a choice of values, and proceeds toward the attainment of these values responsibly and realistically. Obviously these processes are never achieved perfectly—nor would it be good if they were; they indicate, rather, the general aims of the therapeutic process.

But whereas the use of neurotic anxiety as a challenge for problem-solving has been agreed upon, in our day it has often been overlooked that *normal* anxiety also indicates possibility and may be used constructively. The tendency in our culture to regard fears and anxiety chiefly in a negative light, as results of unfortunate learning, is not only an oversimplification. It tends by implication to remove the possibility of the constructive acceptance and use of those day-to-day anxiety experiences which cannot be called specifically neurotic. Jerome Kagan echoes this view when he attacks the falsehood that "signs of anxiety are always bad and are indicators of psychopathology."[8] The judgment "Mental health is living without anxiety" has its valuable ideal meaning; but when it is oversimplified, as it often is in general usage, *to mean that the goal in all life is a total absence of anxiety, the judgment becomes delusive and even dangerous.*

When we are dealing with the anxiety which inheres in such aspects of human contingency as death, the threat of isolation which accompanies the development of individuality, and so forth, the desideratum cannot be the complete absence of anxiety. An officer who had no anxiety for his men in time of battle would be irresponsible, and it would be dangerous to serve under him. Needless to say, living totally without anxiety in a historical period like the present would imply an unrealistic and insensitive view of our cultural situation and would betoken an irresponsible attitude toward our duties as citizens. Many demonstrations could be cited from the rise of fascism in Spain and Germany that the citizens who were unaware of the social danger were the ones who became putty in the hands of the rising dictatorships.[9]

To be sure, neurotic anxiety *is* the result of unfortunate

learning because the individual was forced to deal with threatening situations at a period—typically in early childhood—when he was incapable of coping directly or constructively with such experiences. In this respect, *neurotic anxiety is the result of the failure to cope with the previous anxiety situations in one's experiences.* But normal anxiety is not the result of unfortunate learning. It arises rather from a realistic appraisal of one's situation of danger. To the extent that a person can succeed in constructively meeting the normal day-to-day anxiety experiences as they arise, he avoids the repression and retrenchment which make for later neurotic anxiety.

Our problem, therefore, is *how normal anxiety-creating situations may be used constructively.* Though this question has not generally been attacked in scientific writings, it was confronted directly by Kierkegaard a century ago. Kierkegaard called anxiety a better teacher than reality, for while reality situations may be temporarily evaded, anxiety is an inner function which cannot be escaped short of constriction of the personality. Kierkegaard writes that only he who has been educated in the "school of anxiety"—i.e., has confronted and worked through previous anxiety experiences—is able to meet present and future anxiety experiences without being overwhelmed. In this connection, there is evidence that soldiers who had experienced a fair degree of anxiety in their past lives and were in some cases relatively "high strung" were better able to face the anxiety experiences of combat than soldiers who had experienced relatively little anxiety before combat.[10]

In our times the question of the constructive use of anxiety has been addressed by Goldstein, among others. We recall Goldstein's emphasis, as reviewed in Chapter 3 of the present study, that every human being encounters frequent anxiety shocks in the course of his normal development, and that his capacities can be actualized only through an affirmative response to these threats to his existence. Goldstein's simple illustration is the healthy child's learning to walk despite the fact that he falls and gets hurt many times in the process.

When we consider the constructive use of normal anxiety from the *objective* side, we note that it is characterized by the individual's confronting the anxiety-creating situation directly, admitting apprehensions but *moving ahead despite the anxiety.* In other words, it consists of moving *through* anxiety-creating experiences rather than moving *around* them or *retrenching* before them. This, interestingly enough, is parallel to the ultimate lesson Peer Gynt learns. Ibsen describes the trolls as those who *go around.* Peer Gynt's change of character is shown at the end of the drama when, hearing the trolls singing, "Go back! Go around!" he cries out, "Ah! No! This time straight through."[11] For example, if we may refer again to World War II, the most constructive attitude consisted of the soldier's frankly admitting his fear or anxiety about going into battle, but being subjectively prepared to act *despite* his apprehension.

As a corollary we have pointed out that *courage consists not of the absence of fear and anxiety but of the capacity to move ahead even though one is afraid.* This constructive confronting of normal anxiety in daily life and in crises which require moral rather than physical courage (such as the crises in self-development, often attended with profound anxiety, which occur during psychotherapy), is accompanied by the feeling of adventure. At the other times, however, when the anxiety-creating experience is more severe, confronting it may entail no pleasurable affect whatever but may be accomplished only by the sheerest kind of dogged determination.

When we view this process *subjectively*—that is, when we ask what is going on within one individual which enables him to confront the danger directly whereas others in the same situation may flee—we discover some very significant data. To draw an illustration again from the studies of soldiers, it has been pointed out that often the subjective motivation which enabled soldiers to confront dangers was their conviction that the threat connected with backing out was greater than the threat faced in moving ahead into battle. Put positively, there were values to be achieved in confronting the danger greater than the values in flight. For many a soldier the common value was probably the expectation of his fellow soldiers—he must not let his battalion down. In simple terms this would be verbalized as the desire not to appear "yellow" to one's buddies. In the more sophisticated soldiers it might be articulated as community responsibility. The sometimes platitudinous statement that one confronts and overcomes dangers by having a "cause" which more than counterbalances the threat is profoundly true. The one trouble with the platitude is that only in the more sophisticated soldiers, to continue our example, does the value for which they fight become verbalized in the deeper terms of a "cause" such as patriotism, freedom, or human welfare.

I hope that the above illustrative paragraph has prepared the ground for the following generalized statement: *A person is subjectively prepared to confront unavoidable anxiety constructively when he is convinced (consciously or unconsciously) that the values to be gained in moving ahead are greater than those to be gained by escape.* We have pointed out earlier that anxiety arises when the values the individual identifies with his existence are threatened. Let us picture anxiety as resulting from a conflict between the threat on one hand and the values the person identifies with his existence on the other. Then we can see that neurosis and emotional morbidity mean that the struggle is won by the former (the threat), whereas the constructive approach to anxiety means that the struggle is won by the latter (the individual's values).

The term "values" may seem to many readers to be a vague concept. It is used here purposely because it is a neutral term and gives the maximum amount of psychological leeway for the right of each person to have his own goals. It is thus obvious that the values on the basis of which one confronts anxiety-creating experiences will vary—as, indeed, we have already seen to be the case with soldiers. Most people are motivated by elemental values which they may never articulate—the need to preserve life itself or some elemental trend toward "health," which, as Sullivan has remarked, we always assume (and with pragmatic justification) when doing psychotherapy.

On other levels social prestige is certainly a very important value on the basis of which the individual confronts dangers. Another is the satisfaction to be achieved by the expansion and wider use of one's own powers (as Sullivan, Goldstein, and others have emphasized)—which presumably is operative in the child's learning to walk and many other phases of development through crises. More highly differentiated forms of value occur, for example, in artists and scientists who, in creating new art forms or radically new hypotheses, experience many shocks to their existence. But to the healthy artist and scientist, the discovery of new truth and the adventure of moving into unexplored fields are sufficiently rewarding that they move ahead despite the threat of isolation and anxiety. In the long run, the confronting of normal anxiety depends on what one regards as of value in himself and his existence.

The system of value on the basis of which we confront normal anxiety can be called, as Fromm does call it, our "frame of orientation and devotion."[12] From the theological viewpoint, Paul Tillich expressed this valuing in his term "ultimate concern." Broadly speaking, the values reflect the person's religious attitude toward life, with the term "religious" defined as the basic presuppositions of what is and is not of worth. Such an assumption of value is illustrated in Freud's passionate devotion to science in general and to the discovery of psychological truth in particular. Though, as is well known, Freud attacked the orthodox religious formulations severely, there is no doubt that his own passionate affirmation of value—his "religion of science"—enabled him with remarkable courage to persevere in his lonely, individual investigations for the first ten years, and then to continue in his explorations for several decades despite vilification and attack.[13]

Our point is likewise illustrated by Kierkegaard's devotion to "infinite possibility"—i.e., devotion to his conviction that unless a person pursues with inner integrity and individually sustained courage the intellectual and moral insights which arise as part of his new experience of every day, he is forfeiting his possibilities for expansion and meaning in his existence as a human being. Thus Kierkegaard, in ways not dissimilar to Freud, was able to produce astonishingly creative works despite social misunderstanding, conflict, and very great isolation and anxiety.

We now arrive at a more complete understanding of Spinoza's statement, referred to above, that negative affects like fear and anxiety can be overcome in the long run only by more powerful, constructive affects. The ultimate constructive affect consists, he believed, of the individual's "intellectual love of God." In the context of the present discussion, Spinoza's term "God" may be taken as a symbol expressing that which the individual conceives to be worthy of ultimate concern.

As already pointed out, the values on the basis of which people meet anxiety-creating experiences may vary from simple preservation of physical life to classical hedonistic, stoic, and humanistic values, to the "frames of orientation and devotion" given in the classical religions. It is not my purpose either to imply that all these assumptions of value are of equal efficacy or to make a judgment among them. My interest here is only in indicating that the experiences of normal anxiety are confronted constructively because there is more at stake, more to be achieved in moving ahead than in retrenching. In this discussion I wish to remain on the psychological level by holding to the point that these values will vary greatly from person to person and from culture to culture. The only implicit psychological criterion is, which of these formulations of value will serve a given individual most constructively as a basis for confronting anxiety? Which, in other words, will release the individual's capacities and permit greater expansion in the development of his own powers as well as enhancement of his relation with other human beings?

CHAPTER 12

Anxiety and the Development
of the Self

> ... it is silly
> To refuse the tasks of time
> And, overlooking our lives,
> Cry—"Miserable wicked me,
> How interesting I am."
> We would rather be ruined than changed,
> We would rather die in our dread
> Than climb the cross of the moment
> And let our illusions die.
>
> —W. H. Auden, *The Age of Anxiety*

What happens when a person chooses or feels forced to choose to limit his personality, chooses to construct a wall around himself as a protection from anxiety? A patient of mine, for example, had developed a phobia of open spaces which made it impossible for her to go outside of her house alone or go shopping or drive a car to go to any of the openings of her husband (who was an actor). She had to be chauffeured to my office for her consultations. She literally limited her world, her sphere of activity and her arena for stimulation and development. Neurosis may be called a *negating of possibilities; it is the shrinking up of one's world.* The development of the self is thus radically curtailed. In Tillich's terms, the person has been forced (or has chosen) to accept a greater degree of *nonbeing* in order to preserve some modicum of *being.*

ANXIETY AND THE IMPOVERISHMENT
OF PERSONALITY

The study of Phyllis demonstrates that impoverishment of personality can block off any conflicts that would lead to anxiety. Phyllis submitted entirely to the demands of her environment (especially in the person of her mother), accepted the impoverishment of personality this entailed, and exhibited practically no anxiety. We noted in our discussion of her (in Chapter 8) that Phyllis was glad that the obstetrician would not tell her about her condition, that she placed a positive value on "*not* knowing," and that she used her irrational "faith in science" as a magical incantation to allay anxiety in the same way superstitious persons in other historical periods used a prayer-wheel. Her situation illustrates the effect of structuralized constriction of personality. She accepted constriction and had so thoroughly systematized her activity that (in contrast to Dolores and Brown) her capacities for expansion and development were largely atrophied. The price paid for this avoidance of conflict and anxiety was the surrender of her autonomy, the impoverishment of her thinking and feeling capacities, and a radical and progressive curtailing of her capacity to relate to other people.

Interestingly enough the same thing is seen in an unsuccessful form in the case of Frances, who attempted to constrict her personality and suppress her feelings and her originality as a means of avoiding anxiety-creating situations. But her originality tended to break through the constrictive process. When she was successful in suppressing her originality, anxiety was not present. But when the constrictive processes were unsuccessful—when, for example, her originality emerged—anxiety likewise emerged.

Severe anxiety also tends to impoverish personality. We noted that Brown's first Rorschach, taken while he was in a relatively severe anxiety state, showed a low degree of productivity. There was no originality, very little use of either feeling or thinking capacities, a predominance of vagueness of response, and a lack of capacity for relating to concrete realities. These characteristics can be seen as the direct effects of his anxiety. It was, in general, the picture of one whose relation to himself and to his environment is "blurred." His behavioral symptom of very rapid talking was like the "revving" of a car motor: much noise and activity but no motion or productivity. But the second Rorschach, taken when he was not in anxiety, showed much greater productivity, some originality, marked increase in the use of thinking and feeling capacities, and much greater capacity to deal with concrete, specific realities. The vagueness and blurred relation to reality had vanished.

Another example is Dolores, whose anxiety panic literally paralyzed her productivity on the first Rorschach as well as rendered her in large measure incapable of relating to the other persons at Walnut House.

These instances demonstrate that anxiety involves a paralyzing, to a greater or lesser degree, of the productive activities of the individual on various fronts—his thinking and feeling capacities as well as his capacity to plan and act. This impoverishing effect of anxiety underlies the common dictum that "anxiety cancels out work." The "blurred" relation to one's self and to others, as well as to other aspects of reality, is an illustration of my point that anxiety destroys the capacity to evaluate stimuli realistically or to distinguish between subject and object. This amounts, in Goldstein's phrase, to an experience of the "dissolution of the self," which is the radical opposite of self-realization. Of course, as we saw in the last chapter, if one can work productively the reverse is true: the work tends to cancel out the anxiety.

There is another means of avoiding unbearable conflict which involves some distortion of reality as well as impoverishment of personality. This is psychosis. We noted that in the mildly psychotic state of Charlotte no present problems seemed to exist. If topics arose in the interviews which might touch upon possible conflicts, Charlotte assumed an artificially gay attitude or retreated into periods of vacant silence. In her case the psychotic development covered over any possible conflicts. With respect to those forms of psychosis which are the end result of subjective conflict that is too great to be borne and at the same time insoluble on any other level, the psychotic development represents at one extreme a way out of the conflict and anxiety. In cases like that of Charlotte, this is effected at the price of distortion of her relation to reality, as shown in her attitude toward her pregnancy as well as in the distorted responses in her Rorschach. We have remarked that the presence of anxiety is an indication that severe deterioration has not yet set in. In terms of the present discussion, the presence of anxiety indicates that the individual has not yet been forced to capitulate in the conflict. Charlotte had lost this battle. The healthy state for her would involve the regaining of some anxiety.

Thus, *constriction and impoverishment of personality make it possible to avoid subjective conflict and concomitant anxiety.* But the person's freedom, originality, capacity for independent love, as well as his other possibilities for expansion and development as an autonomous personality are renounced in the same process. By accepting impoverishment of personality, one can buy temporary freedom from anxiety, to be sure. But the price for this "bargain" is the loss of those unique and most precious characteristics of the human self.

CREATIVITY, INTELLIGENCE, AND ANXIETY

Another phase of the problem may be stated in a question: *Are more creative personalities more frequently confronted with anxiety-creating situations?* We have seen that impoverished personalities have relatively little neurotic anxiety. Is the converse of this true? One thesis was set by Kierkegaard in his contention that since anxiety arises as one confronts possibility in his own development as well as in his communicativeness with others, the more creative persons are the ones who confront more situations of possibility; hence they are more often in anxiety-creating situations. In similar vein, Goldstein has held that the more creative person ventures into many situations which expose him to shock and hence is more frequently confronted with anxiety. In our day, Paul Torrance describes how creative children continually seek out anxiety-creating situations to further their own self-realization.[1]

I shall approach this problem by citing the parallel rankings of the young women in this study according to amount of anxiety on the one hand and potential intelligence, originality, and level of differentiation on the other. I am entirely aware that this method leaves much to be desired; the rankings are necessarily a gross method of judgment. Furthermore, it is doubtful whether the factors of potential intelligence, originality, and level of differentiation are adequate as descriptions of what Kierkegaard, for example, meant by "creative." His term was, in German, *Geist*, by which he meant the capacity of human beings, as distinguished from animals, to conceive of possibility and actualize possibility. Or, as Goldstein phrases it in his studies of the brain-injured, the capacity to transcend the immediate, concrete situation in the light of "the possible." Granted the shortcomings of our method, however, I believe the following approach may at least yield suggestive indications.

RANKING ACCORDING TO AMOUNT OF ANXIETY		RANKING ACCORDING TO INTELLIGENCE POTENTIALITY[2]		
Nancy Agnes	*high*	Helen Nancy	(130) (125)	*high*
Helen Hester Frances Irene Ada	*moderately high*	Agnes Frances Hester Irene	(120) (120) (120) (120)	*moderately high*
Dolores Bessie	*moderately low*	Bessie Dolores Phyllis Sarah	(115) (110) (115) (110)	*moderately low*
Louise Phyllis Sarah	*low*	Ada Louise	(100) (100)	*low*

A glance at the comparative rankings for anxiety and for intelligence potentiality shows that the young women who are in the high or moderately-high categories in anxiety are all (except Ada, one of the two young black women) in either the high or moderately-high categories for intelligence potentiality. Conversely, the young women who are in the lower two categories in one list are also in the lower two categories on the other (again, Ada is the one exception). The suggested indication is, therefore, that the girls with the greater intelligence potentiality do have the greater degree of anxiety.

I do not mean that they will necessarily exhibit *overtly* greater anxiety; more intelligent persons presumably have also developed more effective ways of managing and controlling their anxiety. Some readers would prefer to speak of "potential anxiety," but the insertion of that term would not change the above point. Potential anxiety is still anxiety.[3]

When comparing the number of original responses with degree of anxiety (as shown in the chart below), we note that all of the young women except one in high and moderately-high categories with respect to number of original responses are in the high or moderately-high categories in anxiety. The one exception is Sarah, the other black in this study.

All of the young women except one in the high or moderately-high categories according to level of differentiation are also in the upper two categories with respect to anxiety. The one exception is again Sarah.[4] As far as the present methods go, *the results are on the side of the hypothesis that personalities of higher intelligence, originality, and level of differentiation likewise have more anxiety.* As Liddell put it, "anxiety accompanies intellectual activity as its shadow."[5] In proportion to the intellect, I add, there will be anxiety present.[6]

Here are the rankings according to originality (which is simply the number of original responses on the Rorschach) and the level of differentiation.

RANKING ACCORDING TO NUMBER OF ORIGINAL RESPONSES ON THE RORSCHACH			RANKING ACCORDING TO LEVEL OF DIFFERENTIATION AS ESTIMATED FROM THE RORSCHACH	
Helen	15	} *high*	Helen	} *high*
Sarah	15		Irene	
Nancy	8		Frances	
Frances	7	} *moderately high*	Nancy	} *moderately high*
Agnes	7		Sarah	
Irene	6		Agnes	
			Hester	
Hester	4			
Louise	4	} *moderately low*	Bessie	} *moderately low*
Phyllis	3			
Bessie	2		Louise	
			Phyllis	} *low*
Ada	0	} *low*	Dolores	
Dolores	0		Ada	

In the cases in our study, to sum up, impoverishment of personality is related to the absence of anxiety. Anxiety tends to impoverish and constrict the personality, and where impoverishment is accepted and structuralized in the personality—i.e., once one has become impoverished—

subjective conflicts and neurotic anxiety are avoided. The thesis of Kierkegaard, Goldstein, and others is confirmed by this and many other studies that the more creative and productive the personality, the more anxiety-creating situations it confronts. Students who do especially well in their studies and are, presumably, particularly gifted, have more anxiety, i.e., respond to all types of stress with anxiety. Students who are less competitive blame themselves or others for their poor performance, relieving them of anxiety.[7] Furthermore, anxiety can either inhibit or facilitate performance, depending on its strength and the individual's creative potential. Highly creative individuals perform cognitive tasks under stress better than those who are less creative.[8] Many psychologists believe that anxiety facilitates performance up to a point, then as the anxiety rises and tends to become overwhelming, it is debilitating. We agree with J. P. Denny, that perhaps the difficulty of the task itself caused anxiety in the less able.[9] Other persons, presumably the more intelligent and creative, seek anxiety to arouse them to achieve higher quality performances.

There are, likewise, lessons to be drawn from the oft-scorned studies of rats. In a report in *Science*, researchers at Cambridge University found that any general arousal, including pain and anxiety, stimulates learning.[10] It was also found that rats in a crowded pen, which assumedly puts them under stress, warded off disease (tuberculosis) better than those who were not crowded. *When the organism, in other words, is put on its mettle, aroused even by pain and inconvenience, it functions better.* The carry-over to this work could be stated simply: a moderate amount of anxiety has a constructive effect on the organism. Simple contentment, in other words, is not the aim of life. Such things as *vitality, commitment to values, breadth of sensitivity,* I propose, are more adequate goals. Probably this is why parachutists[11] and soldiers who are not "anxiety-free" but experience a realistic degree of anxiety do better than the nonanxious at their respective tasks.

I now wish to present a conceptualization which may draw together some loose ends of the theory of anxiety. We have pointed out in earlier sections of this chapter that neurotic anxiety results from a cleavage or contradiction between expectations and reality, a contradiction which occurred originally in the person's early relations with and attitudes toward his parents. We need now to emphasize that the cleavage between expectations and reality has its normal and healthy form as well as its neurotic form.

This cleavage, indeed, *is present as one condition of all creative activity*. The artist conceives a landscape in his imagination that has significant form. This is always partially in the way he sees the natural scene and partially produced by his own imagination. His painting is the result of his capacity to wed his own expectations—in this case, his artistic conception—with the reality of the scene before him. The man-created picture then has beauty which is richer and more gripping than the inanimate nature from which it was painted. Similarly, every scientific endeavor consists of the scientist's bringing to bear his own expectations—in this case, his hypotheses—upon reality, and when this process is successful he uncovers some reality which was not known in that way before. In ethics, the person brings to bear his expectations—in this case, ideals of more desirable relations—upon the reality of his immediate relations with other people, and by this means some transformation of his interpersonal relations occurs.

This capacity to experience a gap between expectations and reality and, with it, the capacity to bring one's expectations into reality, is the characteristic of all creative endeavor. We have seen this capacity of the human being as the capacity to deal with the "possible" and as the human ability to "plan."[12] In this context the human being may be described as the mammal with imagination.

Now this capacity, however it may be defined, is the condition *both* for anxiety and for creativity. The two are bound together; as Liddell has put it, anxiety is the shadow of intellect and it is the milieu in which creativity occurs. So our discussion now comes full circle. We see that man's creative abilities and his susceptibility to anxiety are two sides of the same capacity, uniquely possessed by the human being, to become aware of gaps between expectations and reality.

But there is a radical difference between neurotic and the healthy manifestations of this capacity. In neurotic anxiety, the cleavage between expectations and reality is in the form of a *contradiction*. Expectation and reality cannot be brought together, and since nobody can bear the constant tension of the experience of such a cleavage, the individual engages in a neurotic distortion of reality. Though this distortion is undertaken for the purpose of protecting the individual from neurotic anxiety, in the long run it makes the contradiction between the individual's expectations and reality more rigid and hence sets the stage for greater neurotic anxiety.

In productive activity, on the other hand, the expectations are not in contradiction to reality, but are used as a means of *creatively transforming reality*. The cleavage is constantly being resolved by the individual's bringing expectations and reality progressively into greater accord. This, as we have endeavored to show at many points throughout this book, is the sound way to overcome neurotic anxiety. Thus our human power to resolve the conflict between expectation and reality—our *creative* power—is at the same time our power to transcend neurotic anxiety and to live with normal anxiety.

THE REALIZATION OF THE SELF

The term "self" is used in two senses by writers on anxiety. In its broader meaning, "self" refers to the sum total of the individual's capacities, which is the way Goldstein uses it. In its more limited sense, "self" refers to the capacity of the human organism to have conscious awareness of its activities and, through this awareness, to exercise a measure of freedom in directing these activities. This is the way Kierkegaard, Sullivan, and Fromm use the term. Anxiety is involved in the development of the self in both of these meanings of the word.

Self-realization—i.e., expression and creative use of the individual's capacities—can occur only as the individual confronts and moves through anxiety-creating experiences. *The freedom of the healthy individual inheres in his capacity to avail himself of new possibilities in the meeting and overcoming of potential threats to his existence.* By moving through anxiety-creating experiences, one seeks and partially achieves realization of himself. He enlarges the scope of his activity and, at the same time, measure of selfhood. It is also a prerequisite to working through the anxiety. This capacity to tolerate anxiety is found least of all in the brain-injured patient, more in the child, and most of all in the creative adult.

Using the term "self" 'in its more limited sense—namely, the function of awareness of one's experience and activities —Sullivan has made a significant contribution. He holds that it is *in anxiety experiences in the young child that the self comes into being.* The infant in its early relations with its mother learns which activities will receive approbation and reward and which will receive disapproval and possible punishment. The latter activities arouse anxiety. The "self-dynamism," as Sullivan terms it, develops as a process by which the anxiety-creating experiences are excluded from activity and awareness and the approved activities are incorporated into the child's awareness and behavior. In this sense, the self comes into being to preserve the individual's security, to protect him from anxiety. This view emphasizes the integrative function of anxiety in the development of the self and illuminates the very common phenomenon, which we have seen above, that anxiety experiences which are dealt with unconstructively lead to a constriction of the self. Sullivan also indicates—pointing toward the constructive use of anxiety—that the *areas in the personality marked by anxiety often become the areas of significant growth when, as in psychotherapy or favorable human relationships, the individual can deal with his anxiety constructively.*

Consider now the positive aspects of selfhood—freedom, enlarged self-awareness, responsibility. The emergence of individual freedom is very closely connected with anxiety; indeed, the possibility of freedom always arouses anxiety, and how the anxiety is met will determine whether the freedom is affirmed or sacrificed by the individual. The child's need to break the original ties of dependence on its parents always involves anxiety. In the healthy child this anxiety is overcome by new relatedness to his parents and others on the basis of a larger degree of self-direction and autonomy. But if independence from parents brings with it an insupportable degree of anxiety (as in the case of the child of hostile or excessively anxious parents), and if the price in increased feelings of helplessness and isolation is too great, the child retreats into new forms of dependency. That particular possibility of enlarged selfhood is sacrificed and the way is set for the later emergence in this person of neurotic anxiety. This means that the capacities for independence and human freedom are necessary if one is to confront anxiety constructively.

An enlarging of self-awareness occurs whenever one confronts and moves through new possibilities. Whereas the first anxiety of the infant is without content, a change occurs in the child after the emergence of self-awareness. Kierkegaard terms this emergence of self-awareness a "qualitative leap"; it is described in a different context in modern dynamic psychology as the emergence of the ego. Now the child becomes aware that freedom involves responsibility. The responsibility is to "be one's self" as well as to be responsible to others. The converse side of this responsibility is guilt feeling. To the extent that individuals seek to avoid anxiety, responsibility, and guilt feeling by refusing to avail themselves of their new possibilities, by refusing to move from the familiar to the unfamiliar, they sacrifice their freedom and constrict autonomy and self-awareness.

"To venture causes anxiety, but not to venture is to lose oneself," Kierkegaard puts it pithily. Availing oneself of possibilities, confronting the anxiety, and accepting the responsibility and guilt feeling involved result in increased self-awareness, freedom, and enlarged spheres of creativity.

> So it is too that in the eyes of the world it is dangerous to venture. And why? Because one may lose. But not to venture is shrewd. And yet, by not venturing, it is so dreadfully easy to lose that which it would be difficult to lose in even the most venturesome venture, and in any case never so easily, so completely as if it were nothing—one's self. For I have ventured amiss—very well, then life helps me by its punishment. But if I have not ventured at all—who then helps me? And, moreover, if by not venturing at all in the highest sense (and to venture in the highest sense is precisely to become conscious of oneself) I have gained all earthly advantages . . . and lose my self! What of that?[13]

The more creative the individual, the more possibilities he or she has and the more they are confronted with anxiety and its concomitant responsibility and guilt feeling. Or, as Kierkegaard again phrases it: "The more consciousness, the more self." Increased self-awareness means increased selfhood. We conclude: *the positive aspects of selfhood develop as the individual confronts, moves through, and overcomes anxiety-creating experiences.*

APPENDICES

BIBLIOGRAPHY

NOTES

Appendices[1]

ANXIETY CHECK-LIST NO. 1:
ANXIETIES I HAD IN CHILDHOOD

Every child has some worries, fears, or anxieties. Will you please check the following list as to whether you had each worry "never," "sometimes," or "often" as a child.

	Never	Some-times	Often
1. Failing a test in school	____	____	____
2. My father losing his job	____	____	____
3. Being scolded by the teacher ...	____	____	____
4. Being in an accident	____	____	____
5. My mother leaving me	____	____	____
6. Not having enough to eat	____	____	____
7. Not having girl friends	____	____	____
8. Being left behind in my grade at school	____	____	____
9. My parents being sick	____	____	____
10. Someone following me at night ..	____	____	____
11. My brother or sister leaving me	____	____	____
12. Not being popular enough	____	____	____
13. Getting struck by a car	____	____	____
14. Making a speech before a group in school	____	____	____
15. Getting sick	____	____	____
16. My father scolding me	____	____	____
17. Having bad dreams	____	____	____
18. Not having boy friends	____	____	____

359

	Never	Some-times	Often
19. Not being able to get a job	___	___	___
20. Dying	___	___	___
21. Not being a success	___	___	___
22. My brother or sister picking on me	___	___	___
23. Having to support my parents some day	___	___	___
24. My mother scolding me	___	___	___
25. Not getting enough presents at Christmas	___	___	___
26. Being in a play in school (stage fright)	___	___	___
27. The house burning down	___	___	___
28. Being poor	___	___	___
29. Being left alone in the dark	___	___	___
30. My sister or brother getting more presents than I at Christmas ...	___	___	___
31. My father leaving me	___	___	___
32. Whether I would get married ...	___	___	___
33. My father punishing me	___	___	___
34. My mother dying	___	___	___
35. When my menstrual period came	___	___	___
36. Robbers breaking in the house ..	___	___	___
37. Not having an attractive home ..	___	___	___
38. My brother or sister dying	___	___	___
39. Being lonely	___	___	___
40. Feeling my parents might not care for me	___	___	___
41. Witches or ghosts coming	___	___	___
42. My mother punishing me	___	___	___
43. My father dying	___	___	___
44. Not being attractive	___	___	___
45. Not being healthy	___	___	___
46. Things I saw in movies, like Frankensteins	___	___	___
47. Being out in lightning and thunderstorm	___	___	___
48. People picking fights with me ...	___	___	___
49. Meeting snakes	___	___	___
50. Meeting large animals	___	___	___
51. Having the dentist pull a tooth ..	___	___	___

	Never	Some-times	Often
52. Someone ridiculing or making fun of me	___	___	___
53. Jumping or falling off a high cliff	___	___	___
54. Being shut in a room by myself	___	___	___

ANXIETY CHECK-LIST NO. 2:
PRESENT ANXIETIES

People worry or have anxiety about different things. Please check this list as to whether you worry or have anxiety about each thing "often," "sometimes," or "never."

	Never	Some-times	Often
1. Being struck by an auto	___	___	___
2. Not being attractive to men	___	___	___
3. Going to the hospital	___	___	___
4. Whether I will be successful at my jobs	___	___	___
5. Getting old too soon	___	___	___
6. Whether my mother is disappointed in me	___	___	___
7. Whether I will be unhappy	___	___	___
8. Not having enough money to get along	___	___	___
9. Being operated on	___	___	___
10. Not having men friends	___	___	___
11. Whether my baby will be healthy	___	___	___
12. What people in the hospital will say to me	___	___	___
13. Being discharged from my work	___	___	___
14. What my brother or sister thinks of me	___	___	___
15. The city being bombed by enemy planes	___	___	___
16. Where I will live	___	___	___
17. Nightmares or bad dreams	___	___	___
18. Whether I will get married some day	___	___	___
19. Being held up by a robber	___	___	___
20. What my baby will look like ...	___	___	___

	Never	Some-times	Often
21. Losing my figure	——	——	——
22. Not having good health	——	——	——
23. What my girl friends think about me	——	——	——
24. Dying	——	——	——
25. The labor pains of birth	——	——	——
26. What my men friends think of me	——	——	——
27. Bad luck	——	——	——
28. Whether I should keep my baby	——	——	——
29. What my father thinks of me ...	——	——	——
30. What kind of work I should follow	——	——	——
31. Being lonely	——	——	——
32. My father or mother dying	——	——	——
33. People being angry at me	——	——	——
34. Being poisoned	——	——	——
35. Not getting the man I love	——	——	——
36. Friends letting me down	——	——	——
37. Drowning	——	——	——
38. Not getting the approval of the employers I work for	——	——	——

ANXIETY CHECK-LIST NO. 3: FUTURE ANXIETIES

People have different worries or anxieties. Please check this list as to whether you worry or have anxiety about each thing "often," "sometimes," or "never."

1. Friends not sticking by me	——	——	——
2. Where and how I will live	——	——	——
3. Being discharged from my job ..	——	——	——
4. Being hurt in an air raid	——	——	——
5. Not having men friends	——	——	——
6. What my sister or brother will think of me	——	——	——
7. My apartment building catching fire	——	——	——
8. How my baby will develop	——	——	——

	Never	Some-times	Often
9. Having an operation	———	———	———
10. Whether I will get married some day	———	———	———
11. Bad dreams or nightmares	———	———	———
12. Not getting the man I love	———	———	———
13. Being poisoned	———	———	———
14. My father or mother dying	———	———	———
15. Being lonely	———	———	———
16. What kind of work I should follow	———	———	———
17. What my men friends will think of me	———	———	———
18. Some calamity befalling me	———	———	———
19. Not having a good figure	———	———	———
20. What my father will think of me	———	———	———
21. What future plans I should make for the baby	———	———	———
22. Dying	———	———	———
23. Not having good health	———	———	———
24. What my girl friends say about me	———	———	———
25. Being run into by a car	———	———	———
26. Getting old too quickly	———	———	———
27. Not being successful at my work	———	———	———
28. What my neighbors will think of me	———	———	———
29. Whether I will be unhappy	———	———	———
30. Whether I will have enough money to get along	———	———	———
31. How my baby's health will be ..	———	———	———
32. Not being attractive to men	———	———	———
33. Not getting the approval of employers I work for	———	———	———
34. People picking fights with me ..	———	———	———
35. A robber entering my house	———	———	———
36. What my mother will think of me	———	———	———
37. Having teeth pulled by a dentist	———	———	———
38. Having to go to the hospital again	———	———	———

NOTE: The above three check-lists are not presented as models for other studies. They were drawn up for the author's study, and the content of the items is specifically related to that study. They are presented here to enable the reader to see more concretely the basis for one approach to the cases in Chapters 8 and 9.

Bibliography

ADAMS, J. DONALD. 1948. *New York Times Book Review.* January 11, 1948, p. 2.

ADLER, ALFRED. 1917. *The neurotic constitution.* English trans. by Bernard Glueck. New York: Moffatt, Yard & Co.

———. 1927. *Understanding human nature.* Trans. by W. Beran Wolfe. New York: Greenberg Publisher, Inc.

———. 1930. *The pattern of life,* ed. W. Beran Wolfe. New York: Cosmopolitan Book Corp.

———. 1930. *Problems of neurosis,* ed. Philippe Mariet. New York: Cosmopolitan Book Corp.

ALEXANDER, FRANZ. 1934. The influence of psychologic factors upon gastrointestinal disturbances. *Psychoanal. Quart.* 3, 501–88.

ALLPORT, G. W. 1942. *The use of personal documents in psychological science.* New York: Social Science Research Council.

ALLPORT, G. W., and VERNON, P. E. 1933. *Studies in expressive movement.* New York: The Macmillan Co.

AUDEN, W. H. 1947. *The age of anxiety: a baroque eclogue.* New York: Random House, Inc.

BAILEY, PEARCE. 1935. *Theory and therapy: an introduction to the psychology of Dr. Otto Rank.* Paris: Jouve et Cie., Editeurs.

BATESON, GREGORY. 1975. *Steps to an ecology of mind.* New York: Ballantine Books.

BECK, AARON. 1972. Cognition, anxiety, and psychophysiological disorders. In Charles Spielberger (ed.), *Anxiety: current trends in theory and research.* Vol. II. New York: Academic Press.

BENDER, LAURETTA. 1950. Anxiety in disturbed children. In Paul Hock and Joseph Zubin (eds.). *Anxiety*. New York: Grune and Stratton.

BERNSTEIN, LEONARD. 1949. Notes on *The age of anxiety,* Bernstein's Second Symphony, in *Concert Bulletin*. Boston: Boston Symphony Orchestra.

BINGER, CARL. 1945. *The doctor's job*. New York: W. W. Norton & Co., Inc.

BOURNE, PETER, ROSE, ROBERT, and MASON, JOHN. 1967. Urinary 17-OHCS levels. *Archives of General Psychiatry*, **17,** 104–10.

BROCK, WERNER. 1935. *An introduction to contemporary German philosophy*. London: Cambridge University Press.

BROWN, LAWRASON. 1933. The mental aspect in the etiology and treatment of pulmonary tuberculosis. *International Clinics,* **3:**43, 151–62.

BURCKHARDT, JACOB. 1935. *The civilization of the Renaissance in Italy*. Authorized trans. from 15th ed. by S. G. C. Middlemore. ("Bonibooks Series.") New York: Albert and Charles Boni, Inc.

CANNON, W. B. 1927. *Bodily changes in pain, hunger, fear and rage*. (2d ed.) New York: Appleton-Century-Crofts, Inc.

———. 1939. *The wisdom of the body* (Rev. and enl. ed.). New York: W. W. Norton & Co., Inc.

———. 1942. Voodoo death. *Amer. Anthrop.*, **44:**2, 169–81.

CASSIRER, ERNST. 1944. *An essay on man*. New Haven, Conn.: Yale University Press.

COATES, D. B., ET AL. 1976. Life-event changes and mental health. In Irwin Sarason and Charles Spielberger (eds.), *Stress and anxiety*. Vol. III. New York: John Wiley and Sons, pp. 225–250.

COUSINS, NORMAN. 1945. *Modern man is obsolete*. New York: The Viking Press, Inc.

DOLLARD, JOHN. 1935. *Criteria for the life history*. New Haven: Yale University Press.

———. 1942. *Victory over fear*. New York: Reynal & Hitchcock, Inc.

DOLLARD, JOHN, and HARTEN, DONALD. 1944. *Fear in battle*. (Rev. ed.) Washington, D.C.: *The Infantry Journal*, 1944.

DU BOIS, CORA. 1944. *People of Alor*. (With analyses by Abram Kardiner and Emil Oberholzer.) Minneapolis: University of Minnesota Press.

DUNBAR, HELEN FLANDERS. 1938. *Emotions and bodily changes*. (Rev. ed.) New York: Columbia University Press.

———. 1942. The relationship between anxiety states and organic diseases. *Clinics,* 1:4, 879–907.

———. 1943. *Psychosomatic diagnosis.* New York: Paul B. Hoeber, Inc., Medical Book Dept. of Harper & Bros.

DUNNE, JOHN S. 1972. *The way of all earth.* New York: Macmillan.

EBON, MARTIN. 1948. *World communism today.* New York: Whittlesey House.

ENDLER, NORMAN. 1975. A person-situation-interaction model for anxiety. In Charles Spielberger and Irwin Sarason (eds.), *Stress and anxiety.* Vol. I. New York: John Wiley and Sons, pp. 145–162.

ENGEL, GEORGE. 1962. *Psychological development in health and disease.* Philadelphia: W. B. Saunders Co.

FORD, CHARLES. 1975. The *Pueblo* incident: psychological response to social stress. In Irwin Sarason and Charles Spielberger (eds.), *Stress and anxiety.* Vol. II. New York: John Wiley and Sons.

FRANK, L. K. 1936. Society as the patient. *Amer. J. Sociol.,* 42, 335.

———. 1939. Projective methods for the study of personality. *J. Psychol.,* 8, 389–415.

FREUD, SIGMUND. 1968. *A general introduction to psychoanalysis.* New York: Liveright. (First published in German in 1916.)

———. 1974. *New introductory lectures in psychoanalysis.* New York: W. W. Norton & Co., Inc.

———. 1964. *The problem of anxiety.* Trans. by H. A. Bunker. (American ed.) New York: W. W. Norton & Co., Inc. (Originally published under the title *Inhibition, symptom, and anxiety* by the Psychoanalytic Institute, Stamford, Conn., 1927.)

———. 1970. *An outline of psycho-analysis.* New York: W. W. Norton & Co., Inc.

FROMM, ERICH. 1939. Selfishness and self-love. *Psychiatry,* 2, 507–23.

———. 1941. *Escape from freedom.* New York: Rinehart & Co., Inc.

———. 1947. *Man for himself, an inquiry into the psychology of ethics.* New York: Rinehart & Co., Inc.

GESELL, A. L. 1929. The individual in infancy. In Carl Murchison (ed.), *The foundations of experimental psychology.* Worcester, Mass.: Clark University Press. Pp. 628–60.

GOLDSTEIN, KURT. 1938. A further comparison of the Moro reflex and the startle pattern. *J. Psychol.*, 6, 33–42.

———. 1939. *The organism, a holistic approach to biology.* New York: American Book Co.

———. 1940. *Human nature in the light of psychopathology.* Cambridge, Mass.: Harvard University Press.

GRAY, G. W. 1939. Anxiety and illness. *Harper's Magazine,* May, 1939, pp. 605–16.

GRAY, J. 1971. *The psychology of fear and stress.* London: Weidenfeld and Nicolson.

GREENACRE, PHYLLIS. 1941. The predisposition to anxiety. *Psychoanal. Quart.*, 10, 66–94, 610–38.

GRINKER, R. R. 1944. Treatment of war neuroses. *J. Amer. med. Assn.*, 126:3, 142–45.

GRINKER, R. R., and SPIEGEL, S. P. 1945. *Men under stress.* Philadelphia: The Blakiston Co.

GROEN, J. J. and BASTIAANS, J. 1975. Psychosocial stress, interhuman communication and psychosomatic disease. In Charles Spielberger and Irwin Sarason (eds.), *Stress and anxiety.* Vol. I. New York: John Wiley and Sons, pp. 27–50.

HAGMAN, R. R. 1932. A study of fears of children of preschool age. *J. exp. Educ.*, 1, 110–30.

HALLIDAY, JAMES L. 1948. *Psychosocial medicine, a study of the sick society.* New York: W. W. Norton & Co., Inc.

HALLOWELL, A. I. 1938. Fear and anxiety as cultural and individual variables in a primitive society *J. soc. Psychol.*, 9, 25–47.

———. 1941. The social function of anxiety in a primitive society. *Amer. sociol. Rev.*, 6:6, 869–87.

HARTZ, JEROME. 1944. Tuberculosis and personality conflicts. *Psychosom. Med.*, 6:1, 17–22.

HASTINGS, DONALD W. 1945. What fear is—and does—to fighting men. *New York Times Magazine,* July 15, 1945, pp. 11, 31–32.

HEALY, W., BRONNER, A. F., and BOWERS, A. M. 1930. *The meaning and structure of psychoanalysis.* New York: Alfred A. Knopf, Inc.

HERSHEY, LEWIS B. 1942. Fear in war. *New York Times Magazine,* September 27, 1942, pp. 5, 6, 36.

HESSE, HERMAN. 1947. *Steppenwolf.* Trans. by Basil Creighton. New York: Henry Holt & Co., Inc.

HOCH, PAUL AND ZUBIN, JOSEPH (eds.). 1950. *Anxiety: proceedings of the thirty-ninth annual meeting of the American Psy-*

chopathological Association. New York: Grune and Stratton. Republished by Hafner Publishing Co., New York, 1964.

HORNEY, KAREN. 1937. *The neurotic personality of our time.* New York: W. W. Norton & Co., Inc.

——. 1939. *New ways in psychoanalysis.* New York: W. W. Norton & Co., Inc.

——. 1945. *Our inner conflicts, a constructive theory of neurosis.* New York: W. W. Norton & Co., Inc.

HOROWITZ, MARDI. 1976. *Stress response syndromes.* New York: Jason Aronson, Inc.

HUIZINGA, JOHAN. 1924. *The waning of the Middle Ages.* London. Edward Arnold & Co.

HUNT, J. McV. (ed.). 1944. *Personality and the behavior disorders.* New York: The Ronald Press Co.

IBSEN, HENRIK. *Eleven plays of Henrik Ibsen.* New York: Random House, Inc.

IBSEN, HENRIK. 1963. *Peer Gynt.* Trans. by Michael Meyer. Garden City, N.Y.: Doubleday, p. 16.

JANIS, IRVING. 1958. *Psychological Stress.* New York: Academic Press.

JERSILD, A. T. 1933. *Child psychology.* (Rev. ed.) New York: Prentice-Hall, Inc., 1940.

——. 1935. Methods of overcoming children's fears. *J. Psychol.*, **1**, 75–104.

JERSILD, A. T., MARKEY, F. V., and JERSILD, C. D. 1933. *Children's fears, dreams, wishes, daydreams, likes, pleasant and unpleasant memories.* Child Develpm. Monogr. No. 12. New York: Teachers College, Columbia University.

JERSILD, A. T., and HOLMES, F. B. 1935. *Children's fears.* Child Develpm. Monogr. No. 20. New York: Teachers College, Columbia University.

JONES, E. S. 1944. Subjective evaluations of personality. In J. McV. Hunt (ed.), *Personality and the behavior disorders.* New York: The Ronald Press Co. **I**, 139–70.

JONES, H. E., and JONES, M. C. 1928. A study of fear. *Childhood Education*, **5**, 136–43.

JUNG, C. G. 1916. *Collected papers on analytical psychology.* Authorized trans. by C. E. Long. London: Baillière, Tindall & Cox.

——. 1938. *Psychology and religion.* New Haven, Conn.: Yale University Press.

KAFKA, FRANZ. 1930. *The castle.* Trans. from the German by Edwin and Willa Muir. New York: Alfred A. Knopf, Inc.

————. 1937. *The trial*. Trans. from the German by Edwin and Willa Muir. New York: Alfred A. Knopf, Inc.

KAGAN, JEROME. 1966. Psychosocial development of the child. In Frank Falkner, *Human development*. Philadelphia: W. B. Saunders.

KARDINER, ABRAM. 1939. *The individual and his society—the psychodynamics of primitive social organization*. With a foreword and two ethnological reports by Ralph Linton. New York: Columbia University Press.

————. 1945. *The psychological frontiers of society*. New York: Columbia University Press.

KIERKEGAARD, SØREN. 1941. *Sickness unto death*. Trans. by Walter Lowrie. Princeton, N.J.: Princeton University Press. (Originally published in Danish, 1849.)

————. 1944. *The concept of dread*. Trans. by Walter Lowrie. Princeton, N.J.: Princeton University Press. (Originally published in Danish, 1844.)

————. 1976. *The concept of anxiety*. Ed. and trans. by Howard V. Hong and Edna V. Hong. Northfield, Minn.

KIMMEL, H. D. 1975. Conditioned fear and anxiety. In Charles Spielberger and Irwin Sarason (eds.), *Stress and anxiety*. Vol. I. New York: John Wiley and Sons, pp. 189–210.

KJERULFF, KRISTEFF, and WIGGIN, NANCY. 1976. Graduate students' style for coping with stressful situations. *Journal of Educational Psychology*, 68:3, 247–254.

KLAUSNER, SAMUEL (ed.). 1968. *Why man takes chances: studies in stress seeking*. New York: Anchor Books, Doubleday & Company.

KLINEBERG, OTTO. 1940. *Social psychology*. New York: Henry Holt & Co., Inc.

KLOPFER, BRUNO, and KELLEY, DOUGLAS. 1942. *The Rorschach technique, a manual for a projective method of personality diagnosis*. Yonkers, N.Y.: World Book Co.

KUBIE, L. S. 1941. The ontogeny of anxiety. *Psychoanal. Rev.*, 8:1, 78–85.

LANDIS, C., and HUNT, W. A. 1939. *The startle pattern*. New York: Rinehart & Co., Inc.

LAZARUS, RICHARD, and AVERILL, JAMES. 1972. Emotion and cognition: with special reference to anxiety. In Charles Spielberger (ed.), *Anxiety: current trends in theory and research*. Vol. II. New York: John Wiley and Sons, pp. 241–283.

LEONARD, A. G. 1906. *The lower Niger and its tribes*. London.

LEVINE, SEYMOUR. 1971. Stress and behavior. *Scientific American*, 224:1, 26–31.

LEVITT, EUGENE. 1972. A brief commentary on the "psychiatric breakthrough" with special emphasis on the hematology of anxiety. In Charles Spielberger (ed.), *Anxiety: current trends in theory and research.* Vol. I. New York: Acadamic Press.

LEVY, D. M. 1938. Maternal overprotection. *Psychiatry,* 1, 561 ff.

———. 1949. The source of acute anxieties in early childhood. In Paul Hoch and Zubin (eds.), *Anxiety.* New York: Grune and Stratton.

LEWIN, KURT. 1936. *Principles of topological psychology.* New York: McGraw-Hill Book Co., Inc.

LIDDELL, HOWARD S. 1949. The role of vigilance in the development of animal neurosis. In Paul Hoch and Joseph Zubin (eds.), *Anxiety.* New York: Grune and Stratton, pp. 183–197.

LIFTON, ROBERT JAY. 1961. *History and human survival.* New York: Random House.

———. 1961. *Thought reform and the psychology of totalism.* New York: W. W. Norton & Co., Inc.

———. 1976. *The life of the self.* New York: Simon and Schuster.

LOWRIE, WALTER. 1944. *A short life of Kierkegaard.* Princeton, N.J.: Princeton University Press.

LUDWIG, WALTER. 1920. Beiträge zur Psychologie der Furcht im Kriege. In Stein and Lipmann (eds.), *Beiträge zur Psychologie des Krieges.* Leipzig.

LURIA, A. R. 1932. *The nature of human conflicts.* New York: Liveright Publishing Corp.

LYND, R. S., and LYND, H. M. 1929. *Middletown.* New York: Harcourt, Brace & Co., Inc.

———. 1937. *Middletown in transition.* New York: Harcourt, Brace & Co., Inc.

LYNN, RICHARD. 1975. National differences in anxiety. In Irwin Sarason and Charles Spielberger (eds.), *Stress and Anxiety.* Vol. II. New York: John Wiley and Sons, pp. 257–272.

MACKINNON, DONALD W. 1944. A topological analysis of anxiety. *Character & Pers.,* **12**:3, 163–76.

MALLER, J. B. 1944. Personality tests. In J. McV. HUNT (ed.), *Personality and the behavior disorders.* New York: The Ronald Press Co. I, 170–214.

MANN, THOMAS. 1937. *Freud, Goethe, Wagner.* New York: Alfred A. Knopf, Inc.

MANNHEIM, KARL. 1941. *Man and society in an age of reconstruction.* New York: Harcourt, Brace & Co., Inc.

MASLOW, A. H., and MITTELMANN, BÉLA. 1941. *Principles of*

abnormal psychology: the dynamics of psychic illness. New York: Harper & Bros.

MASON, JOHN. 1975. Emotion as reflected in patterns of endocrine integration. In L. Levi (ed.), *Emotions—their parameters and measurement.* New York: Raven Press.

MATTHEWS, HERBERT L. 1946. *The education of a correspondent.* New York: Harcourt, Brace & Co., Inc.

MAY, MARK A. 1941. *Education in a world of fear.* Cambridge, Mass.: Harvard University Press.

MAY, ROLLO. 1950. Historical roots of modern anxiety theories. Paper read before the American Psychopathological Association. In Paul Hoch and Joseph Zubin (eds.), *Anxiety.* New York: Grune and Stratton, 1964, pp. 3–16.

———. 1950. *The meaning of anxiety.* First Edition. New York: Ronald Press.

———. 1953. *Man's search for himself.* New York: W. W. Norton & Co., Inc.

———. (ed.). 1960. *Symbolism in religion and literature.* New York: George Braziller.

———. 1967. *Psychology and the human dilemma.* Princeton: Van Nostrand Co.

———. 1969. *Love and will.* New York: W. W. Norton & Co., Inc.

MAY, ROLLO, ANGEL, ERNEST, and ELLENBERG, HENRI (eds.). *Existence: a new dimension in psychiatry and psychology.* New York: Basic Books.

MILLER, N. E., and DOLLARD, J. 1941. *Social learning and imitation.* New Haven, Conn.: Yale University Press.

MITTELMANN, B., WOLFF, H. G., and SCHARF, M. P. 1942. Experimental studies on patients with gastritis, duodenitis, and peptic ulcer. *Psychosom. Med.,* 4:1, 5–61.

MOWRER, O. H. 1939. A stimulus-response analysis of anxiety and its role as a reinforcing agent. *Psychol. Rev.,* 46:6, 553–65.

———. 1939. The Freudian theories of anxiety: a reconciliation. New Haven, Conn.: Institute of Human Relations, Yale University (mimeographed).

———. 1940. Anxiety-reduction and learning. *J. exp. Psychol.,* 27:5, 497–516.

———. 1940. *Preparatory set (expectancy)—some methods of measurement.* Psychol. Monogr. No. 233.

———. 1950. *Learning theory and personality dynamics.* New York: Ronald Press.

———. 1950. Pain, punishment, guilt, and anxiety. In Paul

Hoch and Joseph Zubin (eds.), *Anxiety*. New York: Grune and Stratton.

MOWRER, O. H., and ULLMAN, A. D. 1945. Time as a determinant in integrative learning. *Psychol. Rev.*, **52**:2, 61–90.

MUMFORD, LEWIS. 1944. *The condition of man*. New York: Harcourt, Brace & Co., Inc.

MURPHY, GARDNER. 1932. *An historical introduction in modern psychology*. New York: Harcourt, Brace & Co., Inc.

MURPHY, GARDNER, MURPHY, L. B., and NEWCOMB, T. M. 1937. *Experimental social psychology, an interpretation of research upon the socialization of the individual*. (Rev. ed.) New York: Harper & Bros.

MURRAY, H. A., JR., *et al.* 1938. *Explorations in personality*. New York: Oxford University Press.

NIEBUHR, REINHOLD. 1941. *The nature and destiny of man*. New York: Chas. Scribner's Sons.

NORTHROP, F. S. C. 1946. *The meeting of East and West, an inquiry concerning world understanding*. New York: The Macmillan Co.

OBERHOLZER, EMIL. 1949. Anxiety in Rorschach's experiment. Paper read before the American Psychopathological Association, June 3, 1949.

OPLER, M. K. 1956. Culture, psychiatry, and human values. New York: Thomas.

ORTEGA Y GASSET, JOSÉ. 1946. *Concord and liberty*. Trans. from the Spanish by Helen Wey. New York: W. W. Norton & Co., Inc.

PASCAL, BLAISE. 1946. *Pensées*. Ed. and trans. by G. B. Rawlings. Mt. Vernon, N.Y.: Peter Pauper Press.

PFISTER, OSCAR. 1948. *Christianity and fear, a study in history and in the psychology and hygiene of religion*. Trans. by W. H. Johnston. New York: The Macmillan Co.

PINTNER, R., and LEV, J. 1940. Worries of school children. *J. genet. Psychol.* **56**, 67–76.

PLANT, J. A. 1937. *Personality and the cultural pattern*. New York: Commonwealth Fund, Division of Publications.

PLAUT, PAUL. 1920. Psychographie des Krieges. In Stein and Lipmann (eds.), *Beiträge zur Psychologie des Krieges*. Leipzig.

RADO, SANDOR. 1950. Emergency behavior, with an introduction to the dynamics of conscience. In Paul Hoch and Joseph Zubin (eds.), *Anxiety*. New York: Grune and Stratton, pp. 150–175.

Rank, Otto. 1929. *The trauma of birth.* New York: Harcourt, Brace & Co., Inc.

———. 1936. *Will therapy.* New York: Alfred A. Knopf, Inc.

Rees, J. R. 1946. What war taught us about human nature. *New York Times Magazine,* March 17, 1946, pp. 11, 54–55.

Reich, Wilhelm. 1945. *Character analysis: principles and technique for psychoanalysts in practice and training.* Trans. by T. P. Wolfe. New York: Orgone Press. (First published in German in 1935.)

Reik, Theodore. 1941. Aggression from anxiety. *Int. J. Psycho-Anal.,* 22, 7–16.

Riezler, Kurt. 1944. The social psychology of fear. *Amer. J. Sociol.,* 46:6, 489–98.

Rolland, Roman. 1915. *Michaelangelo.* New York: Albert and Charles Boni, Inc.

Rorschach, Hermann, 1942. *Psychodiagnostics.* New York: Grune and Stratton, Inc.

Sarason, Irwin, and Spielberger, Charles (eds.). 1975 and 1976. *Stress and anxiety.* Vols. II and III. New York: John Wiley and Sons.

Sarason, Seymour, et al. 1960. *Anxiety in elementary school children.* New York: John Wiley and Sons.

Saul, Leon J. 1944. Physiological effects of emotional tension. In J. McV. Hunt (ed.), *Personality and the behavior disorders.* New York: The Ronald Press Co. Pp. 269–306.

Schiche, E. 1920. Zur Psychologie der Todesahungen. In Stein and Lipmann (eds.), *Beiträge zur Psychologie des Krieges.* Leipzig.

Schlesinger, Arthur M., Jr. 1948. Communism: a clear-eyed view (book review), *New York Times Book Review Section,* February 1, 1948, p. 1.

Schmideberg, Melitta. 1940. Anxiety states. *Psychoanal. Rev.,* 27:4, 439–49.

Selye, Hans. 1950. *The physiology and pathology of exposure to stress.* Montreal: Acta.

———. 1956. *The stress of life.* New York: McGraw-Hill Company.

———. 1974. *Stress without distress.* Toronto: McClelland and Stewart Limited.

Spielberger, Charles. 1966. *Anxiety and behavior.* New York: Academic Press.

——— (ed.). 1972. *Anxiety: current trends in theory and research.* Vols. I and II. New York: Academic Press.

Spielberger, Charles, and Sarason, Irwin (eds.). 1975 and

1977. *Stress and anxiety*. Vols. I and IV. New York: John Wiley and Sons.

SPINOZA, BARUCH. 1910. *The ethics of Spinoza and treatise on the correction of the intellect*. London: Everyman Edition.

STEKEL, WILHELM. 1923. *Conditions of nervous anxiety and their treatment*. Authorized trans. by Rosalie Gabler. London: Kegan Paul, Trench, Trubner & Co., Ltd.

SULLIVAN, HARRY STACK. 1947. *Conceptions of modern psychiatry*. Washington, D.C.: William Alanson White Psychiatric Foundation. (Reprinted from *Psychiatry*, **3**:1 and **8**:2.)

———. 1948. The meaning of anxiety in psychiatry and life. *Psychiatry*, **2**:1, 1–15.

———. 1949. The theory of anxiety and the nature of psychotherapy. *Psychiatry*, **12**:1, 3–13.

SYMONDS, JOHN ADDINGTON. 1935. *The Italian Renaissance*. New York: Random House, Inc.

SYMONDS, PERCIVAL M. 1946. *The dynamics of human adjustment*. New York: Appleton-Century-Crofts, Inc.

TAWNEY, R. H. 1920. *The acquisitive society*. New York: Harcourt, Brace & Co., Inc.

TEICHMAN, YONA. 1975. The stress of coping with the unknown regarding a significant family member. In Irwin Sarason and Charles Spielberger (eds.), *Stress and anxiety*. Vol. II. New York: John Wiley and Sons, pp. 243–254.

TILLICH, PAUL. 1944. Existential philosophy. *Journal of the History of Ideas*, **5**:1, 44–70.

———. 1947. *The Protestant era*. Chicago: University of Chicago Press.

———. 1949. Anxiety-reducing agencies in our culture. Paper read before the American Psychopathological Association, June 3, 1949.

TOYNBEE, ARNOLD J. 1949. How to turn the tables on Russia. *Woman's Home Companion*, August, 1949, pp. 30 ff.

TREGEAR, E. J. *Anthrop. Inst.*, 1890, **19**, 100.

VASARI, GIORGIO. 1946. *Lives of the artists*. Abridged and ed. by Betty Burroughs. New York: Simon & Schuster, Inc.

WATSON, JOHN B. 1924. *Behaviorism*. New York: W. W. Norton & Co., Inc.

WILLOUGHBY, R. R. 1935. Magic and cognate phenomena: an hypothesis. In Carl Murchison, ed., *A Handbook of Social Psychology*. Worcester, Mass.: Clark University Press.

WOLF, STEWART, and WOLFF, H. G. 1947. *Human gastric function*. New York: Oxford University Press.

WOLFE, THOMAS. 1929. *Look homeward, angel*. New York:

Chas. Scribner's Sons.

————. 1934. *You can't go home again.* New York: Harper & Bros.

————. 1935. *Of time and the river.* New York: Harper & Bros.

YASKIN, JOSEPH. 1937. The psychobiology of anxiety, a clinical study. *Psychoanal. Rev.*, Supp. to Vols. **23–24**, pp. 1–93.

YOUNG, PAUL THOMAS. 1968. Emotion. In *International encyclopedia of social sciences.* Vol. 5. New York: Macmillan.

ZELIGS, ROSE. 1939. Children's worries. *Sociology and Social Research*, 24:22–32.

ZILBOORG, G. 1932. Anxiety without affect. *Psychoanal. Quart.*, 2, 48–67.

ZINN, E. 1940. Anxiety—clinically viewed. Paper presented before the Monday Night Group, season of 1939–40. New Haven, Conn.: Institute of Human Relations, Yale University (mimeographed).

Notes

FOOTNOTES — CHAPTER 1

1. W. H. Auden, *The age of anxiety* (New York, 1947).
2. *Ibid.*, p. 3.
3. *Ibid.*, p. 45.
4. *Ibid.*, p. 44.
5. *Ibid.*, p. 42.
6. I was excited to find, during the first writing of this book, that Leonard Bernstein had composed a symphony, which had its premiere in 1949, entitled *Age of anxiety*. On the basis of his conviction that Auden's poem truly presents the "state of the age" in general, as well as speaking for the particular individual members of that age like himself, Bernstein translated the poem into the symbols of instrumental music.
7. Quoted in the *New York Times*, December 21, 1947, Sec. 7, p. 2.
8. Max Brod, in Appendix to Kafka's *The castle* (New York, 1930), p. 329.
9. Herman Hesse, *Steppenwolf*, trans. Basil Creighton (New York, 1947); originally published in German in 1927.
10. *Ibid.*, p. 28. Emphasis mine.
11. R. S. Lynd and H. M. Lynd, *Middletown* (New York, 1929), and *Middletown in transition* (New York, 1937).
12. *Middletown*, p. 87.
13. *Ibid.*, p. 493.
14. *Middletown in transition*, p. 315.
15. *Ibid.*, p. 177.
16. This problem is discussed in some detail in Chapter 6, where we discuss the relation between cultural change and anxiety.
17. *Middletown in transition*, p. 315.
18. Robert Jay Lifton, *Thought reform and the psychology of totalism* (New York, 1961).
19. John S. Dunne, *The way of all earth* (New York, 1972).
20. Robert Jay Lifton, *The life of the self* (New York, 1976), p. 141.
21. Robert Jay Lifton, *History and human survival* (New York, 1961), p. 319.
22. Charles Ford. "The *Pueblo* incident: psychological response

to severe stress," in Irwin Sarason and Charles Spielberger (eds.), *Stress and anxiety*, II (New York, 1975), pp. 229–241.

23. Paul Tillich, *The Protestant era* (Chicago, 1947), p. 245.

24. *The education of a correspondent* (New York, 1946).

25. *New York Times*, February 1, 1948.

26. *World communism today* (New York, 1948).

27. To some extent, it might be said, dictatorships are born and come to power in periods of cultural anxiety; once in power, they live in anxiety—e.g., many of the acts of the dictating group are motivated by its own anxiety; and the dictatorship perpetuates its power by capitalizing upon and engendering anxiety in its own people as well as in its rival nations.

28. Several references to "fear of fear" preceding Roosevelt's are cited by J. Donald Adams (*New York Times Book Review*, p. 2, Jan. 11, 1948): Emerson, quoting from Thoreau's *Journals*, "Nothing is terrible except fear itself." Carlyle, "We must get rid of fear; we cannot act at all till then." Sir Francis Bacon, "Nothing is terrible except fear itself." "We have nothing to fear but fear itself" has also been attributed to the Roman, Seneca. Such statements do not make sense on the level of fear. Strictly speaking, a fear does not prevent action; it prepares the organism *for* action. It is doubtful whether the phrase "fear itself" has logical meaning—one is afraid *of* something. "Fear itself" is more logically to be termed anxiety. Indeed, if the term "anxiety" is substituted, all the above quotations make better sense.

29. *Modern man is obsolete* (New York, 1945), p. 1. First printed as an editorial in *The Saturday Review of Literature* and then published in book form. Though Norman Cousins used the term "fear," he is describing what I would call anxiety. "Fear of irrational death" is a good example of anxiety.

30. Arnold Toynbee, How to turn the tables on Russia, *Woman's Home Companion*, August, 1949, 30 ff.

31. Reinhold Niebuhr, *The nature and destiny of man* (New York, 1941), p. 182.

32. *Ibid.*

33. R. R. Willoughby, *Magic and cognate phenomena: an hypothesis*, in Carl Murchinson (ed.), *Handbook of social psychology* (Worcester, Mass., 1935), p. 498.

34. *Ibid.*, p. 500.

35. Statistics furnished by the Center for Policy Research, Columbia University.

36. Discussed in Chapter 4.

37. Sigmund Freud, *Introductory lectures on psychoanalysis*, trans. James Strachey (New York, 1966), p. 393.

38. Sigmund Freud, *New introductory lectures in psychoanalysis* (New York, 1974), p. 113.

FOOTNOTES — CHAPTER 2

1. This assumption, which is implicit in this chapter, is dealt with in some detail in Chapter 6.

2. Cf. Rollo May, Historical roots of modern anxiety theories, in *Anxiety* (New York, 1950).

3. Other aspects of the development of modern culture as it affects the problem of anxiety (e.g., the economic and sociological aspects) are referred to in Chapter 6. A summary of the cultural backgrounds of contemporaneous anxiety is given in Chapter 7 and may serve as a supplement to the discussion in this chapter.

4. Ernst Cassirer, *An essay on man* (New Haven, Conn., 1944), p. 16.

5. This point is discussed in Chapter 6.

6. *The age of anxiety* (New York, 1947), p. 8.

7. Cassirer, *op. cit.,* p. 16.

8. *The Protestant era* (Chicago, 1948), p. 246.

9. Cassirer, p. 16.

10. His definition of emotions is a predecessor of the modern James-Lange theory: "By emotion I understand the modifications of the body by which the power of action in the body is increased or diminished, aided or restrained, and at the same time the ideas of these modifications."—Origin and nature of the emotions, *Spinoza's ethics, Everyman edition* (London, 1910), p. 84.

11. *Spinoza's ethics, The power of the intellect,* p. 203. Spinoza saw the political aspect of "freedom from fear," as mentioned in Chapter 1, p. 12.

12. *Spinoza's ethics, Origin and nature of the emotions,* p. 131.

13. On the basis of this statement of Spinoza's, one can contemplate with profit how greatly the historical situation in which one lives conditions one's anxiety and fear. One could say that living *without* fear in the twentieth century—the day of atom bombs, totalitarianism, and traumatic social change—shows weakness of mind, or, more accurately, insensitivity, atrophy of mind.

14. *Spinoza's ethics, The strength of the emotions,* p. 175.

15. *The power of the intellect,* in *Spinoza's ethics* (London, 1910), p. 208.

16. Cf. Kurt Riezler, The social psychology of fear, *Amer. J. Sociol.,* May, 1944, p. 489. For examples of such psychic conflicts underlying anxiety, see what I describe as the "rift between expectation and reality" which underlay some of the neurotic anxiety of the cases in Part II, page 321, below.

17. It is, however, to be borne in mind that Spinoza's seventeenth-century cultural situation was not only different from the situation of the nineteenth and twentieth centuries, but also that his confidence in reason was different from the deteriorated forms of rationalism in the nineteenth century. These last involved a denial and repression of emotion. Also, since we are chiefly interested in Spinoza as a spokesman for the confidence in reason in the seventeenth century, it is important to emphasize that he was by no means merely a rationalist in the contemporary connotation of that term. His ethical and mystical interests gave a broad and profound context to his thought which was absent in the later and more limited forms of rationalism. For example, if we should follow out to the ultimate step his analysis of how to overcome fear (and anxiety, so far as anxiety appears as a problem), we should discover that each *destructive affect must be overcome by a stronger, constructive one.* We should also find that he defined the ultimate constructive affect in the curiously mystico-rationalistic phrase, the "intellectual love of God." In other words, fear (and

anxiety) can be overcome in the last analysis only by a religious attitude toward one's life as a whole. It should also be mentioned, by the way, that one important consequence of the broad base of Spinoza's thinking was that he was able to avoid the dichotomy between mind and body which characterized other philosophies of his day.

18. *Pascal's pensées,* ed. and trans. G. B. Rawlings (Mt. Vernon, N.Y., 1946), pp. 36, 7.

19. *Pascal's thoughts,* trans. Edward Craig (New York, 1825), p. 110.

20. *Pascal's pensées* (Rawlings ed. and trans.), *op. cit.,* p. 35.

21. It is interesting to note in connection with Pascal's lament that the emotions were not reasonable, that it became Freud's endeavor, more than three centuries later, to extend the domain of reason to include the emotions.

22. Rawlings (ed. and trans.), *op. cit.,* p. 38.

23. Craig (trans.), *op. cit.,* p 84.

24. The question of why he was an exception, and why he experienced inner trauma and anxiety to a much greater degree than his contemporaries, would take us afield from this discussion. We might, however, mention Cassirer's suggestion that Pascal's view of man is really a carry-over from medievalism, and that despite Pascal's scientific genius, he had not really absorbed the new view of man which had emerged at the Renaissance.

25. This term "technical reason" is Paul Tillich's. It refers to the fact that in the nineteenth century reason, in practice, became increasingly applied to technical problems. The theoretical implications of this growing emphasis on the technical aspects of reason were not widely appreciated at the time.

26. *An essay on man, op. cit.,* p. 21.

27. *Ibid.,* p. 22.

28. Freud often wrote of his aim of making unconscious material conscious, and thus increasing the scope of reason. In his more theoretical writings (see *Civilization and its discontents* and *The future of an illusion*), he has a concept of reason and science which is inherited directly from the seventeenth and eighteenth centuries. But in actual practice his concept of reason, involving as it does a union of conscious experience with the vast store of unconscious tendencies within the individual, is a quite different thing from "reason" in traditional rationalism.

29. Paul Tillich, Existential philosophy, *Journal of the History of Ideas,* 1944, 5:1, 44–70. Since Tillich's own thinking participates in the Existentialist tradition, his descriptions of the movement have special cogency and will be quoted frequently in this section.

30. The relationship of this form of thought to American pragmatism, as presented by William James, will be clear. Modern representatives of existentialism include Martin Heidegger, Karl Jaspers, Jean-Paul Sartre, and Gabriel Marcel.

31. Existential philosophy, *op. cit.,* p. 66.

32. *Ibid.,* p. 67.

33. *Ibid.,* p. 54.

34. Walter Lowrie, *A short life of Kierkegaard* (Princeton, N. J., 1944), p. 172.

35. *Ibid.,* p. 116.

36. *The concept of dread,* trans. Walter Lowrie (Princeton, N. J., 1944), p. 123.

37. Tillich, p. 67.

38. Werner Brock, *Contemporary German philosophy* (Cambridge, 1935), p. 75. For an appreciation of Kierkegaard by a twentieth-century psychologist, see O. H. Mowrer, Anxiety, in *Learning theory and personality dynamics* (1950). Mowrer believes that it was necessary for Freud to produce his work before the insights of Kierkegaard could be widely understood.

39. *The concept of dread, op. cit.* Walter Lowrie states that in English "we have no word which adequately translates *Angst*" (preface to above edition, p. ix). Hence, after much deliberation, Dr. Lowrie and the other early translators of Kierkegaard decided to use the term "dread" as a translation into English of Kierkegaard's *Angst*. I certainly agree that the term "anxiety" in English is often used in superficial ways, for example, to mean "eagerness" ("I am anxious to do something") or as a mild form of worry or has other connotations which do not at all do justice to the term *Angst*. But the German *Angst* is the word which Freud, Goldstein, and others use for "anxiety"; and it is the common denominator for the term "anxiety" as used in this book. The question is whether the psychological meaning of "anxiety" (in contrast to the literary meaning) is not very close—in fact much closer than the term "dread"—to what Kierkegaard meant by *Angst*. Professor Tillich, who was familiar with both the psychological meaning of *Angst* and Kierkegaard's works, believed this to be true. I endeavor in this book to preserve both of these meanings, the superficial and the profound, by the two terms "normal anxiety" and "neurotic anxiety." In any case, Professor Lowrie generously gave me permission to render the term "dread" as "anxiety" in the quotations from his translations of Kierkegaard, in order to conform with the usage of terms in this book.

After all these difficulties, I was delighted to discover that the most recent translation by Kierkegaard scholars restores "anxiety" to its rightful place. See *The concept of anxiety,* ed. and trans. Howard V. Hong and Edna V. Hong (Northfield, Minn., 1976).

40. *The concept of dread,* p. 138.

41. *Ibid.,* p. 99.

42. Kierkegaard goes on to insist that, for the realization of selfhood, one must always move ahead: "So it is too that in the eyes of the world it is dangerous to venture. And why? Because one may lose. But not to venture is shrewd. And yet, by not venturing, it is so dreadfully easy to lose that which it would be difficult to lose in even the most venturesome venture, and in any case never so easily, so completely as if it were nothing . . . one's self. For if I have ventured amiss—very well, then life helps me by its punishment. But if I have not ventured at all—who then helps me? And, moreover, if by not venturing at all in the highest sense *(and to venture in the highest sense is precisely to become conscious of oneself)* I have gained all earthly advantages . . . and lose my self! What of that?" Kierkegaard, *Sickness unto death,* trans. Walter Lowrie (Princeton, N. J., 1941), p. 52. (Italics mine.)

43. *The concept of dread,* p. 44.

44. *Ibid.,* p. 38.

45. *Ibid.*, p. 92.

46. *Ibid.*, p. 40.

47. *Sickness unto death, op. cit.*, p. 43.

48. It should be clear that Kierkegaard, like the exponents of modern psychotherapy, is not speaking of what is sometimes called "unhealthy introspection." Such introspection arises not from too much self-awareness (which is a contradiction in terms in Kierkegaard's view) but rather from conditions of blocked self-awareness.

49. In philosophical terms, this is the problem of man's "essence" as over against his "existence."

50. *The concept of dread, op. cit.*, p. 47.

51. *Ibid.*, p. 65.

52. *The concept of dread*, p. 92.

53. *Ibid.*, p. xii, quoted from his Journal (III A 233; Dru No. 402).

54. It is interesting that Otto Rank also holds that the healthy individual is the one who can create despite the inner conflict (between "life will" and "death will," in his terms), whereas the neurotic is the one who cannot manage this conflict except by retrenching and sacrificing his creativity.

55. In contemporary psychopathology it is held that there is always anxiety where there is guilt feeling (fear of punishment) but that the reverse is not necessarily true. It will be seen, however, that Kierkegaard is speaking of a different level—i.e., the relation of guilt feeling to creativity.

56. The process of creativity has not been adequately explored in contemporary psychology. The testimony of the artists would support Kierkegaard at this point: Degas says, "A picture must be painted with the same feeling as that with which a criminal commits his crime," and Thomas Mann speaks of the "precious and guilty secret" which the artist keeps. One can find more insight into this phenomenon in mythology; in the myth of Prometheus, creativity is pictured as a defiance of the gods. One could ask psychologically whether individuation, and the creativity involved, means a progressive breaking from, and defiance of, the mother; or in Freudian terms, whether creativity is a progressive dethroning of the father.

57. *The concept of dread, op. cit.*, p. 96.

58. *Ibid.*, p. 65.

59. This will be discussed frequently in subsequent chapters. For example, see particularly the cases of Phyllis and Frances in Chapter 9; see also Chapter 10.

60. *The concept of dread, op. cit.*, p. 110.

61. *Ibid.* Compare Ibsen's description of inmates of a lunatic asylum: "Each shuts himself in a cask of self, the cask stopped with a bung of self and seasoned in a well of self." *Peer Gynt.*

62. *The concept of dread.*

63. *Ibid.*, p. 114 n.

64. *Ibid.*, p. 109.

65. *Ibid.*, p. 124.

66. *Ibid.*

67. *Ibid.*, p. 129.

68. *Ibid.*, p. 107.

69. *Ibid.*, p. 139.
70. *Ibid.*, p. 139.
71. *Ibid.*, p. 144.
72. *Ibid.*, p. 141. (Italics mine.)
73. *Ibid.*, p. 140.
74. *Ibid.*, p. 142.

FOOTNOTES — CHAPTER 3

1. The only names of unifiers that come to mind are Hans Selye and Ludwig von Bertalanffy. But important as their contributions are, the former is in the field of experimental medicine and surgery, and the latter in theoretical biology. We are still left without our unifying of the heterogeneous researches on anxiety. Stress is similar to anxiety but, as I will indicate later, is not to be identified with it.

2. Eugene E. Levitt, Commentary on the psychiatric breakthrough, in Charles Spielberger (ed.), *Anxiety: current trends in theory and research*, I (New York, 1972), p. 233.

3. Harry Stack Sullivan, *Conceptions of modern psychiatry* (Washington, D.C., 1947), p. 4.

4. Aaron Beck, Cognition, anxiety, and psychophysiological disorders, in Charles Spielberger (ed.), *Anxiety: current trends in theory and research*, II (New York, 1972), p. 349.

5. John W. Mason, Emotion as reflected in patterns of endocrine integration, in L. Levi (ed.), *Emotions—their parameters and measurement* (New York, 1975).

6. C. Landis and W. A. Hunt, *The startle pattern* (New York, 1939).

7. Landis and Hunt, *op. cit.*, p. 23.

8. *Ibid.*, p. 21.

9. *Ibid.*, p. 153.

10. *Ibid.*

11. *Ibid.*, p. 136.

12. *Ibid.*, p. 141. Note that this is the startle *pattern*, meaning it is the response of the total organism. This may explain why in the literature of the last two decades, the researchers, increasingly interested in isolating discrete elements in neurology and physiology, should have neglected the startle pattern.

13. L. S. Kubie, The ontogeny of anxiety. *Psychoanal. Rev.* 1941, **28**:1, 78–85. The startle pattern is applied in different ways. See Stress and Behavior, by Seymour Levine, *Scientific American*, January, 1971, **224**:1, 26–31.

14. Kurt Goldstein, *The organism: a holistic approach to biology* (New York, 1939), and *Human nature in the light of psychopathology* (Cambridge, 1938).

15. A distinction must be made between "biological," referring to the organism as an acting and reacting totality, and "psychological" referring to one level in that totality. It is true, as some writers have held, that a study of brain-injured patients does not yield data on the specifically psychological aspect of neurotic anxiety, since these patients are neurologically impaired to begin with.

For example, Mowrer (1950) holds that the anxiety of Goldstein's patients is more akin to *Urangst* (basic, normal anxiety) than to neurotic anxiety. Indeed, it is doubtful whether the term "neurotic anxiety" has any meaning when applied to these patients. This distinction, however, does not contradict my statement that Goldstein's findings are of great value in providing a biological base for the understanding of anxiety. It is my judgment (as will be indicated in detail later) that the understanding of anxiety on the psychological level is not inconsistent with, but complementary to, Goldstein's findings on the biological level.

16. Though he rejects the concept of "drives," Goldstein holds that one can speak of the "needs" of the organism in its trend to actualize itself.

17. R. R. Grinker and S. P. Spiegel, *Men under stress* (Philadelphia, 1945). The frequent studies, incidentally, of anxiety in soldiers in this book is by no means an overfondness for things military. It is because soldiers, like unmarried mothers, will stay put in their group long enough to be studied. They also, again like the unmarried mothers, are in a purportedly anxiety-creating situation.

18. Bourne, Rose, and Mason, Urinary 17-OHCS levels, *Arc. Gen. Psych.*, July, 1967, 17, 104–110.

19. Of course a "pseudo-object" is often found for the anxiety. This is the function of phobias and superstitions. As is well known, anxiety is often displaced on any acceptable object; there is generally relief from the pain of anxiety if the sufferer can attach it to some thing. The presence of pseudo-objects in anxiety ought not to be confused with the real sources of the anxiety.

20. *The organism, op. cit.*, p. 292.

21. *Ibid.*, pp. 293, 297.

22. *Ibid.*, p. 295.

23. *Ibid.*

24. Readers who wish a clinical illustration of these points are referred to the case of Brown in Chapter 8, especially to the discussion on page 222.

25. Of course, Goldstein does not intend, in this discussion of the objectless nature of anxiety, to divorce the organism from its objective environment. The individual is always faced with an objective environment, and it is only in seeing the organism-in-environment—that is, the organism reacting to tasks which it cannot solve, that we are able to understand the onset of anxiety.

26. *Op. cit.*, p. 295.

27. *Ibid.*, p. 296.

28. See P. M. Symonds, *The dynamics of human adjustment* (New York, 1946), p. 155.

29. *The organism, op. cit.*, p. 297.

30. Gray, reviewing the origin of fears, formulated a fourfold classification of innately fear-producing stimuli: "intensity, novelty, special evolutionary dangers (from generations of experiences with predators) and stimuli arising from social interaction." The first two principles all diminish rapidly with age. The latter seem subject to maturation; they tend to become stronger over time. J. Gray, *The psychology of fear and stress* (London, 1971).

31. *Ibid.*, p. 300.

32. *Ibid.,* p. 303.

33. *Ibid.,* p. 306.

34. Kurt Goldstein, *Human nature in the light of psychopathology,* p. 113.

35. *Ibid.,* p. 115.

36. *Ibid.,* p. 117.

37. Goldstein offers a challenging corrective to much of the discussion in this field: "There are no 'specific' neurophysiological bases for anxiety or fear," he stated in conversation with me. "If the organism reacts at all, the whole organism reacts." This does not imply, of course, that it is not useful to study sympathetic activity—for example, as one important aspect of the neurophysiology of anxiety and fear—but it does imply that such a study must be subsumed under a more comprehensive view of the organism as a reacting totality. Nor does Goldstein's view imply that some reactions of the organism are not more specific than others. For example, fear is a more specific reaction, neurophysiologically as well as psychologically, than anxiety, so the practice of describing the neurophysiology of fear solely in terms of sympathetic activity is less fallacious than the same procedure with anxiety. As we shall later demonstrate, one distinction between fear and anxiety is that anxiety strikes at more fundamental, and hence, more engrossing, "strata" in the organism. Furthermore, the reader should perhaps be warned that while much of great value is known about the neurophysiological reactions of the organism under threat (which knowledge we shall endeavor to review in the remainder of this chapter), there is a great deal about the neurophysiology of anxiety which we do *not* know.

38. This is one distinction between the autonomic system and the other nervous system in the organism, the central (cerebral-spinal) system which is more directly under conscious control.

Recently there have been studies demonstrating that conscious control of the autonomic nervous system is more possible than we had thought. This has been shown by Neil Miller at Rockefeller University and also by the experiments in biofeedback by Barbara Brown. I do not believe, however, that any of these invalidate the basic description we are here making.

39. See Walter B. Cannon, *Bodily changes in pain, hunger, fear and rage,* 2nd ed. (New York, 1927), and *The wisdom of the body* (New York, 1932).

40. *The wisdom of the body, op. cit.*

41. Grinker and Spiegel, *op. cit.,* p. 144.

42. Cannon, *Wisdom of the body, op. cit.,* p. 254.

43. *Ibid.,* p. 253. A later criticism made of Cannon's work is that emotional processes are the function of the entire autonomic nervous system, with the sympathetic and parasympathetic functioning reciprocally and simultaneously in producing what we call emotions. Also Cannon's work is deficient in understanding the role of hormones which was not possible in his day. Other than these additions, Cannon's work is still considered the classic in the field. Paul Thomas Young, Emotion, in *International encyclopedia of social sciences,* V (New York, 1968), pp. 35–41.

44. R. R. Willoughby, Magic and cognate phenomena: an hy-

pothesis, in Carl Murchison (ed.), *Handbook of social psychology* (Worcester, Mass., 1935), p. 466.

45. Walter B. Cannon, "Voodoo" death, *Amer. Anthrop.*, 1942, **44**:2, 169–181.

46. E. Tregear, in *J. Anthrop. Inst.*, 1890, **19**, 100, quoted by Cannon, in "Voodoo" death, 170.

47. *Ibid.*, p. 176.

48. A. G. Leonard, *The Lower Niger and its tribes* (London, 1906), pp. 257 ff.

49. *Ibid.*, p. 178.

50. George Engel, *Psychological development in health and disease* (Philadelphia, 1962), pp. 290, 392–393.

51. *Ibid.*, p. 179.

52. *Ibid.*, p. 180.

53. Engel, *op. cit.*, p. 383, and Aaron Beck, *op. cit.*, 343–354.

54. Leon J. Saul, Physiological effects of emotional tension, in J. McV. Hunt (ed.), *Personality and the behavior disorders* (New York, 1944), Vol. I, pp. 269–305.

55. J. J. Groen and J. Bastiaans, Psychosocial stress, interhuman communication, and psychosomatic diseases, in Charles Spielberger and Irwin Sarason (ed.), *Stress and anxiety* (New York, 1975), Vol. I, p. 47.

56. Engel, *op. cit.*, p. 391.

57. Dunbar, *Emotions and bodily changes*, p. 63.

58. Saul, *op. cit.*, p. 274. This pattern is mentioned to emphasize the interrelation of many anxiety states with dependence on the mother.

59. For another example, see case of Brown, Chapter 8, below, esp. page 229.

60. Saul, *op. cit.*, pp. 281–84.

61. *Ibid.*, p. 294.

62. *Ibid.*, p. 292.

63. Bela Mittelmann, H. G. Wolff, and M. P. Scharf, Experimental studies on patients with gastritis, duodenitis and peptic ulcer, *Psychosom. Med.*, 1942, 4:1, 58. (Quotes are printed by permission of the authors and of Paul B. Hoeber, Inc., Medical Book Department of Harper & Brothers. Copyright, 1942, by Paul B. Hoeber, Inc.)

64. From *Human gastric function* by Stewart Wolf and H. G. Wolff. Copyright 1943, 1947, by Oxford University Press, Inc. (Quotes are printed by permission of Oxford University Press.)

65. *Ibid.*, p. 112.

66. *Ibid.*, p. 120.

67. *Ibid.*, pp. 118–19.

68. *Ibid.*, p. 92.

69. Mittelmann, Wolff, and Scharf, *op. cit.*, p. 16.

70. Engel presents an interesting case of an infant, who, like Tom, had a gastric fistula. When "Monica was outgoing and relating to persons either affectionately or aggressively, her stomach secreted actively." In other words, Monica was similar to Tom without Tom's neurotic tendencies.

71. *Op. cit.*, p. 176.

72. *Op. cit.*, p. 54 (italics mine).

73. *Ibid.*, p. 240.

74. See Jerome Hartz, Tuberculosis and personality conflicts, *Psychosom. Med.*, 1944, **6**:1, 17–22. I suggest that the progression may be roughly as follows: When the organism is in a catastrophic situation, the endeavor to solve the conflict takes place first on the conscious level; then on the specifically psychosomatic level; and if neither of these is effective, the conflict may involve a disease such as tuberculosis representing a more complete involvement of the organism.

75. *Op. cit.*, p. 140.

76. We have indicated above the questionable nature of this assumption.

77. J. C. Yaskins, The psychobiology of anxiety—a clinical study, *Psychoanal. Rev.*, 1936, **23**, 3 and 4, and 1937, **24**, 81–93.

78. Needless to say, we are speaking of the anxiety related to the patient's behavior patterns, not the specific anxiety related to the fact that he has a disease (which may obviously be present during the disease). Many observers have spoken of the "substitution function" of the disease for anxiety. Draper (see Saul, *op. cit.*) mentions also that a neurosis may function as a substitute for organic symptoms.

79. Quoted by Dunbar, *Emotions and bodily changes*, p. 80.

80. This observation, of course, is directed only against oversimplified applications of Cannon's findings, not against Cannon's classical work itself.

FOOTNOTES — CHAPTER 4

1. Howard Liddell, The role of vigilance in the development of animal neurosis, paper read at the symposium on anxiety of the Amer. Psychopath. Ass., New York, June, 1949. (Published in Hoch and Zubin [eds.], *Anxiety* [New York, 1950], pp. 183–197.)

2. We shall see later, in our discussion of anxiety and the impoverished personality, that a person's blocking off his or her anxiety also blocks off creativity. This leaves the personality impoverished. But the converse of this is not necessarily true—that the more anxiety one experiences, the more creative he or she is (cf. Chapter 11).

3. The reasoning which leads Liddell to this conclusion is very similar to that of Sullivan, and it also has much in common with the viewpoints of Freud and of Mowrer on the social origins of anxiety.

4. John B. Watson, *Behaviorism* (New York, 1924).

5. This and following excerpts from *Child psychology* (rev. ed., New York, 1940), p. 254, by A. T. Jersild are reprinted by permission of Prentice-Hall, Inc. Copyright, 1933, 1940, by Prentice-Hall, Inc.

6. A. T. Jersild and F. B. Holmes, *Children's fears* (Child Development Monograph No. 20, Bureau of Publications, Teachers College, Columbia University, New York, 1935), p. 5. By permission of Teachers College. Copyright, 1935, by Teachers College, Columbia University.

7. See Jersild, *Child psychology, op. cit.*, p. 255. Quotations are

from A. L. Gesell, The individual in infancy, in Carl Murchison, ed., *The foundations of experimental psychology* (Worcester, Mass., 1929).

8. Jersild, *op. cit.*, p. 255.

9. Cf. George Engel, *Psychological development in health and disease* (Philadelphia, 1962), p. 50, quoting René Spitz, *Anxiety: its phenomenology in the first year of life*.

10. Jersild, *op. cit.*, p. 256. Whether these reactions—for example, those connected with competition—which Jersild describes as "fears" are really fears or anxiety is a question which can be answered only on the basis of the actual situation. Clinical studies indicate that intrapsychic conflicts may be projected on the environment and give rise to anxiety; one common example of this is the anxiety underlying phobias. This likewise presupposes not only some level of maturation but also intricate conditioning and experiential processes.

11. Based upon interviews with 398 children aged five to twelve years. See A. T. Jersild, F. V. Markey, and S. L. Jersild, *Children's fears, dreams, wishes, daydreams, pleasant and unpleasant memories* (Child Development Monograph No. 12; New York: Teachers College, Columbia University, 1933).

12. Jersild and Holmes, *Children's fears op. cit.*, p. 328.

13. *Ibid.*, p. 308.

14. See page 120.

15. Jersild continues: "For example, a child's apparent fear of being abandoned, exhibited whenever his mother leaves the house on a brief errand, may be associated with other symptoms of distress that first appeared when a new baby came into the household. This particular expression of fear may abate in response to parental efforts to help the child overcome it, only to be followed by other expressions of fear—such as fear of sleeping alone in a dark room—if the underlying uncertainties still persist." *Child psychology, op. cit.*, p. 274.

As an actual case I cite the following: A boy of three was sent to his grandparents' farm for the period during which his mother gave birth to twins. On his mother's arrival with the new babies, the boy began to exhibit a strong "fear" of the tractor on the farm. It was noted by the parents that this "fear" took the form of the boy's running to his parents ostensibly for their protection from the tractor. On the assumption that the underlying cause of the boy's "fear" was feelings of isolation and rejection related to the previous separation from the parents and the advent of the two babies, the parents ignored the item of the tractor as such and devoted their efforts to helping the boy overcome his feelings of isolation. The fear of the tractor shortly vanished. If it had been assumed that the exhibited fear was related specifically to the threat of the tractor, I do not deny that the child could have been conditioned, in the usual meaning of this term, out of the fear of the tractor. But if, as hypothesized by the parents, this fear were really a focus for anxiety which actually had quite different roots, the "fear" would simply have shifted to a new object.

16. Jersild, *Child psychology, op. cit.*, p. 270.

17. Jersild and Holmes, *op. cit.*, p. 305. Several studies indicate that a common, if not the chief, fear of school children is that they

might fail in school. Studies also show this fear of failure to be very much out of proportion to the actual experience or reasonable probability of failure on the part of the student.

18. See the following chapter on Freud, Sullivan, *et al.*

19. The phenomenon of phobias presents in extreme form a demonstration of the above hypothesis. Phobias appear as specific, but are found on deeper analysis to be concentrations of anxiety at one point in the environment in order to avoid anxiety at other points. See Freud's analysis of Hans, the five-year-old boy whose phobia of horses, Freud indicates, was a displacement of anxiety arising out of his relations with his father and mother.

20. Hans Selye, *The stress of life* (New York, 1956), pp. 55–56. Also cf. p. 311.

21. Selye, *op. cit.*, p. vii.

22. *Ibid.*, p. 66. Gregory Bateson questions the use of the term "energy" both in biology and psychology. He writes: "It would have been more fruitful to think of *lack* of energy as preventive of behavior, since in the end a starving man will cease to behave. But even this will not do: an amoeba, deprived of food, becomes for a time *more* active. Its energy expenditure is an inverse function of energy input." Gregory Bateson, *Steps to an ecology of mind* (New York, 1972), p. xxii.

23. Charles Spielberger, *Anxiety: current trends in theory and research* (New York, 1972), II, p. 345.

24. Peter Bourne, Robert Rose, and John Mason, Urinary 17-OHCS levels, *Archives of General Psychiatry*, July, 1967, **17**, p. 109.

25. Hans Selye, *Stress and distress* (Toronto, 1974).

26. M. K. Opler, *Culture, psychiatry and human values* (Thomas, 1956), p. 67.

27. I am especially indebted at this point to my research associate, Dr. Joanne Cooper.

28. Spielberger (ed.), *Anxiety: current trends in theory and research*, Vol. I and II. Irwin Sarason and Charles Spielberger (eds.), *Stress and anxiety* (New York, 1966), Vols. I–IV. Charles Spielberger, *Anxiety and behavior* (New York, 1966).

29. Richard Lazarus and James Averill. Emotion and cognition: With special reference to anxiety, in Spielberger (ed.), *Anxiety: current trends in theory and research*, Vol II, pp. 241–283.

30. Seymour Epstein, The nature of anxiety with emphasis upon its relationship to expectancy, in Spielberger (ed.), *Anxiety: current trends in theory and research*, Vol. II, ch. 8.

31. See my distinction between stress and anxiety earlier in this chapter.

32. Walter D. Fenz, Strategies for coping with stress, in Sarason and Spielberger (eds.), *Stress and anxiety*, Vol. II, pp. 305–335.

33. Seymour Epstein, Anxiety arousal and the self-concept, in Spielberger and Sarason (eds.), *Stress and anxiety*, Vol. III, pp. 185–225.

34. *Op. cit.*

35. Epstein, *op. cit.*, p. 223.

36. Charles Spielberger, Current trends in research and theory on anxiety, in Spielberger (ed.), *Anxiety: current trends in theory and research*, Vol. I, p. 10.

37. Norman Endler, A person-situation-interaction model for anxiety. In Sarason and Spielberger (eds.), *Stress and anxiety*, Vol. I, pp. 145–162.

38. H. D. Kimmel, Conditioned fear and anxiety, in Spielberger and Sarason (eds.), *Stress and anxiety*, Vol. I, pp. 189–210.

39. Yona Teichman, The stress of coping with the unknown regarding a significant family member, in Spielberger and Sarason (eds.), *Stress and anxiety*, Vol. II, pp. 243–254.

40. See my earlier discussion of Robert Jay Lifton's *Protean man* in Chapter 1.

41. Charles Ford, The *Pueblo* incident: Psychological response to severe stress, in Spielberger and Sarason (eds.), *Stress and anxiety*, Vol. II, pp. 229–240.

42. Richard Lynn, National differences in anxiety, in Spielberger and Sarason (eds.), *Stress and anxiety*, Vol. II, pp. 257–272.

43. D. B. Coates, S. Moyer, L. Kendall, and M. G. Howart, Life event changes and mental health, in Sarason and Spielberger (eds.), *Stress and anxiety*, Vol. III, pp. 225–250.

44. O. H. Mowrer, A stimulus-response analysis of anxiety and its role as a reinforcing agent, *Psychol. Rev.*, 1939, **46**:6, 553–65.

45. *Ibid.*, p. 555.

46. Anxiety-reduction and learning, *J. exp. Psychol.* 1940, **27**:5, 497–516.

47. Cf. N. E. Miller and John Dollard, *Social learning and imitation* (New Haven, Conn., 1941).

48. Cf. O. H. Mowrer, *Preparatory set (expectancy)—some methods of measurement* (Psychol. Monogr., 1940), No. 233, pp. 39, 40.

49. I would call the reactions of Mowrer's animals in this experiment fear, and Mowrer himself, from his later perspective, would likewise term the reactions fear.

50. Cf. O. H. Mowrer, Freud's theories of anxiety: a reconciliation. Unpublished lecture given at Yale Institute of Human Relations, 1939.

51. O. H. Mowrer, A. D. Ullman, Time as a determinant in integrative learning, *Psychol. Rev.*, 1945, **52**:2, 61–90.

52. Elsewhere (page 82 and Chapter 6), I discuss these two qualities of the human being as (1) *man is the mammal who lives by symbols* and (2) *man is the historical mammal* in that we possess the capacity for self-awareness of our history. We are, therefore, not just the product of history (as all animals are), but in varying degrees, depending upon our self-awareness of history, we can exercise selectivity toward our history, can adapt ourselves to portions of it and correct other portions. Within limits we can mold history and in other ways use it in our development in self-chosen directions. Cassirer also makes these two qualities distinctive for human beings; cf. *An essay on man* (New Haven, Conn., 1944).

53. O. H. Mowrer, *op. cit.*

54. In the light of this distinction, we raise a question in regard to the implications of the concept of *anxiety as a drive*. That anxiety does operate as a drive, a "secondary" drive, as is emphasized by learning theorists (Miller and Dollard, Symonds, etc.) is indisputable. And its reduction, like the reduction of other

drives, is rewarding and reinforces learning. But strictly speaking, *behavior which occurs chiefly and directly to lessen the drive of anxiety is adjustive, not integrative.* To me, it falls in the same category as the learning of neurotic symptoms. This is Goldstein's point when he holds that all activity which is a direct product of the individual's anxiety (i.e., when the motivation is the reduction of anxiety as a drive) is marked by a stress on partial aspects of action, compulsiveness, and lack of freedom. And, "as long as these activities are not spontaneous, are not outlets of the free personality, but are merely the sequelae of anxiety, they have only a pseudo-value for the personality." (See Chapter 3 above.)

55. Mowrer, *op. cit.*

56. Mowrer, *op. cit.*

57. *Ibid.*

58. *Ibid.*

59. *Ibid.*

60. *Ibid.*

61. *Ibid.*

62. O. H. Mowrer, Anxiety, chapter in *Learning theory and personality dynamics* (1950).

63. Søren Kierkegaard, *The concept of dread,* trans. Walter Lourie (Princeton, N.J., 1944), p. 38.

64. In the previous chapter we discussed the ingenious psychosomatic studies which used physiological, neurological, psychological, and case-history approaches, combining clinical and experimental procedures. The book-length study of Tom likewise falls into this multidimensional category. I would add at this point only that these studies have their great value for the understanding of anxiety because the investigators were able to (1) inquire into subjective as well as objective factors; (2) study each individual as a unit in his life situation; and (3) pursue the study of each over a period of time.

65. These terms are placed in quotation marks because, in the final analysis, I do not believe that genuine autonomy is possible without corresponding responsibility.

FOOTNOTES — CHAPTER 5

1. Cf. Thomas Mann, *Freud, Goethe, Wagner* (New York, 1937).

2. *The problem of anxiety,* trans. H. A. Bunker (New York, 1936), p. 111.

3. *New introductory lectures in psychoanalysis* (New York, 1965), p. 81.

4. *Introductory Lecture on Psychoanalysis,* p. 395. Beyond this brief distinction, Freud does not—either in the chapter on anxiety in the *Introductory lectures* or in his later *Problem of anxiety*—throw much illumination on the problem of fear as such. He treats Stanley Hall's list of allegedly innate fears—fear of darkness, fear of bodies of water, of thunder, etc.—as phobias, which are by definition expressions of neurotic anxiety. In a summary of Freud's views in W. Healy, A. F. Bronner, and A. M. Bowers, *The struc-*

ture and meaning of psychoanalysis (New York, 1930), p. 366, a distinction between real fear and neurotic fear is made which is parallel to Freud's distinction between real and neurotic anxiety. Real fear, it is stated, is the reaction to an objective danger, whereas neurotic fear is the "fear of an impulse claim." Freud is interpreted as holding that "three practically universal childhood fears"—fear of being alone, fear of darkness, and the fear of strangers—arise out of the "unconscious Ego's fear of loss of the protecting object, namely, the mother" *Ibid*. This is synonymous with his definition of the source of anxiety in similar situations. Apparently the terms "fear" and "anxiety" are here used interchangeably, the former being the term for the emergence of anxiety in specific form.

5. *Ibid.*, p. 394.

6. *Ibid.*, p. 395.

7. *Ibid.*, pp. 401–2.

8. *The problem of anxiety*, pp. 51–52.

9. *Introductory lectures*, pp. 403–4.

10. *Ibid.*, p. 409.

11. *Ibid.*, p. 407. Cf. René Spitz, Chapter 4, p. 90.

12. *Ibid.*, p. 410.

13. *New introductory lectures*, p. 85.

14. *The problem of anxiety*, p. 80.

15. *New introductory lectures*, p. 86.

16. *The problem of anxiety*, p. 22.

17. *New introductory lectures*, p. 86. If Hans were merely afraid of his father's punishment (as an external danger), Freud would not call his anxiety neurotic. There are several cases later in this book where the person—Louise, Bessie, *et al.*—is able to judge the parent's action for what it really is. Such a situation leads to objective anxiety, in Freud's terms, not neurotic anxiety. The neurotic element enters because of the ego's perception of the danger inherent in the internal instinctual promptings (Hans's hostility toward his father, for example). Now it is well known that inner promptings in the individual's experience can come easily to stand for external, objective dangers. If hostility toward the parent is met by retaliation, the child will soon be conditioned to experience anxiety whenever the hostile promptings arise intrapsychically.

18. Percival M. Symonds, *The dynamics of human adjustment* (New York, 1946).

19. *Introductory lectures*, p. 406.

20. *The problem of anxiety*, p. 98.

21. *Introductory lectures*, p. 408.

22. *The problem of anxiety*.

23. *Ibid.*, p. 75.

24. *Ibid.*, pp. 99–100.

25. *Ibid.*, p. 105.

26. *Ibid.*, p. 123.

27. Since castration and other aspects of the Oedipus situation are so important in Freudian discussions of anxiety, another question may be raised: Does not neurotic anxiety arise around castration or the Oedipus situation only when there are prior disturbances in the relationship between parents and child? To illustrate in the

case of Hans, are not the boy's jealousy and consequent hatred of his father themselves the product of anxiety? Apparently Hans had exclusive needs for his mother, needs which her loving the father would threaten. Are not such needs (which may fairly be termed excessive) in themselves an outgrowth of anxiety? It may well be true that the conflict and anxiety leading to the particular phobic construction which Freud analyzes are specifically related to ambivalence and hostility toward the father. But I submit that this hostility and ambivalence would not have developed except that Hans was already in a disturbed relationship with his mother and father which produced anxiety and led to exclusive demands for his mother. One can understandably hold that every child experiences clashes with its parents in its development of individuality and autonomy *(vide* Kierkegaard, Goldstein, *et al.),* but in the normal child (defined as the child in a relationship to its parents which is not characterized by pronounced anxiety) such clashes do not produce neurotic defenses and symptoms. I here suggest that Oedipus situations and castration fears do not emerge as *problems*—i.e., do not become the foci of neurotic anxiety—unless prior anxieties already exist in the family constellation.

28. For discussion of the possible relation between birth and anxiety, see Symonds, *op. cit.*

29. Cf. D. M. Levy: "[The] most potent of all influences on social behavior is derived from the primary social experience with the mother." Maternal overprotection, *Psychiatry,* 1, 561 ff. Grinker and Spiegel, whose viewpoint represents a development of Freudianism, point out in their study of anxiety in combat airmen that fear or anxiety will not develop unless the value or object that is threatened in combat is "something that is loved, highly prized, and held very dear." This may be a person (one's self or a loved one) or a value like an abstract idea. *Men under stress* (Philadelphia, 1946), p. 120. I suggest, in line with Freud's discussion above, that the primal form of the prized person is the mother and that the capacity to prize other persons and values is a development from this first prototype.

30. *The problem of anxiety,* p. 100.

31. I agree with those critics of the Freudian libido theory who hold that the theory is a carry-over from nineteenth-century physiochemical forms of thought.

32. *The problem of anxiety,* p. 86. This is the point I make with respect to the function of symptoms (see Chapters 3 and 8).

33. *Ibid.,* p. 152.

34. *Ibid.,* p. 112. In some interpretations of Freudian theory the first emphasis of Freud is still made. Cf. Healy, Bronner, and Browers: "Symptom-formation . . . is now regarded as a defense against or a flight from anxiety" *(The structure and meaning of psychoanalysis,* p. 411). I advanced the view in Chapter 3 above, that the symptom is a protection not from anxiety but from the *anxiety-creating situation.*

35. The confusing implications of Freud's topology are seen in his tendencies to think of the ego and the id as literally geographical regions in the personality. In his last writing, *Outline of psychoanalysis* (New York, 1969), he refers to his "topographical" viewpoint, speaks of the ego as "developed out of the cortical

layer of the id" (p. 55), and uses such phrases as "mental regions" (p. 2) and "the outermost cortex of the ego" (p. 18). The tendency to locate the "ego function" geographically reminds me of the endeavors of Descartes and others of the seventeenth century to locate man's "soul" in the pineal gland at the base of the brain! Again, we can do no better than to quote Freud against himself; the essential thing is to grasp psychological facts psychologically.

36. The concept of the "separation of the individual from the whole" has a long history in human thought, running back to Anaximander in the preclassical period in ancient Greece. It would be agreed that it is a fruitful concept psychologically as well as philosophically, and that Rank has much empirical, experiential data on which to base his psychology.

37. *The trauma of birth* (English trans.; New York, 1929). (Original publication in German, 1924.)

38. Otto Rank, *Will therapy; an analysis of the therapeutic process in terms of relationship* (authorized trans. from the German; New York, 1936), p. 168.

39. *Ibid.*, p. xii.

40. *Ibid.*, pp. 172–73.

41. *Ibid.*, p. 175.

42. Cf. Kierkegaard in Chapter 2.

43. *Will therapy*, p. 175. Apparently Rank means it is not possible to overcome *all* anxiety therapeutically; he indicates clearly that neurotic anxiety may be overcome. As regards normal anxiety, he would hold that it may be *surmounted* in the sense that the healthy individual moves ahead despite anxiety. By creativity one surmounts normal anxiety and overcomes neurotic anxiety.

44. Pearce Bailey, *Theory and therapy: an introduction to the psychology of Dr. Otto Rank* (Paris, 1935). Needless to say, Rank's use of the term "collective values" antedated the appearance in Europe of fascism, a neurotic form of collectivism.

45. Adler here implies a negative view of culture (i.e., civilization is developed because it compensates for weakness), which is not consistent with his general positive valuation of social experience. The above view is similar to the Freudian concept that civilization is a product of man's anxiety (or, more accurately, that anxiety leads human beings to sublimate their natural impulses into cultural pursuits). This general viewpoint is a halftruth and has the implication that all constructive activity is a defense against anxiety. It lacks a comprehension of the fact that the human being may act on the basis of positive, spontaneous powers and curiosity or, as Goldstein puts it, on the basis of the "joy of actualizing one's own capacities."

46. W. Beran Wolfe, Introduction to Alfred Adler, *The pattern of life* (New York, 1930).

47. Alfred Adler, *The neurotic constitution* (New York, 1926), p. xvi.

48. Alfred Adler, *Problems of neurosis* (New York, 1930), p. 73.

49. Alfred Adler, *Understanding human nature* (New York, 1927).

50. See discussion of this problem in Chapter 8.

51. See case of Brown, Chapter 8.

52. *Understanding human nature, op. cit.*, p. 238.

53. Carl G. Jung, *Collected papers on analytical psychology* (London, 1920).

54. Carl G. Jung, *Psychology and religion* (New Haven, Conn., 1938), pp. 14–15.

55. *Ibid.*, p. 18.

56. *Ibid.*, p. 18.

57. *Psychology and religion,* chap. 1. (Italics mine).

58. A viewpoint of Erich Fromm, as phrased by Karen Horney, *New ways in psychoanalysis* (New York, 1939), p. 78.

59. Horney's contention is that Freud's instinct theories, and the libido theory which is derivative from them, are based on the assumption that "psychic forces are chemical-physiological in origin." (*Ibid.,* p. 47). She holds that psychology for Freud seems to be the science of how an individual uses or misuses libidinal forces. Horney does not deny that the outright frustration of a sheer biological need—such as that for food—would menace life and, therefore, be a source of anxiety. But beyond such fairly rare cases, it is to be recognized that biological needs assume a wide divergency of forms in different cultures, depending upon the patterns in the culture; and *the point at which a threat to a biological need arouses anxiety depends in the great majority of cases on the psychological patterns of that culture.* This is clearly indicated in a study of what sorts of sexual frustration arouse anxiety in different cultures. Horney believes that Freud's nineteenth-century biological presuppositions prevented him from seeing the psychological context of such problems (she refers to "biological" in the sense of chemical-physical mechanisms, rather than to Goldstein's use of "biological" in the sense of the organism responding as an entirety to its environmental situation).

60. Karen Horney, *Our inner conflicts* (New York, 1945), pp. 12–13.

61. *New ways in psychoanalysis* (New York, 1939), p. 76.

62. Cf. Goldstein, Kierkegaard, *et al.*

63. *The neurotic personality of our time* (New York, 1937), p. 89.

64. Ibid., p. 199.

65. One is reminded of W. Stekel's central idea that all anxiety is psychic conflict. *Conditions of neurotic anxiety and their treatment.* However, in his epigrammatic statements, some of which show penetrating insight, Stekel did not work out systematically the nature of the psychic conflict as Horney has done.

66. *The neurotic personality of our time, op. cit.,* p. 62. Horney feels it is entirely understandable that Freud in his Victorian culture considered that the expression of various sexual inclinations on the part, let us say, of the upper middle-class girl would incur real dangers in terms of social ostracism. But she warns against taking Freud's culturally conditioned data as the basis for a generalization about personality. Except in unusual cases, her experience has been that anxiety which on superficial observation is related to sexual impulses often turns out to have its source in hostile or counter-hostile feelings about the sexual partner. This is plausible in the light of the consideration that sex is a very ready focus for dependent and symbiotic tendencies and that such tendencies are generally found in exaggerated form in anxious persons.

67. It is not to be implied that all hostility leads to anxiety; conscious hostility does not necessarily produce anxiety, but may be a constructive function, resulting in actions which decrease the threat. Horney is speaking specifically of repressed hostility. Apart from the hostile content of repressions, one could remark that *any* repression sets the intrapsychic stage for anxiety in that the nature of repression itself involves some surrender of the autonomous power of the individual (some curtailment of the "ego," as it would be stated in Freudian topology). The repression, of course, does not result in itself in conscious anxiety—indeed, its immediate purpose is precisely the opposite—but it represents a retrenchment of autonomy on the part of the individual and thereby accentuates his situation of weakness.

68. A criticism frequently made against Horney is that her emphasis on how the patient's conflicts are manifested in his present relationships (an emphasis developed partly in reaction against what she felt to be Freud's too exclusive emphasis on past origins) has led her and members of her school to neglect the origins of psychological conflict in early childhood. In my judgment, this criticism is justified.

69. From Harry Stack Sullivan, *Conceptions of modern psychiatry*, copyright 1940, 1945, 1947, 1953 by William Alanson White Psychiatric Foundation (New York: W. W. Norton & Company, Inc., 1953).

70. "Power motive" is to be sharply distinguished from "power drive," the latter being a neurotic phenomenon which may be motivated by the accumulated frustration of normal needs for achievement. Sullivan's concept of the expansion of the organism in terms of ability and achievement is parallel to Goldstein's concept of self-actualization. Goldstein's interest is more biological, whereas Sullivan's persistent emphasis is that this expansion occurs and has its meaning almost wholly in interpersonal relationships.

71. Sullivan, p. 14.

72. Patrick Mullahy, A theory of interpersonal relations and the evolution of personality, in Sullivan, *op. cit.*, p. 121 (a review of Sullivan's theories).

73. The term "disapproval" may not have a strong enough connotation to suggest the degree of threat involved or the degree of discomfort the infant experiences when this threat cues off anxiety. Certainly "disapproval" does not refer to reproof, a great deal of which, it is known, can be assimilated by the infant if the mother-child relationship is fundamentally secure.

74. *Op. cit.*, p. 34.

75. *Ibid.*, p. 20.

76. *Ibid.*, p. 46.

77. *Ibid.*, p. 22.

78. *Ibid.*, p. 46.

FOOTNOTES — CHAPTER 6

1. A. I. Hallowell, The social function of anxiety in a primitive society, *Amer. Sociol. Rev.*, 1941, 6:6, 869–81.

2. Seymour Sarason, Kenneth Davidson, Frederick Lighthall,

Richard Waite, and Britton Ruebush, *Anxiety in elementary school children* (New York, 1960).

3. *The psychological frontiers of society* (New York, 1945), p. 99.

4. Quoted in Gardner Murphy, *Historical introduction to modern psychology* (New York, 1932), p. 446.

5. Society as the patient, *Amer. J. Sociol.*, 1936, **42**, 335.

6. Karl Mannheim, *Man and society in an age of reconstruction* (New York, 1941).

7. Fromm, *op. cit.*, p. 14.

8. Our concern with the Renaissance, the beginning of the modern period and thus the time when many of the cultural patterns which underlie contemporaneous anxiety received their formative influences, corresponds roughly to the emphasis in individual psychotherapy upon the period of early childhood, when the patterns which underlie the individual adult's anxiety were formed.

9. Jakob Burckhardt, *Civilization of the Renaissance in Italy*, trans. S. G. C. Middlemore (New York, 1935).

10. Johan Huizinga, *The waning of the Middle Ages* (New York, 1924), p. 40.

11. *Ibid.*

12. Karl Mannheim, *Man and society in an age of reconstruction* (New York, 1941), p. 117.

13. In this chapter we refer to the work of artists on the presupposition that the artist expresses the underlying assumptions and meaning of his culture and that artistic symbols are often not only less distorted than the expressions in word symbols but also can communicate the meaning of the cultural period more directly.

14. Quoted in Burckhardt, *op. cit.*, p. 146.

15. John Addington Symonds, *The Italian Renaissance* (New York, 1935), p. 60.

16. Burckhardt, *op. cit.*

17. Symonds, *op. cit.*, p. 87.

18. Burckhardt, *op. cit.*, p. 150.

19. Symonds, *op. cit.*, p. 352.

20. Romain Rolland, *Michelangelo*, trans. F. Street (New York, 1915), p. 161.

21. Symonds, *op. cit.*, p. 775.

22. Fromm, *op. cit.*, p. 48.

23. Fromm points out that "if one's relations to others and to one's self do not offer full security, then fame is one means to silence one's doubts."

24. *Ibid.*, p. 48.

25. Kardiner, *op. cit.*, p. 445.

26. R. H. Tawney, *The acquisitive society* (New York, 1920), p. 47.

27. *Ibid.*, p. 47.

28. *Ibid.*, p. 49. From a historical perspective, it becomes clear that Freud was accepting the common prejudice of our culture since the Renaissance, that the triumphant individual who was able to achieve his own ends of gratification, to a large extent despite society, was the healthy personality. This is the psychological form of what Tawney, speaking from the economic viewpoint, has called the apotheosis of the individual's self-interest and "natural instinct"

for aggrandizement which has characterized industrialism in the past several centuries. This is one example of how the ideals in practice by our modern culture run counter to our long-time ethical traditions.

29. R. S. Lynd and H. M. Lynd, *Middletown* (New York, 1929), p. 87.

30. *Op. cit.*, p. 72.

31. This is very important in understanding the totalitarian developments in our own day.

32. *Ibid.*, pp. 72 ff.

33. *Ibid.*, pp. 81–82.

34. Fromm, *op. cit.*

35. *Ibid.*, p. 240.

36. *Ibid.*, p. 29.

37. *Ibid.*, p. 63.

38. *Ibid.*, p. 62.

39. See Horney, Chapter 4.

40. I have described this same need for frantic activity among Vietnam soldiers in combat in Chapter 11.

41. Fromm, *op. cit.*, p. 94.

42. W. H. Auden, *The age of anxiety* (New York, 1947), p. 42.

43. Erich Fromm, *Man for himself: an inquiry into the psychology of ethics* (New York, 1947), p. 72.

44. Fromm, *Escape from freedom*, p. 185.

45. *Ibid.*, p. 186.

46. *Ibid.*, p. 105.

47. *Ibid.*, p. 152.

48. *Escape from freedom*, p. 217.

49. Cf. Kurt Goldstein, Chapter 3 above. Also cf. Kurt Riezler, The social psychology of fear, *Amer. J. Sociol.*, 1944, 49, 489.

50. Abram Kardiner, *The psychological frontiers of society* (New York, 1945).

51. *Ibid.*, pp. 411–412.

52. *Ibid.*, p. 376.

FOOTNOTES — CHAPTER 7

1. See Chapter 3, page 74.

2. The literal translation of *Urangst* into English is "original anxiety."

3. I suggest that the reason death, whenever it is discussed in our culture, may be a symbol for neurotic anxiety is that the normal recognition of death as an objective fact is so widely repressed. In our culture one is supposed to ignore the fact that he will sometime die, as though the less said about it the better and as though the experience of living is somehow enhanced if one can remain oblivious to the fact of death. Actually, the exact opposite occurs: the experience of living tends to become vacuous and to lose its zest and savor if the fact of death is ignored. Fortunately, this repression of the fact of death is now being changed to a greater openness on the topic.

4. It tends to paralyze the person, and thus does not make for constructive and creative activity.

5. This ambiguity is one of the reasons it is important to make a clear distinction between the two kinds of anxiety.

6. Cf. next section.

7. In dealing with persons in situations with which their age and objective capacities fit them to cope adequately, a handy distinction between normal and neurotic anxiety is *ex post facto*—i.e., how the anxiety is used—normal anxiety being that which is used for a constructive solution to the problem which causes the anxiety, and neurotic anxiety being that which results in defense from and avoidance of the problem.

8. Chapters 8 and 9, and the discussion on p. 317.

9. Cf. Jersild in Chapter 4, note 6.

10. Quoted by permission.

11. The term "castration" is often used by present Freudian analysts as equivalent to punishment. This generalized meaning of the term has the merit of placing the emphasis on the relationship between the child and his parents, but it still leaves open the question of what values are threatened by the punishment.

12. *Dynamics of human adjustment* (New York, 1946).

13. I am using "dialectical" as meaning a relationship in which each pole reciprocally influences and conditions the other pole. A influences B and B, in turn, influences A; each becomes a different entity by knowing the other. The term "community" is used rather than "society" because it implies a positive quality of relatedness, achieved by the individual by means of his own self-awareness.

14. Karen Horney, *The neurotic personality of our time* (New York, 1937), p. 284.

15. The term "dispelled" is used here in connection with an attitude which realistically obviates anxiety, and "allay" for an attitude which permits the avoidance of anxiety without solving the problem underlying the anxiety. The same attitude may dispel anxiety at one period but become a means of allaying (avoiding) anxiety at another. For example, the assumption that individualistic economic striving furthers community well-being *was* realistically true, and did dispel anxiety during the expanding stages of capitalism. In recent economic developments the assumption is considerably less efficacious, but it still persists as a means of allaying anxiety.

16. *Neurotic personality of our time*, p. 289 (italics mine).

17. Kardiner, *op. cit.*, p. 264.

18. Kurt Riezler, Social psychology of fear, *Amer. J. Socio.,* 1944, 44, 496.

19. Karl Mannheim, *Man and society in an age of reconstruction* (New York, 1941), p. 6. Mannheim sees the "phase of disintegration" through which Western society is now passing as consisting of a conflict between traditional principles of "laissez-faire" and "planless regulation" (totalitarianism). Laissez faire, as an economic and social principle, was serviceable during the major part of the modern period. When, due to various developments in the late industrial age, the principles of laissez faire were no longer serviceable, some form of regulation was bound to appear. The "morbid" forms of regulation which did appear are, in his terms, "dictatorship, conformity and barbarism." Mannheim is convinced that the endeavor to return to laissez-faire principles is neither a possible nor a constructive solution, nor obviously is acquiescence

to planless regulation. His recommendation is democracy based upon economic planning. In many respects the analysis in my study parallels Mannheim's analysis, his term "laissez-faire" being related to the term "competitive individualism" as used here.

20. *Ibid.*, p. 128.

21. *Ibid.*, p. 130 (italics mine).

22. See Rollo May, Historical roots of modern anxiety theories, paper delivered at symposium on "Anxiety" of the Amer. Psychopath. Ass., June 3, 1949 (rpt. in *Anxiety* [New York, 1964]).

23. The term is B. Malinowski's, used in a lecture.

FOOTNOTES — CHAPTER 8

1. Mardi Horowitz, *Stress response syndromes* (New York: Jason Aronson, 1976).

2. I use the term in this way. It includes Jung, Adler, Rank, Sullivan, and all the psychotherapists, as well as many others. There is historical justification for the assumption that practically all methods which get at unconscious motivations, such as the Rorschach, stem from the great impetus given by Freud and his successors.

3. If we speak in diagnostic terms, this case might be described as severe anxiety neurosis or as schizophrenia. If the latter term is used, it should be made clear that it refers not to a distorting of reality, but to the fact that the person is so radically incapacitated by his anxiety that he cannot take care of himself in the real world. In such conditions, the diagnosis of severe anxiety neurosis may be interchangeable with a diagnosis of schizophrenia. In any case, we are concerned here primarily with the psychological dynamics rather than the diagnostic label.

4. *The concept of dread*, p. xii.

5. For those familiar with the Rorschach projective test, we append these technical details: total responses, 18: 1 M, 2 FM, 1 k, 6 F, 3 Fc, 3 FC (of which 2 were F/C), 2 CF; 13 responses (76%) were W, 5 responses (28%) D.

6. If I do not say much about Harold's relation to his father, it is because I must select, and the mother relation seems to me crucial in the case. I do not mean to imply, however, that the father's problems, his psychosis and eventual suicide, were not exceedingly important influences on the young man. Brown's relation to his father, from childhood on, was characterized by (1) identification with his father, (2) belief that his father was excessively strong, (3) subsequent feelings of being pushed down by the father, and finally (4) being convinced by his father's suicide that "my father, whom I thought was so strong, turned out to be so weak —so how can there be any hope for me?" Thus his relation to his father exacerbated his own profound dilemma of weakness.

7. Anxiety has a way of seemingly operating under self-generated power. I say "seemingly" because the occasion of the anxiety must have some element in it which pertains to the conflict that is its cause; only we cannot at the moment see this connection. It is the nature of anxiety to keep this connection hidden. In therapy, the client cannot permit himself to see the connection until he is ready

to give up the neurotic element in the anxiety; and often, when he can permit himself to see the connection between the anxiety and his fundamental conflict, there is a dramatic, sudden easing of tension.

8. Physical examinations of Brown had always been negative. A special neurological conference was held concerning this symptom of dizziness, the conclusion of which was that it was in all probability a psychogenic symptom of anxiety. The dizziness almost always occurred in the context of an anxiety situation, such as on his assumption of some responsibility he dreaded. The similarity of the phrase "being struck in the back of the neck" with the anxiety dream of being killed (in which his assailant also struck him in the back) is obvious. The neurologist remarked, incidentally, to me that the therapy was doing well if it kept Brown out of a mental hospital.

9. The fear that he had cancer was associated wtih a dream of being a patient in a hospital with nurses taking care of him. This suggests one of the functions, or purposes, of the symptom.

10. The scoring on the second Rorschach: there were 50 responses; W percentage was reduced to 44 (almost normal); D was 40 per cent, and d, Dd, and S together were 16 per cent. The number of M had risen to 6 and FC to 4, which indicates much more use of intratensive productivity and also more effective extratensive productivity. There were 3 original responses on the second record, compared to no originality at all and much banality of response on the first.

11. The meaning of cancer as symbolic, and the importance of symbols in general for revealing unconscious material, emerges at this point. After all, Brown's relation to his mother *was* a form of "psychic cancer."

12. There is a sad addendum to the case of Brown. He got along well for a number of years. Then I received a phone call from him in another part of the country saying that he had gone into an anxiety spell so severe that he could not stand it; would I meet him at the train station and help him get into a mental hospital? This I did. He was transferred to another hospital and, unbeknown to me, was given a lobotomy. I had lunch with him several years later. He was then a Coca-Cola salesman and seemed relatively contented.

Practically speaking, if drugs had been available when he was in the hospital, this would have been one time they would have been useful to tide him over that episode. There can be endless arguments about what should have been done, most of them meaningless because they are "oblique"—that is, they argue from our present knowledge and armamentarium back to the past of thirty years ago when such methods of treatment were not available. I am personally against lobotomies on principle; but whether it is better to suffer the reduction of one's potentialities by half and live with some contentment is a question I will not try to answer here.

I only want to make clear that none of these later facts negates what we have said above. Goldstein's brain-injured soldiers, or schizophrenics, or neurotics, or persons of all sorts, react to anxiety in certain similar patterns. Some of these we have illustrated in Harold Brown's experience.

FOOTNOTES — CHAPTER 9

1. Walnut House is a fictitious name employed for the customary purposes of anonymity. These young women were between the ages of fourteen and the mid-twenties. Most of them chose Walnut House more or less voluntarily, though some were sent by social-work agencies. None were in therapy, though a psychiatrist connected with the courts of New York was in legal charge although she was not there often. The psychologist sometimes referred to is myself. The staff consisted of three full-time social workers and several nurses.

2. Pregnancy outside of marriage is surely less anxiety-creating in our present period, chiefly due to the change in social attitudes toward the situation. I am not suggesting that the experience itself, apart from the social status, carries less anxiety. For a more thorough discussion of anxiety and other emotions in abortion, see Magda Denes, *In necessity and sorrow* (New York, 1976).

3. The work of Kierkegaard yields pertinent and profound insights which are applicable to many kinds of people in many situations. Yet Kierkegaard gained his insights chiefly by the intensive study of one person—namely, himself. The same is true of Freud's early theories on dreams, which have been very widely accepted and have proven applicable to many different kinds of persons; Freud arrived at these theories chiefly through a study of his own dreams.

4. Every young woman was interviewed on entering Walnut House by the head social worker, and the young woman then became the case of one of the other social workers, who held conferences with her regularly during her stay (lasting on the average between three and four months) at the house.

5. Copies of these check-lists are given in the Appendix. One purpose in using the second Rorschach and the third check-list was to discover if there were changes in the foci of anxiety after birth. To this end, the items in the third check-list are almost identical, except for rewording, with the items in the second check-list. In some cases it was not possible to administer the second Rorschach because some women did not return to Walnut House after the birth of their babies. Similarly it was not possible to administer the third check-list to the majority of them. Hence we have only limited data on the changes in foci of anxiety after the birth. Where the tests were given after parturition, the chief use of the results has been to show the shifts in that particular person's attitudes and anxiety.

6. The rating is from 1 to 5, 1 equaling the optimum, or lowest, degree of anxiety. "Depth" refers to how penetrating and profound the anxiety is; this is *intensity in its qualitative sense*. "Width" refers to whether the anxiety is generalized or limited to special areas; this is intensity in the sense of the *quantity of symptoms*. "Handling" refers to the degree of efficient effort of the subject in managing her anxiety.

7. The items in these check-lists were classified independently

by three persons: Dr. P. M. Symonds, a social worker at Walnut House, and myself.

8. The ratings for anxiety in the Rorschach are given separately in the discussion of the Rorschach in each case, and a summary rating of the anxiety of each individual against the others in the Rorschach is also given. In the latter, the rating for *depth* and *width* of anxiety are combined; the *handling* is omitted, since it refers to something different from quantity or kind of anxiety. Though the Rorschach ranking often agrees, or closely agrees, with my over-all anxiety ranking for the woman, the two are not to be confused.

9. See G. Allport, *The use of personal documents in psychological science* (New York, 1942).

10. Total responses, 46: 10 *M*, 7 *FM*, 1 *m*, 2 *k*, 1 *K* (with three additionals), 4 *FK* (with four additionals), 8 *F*, 4 *Fc*, 4 *FC*, 5 *CF*; popular responses 7, originals 15; *W%* 66, *D%* 34; intelligence estimate on basis of Rorschach: potentiality 130 (or higher), efficiency 120. This intelligence estimate accords with the reports received of two intelligence tests she had taken in school and college.

11. These methods of coping are often effective when a person is up against it. They are, for example, tried and true methods in the army, as we have seen in previous chapters.

12. As a matter of actual fact, Helen's labor turned out to be not at all what she had dreaded. After parturition she remarked to the psychologist, "If your wife tells you women suffer in childbirth, just tell her it ain't so." It is impossible, of course, to reason from the fact that her fear *actually* turned out to be unrealistic to a conclusion that *therefore* the fear was neurotic. But nevertheless the relief Helen expressed after parturition seemed to be more similar to the "what-was-I-afraid-of?" feeling of people after a neurotic fear has been dispersed than the relief after escaping a real threat: "It was dangerous, but I was fortunate."

13. Though the second Rorschach shows less anxiety than the first, there is still a substantial amount of anxiety present. I believe that Helen would have a moderate to moderately high degree of anxiety in any situation in which her subjective conflicts, such as we have been discussing, are cued off.

14. It is perhaps needless to emphasize that we are not referring to a genuinely scientific and rational attitude toward anxiety and guilt feelings; we are rather speaking of intellectualizing as a defense, an attitude of rationalization rather than a rational attitude.

15. Total responses, 41: 6 *M*, 3 *FM*, 1 *K*, 22 *F*, 7 *Fc*, 1 *C'*, 1 *CF*; popular responses, 5; originals, 8; *W%* 10, *D%* 41, *d%* 24½, *Dd%* 24½; (*H* plus *A*): (*Hd* plus *Ad*) is 12:13.; percentage of responses in wholly colored cards, 29; intelligence estimate from Rorschach: efficiency 115, potentiality 125.

16. This was not only evidenced in her attitudes toward her mother, but also in her present situation: she stated that whenever she now felt worried, she put the worry out of her mind by thinking about her fiancé and "what a nice future we will have."

17. Compare, in this respect, with the case of Phyllis, who, at the price of impoverishment of personality, was able actually to

escape anxiety by avoiding emotional involvement with other persons.

18. Total responses, 13: 6 *M*, 2 *FM* (5 additional *m*), 2 *F*, 1 *Fc*, 2 *CF*; popular responses 3, originals 7; *W%* 62, *D%* 30; *Dd%* 8. Intelligence estimate; potentiality 120, efficiency 110.

19. Total responses, 22: 1 *K*, 11 *F*, 4 *Fc*, 1 *c*, 3 *FC*, 2 *CF*; *W%* 45, *D%* 55; popular responses 2, originals 4. Intelligence estimate from Rorschach: potentiality 100, efficiency 100.

20. The quantity of anxiety on the childhood list seems partly to be a function of Louise's conscientiousness and her considerable desire to please the psychologist, in whose study she wished to cooperate. (See subsequent discussion of her being a deferential, compliant personality with people she considered her "superiors.") The "present anxiety" check-list, filled out in the presence of a social worker, seems to be a fairer indication of her quantity of anxiety.

21. Total responses, 20: 1 *M*, 5 *FM*, 3 *FK*, 7 *F*, 2 *Fc*, 2 *FC*, popular responses 4, originals 2; *W%* 50, *D%* 40; *S%* 10; percentage of responses in last three cards, 25. Intelligence estimate: potentiality 115, efficiency 100. (This accords with an I.Q. of 101, from the report of psychometric tests given Bessie at the Children's Court during her stay at Walnut House.)

22. It will be noted several times in these cases that the quantity of items checked on these lists seemed to be partly a function of the conforming, compliant tendencies of the girl in question (i.e., her being influenced by the belief that checking a large number would please me, the psychologist). The fact that Bessie did not check many items is support of this hypothesis in the respect that she was not a conforming type but was relatively self-assertive and was not noticeably influenced by the need to please other people.

23. It turned out not to be necessary that she go to court in the father's trial, and she carried through the second instance successfully when the social worker and foster mother went with her.

24. Response to Card I: *W-F-A-P;* to Card II: *W-M-H-P;* to Card VIII: *D→W-FM-A-P.* In the testing-the-limits phase, she revealed she could use the color and also could employ the details of the blots without difficulty. This phase of the test corroborated the above hypothesis that the disturbance was not psychotic or due to organic deterioration but rather to severe psychological conflict. Dolores had a slight handicap in the use of the English language, but it was clear that this did not materially contribute to her block on the Rorschach, since the responses she did give, as well as her answers to the tester, were made entirely intelligibly.

25. It would have been desirable to take a Rorschach directly after the "confession," but this was not possible. We assume it is amply demonstrated in her behavior, however, that the radical change occurred at the time of her telling the truth about her pregnancy.

26. Total responses, 15: 2 *M*, 4 *FM*, 8 *F*, 1 *FC; A%* 60; popular responses 4, no originals; *W%* 33, *D%* 60, *d%* 7; total time 14', as compared to 35' on first Rorschach. Intelligence could not be estimated on the first record; on this one it is: potentiality 110, efficiency 90 to 100. (Her intelligence tests in the New York schools —fifth grade—indicated an I.Q. of 80, but this was considered unreliable because of her language handicap.)

27. It is significant that her first two check-lists, taken when she was in her period of paralyzing conflict, show a fairly high degree of response (i.e., a large number of items checked), whereas in the same period she refused to respond to the Rorschach. The plausible explanation seems to be that one knows what one is saying on the check-lists; there is no danger of unwittingly revealing her secret. Hence the check-lists would not be a threat to Dolores.

28. This rating of *moderately low* anxiety, based on the second Rorschach and her behavior after the relief of the conflict, is taken as our base in comparing Dolores with the other girls in the concluding chapter.

29. Total responses, 39: 2 *M*, 1 *FM*, 2 *K*, 18 *F*, 13 *Fc*, 1 *c*, 1 *FC*, 1 *CF*; total percentage in *F* area 80; *W%* 15, *D%* 59, *d%* 5, *Dd%* 21; *(H* plus *A): (Hd* plus *Ad)* equals 9: 14; popular responses 5, originals 3. Intelligence estimate: efficiency 110, potentiality 115.

30. My feeling in working on these notes was one of wanting to explode.

31. Total responses, 37: 2 *M*, 4 *FM*, 1 *k*, 4 *K*, 21 *F*, 3 *Fc*, 1 *c*, 1 *CF*; percentage in *F* area, 65; popular responses 6, originals 7; percentage of responses in Cards VIII, IX, and X, 51; only one *H* response in entire record; succession rigid; *W%* 16, *D%* 68, *d%* 8, *dd%* 8. Intelligence estimate: efficiency 110, potentiality 125.

32. Though the crucial element in Charlotte's Rorschach was the rationally distorted responses, we are including the numerical scoring because that has been our form of presentation with the other cases. Total responses, 36: 9 *M*, 4 *FM*, 4 *FK*, 9 *F*, 3 *Fc*, 4 *FC*, 3 *CF*; average time per response, 1'45''; popular responses 8, originals 7; *W%* 44, *D%* 42, *d%* 3, *Dd%* 11.

33. We are, of course, speaking here only of the forms of psychosis which are psychogenic—i.e., have their origin in subjective, psychological conflict rather than organic deterioration. The general statement that these psychotic states are characterized by a lack of anxiety is not contradicted by the fact that anxiety is present in some forms of paranoia; the latter is a different configuration within the general pattern.

34. Total responses, 22: 1 *M*, 6 *FM*, 1 *K*, 3 *FK*, 5 *F*, 1 *Fc*, 1 *FC*, 4 *CF*; popular responses 6, originals 4; *W%* 50, *D%* 50. Intelligence estimate: potentiality 120, efficiency 110.

35. The fact that the *W%* on the Rorschach was not high is a corroborating datum for the statement that her ambition was not aggressively competitive.

36. Total responses, 40: 1 *M*, 6 *FM*, 1 *FK*, 14 *F*, 10 *Fc*, 2 *FC'*, 6 *FC*; *W%* 20, *D%* 70, *Dd%* 5, *S%* 5; popular responses 5, originals 15. Intelligence estimate: potentiality 110, efficiency 110.

37. Total responses, 12: 1 *M*, 5 *F*, 2 *Fc*, 2 *FC*, 1 *CF*, 1 *C*; popular responses 4, no originals: *W%* 67, *D%* 33. Intelligence estimate: potentiality 100, efficiency 100 (or less).

38. I am assuming the internalized expectations of Ida and her mother's authoritative rules and standards are very much the same thing.

39. Total responses, 23: 3 *M*, 6 *FM*, 5 *F*, 6 *Fc*, 3 *FC*; *A%*, 70; popular responses 6, originals 6; *W%* 39, *D%* 61; average reaction time, 2', 17''; percentage of responses in last three cards, 48. Intelligence estimate: potentiality 125, efficiency 110.

FOOTNOTES — CHAPTER 10

1. Cases of Brown, Helen, Nancy, Ada, Agnes, Hester, Frances, Irene, and, most dramatically, Dolores.

2. Though the case of Brown is not in this series of unmarried mothers, it is illuminating to note that he exhibited the same conscious incapacity to see his mother as the tyrannical person she was, but interpreted her dominating acts as "loving" behavior. The conflict this involves is seen clearly in the respect that his dreams revealed that on a deeper level he actually was aware of her as dominating and tyrannical.

3. This is the ground for assuming a causal relationship between the rejection by parents, which generally occurs significantly in the early years, with present predisposition to neurotic anxiety. The *a priori* rationale behind such an assumption of causality has been given in previous chapters (along with the clinical data supporting the assumption) in the discussion of the viewpoints of Sullivan, Horney, Fromm, and, in fact, practically every psychoanalytic writer from Freud onward. All the above reasoning presupposes a continuity in individual character structure.

4. Curiously, this insight in 1950 is a prediction of the double-bind, formulated chiefly by Gregory Bateson later in the middle 1950's. I have talked this over with Bateson since that time. He compared the situation with Darwin and Wallace—Darwin (Bateson) saw the breadth of the application of the new idea, and Wallace (me) did not. It is certainly true that I was not aware of the universal application of the concept at that time. It is also true that certain seminal ideas are "in the air" at certain times, as expressions of the "collective unconscious" of the age. They come out in a number of different thinkers more or less simultaneously. I suppose the "genius" is the one who recognizes the significance of the fish he has caught.

5. Cf. Kardiner's point that the stage is set for the development of neurotic anxiety in Western man's psychological growth pattern by, among other things, the inconsistency in the parental training of the children (Chapter 7 above).

6. If the rejection is complete—if, that is, the child in its infant months has no experience of relatedness, even of a hostile nature, with parents or parent surrogates—the result is the psychopathic personality. This type is also characterized by a lack of neurotic anxiety. The reader may remember that we had to rule out this possibility with Louise and Bessie. For an excellent discussion of this point, see Lauretta Bender, Anxiety in disturbed children, paper delivered at the American Psychopathological Association symposium on anxiety, June 4, 1949, published in the proceedings of that symposium, Paul Hoch and Joseph Zubin, *Anxiety* (New York, 1950).

7. These findings are contained in a summary of an unpublished paper, Some conditions of love in childhood, by Anna Hartoch Schachtel, March, 1943.

8. Donald W. MacKinnon, A topical analysis of anxiety, *Character & Pers.*, 1944, 12:3, 163–76.

FOOTNOTES — CHAPTER 11

1. Blaise Pascal, *Pensées* (italics mine).
2. Bourne, Rosen, and Mason, Urinary 17-OHC Levels, reprinted from the *Archives of General Psychiatry*, August 1967, **17**, 104–10.
3. *Ibid.*, 138.
4. *Ibid.*, 137.
5. Henrik Ibsen, *Peer Gynt*, trans. Michael Meyer (Garden City, N.Y., 1963), p. 16.
6. *Ibid.*, p. 34.
7. See his *Character analysis: principles and technique for psychoanalysis in practice and training*, trans. T. P. Wolfe (New York, 1945).
8. Jerome Kagan, Psychosocial development of the child. In Frank Falkner, *Human development* (Philadelphia, 1966).
9. Irving Janis of Yale, in his study of persons in a hospital about to go into operation, found that those who had "no anxiety" and those who had excessive anxiety both fared poorly. Those who fared best were the ones who had a moderate amount of anxiety and performed what Janis calls their "work of worrying" adequately. (Cf. *Psychological stress* [New York, 1974].)
10. R. R. Grinker and S. P. Spiegel, *Men under stress* (Philadelphia, 1945).
11. *Op. cit.*, p. 126.
12. Erich Fromm, *Man for himself, an inquiry into the psychology of ethics* (New York, 1947).
13. Both Freud's critical attitude toward religious formulations and his own passionate devotion to science as the means of attaining human happiness are given in his two books: *The future of an illusion* (London and New York, 1961) and *Civilization and its discontents* (London and New York, 1961).

FOOTNOTES — CHAPTER 12

1. E. Paul Torrance, Comparative studies of the stress-seeking in the imaginative stories of preadolescents in twelve different subcultures, in Samuel Klausner (ed.), *Why man takes chances: studies in stress seeking* (New York, 1968).
2. These two rankings were done by Dr. Bruno Klopfer, a Rorschach expert. The intelligence potentiality is based upon the Rorschach and is to be distinguished from efficiency of intelligence. It is very doubtful whether results from tests which measure efficiency of intelligence would be useful in the present problem.

The case of Charlotte is omitted, since the psychotic development brings other elements into the picture, chief of which is the withdrawal from any conflicts which would make for anxiety.

I am aware of the present controversy about the measurement of intelligence. The term "intelligence potentiality" can be "creative potentiality" without changing the main point I am making.

3. "I might be anxious" is simply a less intense form of "I am anxious."

4. In the case discussion of Sarah it was pointed out that, for her, extramarital pregnancy was not so much of an anxiety-creating situation as it was for the white women. Hence it is doubtful whether much weight should be given to her as the exception in these comparisons.

5. See p. 45.

6. As a demonstration of the relation of anxiety to intelligence, Amen and Renison's study of children's fears concluded that the more intelligent child can recall frightening experiences vividly and project them into the future as potential sources of threat. E. N. Amen and N. Renison, A study of the relationship between play patterns and anxiety in children, *Gen. Psychol. Mon.*, 1954, **50**, 3–41.

7. Kristen Kjerulff and Nancy Wiggins, Graduate students style for coping with stressful situations, *J. of Ed. Psych.*, 1976, **68** (3), 247–254.

8. John Simpowski, The relationship of stress and creativity to cognitive performance. *Diss. Abs. Int.*, 1973, **34** (5–A), 2399.

9. J. P. Denny, Effects of anxiety and intelligence on concept formation. *Journ. of Exp. Psych.*, 1966, **72**, 596–602.

10. From *Brain-Mind Bulletin*, January 3, 1977, **2** (4).

11. W. D. Fenz and S. Epstein, Gradients of physiological arousal in parachutists as a function of an approaching jump, *Psychosom. Medicine*, 1967, **29**, 33–51.

12. See Liddell, p. 52.

13. Søren Kierkegaard, *Sickness unto Death*, trans. Walter Lowrie (Princeton, N.J., 1941), pp. 43–44.

FOOTNOTE — APPENDICES

1. The three check-lists included here were used in studying the foci of anxiety of unmarried mothers as described in the text, and are not meant for any other purpose.

INDEX

Index

411